# Phaedra and Hippolytus

## Myth and Dramatic Form

❖ ❖ ❖ ❖
❖ ❖ ❖
❖

# Phaedra and Hippolytus

## Myth and Dramatic Form

EDITED BY

James L. Sanderson · Irwin Gopnik

RUTGERS UNIVERSITY

*Houghton Mifflin Company* · *Boston*

NEW YORK · ATLANTA · GENEVA, ILL. · DALLAS · PALO ALTO

# PREFACE

◇◇◇◇◇◇◇◇◇◇◇◇◇◇◇◇◇◇◇◇◇◇◇◇◇◇◇◇◇◇◇◇◇◇◇◇

THIS ANTHOLOGY of plays and critical comment attempts to provide the materials for an interesting and unusual classroom exercise in the study of drama. It is concerned with five dramatic forms which an ancient Greek myth has assumed during more than two thousand years.

Myth has become an important term in the vocabularies of several disciplines, including religion, anthropology, sociology, psychology, classical studies, art, and literature. But it has also become an omnibus term taking on as many meanings as there are disciplines — and exponents of those disciplines — that have concerned themselves with myth. It is not within the scope of this book or our capabilities to resolve the semantic complexities and conflicts surrounding the term. For our purposes here we have accepted Philip Wheelwright's definition of myth as "a story or a complex of story elements taken as expressing, and therefore as implicitly symbolizing, certain deep-lying aspects of human and transhuman existence."

The myth with which we are concerned is the story of Phaedra and Hippolytus. Hippolytus was the object of cults in Troezen and in Attica and was reverenced by sacrifice and ritual. Girls in Troezen, Euripides notes, cut their hair before their marriage and dedicated it to Hippolytus. Hippolytus became connected with the legendary material of Phaedra and Theseus, which first appears in dramatic form in the fifth century B.C. The early accounts agree in certain basic aspects: Hippolytus, chaste and dedicated to the hunt and outdoor interests, is the son of Theseus. Unwittingly, Hippolytus arouses the lustful passions of his stepmother, Phaedra, who when rebuffed and frustrated in satisfying her desires for him, accuses him to his father of rape or attempted rape. Enraged, Theseus curses his son and prays to Poseidon for the death of Hippolytus, a petition which the god grants.

This story of human desire, hate, revenge, and innocence has been the subject of poems, novels, operas, motion pictures, and, most memorably, dramas. Three of the plays included here, Euripides' *Hippolytus*, Racine's *Phaedra*, and O'Neill's *Desire Under the Elms*, are familiar standard works of dramatic literature; the remaining two, Seneca's *Phaedra* and Jeffers' *The Cretan Woman*, are perhaps less well known. But each play merits and rewards careful study and

v

analysis. And to their interest as separate, independent aesthetic entities is added that deriving from their interrelationships. Being dramatizations of the same basic subject, the plays are related as variations on a dominant theme. With a constant element in common, they may be profitably compared. And such comparisons will reveal significant differences among the plays in formal characteristics, dramatic techniques and conventions, and subtle and profound variations in emphasis and interpretation which reflect the cultural and intellectual milieux as well as the individual talents of the writers.

The book is divided into three parts: a summary account of the Phaedra-Hippolytus story; the plays; and comment. Each play is introduced by a brief biographical notice of the dramatist, an account of the stage history of his play, and a selective bibliography. The "Study Aids" and "Discussion Topics" which follow each play seek to promote first a mastery and then a synthesis of the details of the play.

The essays in the third part of the book are by recognized scholars and critics. These essays may be used as supplementary aids in the study of the plays and as materials for student papers requiring the utilization of secondary sources. Concluding the volume are a number of suggestions for student research and writing projects.

We have acknowledged elsewhere in the book our indebtedness to authors and publishers for permission to reprint their works. We wish here to express our appreciation to Professor Wesley D. Smith, Department of Classical Studies, University of Pennsylvania, and to Professor Walter K. Gordon, English Department, Rutgers University, for suggestions which we have incorporated in this book, and to our wives, Myrna Gopnik and Rosamond Sanderson, for their assistance in preparing the manuscript and in proofreading.

J.L.S.
I.G.

# CONTENTS

## PART ONE · THE MYTH

Robert Graves *The Myth of Phaedra and Hippolytus*   3

## PART TWO · FIVE PLAYS

Euripides   11
  *Hippolytus* (translated by Philip Vellacott)   14
  STUDY AIDS   50
  DISCUSSION TOPICS   57

Seneca   59
  *Phaedra* (translated by F. J. Miller)   62
  STUDY AIDS   102
  DISCUSSION TOPICS   107

Jean Racine   109
  *Phaedra* (translated by Robert Lowell)   114
  STUDY AIDS   161
  DISCUSSION TOPICS   165

Robinson Jeffers   167
  *The Cretan Woman*   169
  STUDY AIDS   204
  DISCUSSION TOPICS   209

Eugene O'Neill   211
  *Desire Under the Elms*   213
  STUDY AIDS   265
  DISCUSSION TOPICS   268

## PART THREE · COMMENT

Sir James George Frazer  *The King of the Wood*  273

Richmond Lattimore  *Euripides' Phaedra and Hippolytus*  283

Norman T. Pratt, Jr.  *Tragedy and Moralism: Euripides and Seneca*  297

Henri Peyre  *The Tragedy of Passion: Racine's* Phèdre  308

Edgar F. Racey, Jr.  *Myth as Tragic Structure in* Desire Under the Elms  329

WRITING SUGGESTIONS  335

# PART ONE

# The Myth of Phaedra
## and Hippolytus

# ❧ ❧ ❧ The Myth of Phaedra and Hippolytus

## *Robert Graves*

AFTER marrying Phaedra, Theseus sent his bastard son Hippolytus to Pittheus, who adopted him as heir to the throne of Troezen. Thus Hippolytus had no cause to dispute the right of his legitimate brothers Acamas and Demophoön, Phaedra's sons, to reign over Athens.[1]

*b.* Hippolytus, who had inherited his mother Antiope's exclusive devotion to chaste Artemis, raised a new temple to the goddess at Troezen, not far from the theatre. Thereupon Aphrodite, determined to punish him for what she took as an insult to herself, saw to it that when he attended the Eleusinian Mysteries, Phaedra should fall passionately in love with him. He came dressed in white linen, his hair garlanded, and though his features wore a harsh expression, she thought them admirably severe.[2]

*c.* Since at that time Theseus was away in Thessaly with Peirithous, or it may have been in Tartarus, Phaedra followed Hippolytus to Troezen. There she built the Temple of Peeping Aphrodite to overlook the gymnasium, and would daily watch unobserved while he kept himself fit by running, leaping, and wrestling, stark naked. An ancient myrtle-tree stands in the Temple enclosure; Phaedra would jab at its leaves, in frustrated passion, with a jewelled hair-pin, and they are still much perforated. When, later, Hippolytus attended the All-Athenian Festival and lodged in Theseus's palace, she used the Temple of Aphrodite on the Acropolis for the same purpose.[3]

*d.* Phaedra disclosed her incestuous desire to no one, but ate little,

[1] Apollodorus: *Epitome* i. 18; Pausanias: i. 22. 2; Ovid: *Heroides* iv. 67 ff.
[2] Pausanias: ii. 31. 6; Ovid: *loc. cit.*
[3] Ovid: *loc. cit.*; Seneca: *Hippolytus* 835 ff.; Pausanias: ii. 32. 3 and i. 22. 2; Euripides: *Hippolytus* 1 ff.; Diodorus Siculus: iv. 62.

From *The Greek Myths* (New York, 1955), I, 356–360. Reprinted by permission of Willis Kingsley Wing. Copyright © 1955, by International Authors N.V.

slept badly, and grew so weak that her old nurse guessed the truth at last, and officiously implored her to send Hippolytus a letter. This Phaedra did: confessing her love, and saying that she was now converted by it to the cult of Artemis, whose two wooden images, brought from Crete, she had just rededicated to the goddess. Would he not come hunting one day? "We women of the Cretan Royal House," she wrote, "are doubtless fated to be dishonoured in love: witness my grandmother Europe, my mother Pasiphaë, and lastly my own sister Ariadne! Ah, wretched Ariadne, deserted by your father, the faithless Theseus, who has since murdered your own royal mother — why have the Furies not punished you for showing such unfilial indifference to her fate? — and must one day murder me! I count on you to revenge yourself on him by paying homage to Aphrodite in my company. Could we not go away and live together, for a while at least, and make a hunting expedition the excuse? Meanwhile, none can suspect our true feelings for each other. Already we are lodged under the same roof, and our affection will be regarded as innocent, and even praise-worthy." [4]

e. Hippolytus burned this letter in horror, and came to Phaedra's chamber, loud with reproaches; but she tore her clothes, threw open the chamber doors, and cried out: "Help, help! I am ravished!" Then she hanged herself from the lintel, and left a note accusing him of monstrous crimes.[5]

f. Theseus, on receiving the note, cursed Hippolytus, and gave orders that he must quit Athens at once, never to return. Later he remembered the three wishes granted him by his father Poseidon, and prayed earnestly that Hippolytus might die that very day. "Father," he pleaded, "send a beast across Hippolytus's path, as he makes for Troezen!" [6]

g. Hippolytus had set out from Athens at full speed. As he drove along the narrow part of the Isthmus a huge wave, which overtopped even the Molurian Rock, rolled roaring shoreward; and from its crest sprang a great dog-seal (or, some say, a white bull), bellowing and spouting water. Hippolytus's four horses swerved towards the cliff, mad with terror, but being an expert charioteer he restrained them from plunging over the edge. The beast then galloped menacingly be-hind the chariot, and he failed to keep his team on a straight course. Not far from the sanctuary of Saronian Artemis, a wild olive is still shown, called the Twisted Rhachos — the Troezenian term for a barren olive-tree is *rhachos* — and it was on a branch of this tree that

---

[4] Ovid: *loc. cit.*; Pausanias: i. 18. 5.
[5] Apollodorus: *Epitome* i. 18; Diodorus Siculus: iv. 62; Hyginus: *Fabula* 47.
[6] Plutarch: *Parallel Stories* 34; Servius on Virgil's *Aeneid* vi. 445.

a loop of Hippolytus's reins caught. His chariot was flung sideways against a pile of rocks and broken into pieces. Hippolytus, entangled in the reins, and thrown first against the tree-trunk, and then against the rocks, was dragged to death by his horses, while the pursuer vanished.[7]

*h*. Some, however, relate improbably that Artemis then told Theseus the truth, and rapt him in the twinkling of an eye to Troezen, where he arrived just in time to be reconciled to his dying son; and that she revenged herself on Aphrodite by procuring Adonis's death. For certain, though, she commanded the Troezenians to pay Hippolytus divine honours, and all Troezenian brides henceforth to cut off a lock of their hair, and dedicate it to him. It was Diomedes who dedicated the ancient temple and image of Hippolytus at Troezen, and who first offered him his annual sacrifice. Both Phaedra's and Hippolytus's tombs, the latter a mound of earth, are shown in the enclosure of this temple, near the myrtle-tree with the pricked leaves.

*i*. The Troezenians themselves deny that Hippolytus was dragged to death by horses, or even that he lies buried in his temple; nor will they reveal the whereabouts of his real tomb. Yet they declare that the gods set him among the stars as the Charioteer.[8]

*j*. The Athenians raised a barrow in Hippolytus's memory close to the Temple of Themis, because his death had been brought about by curses. Some say that Theseus, accused of his murder, was found guilty, ostracized, and banished to Scyros, where he ended his life in shame and grief. But his downfall is more generally believed to have been caused by an attempted rape of Persephone.[9]

*k*. Hippolytus's ghost descended to Tartarus, and Artemis, in high indignation, begged Asclepius to revive his corpse. Asclepius opened the doors of his ivory medicine cabinet and took out the herb with which Cretan Glaucus had been revived. With it he thrice touched Hippolytus's breast, repeating certain charms, and at the third touch the dead man raised his head from the ground. But Hades and the Three Fates, scandalized by this breach of privilege, persuaded Zeus to kill Asclepius with a thunderbolt.

*l*. The Latins relate that Artemis then wrapped Hippolytus in a thick cloud, disguised him as an aged man, and changed his features. After hesitating between Crete and Delos as suitable places of concealment, she brought him to her sacred grove at Italian Aricia.[10] There, with

[7] Pausanias: ii. 32. 8; Euripides: *Hippolytus* 1193 ff.; Ovid: *Metamorphoses* xv. 506 ff.; Plutarch: *loc. cit.*; Diodorus Siculus: iv. 62.
[8] Euripides: *Hippolytus* 1282 ff. and 1423 ff.; Pausanias: ii. 32. 1–2.
[9] Pausanias: i. 22. 1; Philostratus: *Life of Apollonius of Tyana* vii. 42; Diodorus Siculus: iv. 62.
[10] Ovid: *Metamorphoses* xv. 532 ff. and *Fasti* vi. 745.

her consent, he married the nymph Egeria, and he still lives beside the
lake among dark oak-woods, surrounded by sheer precipices. Lest he
should be reminded of his death, Artemis changed his name to Virbius,
which means *vir bis*, or "twice a man"; and no horses are allowed in
the vicinity. The priesthood of Arician Artemis is open only to runaway slaves.[11] In her grove grows an ancient oak-tree, the branches of
which may not be broken, but if a slave dares do so then the priest,
who has himself killed his predecessor and therefore lives in hourly
fear of death, must fight him, sword against sword, for the priesthood.
The Aricians say that Theseus begged Hippolytus to remain with him
at Athens, but he refused.

   *m.* A tablet in Asclepius's Epidaurian sanctuary records that Hippolytus dedicated twenty horses to him, in gratitude for having been
revived.[12]

❖

*1.* The incident of Phaedra's incestuous love for Hippolytus, like
that of Potiphar's wife and her adulterous love for Joseph, is borrowed
either from the Egyptian *Tale of the Two Brothers,* or from a common Canaanite source. Its sequel has been based upon the familiar icon
showing the chariot crash at the end of a sacred king's reign. If, as in
ancient Ireland, a prophetic roaring of the November sea warned the
king that his hour was at hand, this warning will have been pictured
as a bull, or seal, poised open-mouthed on the crest of a wave.
Hippolytus's reins must have caught in the myrtle, rather than in the
sinister-looking olive later associated with the crash: the myrtle, in
fact, which grew close to his hero shrine, and was famous for its perforated leaves. Myrtle symbolized the last month of the king's reign;
as appears in the story of Oenomaus's chariot crash; whereas wild olive
symbolized the first month of his successor's reign. *Vir bis* is a false
derivation of Virbius, which seems to represent the Greek *hierobios,*
"holy life" — the *h* often becoming *v*: as in *Hestia* and *Vesta,* or
*Hesperos* and *Vesper.* In the *Golden Bough* Sir James Frazer has
shown that the branch which the priest guarded so jealously was mistletoe; and it is likely that Glaucus son of Minos, who has been confused with Glaucus son of Sisyphus, was revived by mistletoe. Though
the pre-Hellenic mistletoe and oak cult had been suppressed in Greece,
a refugee priesthood from the Isthmus may well have brought it to

   [11] Virgil: *Aeneid* vii. 775; Ovid: *Fasti* v. 312 and *Metamorphoses* xv. 545;
Strabo: iii. 263 ff.; Pausanias: ii. 27. 4.
   [12] Servius on Virgil's *Aeneid* vi. 136; Strabo: v. 3. 12; Suetonius: *Caligula*
35; Pausanias: *loc. cit.*

Aricia. Egeria's name shows that she was a death-goddess, living in a grove of black poplars.

2. Hippolytus's perquisite of the bride's lock must be a patriarchal innovation, designed perhaps to deprive women of the magical power resident in their hair, as Mohammedan women are shaved on marriage.

3. The concealment of Hippolytus's tomb is paralleled in the stories of Sisyphus and Neleus, which suggests that he was buried at some strategic point of the Isthmus.

# PART TWO ◇◇◇◇◇◇◇◇◇◇◇◇◇◇◇◇◇◇◇◇◇◇◇

## *Five Plays*

# EURIPIDES

◇◇◇◇◇◇◇◇◇◇◇◇◇◇◇◇◇◇◇◇◇◇◇◇◇◇◇◇◇◇◇◇◇◇◇

BIOGRAPHIES of Euripides (485?–406? B.C.) usually include a number of phrases such as "tradition tells us," "some think," and "it is not impossible that" — signals that very little is definitely known about the life of one of the three greatest Greek tragedians. But this lack of dates and details is well compensated for by the existence of the most important kind of fact of a great dramatist's life — his plays. Although the nineteen plays of Euripides (assuming that the disputed *Rhesus* is his) represent only a fraction of the eighty or ninety plays he is credited with writing, they exceed the combined total of extant plays of Aeschylus and Sophocles.

The theatre for which Euripides wrote differed considerably from that with which we are most familiar. The plays were performed in daylight in large, open-air amphitheatres before audiences numbering in the thousands as a kind of civic-religious festival observance. The Greek stage sometimes utilized fairly elaborate and ingenious stage machinery, but it did not strive for a meticulous realism in staging. It lacked a curtain and the easy facility for set changes customary in modern theatres. What would be accomplished today by a rheostat off-stage or a painted flat lowered as a backdrop would have been accomplished on the Greek stage chiefly through the dramatist's poetry stimulating the imagination of the audience. It is perhaps owing to certain practical limitations of the Greek stage for realistic staging that violent deeds and actions were not exhibited on-stage and that their occurrence and results were reported, as in the *Hippolytus* by the Messenger.

The performance of Greek plays observed other conventions unfamiliar to us. All the roles were played by male actors. Each of the actors, including those in the chorus, wore masks expressive of their rank or attitude, thereby submerging the individuality of the actor in the role he was portraying. While modern dramatic technique has utilized some of its functions through other means, the chorus remains

11

one of the conventions of Greek drama most alien to modern theatrical experience. The chorus was continuously present on-stage during a performance and combined dancing, singing, chanting, recitative, and perhaps mime with dramatic speech. Constituted of "Theban Elders" as in the *Oedipus Rex* or "Women of Troezen" as in the *Hippolytus*, it served many functions, both obvious and subtle. As an interlocutor it provided the actor on-stage with someone to talk to and with. It aided in exposition by introducing entering characters and recalling background information needed to understand the dramatic situation on-stage. The chorus also provided continuity between episodes and facilitated the dramatist's handling of "time": the time ostensibly required for some action to occur off-stage, in the *Hippolytus*, for example, the operation of Theseus' curse placed upon his son, was filled on-stage with the singing of the chorus. More subtly, its expressions of foreboding or anxiety could heighten dramatic tension just as its odes could ease or release it. Finally, the chorus was a medium for interpretive comment, a means of generalizing from the particulars of the play, of drawing from the legends and myths, which were the subjects of Greek tragedy, the wisdom and human significance which the dramatist had discovered, or embodied, in them.

The famous legend of Phaedra, wife of Theseus, and her unlawful, death-bringing passion for her stepson, Hippolytus, was the subject of three different tragedies in the fifth century B.C., one by Sophocles and two by Euripides. Sophocles' *Phaedra* has not survived, and its date and the details of its treatment are largely matters of conjecture. The *Hippolytus* is believed to have been the later of Euripides' two plays on this subject. Although the first has survived only in fragments, these fragments plus early comments about the play provide some idea of its general features. The most important difference between the two plays lies in the character of Phaedra. In the earlier play she was a wicked, assertive, and abandoned woman who strove, not as in the later play to overcome her passion for Hippolytus, but to satisfy it. She was probably much nearer the Phaedra of Seneca's play than that of the *Hippolytus*.

The first play seems to have displeased the Athenians, and there is some suggestion that the second was designed to meet criticism aroused by the first. What had offended the audience was apparently corrected, for the *Hippolytus* won a first prize when it was performed in 428 B.C. The play has been regarded in modern times as one of Euripides' best constructed and most interesting plays.

Discussions of the origins, stage, and production of Greek drama are contained in A. E. Haigh and A. W. Pickard-Cambridge, *The Attic Theatre* (Oxford, 1907); Roy C. Flickinger, *The Greek Theater and*

*Its Drama* (Chicago, 1936); and Margarete Bieber, *The History of the Greek and Roman Theatre* (Princeton, 1939). Comment on Euripides, including the *Hippolytus*, can be found in Gilbert Murray, *Euripides and His Age* (New York, 1913); Gilbert Norwood, *Greek Tragedy* (London, 1928) and *Essays on Euripidean Drama* (Berkeley, 1954); H. D. F. Kitto, *Greek Tragedy: A Literary Study* (London, 1939); and G. M. A. Grube, *The Drama of Euripides* (London, 1941). Special studies are David Grene, "The Interpretation of the *Hippolytus* of Euripides," *Classical Philology*, XXXIV (1939), 45–58; Bernard M. W. Knox, "The *Hippolytus* of Euripides," *Yale Classical Studies*, XIII (1952), 3–31; and Hazel E. Barnes, *Hippolytus in Drama and Myth* (Lincoln, Nebraska, 1962). Translations of Euripides' plays are included in *The Complete Greek Tragedies*, ed. Richmond Lattimore and David Grene (Chicago, 1955).

# Hippolytus

### Translated by Philip Vellacott

◇ ◇ ◇

CHARACTERS IN ORDER OF APPEARANCE

APHRODITE, *the Goddess of Sexual Love*
HIPPOLYTUS, *bastard son of Theseus*
CHORUS *of Huntsmen attending Hippolytus*
SERVANT *of Hippolytus*
CHORUS *of Women of Troezen*
NURSE *attending Phaedra*
PHAEDRA, *wife of Theseus*
THESEUS, *King of Athens and Troezen*
MESSENGER
ARTEMIS, *the huntress Goddess of Virginity*

*The scene is before the royal palace at Troezen, where Theseus is spending a year of voluntary exile to atone for bloodshed. On one side of the stage is a statue of Aphrodite, on the other a statue of Artemis. In the centre is the door of the palace.*

(*Enter* APHRODITE.)

APHRODITE. Powerful among mortals, glorious among the gods,
I am Aphrodite, named in heaven The Cyprian.
On earth, from the Eastern shore to the outward ocean of the West,
Over all that see the light of the sun my rule extends.
To those who reverence my powers I show favour,
And throw to the earth those I find arrogant and proud.
For gods too have their pride; and it is their nature
To enjoy receiving honour from the mortal race.
And that my words are true I shall show this very day.

Hippolytus, the son whom the Amazon bore to Theseus,
Who was trained from a child by Pittheus the Severe,—
Hippolytus, alone among the inhabitants of Troezen,
Calls me the most pernicious of the heavenly powers;
He abhors the bed of love; marriage he renounces;
Honours Apollo's sister, Artemis daughter of Zeus.
All day with her, the virgin, he ranges the green woods,
With his swift hounds emptying the earth of beasts,
Too fond of company too high for mortal men.
I do not envy them their sport — I have little cause;
But Hippolytus has insulted me and shall suffer for it
This very day. My plans, long laid, are well begun,
And little work remains.             Two years ago Hippolytus
Left Pittheus' house for Athens, the city of Pandion,
To attend the holy Mysteries and complete his initiation;
And there the noble Phaedra saw him, his father's wife, —
And a terrible lust, by my contrivance, captured her heart.
The prince came home to Troezen: Phaedra was Queen of Athens.
There on the Acropolis, on the very Rock of Pallas,
She built a temple of Love looking seaward towards Troezen,
Where her heart wandered with her beloved far away; —
Still from that time this temple bears Hippolytus' name.
But Theseus, his hands stained with the blood of the Pallantides,
To purge his guilt, consented to live one year in exile,
And sailed with Phaedra his wife from Athens here to Troezen.
She now, poor wretch, groaning and maddened with the stabs of
    love,
Is dying, and in silence. No one in the palace knows
Her sickness. But not in secret shall her lust's full course be run.
I will reveal the truth to Theseus; all shall be shown.
This youth, who makes war with me, his own father Theseus
Shall kill with curses, by the power Poseidon King of the Sea
Gave him, that three requests of Theseus should not fail.
Phaedra shall save her honour, but must lose her life;
For I will not yield my rights through regard for her misfortunes,
But my enemies shall pay what they owe till I am satisfied.
Now I'll retire. Here comes Hippolytus, son of Theseus,
Home after his exertions in the hunting field, and with him
His whole pack of followers in full cry at his heels,
Singing hymns to Artemis! Little he knows that Death's gates
Are open now, and to-day's light is the last he shall see.

                            (*Exit.*)

(*Enter* HIPPOLYTUS *with Huntsmen; also an Old Servant.*)

HIPPOLYTUS.  Follow, and sing!
    Follow the bright Daughter of Heaven!
    Follow our guardian Maid,
        Artemis!
HUNTSMEN.  Child of Leto and of Zeus,
    Virgin Goddess Artemis,
    Great and holy, hear our song!
    Greeting, joyful greeting,
        Loveliest of maidens!
    You who haunt your kingly father's court,
    Tread at ease the broad sky's golden floor,
    Loveliest of immortal maids,
        Joyful greeting, Artemis!
HIPPOLYTUS.  Goddess, for you I have twined this crown of flowers,
    gathered
    Fresh from a virgin meadow, where no shepherd dares
    To graze his flock, nor ever yet scythe swept,
    But bees thread the Spring air over the maiden meadow.
    There from the running stream Chastity waters the flowers;
    And those whose untaught natures Holiness claims entire
    May gather garlands there; and the impure may not.
    Dear Mistress, take this flowery band for your bright hair,
    Offered with reverent heart. I alone among mortals
    Enjoy this honour; I am your companion, speak with you,
    Hear your voice; only your face I do not see.
    And may the end of my life's course be as the beginning!
SERVANT.  My lord! — or, Prince! for only gods must be called lord, —
    would you accept a word of good advice from me?
HIPPOLYTUS.  Of course! I should plainly be a fool if I would not.
SERVANT.  Then — you know an old law that is laid down for men —
HIPPOLYTUS.  No! What do you mean? Why are you asking me this?
SERVANT.  The law that says: Abhor pride and all unfriendliness.
HIPPOLYTUS.  Yes; a good law: haughtiness is always a hateful thing.
SERVANT.  And surely there is a charm in being open and unreserved?
HIPPOLYTUS.  Great charm; great profit too, and with little trouble.
SERVANT.  Do you not think this is as true for gods as for men?
HIPPOLYTUS.  Why, yes; if our mortal ways are like theirs.
SERVANT.  Then why have you no prayer for — a great goddess?
HIPPOLYTUS.  Be careful! A word may do harm. What goddess do you
    mean?
SERVANT.  She stands here at your own door — Aphrodite!
HIPPOLYTUS.  I greet her from far off: I am untainted.

SERVANT. Yet she is great; and her power is known and feared.

HIPPOLYTUS. I have no love for gods worshipped by night.

SERVANT. My son, we must not neglect the honour due to the gods.

HIPPOLYTUS. Gods may choose whom they will honour: so may mortals.

SERVANT. May the gods grant you wisdom, and good fortune too!

HIPPOLYTUS. Come, men, we'll go in; it is time for food. A loaded table's a cheerful sight after hunting. Rub down the horses: when I've had a good meal I'll take them out with the chariot and exercise them hard. — Your Aphrodite? No! To me she is nothing at all!

(*Exit* HIPPOLYTUS *with Huntsmen.*)

SERVANT. The ways of young men are not for us to copy. Queen Aphrodite! with humble hearts, as befits your servants, we worship you. You must forgive young blood, and the bold spirit that blurts foolish words against you. Forget that you heard him speak! You are a god: and the wisdom of gods must be wiser than men.

(*Exit.*)

(*Enter* CHORUS *of Troezenian Women.*)

CHORUS. You have heard of the rocky fountain　　　　[*Strophe* 1
Where water gushes streaming from the heart of the earth,
Where they dip pails in the pool:
A friend of mine was there,
Rinsing rich-coloured clothes in the rill-water
And laying them to dry on the sun-baked rock:
She was the first to tell me about the Queen,

How she pines on a sick bed,　　　　　　　　[*Antistrophe* 1
Keeps always within doors,
Clouding her golden head in the fine folds of her veil.
This is the third day, they say,
That her lovely lips refuse the gift of the Earth-Mother,
The innocent body of bread.
What storm is wrecking her life she will not tell;
But she longs to moor in the sad harbour of death.

Hers is no wild ecstasy　　　　　　　　　　[*Strophe* 2
Sent by Hecate or Pan,
Mountain-frenzy, Corybantic wandering
By Cybele's power possessed.
Has she sinned, neglecting

Immemorial offerings,
Oil and honey for the Huntress Artemis?
Wrath of gods can range and reach
Every shore and island
Through the salt sea's eddies.

Or is Theseus' heart beguiled?                    [*Antistrophe* 2
Is your kingly husband false,
Following pleasure in some slave-girl's secret bed?
Has some traveller from Crete
Sailed with news of sorrow
To our friendly harbour?
Are your kindred torn with trouble far away,
That such bitter anguish
Makes your bed your prison?

But women are always weak, and their ways are strange;    [*Epode*
Their very being is a blend of terror and helplessness
At the pains and follies their sex inherits.
I have felt this fear thrill through my own womb;
But I cried to the heavenly helper of all women,
Artemis of the arrows;
And always — the gods be praised! — she came to my deep need.

Look! The old Nurse is coming to the door,
Bringing Queen Phaedra into the fresh air.
Her sad face is more clouded than before.
The Queen! How weak she is, how pale!
I long to know what has so wasted her.

(*Enter, from the palace,* PHAEDRA *supported by the* NURSE. *Attendants bring a couch for her.*)

NURSE. Oh, the sickness and pain of this cruel world!
What can I do for you? How can I tell?
Here you are, in the light, under the clear sky;
We have brought your bed from the palace.
It was here that you begged and longed to come;
Soon you will change your mind and fret for your room again.
Each minute cheats you, nothing gives you pleasure;
You hate what you have, and crave for what you have not.
Better to be sick, which is a single trouble,
Than wait on the sick, which troubles both heart and hand.
Man's life from birth to death is sorrow and pain,
With never pause or relief;

And when we are dead, is there a happier world?
Knowledge is hidden from us in clouds and darkness.
Since we can know no other kind of life,
Since the world of the dead is a mystery,
It seems we must blindly love, for what it is worth,
Our little gleam of light,
And follow our foolish course content with tales.

PHAEDRA. Support me, my friends, and lift my head;
The strength of my limbs has melted away.
Hold my white hands, my shapely arms!
This braided veil is a weight on my head, —
Off with it! Now let my hair fall round my shoulders.

NURSE. Patience, my child! Lie still, you will tire yourself!
If you are quiet and keep a brave heart
Your illness will be easier to bear.
We are mortal, and so must suffer.

PHAEDRA. If I could kneel by a well-side in the fresh dew
And drink a cupful of clear water!
If I could lie under the poplar-trees
And rest deep in the waving grass!

NURSE. Speak low, child! You must not scatter your words
So loud and recklessly! There are people here!
Your speech careers wildly on wheels of madness.

PHAEDRA. Come, take me! I am going
Out to the hills and the woods, the pine-forests
Where hounds pace after blood
And press close on the spotted deer!
O gods! were I there, shouting to the pack,
Lifting the lance to my hair bright in the wind,
Hurling the barbed blade!

NURSE. What is it, child, you are fretting for?
What are hounds and the hunt to you?
Why so in love with water from a spring?
If you are thirsty,
Here by the palace-wall a stream runs down the hill!

PHAEDRA. Lady of the Salt Mere,
Artemis, lover of bold horsemanship!
O for your level rides,
And the tamed strength of a Thessaly horse under my hand!

NURSE. What next will you say? This is madness, child!
You were craving first
To hunt wild beasts in a mountain glade;
Now, for a horse on the dry sandy track.

Here's a task for a prophet indeed, to guess
What god drives you beside yourself
And strikes your senses from you!
PHAEDRA. What have I done? I have been wandering.
My mind went from me — where? where? I was mad,
A god touched me with madness. Oh, my grief!
Dear Nurse, my veil again; I am ashamed
To think what I have said. Cover my face.
My tears fall down, and I am hot with shame.
To come back to a right mind is agony,
And no less agony to remain mad.
It is best, then, to feel nothing, and so die!
NURSE (*veiling her*). There, child, there! How soon
Shall my face too be veiled with death?
I have lived long, and learnt much.
Since we must die, it would be better,
In making friends, never to go too far,
Or open the depths of our heart to anyone.
The ties of love ought to lie loosely on us,
Easy to break or bind.
For one heart to endure the pain of two,
As I suffer for her, is a cruel burden.
They say that steadfast devotion
Brings with it more trouble than pleasure,
And is an enemy to life and health.
So I think that in this as in other things
It is best not to go too far;
And any wise man will say the same.
CHORUS. Madam, we see the Queen's distress and are sorry for her;
but what her illness is we cannot understand. We would like to
ask you, her old and trusted servant: will you not tell us?
NURSE. I know nothing. I have questioned her, but she will not speak.
CHORUS. Do you not know how, or when, this trouble first began?
NURSE. The answer is still the same: to all such questions she is silent.
CHORUS. How frail and wasted she looks!
NURSE. No wonder: she has eaten nothing for three days.
CHORUS. Is she out of her mind? Or does she mean to die?
NURSE. She means to die. She is starving herself to death.
CHORUS. Strange that her husband should accept it calmly!
NURSE. She hides her illness from him, tells him she is well.
CHORUS. Does he not look at her face and see for himself?
NURSE. Just now it happens he is away from Troezen.

CHORUS. Can you not compel her to speak? Anything, to discover the cause of this sickness and these delusions!

NURSE. I have tried everything and achieved nothing; but I want to do my best, and I will not give up even now. And you, friends, are here to witness that I am one to stand by my lady in time of trouble. (*She turns to* PHAEDRA.) Dear child, let us both forget the things we said before. Smooth away this terrible look from your brow: be my dear daughter! Don't wander any more — I was wrong to follow you, prying into your thoughts; I will be wiser. Is your sickness something you cannot speak of openly? There are women here to help with remedies. But if your trouble can be told to a man, only speak, and we will consult doctors. Well: not a word? My dear, if I have spoken foolishly, correct me; if well, say you agree. Do not sit there dumb! Speak! One word! Look at me! It is no use. (*She weeps.*) All our trouble leads to nothing, and we are as far off as ever; she would not soften before, and still refuses. Listen to me, my lady: be if you will more stubborn than the sea, — but what of your sons, if you should die? Who will take their part? They will never inherit their father's palace — no, by Hippolyta, Queen of the riding Amazons! She has a son whom your boys will serves as slaves, a bastard nursing the ambition of his royal birth, one you know well: Hippolytus!

PHAEDRA. No! No!

NURSE. Ha! Does that touch you?

PHAEDRA. You kill me! Nurse, by all the gods I implore you never again to speak of him!

NURSE. There! You are not out of your mind, far from it! And yet you still refuse both to save your own life and to help your children.

PHAEDRA. I love my children; but something else is drowning me in despair.

NURSE. My daughter, — your hands are free from blood?

PHAEDRA. My hands are pure; but my heart is defiled.

NURSE. Defiled? What? With some wrong done to you by an enemy?

PHAEDRA. No, no enemy! It is no more his will than mine that he should destroy me.

NURSE. Theseus! Has he done you some injury?

PHAEDRA. No! May I prove as guiltless towards him!

NURSE. What then is this terror that is dragging you to your grave?

PHAEDRA. Leave me to my sin. I do not sin against *you*.

NURSE. I will not leave you if I can help it. If I fail it will be your fault.

PHAEDRA. Will you try to force me? Let my hand go!

NURSE. I will not! I will cling to you until you tell me!

PHAEDRA. Poor soul! The truth would be terrible to you too.

NURSE. What could be worse to me than to see you suffer?

PHAEDRA. To tell would kill you; but what I am doing is for my honour —

NURSE. If so, to speak of it will add to your honour before the world.

PHAEDRA. — I am finding a way to bring honour out of shame.

NURSE. Then I am right in begging you to tell me — how can you hide it?

PHAEDRA. For the gods' sake leave me and let go my hand!

NURSE. Never, while you refuse what you owe to me!

PHAEDRA. It is true! I owe it. I will tell you what you ask.

NURSE. I will be quiet. Now it is for you to speak.

PHAEDRA. O my mother! What dreadful, pitiful lust raged within you!

NURSE. You mean her lust for the bull? Or what do you mean, my child?

PHAEDRA. And you too, O my sister, whom Dionysus desired — how love made you suffer!

NURSE. Why speak of them? Those tales are best forgotten.

PHAEDRA. The curse that destroyed them I now inherit.

NURSE. You frighten me! What are you going to say now?

PHAEDRA. My misery began with them. It is no new thing.

NURSE. You tell me no more of what I long to hear.

PHAEDRA. The words that you want me to say — if only you could speak them for me!

NURSE. I am no magician to read hidden thoughts.

PHAEDRA. When they say that one is in love, what do they mean by love?

NURSE. Oh, my child! It is the sweetest of all things, — yet full of pain.

PHAEDRA. It seems I have found the pain, but no sweetness.

NURSE. What are you saying? You love a man? What man?

PHAEDRA. Why, who should it be? It is he! The Amazon's son!

NURSE. Hippolytus!

PHAEDRA. You spoke his name, not I.

NURSE. Oh, my child! What are you saying? Oh! you have broken my heart! Oh, friends, how can I bear it? How can I go on living? Oh! this hateful life, this accursed day! (*She collapses to the ground, and the* CHORUS *come to help her.*) No! Let me fall, leave me alone; I want to die and be at peace! I am dying, my life is over! . . . What does it mean? Here is a pure-hearted woman, with no desire to do wrong, yet lusting after wickedness against her will! (*Defiantly*) Aphrodite is no goddess! No! She has brought this disaster on Phaedra and on me and on the royal house, — she is something more than a goddess — something greater!

CHORUS. Did you hear? Oh, did you hear
The Queen's pitiful cry,
Born of a crueller blow
Than human heart can bear?
Beloved Queen, let me die
Before my heart should know
Your heart's despair!
Oh, Phaedra, daughter of sorrow!
Oh, sorrow, nurse of our race!
Deadly calamity, dragged into sudden light!
How can you live to face,
Hour by hour, the horror that hangs its threat
Over your house, unknown as yet?
The Queen of Love sent you a strange star,
Princess of Crete!
We see now where it will sink and set.

PHAEDRA. Women of Troezen, who live here on the outer threshold of Peloponnese: I have at times lain long awake in the night, thinking how other lives than mine have been shattered; and I believe that such misfortune does not arise from inborn folly, since often those who suffer are wise and good. But this is how we should regard the matter: we know and see what is right, yet fail to carry it out. Some fail through sloth, others through valuing some pleasure more than goodness; and life offers us many pleasures.

Listen: I will tell you the path my thoughts followed. When love struck me, I searched for the best way to endure the wound. My first resolve was to let slip no word, to hide what I suffered; for there is no trusting the tongue, which knows how to instruct others in wisdom, but invites disaster by its own folly. Next, I prepared to endure this madness as I ought, by overcoming it with self-control. Finally, when I still did not succeed in mastering this love, I determined that the best plan for me, beyond all contradiction, was to die. That is the decision I have taken; that is why I did not choose to thwart my own purpose with any kind of healing drug. If I do what is right, I would not wish to hide it, any more than to display my sins before witnesses. I knew that both the thing I craved, and the craving itself, was a sin. I knew also, too well, that I was a woman: a mark for the world's contempt. Whatever woman first was false to her husband with other men, misery and death destroy her! It was from noble houses that this plague first spread among women: when the great choose dishonour, the common herd will do the same. I hate women whose tongues talk of chastity, who in secret are bold in every sin! Queen Aphrodite, born from the sea's purity! how can they look into their husband's eyes, and not shudder lest sheltering darkness and guilty walls should speak? . . . Friends, it is for this I am dying, that I may never be found guilty of disgracing my husband and my children. I want my sons to go back to the city of cities, to Athens, and hold their heads high and speak like free men there, and not blush for their mother. To live burdened with the secret of a parent's sin will enslave the boldest spirit. Only an upright heart and a clear conscience, they say, gives a man strength to wrestle with life; while those whose hearts are evil, sooner or later — as a young girl sees the truth in her glass — so they, when Time holds up his mirror, find their own sin revealed. May I never be found among them!

CHORUS. It is true: virtue, wherever it appears, is a beautiful thing; and the fruit of virtue in this life is a good name.

NURSE. My lady, when I heard what had happened to you, at the first shock I was terrified: now I begin to reflect how foolish I was. In human life second thoughts often prove to be wiser. What has happened to you is nothing extraordinary or hard to understand. The fever of Aphrodite has fastened on you: you are in love. What is strange in that? Why, so are countless others! And do you therefore mean to lose your life for love? Then surely there is a hard road ahead for all lovers now and to come, if their duty is to die! When Love sweeps on in the fulness of her power, there is no resisting. She steals gently on those who yield to her; but those she finds arrogant and haughty she takes and — what do you suppose? — tramples in the dust! Love rides on clouds and strides through the swollen sea. The whole world was born from Love; she sows every seed; every living creature on earth sprang from that sweet desire which is her gift to us. Those who possess pictures drawn in times past, or who spend their days pursuing the arts, — they know that Zeus once lusted for Semele, they know that once the lovely goddess of the glowing dawn stole away Cephalus and took him to live among the gods, because she loved him. Yet Cephalus and she live in the sky, and show no haste to quit the company of gods. Events have proved too strong for them; and they, believe me, are content. And you: do you refuse to submit? Your father, it seems, should have begotten you upon terms, or looked for other gods, if you're resolved to find fault with the laws of Nature. I ask you: how many good and sensible husbands see their wives unfaithful and look the other way? How many fathers help their love-sick sons to get what they want? Why, the true wisdom for mortals is to keep faults well hidden. A builder doesn't plane and polish the rafters in the roof! and it's not for us mortals to struggle after a tiresome perfection. In any case, how do you think you're going to swim clear of this flood of trouble you've met with? You are mortal, child: if the good you find in life outweighs the ill, you will be extremely fortunate. My dear daughter, soften your stubborn heart; do not blaspheme! What is it but blasphemy, to wish yourself stronger than a god? You are in love: then bear — and dare — what the god has willed. You are stricken: turn the stroke to your own good. Why, there are spells and soothing charms; we'll find a medicine for you. Trouble may wait a long time for men to mend it, if we women take no hand in the matter.

CHORUS. Her advice is more practical, Phaedra, for your present need; yet you, I feel, are right. Though it may be my approval is harder for you to accept, and more painful to hear, than her reproaches.

PHAEDRA. This is what brings ruin on fine cities and ancient houses — fair speech, too fair by far! Instead of saying what you think will please me, show me a way to save my honour.

NURSE. This is mere high-flown talk. Fine sentiments will not help you: you must have your man! He must be told in plain words what has happened, and won over without delay. If this were not a matter of life and death, if you were still a chaste-minded woman, I would never encourage you so far for your own lust and pleasure; but now we must fight for your life, — and there is nothing wrong in this.

PHAEDRA. Nothing wrong! It is horrible! Be silent, never speak such shameful words again!

NURSE. Shameful, — maybe; but more use to you than good words. Better do what I say, and live, than die for a vain boast of chastity.

PHAEDRA. No, for the gods' sake! What you say is plausible, but vile. Go no further! I have disciplined my heart to endure this. If you are so eloquent for evil, I shall fall now into the very pit I shrink from.

NURSE. If you feel so, — you should not have sinned at heart. Well, you did: now obey me — and be as ungrateful as you like. I have indoors a drug for the soothing of love — I have only now thought of it; it will bring you into no disgrace, no distress of mind, but it will cure you of your passion, if only you are not faint-hearted.

PHAEDRA. This drug — is it an ointment, or a draught?
NURSE. I don't know. Look for help, my girl, not explanations.
PHAEDRA. You may be too clever, and ruin me. I dread it.
NURSE. Then you would dread anything. What is it you are afraid of?
PHAEDRA. Of your saying any word about me to Hippolytus.
NURSE. Leave that to me, child. I know what to do. (*Aside*) Great
    Queen Aphrodite, only stand by me now, and help! For what
    else I have in mind, a word to our friend in the palace will be
    enough.

                            (*Exit* NURSE. PHAEDRA *remains.*)

CHORUS.

    O Love, immortal Power,                               [*Strophe* 1
    Love, dropping desire like dew on yearning eyes,
        Love, whose triumphant arms
    Ravish the conquered soul with sweetest ecstasy!
        Come not in cruelty,
    Never with ruthless violence invade my life!
        Fiery stroke of star or sun
    Is less to fear than Aphrodite's dart
    Which flies from the hand of Love, the child of Zeus,
        To madden a mortal heart.


    In vain by Alpheus' banks,                            [*Antistrophe* 1
    In vain at the Pythian shrine shall sacrifice multiply,
        And the blood of bulls pour forth,
    Toll from the pastures of Greece to Apollo and Artemis;
        While Eros, Master of man,
        Who holds Aphrodite's key
        To her chamber of sweet delight, —
        Him in our prayers we slight:
    Love, whose coming has brought, since the world began,
        Death and calamity!


    Iole, Princess of Oechalia,                           [*Strophe* 2
    Was once a free and taintless virgin,
    A maiden unmatched with man;
    But Aphrodite tore her from her home,
    A wild nymph, helpless and frantic;
    And there, amidst blood and smoke,
    With dying groans for her bridal-hymn,
    Gave her to the son of Alcmene
    To carry weeping across the sea.

O holy wall of Thebes, [*Antistrophe* 2
O lips of the Dircean spring,
You with one voice could tell
How terrible is the advent of Aphrodite!
When upon Semele thunder and flame descended,
And her womb gave birth to Bacchus, the child of Zeus,
Aphrodite laid her to sleep,
A bride in the bed of Death.
For the breath of her terror is felt in every land,
And swift as a bee's flight
Is the path of her power.

PHAEDRA. Women, be quiet! . . . Oh, the last blow has fallen!

CHORUS. We will be quiet. But this sounds ominous!

PHAEDRA. Wait! I want to hear exactly what they are saying.

CHORUS. Something terrible is happening in the palace. Phaedra, what is it?

PHAEDRA. Oh! Why must I suffer so? It is unbearable!

CHORUS. What is unbearable?
What is this anguished cry?
Tell us, what fearful word
Fell on your ears like Fate?

PHAEDRA. It is — my death! Come, stand near the door and listen. Do you hear what an uproar is rising there?

CHORUS. You are beside the door:
For you the house utters a voice! Tell me, then,
What horror you heard,
Tell me, what has been done?

PHAEDRA. It is the son of the riding Amazon, Hippolytus, cursing and abusing my old servant.

CHORUS. Yes, I can hear the sound,
Yet not a word is clear!
How can I tell? Oh, it was clear to you,
The cry that came from the house!

PHAEDRA. Ah, listen! Yes, too clear! He calls her "filthy bawd," damns her for treason to her master's bed!

CHORUS.
No, no! What shall we do?
Lady, you are betrayed!
What plan can I offer?
Your secret shown to the world,
Your life and hope laid in the dust by the hand of a friend!

PHAEDRA. She has told him the fatal truth about me. She did it for love, to cure my suffering; but it was wrong!

CHORUS. What now? What way out is there? What will you do?

PHAEDRA. I do not know, — only this: that to die at once is the sole escape from this torture.

(*Enter* HIPPOLYTUS, *followed by the* NURSE.)

HIPPOLYTUS. O Mother Earth! O unfolding radiance of the sun! What things I have heard! What words unspeakable have been spoken!

NURSE. Be quiet, lad, or someone will hear this clamour!

HIPPOLYTUS. How can I be quiet after what I have listened to?

NURSE. I beg you, I kiss your hand — dear boy, be quiet!

HIPPOLYTUS. Keep your hands off my clothes! You shall not touch me.

NURSE. For the gods' sake, have pity! Don't tell what I said to you! It would kill me.

HIPPOLYTUS. Kill you? Your words were harmless, you said!

NURSE. What I said, my son, was not for everyone to hear.

HIPPOLYTUS. Honest words should not be hushed up: let everyone hear!

NURSE. My boy, do not slight the oath you swore me!

HIPPOLYTUS. My tongue swore: the oath does not bind my heart.

NURSE. What will you do, child? Destroy your friend?

HIPPOLYTUS. Friend? God forbid I should have any such friend!

NURSE. Forgive! We are human; we cannot help doing wrong.

HIPPOLYTUS. O Zeus! Why have you plagued this world with so vile and worthless a thing as woman? If it was your pleasure to plant a mortal stock, why must women be the renewers of the race? Better that men should come to your temples and put down a price, each what he could afford, — buy themselves children in embryo for gold or silver and get their money's worth; then they could live at home like free men, without women! Why, for proof that woman is an evil pest, — her father, after begetting and bringing her up, pays out a dowry to find her a home, and so gets rid of her; while whoever welcomes the viper to his bosom glee-fully decks her out with gauds and gowns like a sacred statue, heaping beauty upon hatefulness, poor wretch, and squanders his inheritance. What choice has he? If he marries noble blood, he beds with his shrew and makes the best of it; or if he finds a good wife in a worthless family, with that much comfort he counters his ill-luck. For an easy life, marry a nobody, and keep her worth-less and witless on a pedestal. I hate a woman who is clever — a woman who thinks more than becomes a woman; I would not have her in my house! For passion engenders wickedness the more readily in clever women; while the simple are kept from wanton-ness by lack of wit. A wife should have no servant ever come near her, she should live attended by dumb savage beasts, who could neither understand her nor speak to her. As it is, unchaste wives sit at home scheming lechery, while their servants traffic their schemes out to the world: — you for one, coming like a she-devil to invite me to incest with my father's wife! I'll flush your filthy words from my ears with floods of water! Do you think I could so sin, when I feel polluted merely by hearing you? Listen: I let you trap me into swearing silence. I fear the gods, and that saves you; otherwise I would at once have told my father the whole story. Instead, I shall now leave the palace until he comes back; and I shall say nothing; but I shall come back with my father, and then I shall observe how you and your mistress meet his eye. You at least will brazen it out — I know what you're made of. — Curse the whole race of you! I can never hate you enough. Ha! They tell me I always say the same thing: well, women, it seems, always *are* the same thing. So whoever can teach women to be chaste may forbid me to tread their name in the dust!

(*Exit.*)

CHORUS. How cruel a curse it is to be born a woman!
Who would not pity us?
What shift, what turn, what plea,
After the first faltering,
Can loose us from the clamp of guilt?

PHAEDRA. I have met what I deserved.
Earth and sunlight, show me where to fly
Out of the clutch of Fate!
Where can I hide my anguish?
What god or man can give to my guilty soul
Safety or help or counsel?
I am caught in toils of torment;
There is no escape for the living:
I sink under the scourge of Chance.

CHORUS. Lady, I weep with you. The harm is done; your servant's plans have failed disastrously.

PHAEDRA (*to* NURSE). You vile, treacherous murderess, see what you have done to me! May Zeus who gave me life blast you with fire and grind you to dust! Did I not try to prevent what you were plotting? Did I not forbid you to speak a word of what now drags me in the dirt? You spoke: and your treason robs even my death of honour. Now — some new plan. Hippolytus, white-hot with rage, will carry your foul words to his father and denounce me; go complaining to old Pittheus, fill the whole land with his

outrageous tale! Curse you! Curse all officious fools who thrust
their wicked help on their friends to ruin them!

NURSE. My lady, I have done you wrong; you may well blame me.
The wound pricks, and overcomes your judgement. Yet, if you'll
listen to me, I can speak for myself. I nursed you; I am your
friend; I tried to find a remedy for your trouble; and I was unlucky. With better luck, I would have been called a wise woman.
After all, wisdom is only happening to guess right.

PHAEDRA. So! This is your just amends to me — to follow up your
treachery with argument!

NURSE. We are wasting time in talk. I admit I was unwise; but, my
daughter, there's hope, there's life, even now!

PHAEDRA. Stop! Not another word! You gave me advice before, and
help too; and both were wicked. Get out of my sight! Scheme
for your own affairs, and I will set mine in order!

(*Exit* NURSE.)

Noblewomen of Troezen, I ask you to do me this favour: bury
deep in silence all that you have heard here today.

CHORUS. By holy Artemis, daughter of Zeus, I swear to disclose nothing of what has happened to you.

PHAEDRA. That is well. Listen, my friends — I have said this before — :
I have a remedy for my present plight; one that will ensure an
honourable future for my sons, and help me in face of to-day's
calamity. The royal house of Crete shall forfeit no reputation
through me. After this shame, to face Theseus would be too high
a price for one life.

CHORUS. What are you going to do, that is so dreadful and so final?

PHAEDRA. To die. By what means, I will decide for myself.

CHORUS. In God's name, no!

PHAEDRA. You too must school me; I know my part. To-day I'll be
rid of life, and give joy to my immortal murderess. Love is without mercy: I shall die defeated. Yet my death shall be a curse on
another's life, and teach him not to trample on my agony. He
shall have an equal share in my suffering, and learn to be gentle!

(*Exit* PHAEDRA.)

CHORUS.

O to escape and hide                                        [*Strophe* 1
High among steep and secret rocks!
At the touch of a god to change,
To rise as a bird and ride
On feathered wings among soaring flocks!
To wander far and free

Where the lost waters of Eridanus flow deep
Down to an unknown sea;
Where for dead Phaethon the Sun's daughters weep,
  Dropping piteous tears that gleam
  Like amber in the purple stream!

And O for that quiet garden by the Western sea   [*Antistrophe* 1
  Where the daughters of Evening sing
  Under the golden apple-tree;
  Where the bold sailor wandering
  Finds the Ocean-god has barred
His Westward path over the purple waste!
  Where huge Atlas lives to guard
  The solemn frontiers of the sky;
Where in Zeus' palace fountains of ambrosial wine
  Flow by the festal couch divine,
  While holy Earth heaps high
  Her fruits of rarest taste
To bless the immortal feast with bountiful supply!

  White-winged Cretan ship,   [*Strophe* 2
That brought my lady Phaedra from her wealthy home
Over the salt swell of the pounding sea, —
  White sails for the joy of a bride,
  To veil the black fate waiting!
Heavy with omen was her course
From Crete to Athens, queen of mainland cities,
When at Peiraeus her seamen leapt ashore
And looped their plaited hawsers on the quay;
  Dark again was the hour
When from the rocky harbour of Munychion
The royal progress parted for Troezen.

Thence on Phaedra fell the fatal curse,   [*Antistrophe* 2
When Aphrodite with a cruel unholy lust
  Shattered her helpless heart!
  Now the storm of her distress
  Drives her, a sinking wreck,
  Alone to her marriage-chamber.
From the high beam she will tie
  Close round her white neck the noose:
  This her one choice, to die!
Thus with reverence learnt for her immortal enemy,

And prizing a fair name above her life,
She will win release of heart from her tormenting love.

(*A voice is heard shouting from the palace.*)

VOICE. Oh, help, help! Anyone who is in the house, come and help! She is hanging — the Queen, the wife of Theseus!

CHORUS. Oh! She has kept her word! Oh, Phaedra, Phaedra! She is dead, dead! the Queen! Hung high in a strangling rope!

VOICE. Come quickly! Bring a knife, a sword, anything to cut this cord from her neck!

CHORUS. A. Friends, what shall we do? Ought we to go inside and untie the noose and free her?

B. Why, where are the young men who attend her? It is never safe to interfere.

VOICE. Poor lady, she is dead! Lay her limbs out straight. Oh, what a tale to have to tell my master!

CHORUS. Did you hear? Poor Phaedra, she is dead; they are already laying out her body.

(*Enter* THESEUS, *attended by the royal guard. His head is crowned with the garland worn by those who have received a favourable answer from an oracle.*)

THESEUS. Tell me, women, — what was that outcry in the palace? What I heard was the voices of servants weeping. (*There is silence.*) This is strange: I return home from a solemn mission of piety — and my home receives me with shut doors, not a word of welcome or greeting! . . . I hope nothing has happened to Pittheus? He is well advanced in years; yet his departure from this house would be a grief to me.

CHORUS. What has happened, Theseus, has not touched the old. It is the young whose death will break your heart.

THESEUS. What? Is one of my children's lives stolen from me?

CHORUS. No, it is still more terrible: their mother is dead.

THESEUS. What do you say? My wife dead? What happened?

CHORUS. She made a noose with a rope and hanged herself.

THESEUS. But why? Was it some numbing stroke of grief? What could cause so dreadful an act?

CHORUS. That is all I know, Theseus. I have just now come to the palace to mourn for your loss.

THESEUS. Phaedra — dead! . . . Why have I crowned my head with this garland of leaves? *Here* is my answer from the oracle! — Ho, there! Servants! Unbar the doors and open! Open them wide, let me see my dead wife, whose death is death to me!

(*The doors open, showing* PHAEDRA *dead.*)

CHORUS.
Weep for the Queen, tears for her tears!
Phaedra, your agony and your act alike
Must banish peace from this house!
How could you dare a death so hideous, so unholy,
A prey to your own pitiless hand?
Poor soul, what power dims your brightness in death?

THESEUS. O the torture of life! In this city of exile
I have seen surely the utmost of the grief appointed for me!
O Fate, like a cruel heel crushing me and my house,
A nameless foul infection from some pursuing fiend,
Corrupting, annihilating life and the love of life!
I strain despairing eyes over my sea of misery,
And my hope of safety vanishes, for the shore is out of sight
And life is a mounting wave I have not strength to surmount.
    What reason, Phaedra, what malicious chance,
    What fated cruelty can I accuse?
    As a bird from my hand you have vanished,
Swooped swift and daring into the pit of darkness
And left me tears for your death and anguish for your despair!
    Far from here this harvest grew;
    Long ago a sin was sown;
        Fruit the gods have ripened
        For my grief I gather.

CHORUS. King, this sorrow falls not on your soul alone:
        Many share it, weeping
        A dear wife departed.

THESEUS.
To go into the dark! Now let me die, and pass
To the world under the earth, into the joyless dark!
Since you, dearer than all, are at my side no longer,
And the death you have dealt is more than the death that has swal-
    lowed you.
Who will tell me the truth? Whence, my wife, could it come, —
This chance, whose murderous blow fell on your tortured heart?
What happened? Shall I be told? Or does my palace harbour
A horde of lying lackeys? Phaedra! my heart is broken!
Friends, pity me, who have lived to see such pain
Ravage my home! No words can speak of it,
No human heart bear it. My life is over.
    Now my house is desolate,
    And my children motherless.
    You, the dearest, best, of all

That the dazzling sun surveys
Or the star-eyed evening, —
You are gone for ever!

(*As* THESEUS *has been speaking, the* CHORUS *have noticed a letter tied to* PHAEDRA'S *wrist.*)

CHORUS. Theseus, I pity you for the storm that wrecks your home.
Yet, while I have watched your sorrow with tear-filled eyes,
Still I tremble with deeper dread for the terror to come!

THESEUS. Look! Look here! A letter fastened to her dear hand! What does this mean? Will it tell me something new? Surely, she has written her dying wishes, begging me to remember our marriage and our children. Rest easy, Phaedra! My house and bed shall never be entered by another woman! See, the impression of her golden signet brings me her greeting from the dead! Now to untwist the cord from the seal, and see what this letter has to tell me.

CHORUS. Here is a crueller pain, a deeper horror
Sent by the gods to crown the rest! If it were I, —
Knowing the truth, how could I bear my life?
The royal house heaped in ruin, never to rise!
Gods have pity! Strike not down!
Hear and help us! . . . In his eyes,
See, so grimly staring,
Portents of disaster!

THESEUS. Oh, oh! Horror upon horror, blow upon blow! Beyond endurance, beyond speech! Oh!

CHORUS. What now? If it is for us to hear, tell us!

THESEUS.
The letter! It shrieks, it howls, horrors indelible!
I am crushed; where can I escape? What I have seen has killed me.
A voice from the letter speaks, and tells — what things! what things!

CHORUS. What are you saying, Theseus? Something dreadful must follow.

THESEUS. A thing so dreadful that I scarcely can force my tongue
To utter it. Yet I will speak now. Listen, O city!
Hippolytus has braved the holy eye of Zeus and done violence to my wife's honour!
Yes, Poseidon my father, you promised me three curses: with one of them strike down my son! If they were good curses you gave me, let him not live out this day!

CHORUS. My lord, in heaven's name, take your prayer back! You are wrong — you will know it later; only trust me!

THESEUS. There is no taking back. I will not only curse but banish him from the land. If the one fails he shall feel the other. Either

Poseidon will honour my curse and send his corpse below, or else as a stranger wandering the earth, an outcast from his country, he shall drain his despicable life to the dregs.

CHORUS. Why, look! Here, this very moment, comes your son himself, Hippolytus! King Theseus, calm this dangerous anger, and consider what will be best for yourself and your family.

(*Enter* HIPPOLYTUS, *with Huntsmen.*)

HIPPOLYTUS. Father, I heard your outcry and came at once. What trouble has caused your distress I do not know; but I wish you would tell me. . . . Oh! What do I see? It is your wife, Father — dead! Dead? How is it possible? I had only just left her; a short time ago she was alive! What has happened to her? How did she die? . . . Father, I am asking you to tell me! Will you not speak? This is no time to be silent! I know that to insist out of season on being told everything is called idle curiosity; but I am a friend — something more than a friend. Surely, Father, you should not hide trouble from me!

THESEUS. Oh, the futile folly of men! Why do they teach arts innumerable, contrive and search out every other thing, — when one knowledge they cannot win, one quarry they have not caught: the skill to teach wisdom to the brutish.

HIPPOLYTUS. He would certainly be a clever instructor who could drive sense into a fool. But, Father, this is not the time for philosophical discourse. Sorrow, I fear, is making you talk wildly.

THESEUS. Oh, there should be somewhere a touchstone of human hearts, which men could trust to tell them the truth about their friends, who is loyal and who treacherous! Every man should have two voices, the one truthful, the other — natural; so that his lying voice might be refuted by the true; and we should not be duped.

HIPPOLYTUS. What? Has one of your friends contrived to slander me to you and make you suspect my innocence? I am bewildered, astonished! Your words are crazed, you have taken leave of your wits!

THESEUS. The heart of man! Is there any vileness it will turn from? Will barefaced wickedness ever find its limit? If crime is to bulk bigger with each new generation, new depths of villainy be revealed age after age, the gods will need to create a second earth to house liars and lechers. Look at this man! my own son, who would pollute my marriage-bed, — and is proved guilty by the damning witness of her dead hand. Come, show your face — foul as you are, look your father in the eyes! So you — you are the man above men who keeps the company of gods! Yours is the

chaste life unsmirched with evil! Who believes your bragging?
Who charges gods with such ignorance and folly? Not I! So,
now flaunt your purity! Play the quack with your fleshless diets!
Take Orpheus for your lord and prophet and wallow in frenzied
adoration of his wordy vapourings! Yes, you are exposed! Of
such men let the world take warning and beware! They pursue
their prey with lofty words and low cunning. — Oh, she is dead:
do you think that will save you? No, vile criminal, it is the
prime evidence of your guilt. What oaths or arguments could
outweigh her witness and acquit you? You will say that she hated
you; that there will always be war between the bastard and the
true-born. Was she so poor a bargainer with her life, that she
would throw away all its sweetness to spite you? Or will you
tell me that young men are free from folly, women born to it?
Well I know that young men are no steadier than women, when
Aphrodite stirs the hot blood in them. Indeed, their sex makes
them even more headstrong.

Ah! why should I fight down your defence, when her dead
body blazons its evidence to my eyes? Out of this land to exile!
Go, I say! Never come near the god-built walls of Athens, cross
no frontier that my sword guards! I tell you, if I weaken before
this outrage, the Isthmian bandit Sinis shall deny that I killed
him, and call me boaster; and the sea-washed rocks where Sciron
met his end shall forget the weight of my hand against evildoers!

CHORUS. How can any mortal man be called happy? Until to-day,
Hippolytus, you were first in good fortune: now everything is
reversed.

HIPPOLYTUS. Father, your passionate anger is terrible; and though
what you say at first appears just, you will find it does not bear
closer scrutiny. Though I have no skill to address a crowd, among
a few equals I can speak with more confidence. And this is
natural; just as those who seem fools among wise men can be
eloquent before crowds. So, now that my whole life is in danger,
I must be bold and speak.

And I will begin with the first charge you levelled at me, which
you thought would leave me shattered and speechless. Look at
this sky, this earth: in the length and breadth of them there is
no man — deny it as you will — more pure in heart than I! I
have learnt, first, to reverence the gods; then, to choose friends
who keep their hands innocent, whose honour forbids them either
to render me or expect from me any discreditable service. I do
not mock those I live among, Father; I am the same to my friends
absent or present. One sin you now think me convicted of has

never touched me: to this day my body is chaste; I have not known a woman. I know nothing of such matters, more than I have heard men tell, or seen in pictures; which I have little desire to look at, for my mind is virgin. Perhaps you refuse to believe that I am pure: then it is for you to show what temptation was too strong for me. Was your wife more beautiful than all other women? Or did I hope, by winning her love, to become your heir? Any such hope would have been less vain than mad! Did I covet your place as king? For a wise man a throne has no attraction; to find pleasure in power is to be corrupted by it — there are many examples. No; my ambition is a different one: let me be first in the Grecian Games, and in politics take second place, and be happy with honest friends. In this way I am able to live my own life — and to live free from danger, which is a greater blessing than a crown.

That is all I have to say, except one thing: if a witness to my innocence were here to speak, and if Phaedra were alive to listen to my defence, then the event would guide your search for the guilty. As things are, I swear to you by Zeus, Guardian of oaths, and by the Earth, that I never touched your wife, never could have wished even to think of it. I pray that I may die in nameless dishonour, cityless, homeless, exile and vagabond, — may neither sea nor land receive my dead flesh, if there is sin in me! Whether it was fear that made Phaedra take her life I do not know; further than this it is impossible for me to speak. She kept her chastity, without possessing the virtue of chastity; I possess it, and have practised it to my own ruin.

CHORUS. Surely what you have said will suffice to clear you! Your solemn oaths to the gods must be believed.

THESEUS. Is he not a spellmonger, a cheat, hoping to master my mind with his smooth temper, after putting his father to open shame?

HIPPOLYTUS. It is *your* smooth temper that I wonder at, Father. If you were my son, and I in your place, I would have killed you, not corrected you with exile, if you had dared to touch my wife.

THESEUS. Indeed! How justly! No, you shall not die like that. Many a criminal would be glad of a quick death. No: since you have passed sentence on yourself, you shall wander an outcast from your country, on alien soil you shall drain the bitter lees of life, and earn a criminal's reward.

HIPPOLYTUS. What? You will do that? You will not wait for the witness of time to condemn me, but drive me out to-day?

THESEUS. Yes! beyond the outer ocean and the ends of the earth, if I had the power, so abominable to me is the sight of you!

HIPPOLYTUS. You spurn my sworn oath, you seek no guidance of priests, but banish me unjudged?

THESEUS. Priests! with their omens from birds that fly about over-head! To me they are nothing at all! This letter here is no soothsayer's riddle, and it proves you guilty.

HIPPOLYTUS. Why do I not unlock my lips? You gods, whom my silence honours, it is you who destroy me! — No: I will not speak. Nothing I might say now could carry weight where it would help me. To tell the truth would be to break my oath and gain nothing.

THESEUS. Still your cursed piety! It chokes me! What are you waiting for? Out of my land, I say!

HIPPOLYTUS. Out of your land? Which way shall I turn? Who of my friends will receive me, exiled on such a charge?

THESEUS. Who? Any that has a warm welcome for the defiler of men's wives, the bosom-friend of all iniquity!

HIPPOLYTUS. Oh, it is time indeed for tears and a broken heart, when my father thinks and truly believes that I am guilty.

THESEUS. The time for you to weep and be wise was the time when you cast off shame to dishonour your father's wife!

HIPPOLYTUS. Oh, if these walls could but cry out and speak for me, and witness whether I am so vile a man!

THESEUS. You are careful to fly for help to dumb witnesses; but the fact needs no tongue to prove you guilty.

HIPPOLYTUS. I wish for very pity that I could stand apart and behold myself, to shed tears for my own suffering!

THESEUS. No doubt! You are far more practised in self-worship than in self-control and honourable conduct to your father.

HIPPOLYTUS. My unhappy mother! I was born in bitterness of sorrow. May no one that I love ever be called bastard!

THESEUS. Guards! take him away! Do you not hear? I have already pronounced him banished.

HIPPOLYTUS. It will be the worse for any of them that touches me. Since you're so minded, thrust me out yourself!

THESEUS. I will do so, unless you obey me. Your exile does not touch my tears.

*(Exit* THESEUS.*)*

HIPPOLYTUS. My fate, then, is fixed. It is sad and cruel, that I know the truth, yet know no way to speak it. *(He turns to the figure of* ARTEMIS.*)* Goddess, daughter of Leto, most dear companion, and comrade in the hunt, I shall live exiled for ever from glorious Athens! Farewell, my city; farewell, land of Erechtheus; farewell, plain of Troezen, rich in the vigorous delights of youth! I take my last look now, speak my last word to you. And you too, lads that have grown up with me here, — come, say good-bye to me and see me to the border. Though even my own father denies it, you will never meet a man more honourable.

(*Exit* HIPPOLYTUS *with his men.*)

CHORUS.

When I remember that the gods take thought          [*Strophe* 1
For human life, often in hours of grief
  To me this faith has brought
  Comfort and heart's relief.

Yet, though deep in my hope perception lies
Wistful, experience grows and faith recedes:
  Men's fortunes fall and rise
  Not answering to their deeds.

Change follows change; Fate purposeless and blind
Uproots us from familiar soil:
  The longest life can find
  No rest from travel and toil.

This is my prayer: may divine providence fulfil          [*Antistrophe* 1
  All my heart's will,
  And bless my days with wealth, and guard
My life from pain, and keep my soul unscarred.

The dauntless stern resolve is not for me,
Nor the fair face masking the false intent;
  Rather my choice would be
To change my ways, adapt my easy creed
  To suit to-morrow's need,
And pass my quiet days in long content.

I cannot think clearly now:          [*Strophe* 2
I have seen a thing that I never thought to see, —
I have seen the brightest star of the city of Athens
Driven out by his father's anger
To look for another country.
Sandy shore fringing the city-wall,
You will not see him now;
Nor you, oak-forests of the mountain-side,
Where in the train of the immortal Huntress
He followed with swift-footed hounds to make his kill!

We shall not see him now                                    [*Antistrophe* 2
Leap up behind his trained Thessalian team,
Holding the smooth track round the shore-marshes
Breathless with the tense drumming of hooves.
The music that sang unsleeping from the plucked string
Shall be dumb in his father's palace.
The garlands will wither now
That you strewed in the deep Spring grass
Where Artemis loved to rest;
And the jealous war of girls who longed for your love,
Now you are gone, sinks into hopeless peace.

To me, Hippolytus, your fate has left                          [*Epode*
A life unreal, empty of all but tears.
  Dead are the dreams that lit
  Your mother's pains with joy.
Gods immortal, mortal rage reproaches you!
  How, you sister Graces,
Can you see him hounded from his father's home,
  Innocent, and outcast —
  Righteous, and uprooted?

CHORUS.  Look!  Someone is running this way!  It is one of Hippolytus'
    men!  And his eyes are full of horror!

(*Enter* MESSENGER.)

MESSENGER.  Women, where can I find the King?  Where is Theseus?
    If you know, tell me.  Is he indoors?
CHORUS.  Here is the King.  He is coming out now.

(*Enter* THESEUS.)

MESSENGER.  Theseus, I bring grave news — grave both for you and
    for all your people, whether of Athens or of Troezen.
THESEUS.  What is your news?  Can yet another calamity have fallen
    upon our two cities?
MESSENGER.  Hippolytus is dead — or dying.  His life hangs in the
    balance.
THESEUS.  Who struck him?  Was it the vengeance of some man whose
    wife he had dishonoured as he did his father's?
MESSENGER.  It was his own chariot that killed him — and the curses
    which your lips called down from your father the sea-god upon
    your son.
THESEUS.  By the gods! — so you have proved a true father to me,
    Poseidon: you heard my curse!  And how did it happen?  Tell

me! How did the trap of justice close on the man who shamed me?

MESSENGER. We were on the shore, near the water's edge, combing down the horses and smoothing their manes; and we were weeping, for we had been told that Hippolytus was no longer free to come and go in Troezen, but was condemned by you to the miseries of exile. He came to us there, bringing the same tale of tears; and a great troop of friends and followers, young men like himself, came with him. After some time he stopped weeping and said to us, "This is folly; my father must be obeyed. Men, yoke my horses, harness them to the chariot. This is not my country any more." Then every man of us came with a will, and sooner than you could say it we had the team harnessed and standing ready at the prince's side. He caught up the reins from the driving-rail, and, dressed as he was for hunting, took his stand on the chariot. And first he held up his hands and prayed: "Zeus, may I die if I am a guilty man! And may my father know how he has wronged me, — if not while I live, then after I am dead!"

And now he had gripped the goad and was urging his horses; and we servants began running beside the bridles, to escort our master along the straight road to Argos and Epidauria. We sped on, across the Troezenian frontier, and reached a deserted part of the coast, beyond which, as you know, a beach runs down to the Saronic Sea. It was there that we heard a heavy rumbling sound, like the thunder of Zeus, but rising out of the earth, with a deep roar that was horrible to hear. The horses pricked their ears, lifted their heads. We youths were terrified, wondering where the sound came from. We looked out to the breaking surf, and there we saw a wave of unearthly size, rearing to the sky; it hid from my view not only the Scironian headland but the Isthmus and the Rock of Asclepius. Then, swelling still huger, and spattering foam on every side, it rushed seething and hissing to the shore, and straight towards the chariot and the four horses. And in the very moment of bursting and crashing, the wave threw forth a monstrous savage bull, whose bellow filled the whole earth with an appalling echo, while the sight of him was too tremendous for mortal vision. The horses were seized with a frenzy of terror. Hippolytus, using his long experience in the ways of horses, gripped the reins, twisting them round behind his back and dragging on them as a rower tugs on his oar. It was no use: the beasts took the wrought-iron bits between their teeth and careered on, as though the driver's hand and the reins and harness and the

heavy chariot were nothing at all! When he struggled to steer
their hurtling course up towards the soft grass, there was the bull
in front to craze them with terror and turn them back; when they
went madly tearing towards the rocks, then the bull kept close
beside them, silent, and swerving right in upon the chariot, until
the moment when he crashed the boss of the wheel against a
rock and flung the chariot tossing in the air. Then there was
wild confusion — wheels, axle, bolts, and frame leaping high.
Hippolytus, tangled in the reins, strung fast in an inextricable
knot, was dragged along, his head dashed on the rocks, his flesh
torn; while in a voice terrible to hear he shouted to his horses,
"Stop! You were reared in my own stables — will you grind
me to death?" Then he cried, "Father, why did you curse me?
I am innocent! Will no one come to help me?"

Indeed, there were many of us willing enough, but run as we
might we were left behind. At last — how I do not know — he
fell clear of those fine reins that bound him. He still breathed;
though there was little life left in him. The horses had vanished
away over the rocky ground, I cannot tell where; so had the
dreadful prodigy of a bull.

My lord: I am only one of your palace slaves; but I never can
nor will believe that your son was guilty of so terrible a crime —
no, not if the whole race of women hanged themselves, not if a
mountain of letters were written to accuse him: I know that
Hippolytus is a good man.

CHORUS. The wheel has turned; disaster follows disaster. Fate is inevitable; there is no escape.

THESEUS. Because I hated the man who has suffered this, I was glad
when I heard it; but remembrance of the gods awes me: Hippolytus is my own flesh. What has happened gives me neither
pleasure nor grief.

MESSENGER. What shall we do? Shall we bring him to die here? Or
what would please you? Consider: your son is struck down.
Listen to my advice and do not be harsh to him.

THESEUS. Bring him. Let me see face to face the man who denies
that he dishonoured my bed; so that my words and the hand of
heaven may convict him.

(*Exit* MESSENGER.)

CHORUS. Aphrodite! You lead captive
Stubborn hearts of gods and mortals!
At your side with glinting wing
Eros, round his victim swiftly circling,
Hovers over earth and the salt sea's clear song.

When on the maddened spirit
He swoops with sweet enchantment,
Whelps of the mountain know the power of his golden wing;
Fish, and the unnumbered beasts that draw
Life from the earth's breast, warmth from the sun's eye, —
Yes, and the hearts of men,
Yield to the universal spell.
Aphrodite, you alone
Reign in power and honour,
Queen of all creation!

(THESEUS *and the* CHORUS *are facing the statue of* APHRODITE; ARTEMIS *appears beside her own statue on the other side of the stage. As she speaks all turn towards her.*)

ARTEMIS. Theseus, royal son of Aegeus! I command you,
Listen! It is Artemis, Leto's daughter, who speaks.
Why do you, wretch, rejoice at what you have heard?
You have most sinfully murdered your own son.
You believed your wife's lies without witness: now
Witness the world how you reap your own undoing!
Will you not cower shamed in the depths of hell?
Soar to the sky to escape this chain of misery?
In the common life of good men
There is no place for you now.

(*She moves to centre of stage.*)

I will tell you, Theseus, the true state of your unhappy life; and my words will not smooth your path, but sharpen your pain. My purpose in coming is to disclose, first, your son's uprightness of heart, that he may die with a good name; then, your wife's frenzy — or, in some sense, her nobleness. Phaedra, plagued and goaded by that goddess whom I, and all who love virginity, most hate — Phaedra loved your son. Reason struggled to subdue passion. She died through schemes plotted against her will: her nurse told Hippolytus, under oath of secrecy, the Queen's affliction. He honourably resisted her persuasions; even when you so wronged him, still for reverence of the gods he would not abjure his oath; but Phaedra, in terror lest she be exposed, wrote that lying letter and by fraud killed your son — yes, for you believed her!

THESEUS. My son, my son!

ARTEMIS. Do my words hurt, Theseus? Listen further, for you have more to suffer. You know that your father promised you the fulfilment of three curses? The first you have most wickedly mis-

used, cursing your son when you might have cursed an enemy.
Your father the sea-god gave all that he was bound to give. He
had promised; and the folly was not his. Now in his eyes and in
mine you are condemned. Instead of waiting for proof, or prophetic guidance, giving no room for question or the slow scrutiny
of Time, with unrighteous haste you flung your curse and killed
your son.

THESEUS. Goddess, let me die!

ARTEMIS. Your sin is great. Yet even you may still find pardon for
what you have done. For it was Aphrodite who, to satisfy her
resentment, willed that all this should happen; and there is a law
among gods, that no one of us should seek to frustrate another's
purpose, but let well alone. I tell you, but that I fear Zeus and
his laws, I never would have submitted to such dishonour, as to
stand by and see Hippolytus go to his death; for he was dearest to
me of all mortals. You did not know the truth: this, first, frees
your fault from the deepest guilt. Then, your wife by her death
prevented any test of what she alleged, and thus made sure that
you would believe her. So this flood of misfortune has burst
chiefly upon you; but I too suffer. For a good man's death is no
joy to the gods; but the impious man we utterly destroy, and his
house and children with him.

CHORUS. Ah, look! Here comes the piteous prince,
His young flesh torn, his fair head bruised.
Ah, suffering house! The hand of heaven has struck
Twice in one day, accomplishing
The heavy doom of your appointed pain.

    (*Enter* HIPPOLYTUS, *supported by huntsmen.*)

HIPPOLYTUS. Weep for me, weep for me,
Scarred, broken, trampled under foot
By man and god alike unjust, —
My father's curse, Poseidon's power;
Weep for my death!
My forehead is pierced with the fierce pain,
My brain convulsed with the pulse of anguish.
Enough now! I am fainting; let me lie.

        (*They lay him down.*)

O horses my own hand fed,
Your cursed strength has crushed the breath from my body,
Torn the life from my limbs!
Men, for God's sake have careful hands
And touch me gently where the flesh is raw.

Who stands at my right side?
Lift me softly, with a steady grip.
Fallen cursed by my father's fault —
Zeus, do you see my agony?
I, that revered the gods with a holy heart,
I that was first in innocence,
Tread my way from life to the dark world,
And Death's eyes meet me as I go.

In vain I strove with patience
To love and serve my neighbour:
Now pain sets painful foot upon my body.
Let go, hold me no longer,
But let Death come to heal me;
And, if you pity me, help me to die quickly!
I am in love with the rending spear: come, cruel edge,
Shatter my heart and lull my life asleep!
Now, through my father's fatal curse,
The hellish heritage of bloodguiltiness
Won by forgotten ancestors
Descends impatient to the appointed heir —
On me it falls! Why? Why? I have done no wrong!
What shall I say? How can I ease my soul
And reach the end of anguish?
Lay me deep for evermore,
Death, with sore unyielding hand,
In the land of night and sleep!

ARTEMIS. Poor soul, galled with a bitter yoke! It was your noble heart that destroyed you.

HIPPOLYTUS. Ah, breath of divine fragrance! Goddess, I hear you, and my torment lightens. Is it truly Artemis, here in this place?

ARTEMIS. Poor soul, it is. You have no better friend among the gods.

HIPPOLYTUS. Lady, you see how it is with me?

ARTEMIS. I see; but my eyes are forbidden to shed tears.

HIPPOLYTUS. No one now to attend you in the hunt. . . .

ARTEMIS. No: you were my dear attendant; and you are dying.

HIPPOLYTUS. None to graze your horses, or guard your statues.

ARTEMIS. The wicked craft of Aphrodite has done this.

HIPPOLYTUS. Aphrodite! So, I know what god has killed me.

ARTEMIS. She resented your neglect and hated your purity.

HIPPOLYTUS. It is clear to me now: she has destroyed us all three.

ARTEMIS. You, and your father, and your father's wife.

HIPPOLYTUS. Though my father wronged me, yet I weep for him.

ARTEMIS. He was deceived: a god had planned it so.
HIPPOLYTUS. Father, how you have suffered to-day!
THESEUS. My son, my heart is broken; life is loathsome to me.
HIPPOLYTUS. Though the fault was yours, I weep for you more than
    for myself.
THESEUS. Would God I might die for you, my son!
HIPPOLYTUS. You too had little joy of your father's gifts.
THESEUS. O that that curse had never passed my lips!
HIPPOLYTUS. Why? You would have killed me, you were so angry
    then!
THESEUS. I was cheated by the gods out of my right mind!
HIPPOLYTUS. Oh, if only a man's curse could touch a god!
ARTEMIS. You need not curse. Not even the black depths
  Beneath the earth shall thwart the vengeance due
  For this cruel wrong that Aphrodite's rage
  Wreaked on your body for your pure soul's sake.
  I will requite her: with this unfailing bow
  My own hand shall strike down in just return
  The man her heart holds dearest in the world.
    On you, poor youth, I will bestow a place
  Of highest honour in the city of Troezen.
  The unmarried virgins shall, before their marriage,
  Cut off their hair for you; age after age
  Harvest of tears and mourning shall be yours,
  Music of maidens' sorrow for your death.
  And Phaedra too shall give her name to memory,
  And songs shall celebrate her love for you.
    Theseus, remember your own father Aegeus:
  Embrace your son and clasp him to your heart.
  His death was not your will: men may well sin,
  When the gods so ordain.
                   Hippolytus,
  You must not hate your father; you know now
  The destiny which has destroyed your life.
  Farewell: I may not look upon the dead,
  Nor stain my sight with death's last agony;
  And now I see that you are near your end.
HIPPOLYTUS.
    Farewell, immortal Virgin! Easy it is
    For you to sever our long fellowship.
    Since you desire it, I forgive my father,
    As in days past I have obeyed your word.
    Ah!

Darkness is closing now over my eyes.
Father, take hold of me; lift me upright.
THESEUS. What is it, dear son? Will you break my heart?
HIPPOLYTUS. I stand before Death's gates; I see them open.
THESEUS. And will you leave me guilty and defiled?
HIPPOLYTUS. No, no! I here absolve you of my death!
THESEUS. What? You will free me from the stain of blood?
HIPPOLYTUS. I swear it by the conquering bow of Artemis.
THESEUS. Dear son, how noble a heart you show your father!
HIPPOLYTUS. Pray that your true-born sons may be like me!
THESEUS. O generous soul, dying in innocence!
HIPPOLYTUS. Farewell, my father! Farewell, and farewell!
THESEUS. Do not forsake me now! Courage, my son!
HIPPOLYTUS.

My time for courage is past. I am gone, Father.
Cover my face now quickly with my cloak.

*(He dies.)*

THESEUS.

Land of Athens, frontiers of a famous city!
    When was man more noble?
    When was loss more bitter?
Aphrodite! with what endless tears and anguish
    Shall your cruel contriving
    Haunt my heart for ever!

CHORUS.

Grief unlooked-for now fills every heart alike;
    Tears from all eyes falling
    Shall make mournful music.
He was noble: loudly then from every tongue
    Praise and lamentation
    Through the world shall echo!

## TRANSLATOR'S NOTES

(These notes have been kept as few and as brief as possible. In general, I have not included information which can be more satisfactorily found in a small Classical Dictionary.)

Page 14. *The Cyprian:* the Greek name "Aphrodite" is native to Homeric verse and fits awkwardly into iambics; so that "Kupris," "The Cyprian," is almost everywhere used in tragedy. (This name, in fact, frequently drops its personal meaning and becomes an abstract noun for "sexual love.") In the translation I have kept "Aphrodite" throughout for the sake of clarity.

Page 15. *The Amazon:* the Queen of the Amazons, Hippolyta, captured in war by Theseus. Shakespeare in *A Midsummer Night's Dream* makes her Theseus' honoured bride; but in the original legend she was a virgin queen subdued by force to the bed of her conqueror. Euripides plainly has this less happy situation in mind as the psychological background of the character of Hippolytus.

Page 17. *To me she is nothing at all:* the Greek phrase is an ironically polite dismissal, "Many good-byes to her!" This blasphemy is unconsciously echoed by Theseus on p. 38, in reference to divination by means of birds. As there seems to be no suitable ironic phrase in English to fit both passages, I have used a plain and flat statement.

Page 22. *O my mother!* Phaedra was the daughter of Pasiphaë, who gave birth to the monster called the Minotaur. For this sense of hereditary guilt compare Theseus' words on p. 33, "Far from here this harvest grew," etc.

Page 23. *The Queen's pitiful cry:* this may refer to Phaedra's words, "It is he, the Amazon's son!" But presumably during the Nurse's speech Phaedra would be audibly weeping.

Page 23. *And life offers us many pleasures:* here follow four lines which I have ventured to omit. Their meaning is as follows: ". . . many pleasures: long gossipings and idleness, a pleasant evil; and the sense of shame. Now there are two qualities called 'sense of shame'; the one is not evil [i.e. probably, conscience, which deters men from evil]; the other is a curse to families [i.e. shameful deeds]. If these two different qualities were clearly and aptly named, they would not be represented by the same letters."

There are several passages in other plays where Euripides refers to "gossip" as a thing likely to corrupt women (e.g. Andromache in *The Women of Troy*). There are also passages where he makes a character discuss the meaning of some word. Both kinds of passage were noted as characteristic of him, and no doubt often parodied. Here, in the middle of Phaedra's agonized confession, such banal irrelevance seems to me to go beyond anything found elsewhere in Euripides, and I therefore regard these lines as possibly or probably spurious.

Page 26. *Of your saying any word about me:* the question how far Phaedra understands the Nurse, whether she tries to deceive herself or remains innocent in intention, is purposely left ambiguous by Euripides, who thus achieves an effect far more dramatic than that of a clear decision either way.

Page 26. *Love, the child of Zeus:* Eros.

Page 27. *You are beside the door:* the door is, of course, at the back of the stage; the Chorus are in the *Orchestra*, below and in front of the stage.

Page 32. *A solemn mission of piety:* Theseus has been enquiring formally from an oracle (probably that of Delphi) whether his expiation is now complete (see p. 15, "His hands stained with the blood of the Pallantides"), and has, ironically enough, returned assured of the favour of Heaven.

Page 32. *That is all I know, Theseus:* it was a dramatic convention that the Chorus must keep secrets entrusted to them. For them to tell at this point all that they know would be to prevent the tragedy. They are provided with an excuse for their silence by Phaedra's solemn charge to them before her last exit. Their failure to save Hippolytus by telling Theseus the truth has often been quoted as an instance of Euripides' failure to reconcile his matter with his medium. But in actual production no difficulty is felt here, because it is plain to the audience that the Chorus are partly outside the action of the plot. Besides, if Hippolytus will not break his oath, why should the Troezenian women?

Page 36. *Take Orpheus for your lord and prophet:* there seems to be no evidence for any connexion between Hippolytus and Orphism; neither does Hippolytus' remark on p. 17 ("A loaded table's a cheerful sight after hunting"), nor indeed his occupation as a hunter, suggest that he was a vegetarian. Rather Euripides presents Theseus as a middle-aged man who is ready enough to regard fancy cults as responsible for lack of principle in the younger generation — by no means an out-of-date characteristic of middle-aged man.

Page 38. *To me they are nothing at all:* see note for p. 17.

Page 38. *My unhappy mother:* the fact that it is this remark which rouses Theseus to a climax of fury gives another strong hint of the tangled emotional relationship implied by Euripides as existing between Theseus and his son. Euripides is following his usual practice of making heroic characters think and feel like fifth-century Athenians. It is noticeable that Theseus realizes he has lost control, quickly recovers himself, and goes out on a rather lame threat.

Page 40. *You have proved a true father to me:* this is the second time (see p. 34) that Theseus has claimed Poseidon for his father; but Artemis twice (pp. 43 and 46) reminds him firmly that his father was the mortal Aegeus, though in her second speech she refers to the giver of the three curses as "your father."

Page 44. *I never would have submitted to such dishonour:* the impregnable callousness of this and other remarks of Artemis (especially, "My own hand shall strike down," etc., p. 46) convey Euripides' emphatic valuation of the comforts of religion. Man in extremity must look to himself alone.

Page 47. *When was man more noble?* it is generally supposed that these words carried a reference to Pericles, who died the year before this play was produced.

❖ ❖ ❖

## STUDY AIDS

*Pages 14–15.* Among the recurrent conventions of Euripides' technique are the Prologue, the Messenger, the Chorus, and the "*Deus ex Machina*," the appearance of a god or goddess at the conclusion of the play. Consider the prologue by Aphrodite. What is expository about it? What information, specifically, does it provide? Why is Aphrodite involving herself in the affairs of mortals? What were the conditions under which Phaedra first fell in love with Hippolytus? How long has her love for him persisted? How do Theseus and Phaedra happen to have returned to Troezen?

Does the placing of so much expository material in this initial speech seem unartful? Might the prologue be said to further the compression characteristic of dramatic form? If so, in what way? Gilbert Murray has suggested that such an expository prologue can also contribute to the "atmosphere," that is, the general emotional climate of the play. Does Aphrodite's speech do this? What is her tone or attitude in this speech? What does her attitude toward her intended victims contribute to the atmosphere?

The prologue also foreshadows the major events to come in the play. Does such a revelation destroy the possibilities for suspense? Is suspense an important element in this play? What might be some positive advantages in grasping the play as a whole from the very beginning? Might the greater knowledge of the audience give added dimensions or a sense of irony to actions and speeches of the characters? Does it in this play? If so, where?

Despite the fact that the outcome is revealed so early, does some "plot-interest" remain?

*Page 15.* Is there some irony in the fact that the temple of Love which Phaedra built came to bear Hippolytus' name?

Images of the woods and hunting appear in Aphrodite's speech. Where else in the play do similar images occur? What value does the recurrence of such images have?

*Page 15.* What clues do the closing lines of Aphrodite's speech provide for the staging of Hippolytus' entrance? What is his mood? How does the prologue qualify the audience's response to his mood?

The character of Hippolytus is one of the more difficult problems posed by the play for modern audiences. What are the reasons for his chastity? Has he simply directed all his energies to his religious

devotion? Might he be revealing his immaturity? innocence? ignorance? Would you regard his attitude as one of adolescent idealism,
perhaps not unlike that of Holden Caulfield? Could the excess of
this virtue be regarded as his "tragic flaw"?

*Pages 16–17.* What is accomplished by the interview between Hippolytus and the Servant? What is ironical about Hippolytus' statement: "Yes . . . haughtiness is always a hateful thing"?

*Page 17.* Hippolytus' arrogant and rash dismissal of the honor due
Aphrodite might be said to represent a form of *hubris*, an overween-
ing pride or an undue confidence in the self-sufficiency of man, seldom
unpunished by the gods in Greek drama. Consider his statement:
"Your Aphrodite? No! To me she is nothing at all!" Later in the
play there is a close verbal echo of this line. Where does it occur?
What is the force of this repetition?

In what sense is the Servant's speech directed towards Aphrodite
really a sharp criticism of the goddess as she has revealed herself in
the prologue? Might the speech not represent a rather fundamental
ethical criticism of the overt religious premise of the action?

The chorus, one of the conventions mentioned above, deserves
special attention. Examine the several speeches which it delivers in
this play, and attempt to generalize about its various functions. For
example, what seems to be the function of its first speech? How
much of the speech is exposition? How does its purpose here differ
from that of the choral odes on pp. 30–32, beginning "O to escape
and hide"? What does the chorus contribute in the scene in which
Phaedra and the leader of the chorus listen to the interview between
the Nurse and Hippolytus?

*Pages 17–18.* Around what themes are the chorus's questions about
Phaedra's condition organized? What irony, if any, is involved in
the questions and assumptions?

*Page 18.* The Nurse is one of the early representatives of the
confidante and go-between so useful to dramatists. Comment on her
function in the play. What are the primary attributes of her character? Does her first speech seem "in character"? How do her out-
look and manner contrast with those of Phaedra?

Phaedra will eventually commit a vicious deed. How does Euripides
enlist audience sympathy for her? How does he prevent her from
degenerating into a melodramatic villainess? As noted in the introduction, the Phaedra of Euripides' first play on the subject was a
shameless creature who deliberately attempted to seduce Hippolytus.
How does the Phaedra of this play differ in conception from the earlier
Phaedra?

*Page 19.* Comment on the imagery of Phaedra's opening speeches with the Nurse.

*Page 21.* To what extent may Phaedra's actions be regarded as motivated by her consideration or lack of consideration for her children's fortunes? What is the political situation under Theseus' rule? To what extent does it impinge on the emotional conflict of the play?

*Pages 21–22.* Comment on the dramatic function of the dialogue of single alternating lines (known as "stichomythia") between the Nurse and Phaedra. Consult Robert Graves' *The Greek Myths* for the stories connected with Phaedra's mother and sister. In what sense can Phaedra's passion be explained as hereditary? Might such an explanation of her "disease" be a form of rationalization for her? Is it equal in cogency and importance to a religious or psychological explanation? Are these explanations necessarily mutually exclusive? Might they serve to manifest the intricate combination of motives driving Phaedra to her ruin?

*Page 22.* Why does Phaedra not answer the Nurse directly about the identity of her love? What subtlety of motivation does she reveal in having the Nurse pronounce Hippolytus' name? Does Phaedra's refusal to speak his name follow from shame? from fear? from a feeling that she might thereby confer some objective reality on her subjective longing?

*Pages 23–24.* Speaking to the Women of Troezen, Phaedra comments on the discrepancy between human knowledge and action: "we know and see what is right," she says, "yet fail to carry it out." How have her efforts to subdue her passion led her to this profound pessimism? Would you say that the sense of moral helplessness conveyed in these lines constitutes a major theme of the play? If so, what other evidence for its presence can you cite?

In what terms does Phaedra conceive of her own uprightness? Is it shame or righteousness which leads her to plan her suicide? Does the imagery of her lines suggest that her rectitude is akin to vanity and pride? At what point in the action has Phaedra decided on suicide? Where is the audience informed of her decision? In terms of conventional plotting is this revelation premature?

*Page 25.* After the Nurse has had an opportunity to think about her discovery of Phaedra's love, is her advice merely a form of sophisticated cynicism concerning the ethos of sexual love, or do her recommendations represent a truly human, tolerant, and moderate solution for Phaedra in her predicament?

*Pages 24–25.* The Nurse warns Phaedra about being arrogant and haughty toward Love, the "fever of Aphrodite." How is her warning reminiscent of the advice given by the Servant to Hippolytus? How is it different?

*Page 26.* Phaedra fears that the Nurse will reveal her love to Hippolytus. Is it possible, however, that she has an inkling of the Nurse's intentions? If you were directing the play, would you have Phaedra seem, at least indirectly, to encourage the Nurse? Do her weakness and vacillation at this point indicate her complicity (perhaps unconscious) in the Nurse's plan? How might such complicity bear on her indignant remarks to the Nurse later (p. 29), when Hippolytus has rebuffed her?

*Page 26.* How is the "love-death" theme developed in the choral ode? What religious and sexual images occur here? How and why are they fused? How do the mythical allusions function in the ode? How does this *lyric* poetry enrich the *dramatic* poetry of the play?

*Pages 27–29.* Work out the staging of the scene in which the Nurse is scorned by Hippolytus. Consider it first in terms of the classical Greek theatre and then in terms of a typical modern theatre. What are the positions and movements of the players as the scene develops? Where is Phaedra when the Nurse and Hippolytus appear on the stage? Where is she and what are her actions during the rest of the scene? Does she hear Hippolytus reaffirm his oath of silence? Why is it important whether she does or not? Do her words "Hippolytus, white-hot with rage, will carry your foul words to his father and denounce me" indicate that she does not believe that he will be true to his oath?

*Page 28.* Some of Euripides' contemporaries were offended by the following exchange after the Nurse has sworn Hippolytus to silence:

NURSE. My boy, do not slight the oath you swore me!

HIPPOLYTUS. My tongue swore: the oath does not bind my heart.

What is the meaning of Hippolytus' reply? Does it qualify somewhat the moral purity of which Hippolytus has boasted, especially where sex is concerned? Is it possibly a tactic intended only to frighten the Nurse?

*Pages 28–29.* Is Hippolytus' long misogynistic speech motivated as much by fear of women as by cynical disillusioned knowledge of their all-too-human weaknesses? How does one reconcile Hippolytus' love of Artemis and his hatred of females in general? Is the harsh cruelty of this speech one of the factors that move Phaedra to take revenge on Hippolytus through her note? What are other factors (see p. 30)?

*Page 30.* Is the Nurse's defense of herself a mere rationalization, or is there a hard-won wisdom in her words?

*Page 30.* What are Phaedra's motives for committing suicide and for implicating Hippolytus in her death? To what extent is she attempting to guide her own destiny by planning for the future of her sons and protecting the reputation of the royal house of Crete? Is hurt or offended feminine pride a possible factor?

*Pages 30–31.* How are the first two stanzas of the choral ode related to Phaedra's suicide? Do they help to explain some of her motives? Of what elements in her motivation are they an elaboration? Might the images of flight and escape in Strophe 1 be said to offer a momentary "flight" for the audience from the tension of the preceding scene? In the second two stanzas, how does the imagery of the sea and ships function? What implicit comment on the action of the play does this imagery offer?

*Page 32.* Theseus makes his first appearance returning from a pilgrimage. He is immediately confronted with the news of his wife's suicide. What is ironic about this reception, especially after his religious endeavors? How is this episode related to the theme of the gods and their concern with human affairs?

*Page 33.* Comment on the predominant imagery of the following lines, and indicate how it recalls similar imagery elsewhere in the play:

I strain despairing eyes over my sea of misery,
And my hope of safety vanishes, for the shore is out of sight
And life is a mounting wave I have not strength to surmount.

Does Theseus feel that his own guilt is somehow involved in Phaedra's fate? What is the "long-ago sin" to which he refers?

*Page 35.* Analyze the tone of Hippolytus' speeches as he enters and sees Phaedra's body and his father. Is he feigning total ignorance of what has transpired? Might he be attempting to escape any guilt for Phaedra's death which his speech of loathing has precipitated? Is it part of Hippolytus' character always to be presenting to the world his own innocence? Or does his oath sworn to the Nurse demand this posture? Might it be that Hippolytus is actually as innocent and shocked in his reactions as he seems to be? Might he have been so absorbed in the abstraction of an unhuman ideal that the reality of human need and the consequences of human desperation revealed in Phaedra's death actually stun him?

What dramatic irony is contained in Hippolytus' words, "I had only just left her; a short time ago she was alive!" What interpretation is Theseus prepared to place upon them?

How is dramatic tension generated, during this confrontation, by the fact that Theseus and Hippolytus have only imperfect knowledge of the truth, whereas the audience has complete knowledge?

*Pages 35–36.* To what extent is the long accusation of Hippolytus framed in terms of the conflict between generations? In what ways would Theseus' own background and youth lead him to be particularly suspicious of or unsympathetic to Hippolytus' personality and religious interests? In this father-son confrontation what weaknesses does Theseus reveal in attempting to deal with the complexities of life? Consider his yearning for a "touchstone" to indicate "who is loyal and who treacherous!" Is there a similarity between father and son in their search for simplifying absolutes?

*Pages 35–39.* The fact of Hippolytus' innocence of the accusations made against him is known by the audience. Is there, however, something unsatisfactory about his defense of himself? Is Hippolytus' high boast of his purity a manifestation of pride similar to that which he displayed earlier in the play?

*Page 37.* Hippolytus realizes that the political situation helps to make him suspect in his father's eyes. Where else in the play does the political situation figure as a significant background to events?

*Page 38.* What rashness of Hippolytus is recalled by Theseus' refusal to consult religious counsel concerning the guilt of his son?

Who has won the upper hand in the psychological conflict between father and son? Why? Does Hippolytus sense that Theseus is not sure of himself? How is this related to Theseus' invoking Poseidon's curse instead of acting against his son himself? Is the curse largely an emotional release for Theseus rather than an act whose fulfilment he really expects to see? Why, for example, does he also include the penalty of banishment? What is his attitude when he learns of Hippolytus' fate?

In what sense is Hippolytus' fate the result of his own moral rectitude?

Is there any reason for the chorus not to reveal to Theseus the truth concerning his son?

*Pages 39–40.* What is accomplished by the choral odes at this point? How do the following lines relate to the action of the play as a whole?

> The dauntless stern resolve is not for me,
> Nor the fair face masking the false intent.

According to this ode, does the experience deepen or destroy faith? How do Strophe 2 and Antistrophe 2 prepare for the report of Hippolytus' fate?

*Page 40.* The Messenger is another of the conventions of Euripides' theatre. Comment on the effectiveness of describing the violent accident rather than attempting to represent it on the stage. Is such a description simply a necessary device imposed upon the dramatist by the limitations of the Greek stage, or might there be some positive value in handling violence in this manner? How does Euripides provide a dramatic context for the long speech by arousing interest in what the Messenger has to say?

Page 41. Instances of sea imagery, particularly as it relates to love, have been noted above. How is such imagery recalled by the report of the Messenger? To what degree does this pattern of imagery have a cumulative impact?

Page 42. After the Messenger's report why does the chorus sing a hymn of praise to Aphrodite? What is the effect of having Artemis appear on-stage at just the moment the chorus concludes its song? How does the appearance of Artemis contribute to the play? Does she simply provide the dramatist with an easy escape from an entangled plot, or does she have intrinsic relevance? Is it ironic that Artemis has so much useful information to reveal to Theseus at this point in the play? Gilbert Murray has praised this appearance of Artemis because it achieves an effect "which could scarcely be reached in any other way, a strange poignant note amid the beauty, where mortal emotion breaks against the cliffs of immortal calm." What particulars in the speeches of Artemis support Murray's generalization?

Page 44. Is Artemis' explanation of the "law" of the gods mere sophistry? How does it square with her words, ". . . a good man's death is no joy to the gods"; with the action of the play; and with Aphrodite's prologue? Might Artemis' words be the culmination of a condemnation of the gods which has been implicitly a major theme of the play from the beginning?

Theseus' cry "My son, my son!" and his later yearning "Would God I might die for you, my son!" (pp. 43, 46) recall King David's lament at the death of Absalom (II Samuel 18). Compare the situations of these two bereaved fathers.

Pages 45–46. How does Hippolytus' final declaration of innocence contrast with Artemis' speech about the "law" of the gods? The Book of Job vividly portrays the inner agony as well as the outer suffering of the innocent Job. Does Hippolytus reveal a comparable inner anguish? If so, what are its causes?

Pages 44–47. How does Hippolytus reveal at this point a humility new to him in the play? How does this quality affect one's attitude toward him?

In an attempt to soothe Hippolytus, Artemis pledges revenge against Aphrodite, saying:

I will requite her: with this unfailing bow
My own hand shall strike down in just return
The man her heart holds dearest in the world.

How does this arbitrary vindictiveness relate to the religious theme in the play?

## DISCUSSION TOPICS

1. Analyze the dramatic action involving the mortals in this play, and indicate the points at which the initial stability of their relationships is first clearly disturbed; the point of crisis, where an irreversible turning in the action occurs; and the resolution, where the consequence of the crisis manifests itself in catastrophe.

2. What is the source (or sources) of unity in this play? According to what principle is the play organized? Is there, for example, a central character whose personality dominates the whole? Some readers, such as G. M. A. Grube, consider Hippolytus the focal character. David Grene, on the other hand, has argued that Phaedra is dominant, that the play is chiefly a study in the character of Phaedra — "this simple and cowardly woman transformed into an incestuous harlot and a murderess." Still others have held that the play is constructed about a symbolic conflict between two extremes: austere chastity, represented by Hippolytus, and uncontrollable desire, represented by Phaedra. Comment on the validity of these interpretations and indicate why you agree or disagree with them.

3. Other readers have seen the play's unity produced by a pervasive theme. Professor Kitto, for example, interprets the *Hippolytus* as a step-by-step embodiment of the "victimizing power of Aphrodite over mortals." Bernard Knox sees a unity in the situations of the characters, in that each demonstrates "the meaninglessness of the moral choice." What thematic possibilities do you find in the play? How do they promote the unity of the work?

4. What do you take to be the function of the two deities who, as it were, stand at either side of the play? Do the pronouncements of Aphrodite turn the play into a series of predetermined events in which the characters are the victims of a whimsical goddess? Might Aphrodite be said to "foreknow" but not to predestine the events of the play? To what extent might Aphrodite and Artemis be regarded as projections of psychological traits within Hippolytus and Phaedra?

5. In *Euripides and His Age*, Gilbert Murray writes: "A good

Greek play moves almost always in a curve of steadily increasing tension — increasing up to the last scene but one and then, as a rule, sinking into a note of solemn calm. It often admits a quiet scene about the middle to let the play take breath; but it is very chary indeed of lifting and then dropping again, and never does so without definite reason." How precisely does this statement describe the development of the *Hippolytus*?

6. There are many definitions of "tragic" and "tragedy." Using this play as the basis for an inductive definition, how would you define "tragic" and "tragedy"?

7. Discuss the *Hippolytus* as poetic drama. In considering this question, consult T. S. Eliot's excellent essay "Poetry and Drama" in his collection of essays *On Poetry and Poets* (New York, 1957), pp. 75–95.

8. Turn to the essay "Euripides' Phaedra and Hippolytus" by Richmond Lattimore, in Part Three of this book. What does the essay contribute to your understanding of Euripides' play? Where do you agree and where do you disagree with Professor Lattimore? Why?

# SENECA

◇◇◇◇◇◇◇◇◇◇◇◇◇◇◇◇◇◇◇◇◇◇◇◇◇◇◇◇◇◇◇◇◇◇◇◇◇◇◇

"THE RISING unto place is laborious. . . . The stand-
ing is slippery, and the regress is either a downfall, or at least an
eclipse, which is a melancholy thing." The truth of these familiar
words from Sir Francis Bacon's essay "Of Great Place" is well exem-
plified in the career of Lucius Annaeus Seneca (4 B.C.–65 A.D.). A man
of many talents, Seneca impressed his own times as orator, essayist,
naturalist, dramatist, philosopher, courtier, and efficient government
official. The pattern of his life, his Stoic philosophy, and his literary
works exerted a strong influence on Western European thought and
literature in later times, especially during the Renaissance.

Born in Cordoba, Spain, to well-to-do parents, he was brought to
Rome to be educated and trained for work in government. Presumably
he held minor posts in the court of Tiberius preparatory to his more
prominent positions in the governments of Caligula, Claudius, and
Nero. But his rising unto place was not without dangers along the
way and mortal consequences at the end. Having displeased Caligula,
he escaped a sentence of death, it is said, only because the emperor
believed that Seneca's death from natural causes was imminent. In
Claudius' reign he was banished to Corsica for eight years. Recalled
to Rome in 49 A.D., he became tutor to Nero. Seneca rose to his most
powerful position in the government when Nero became emperor in
54 A.D. But he did so only to find the standing exceedingly slippery.
After years of effective service in the government of Nero, he was
forced by the emperor to commit suicide, an event impressively described in the *Annals* of Tacitus.

The date of composition of Seneca's plays is uncertain, but some
scholars believe that they were written during Seneca's exile on Corsica
between 41 and 49 A.D. Eight of the nine plays usually attributed to
him are based on works by Aeschylus, Sophocles, or Euripides. A
comparison of a Senecan play with its presumed model will reveal
many similarities and suggest a continuity between the great age of

drama in Greece and Seneca's time. But it will also reveal major differences: differences in characterization, interpretation, and, especially, dramatic form or type, which are frequently baffling to a modern reader. Some writers insist that these plays are not plays at all and that they lack the basic components of the "dramatic." But T. S. Eliot has rightly cautioned against attaching too narrow a meaning to "dramatic," which, while it might permit one to see what Senecan drama *is not*, would also prevent one from seeing what it *is*. The question has been debated at length, but the scholarly consensus is that these plays were not written to be staged in the usual sense. A number of reasons support this view. To a marked degree, they seem to be works primarily of verbal art and rhetorical display, to exist more for the manner in which something is said than for what is said. The language often seems more important than the character who is speaking it. As Eliot has aptly observed, "the characters in a play of Seneca behave more like members of a minstrel troupe sitting in a semicircle, rising in turn each to do his 'number,' or varying their recitations by a song or a little back-chat." In addition, the plays contain a considerable amount of description of attitudes, gestures, and actions which would seem unnecessary and redundant were the plays acted on a stage.

Rather than plays to be staged and acted, it is more likely that these were plays written to be recited, and perhaps to be read in private. Senecan drama is, thus, another kind of drama, and one that is not actually so far removed from modern experience as might at first appear. As Eliot has noted, Senecan drama has something in common with the modern "broadcast dramas," such as *The Fall of the City* and *Air Raid* by Archibald MacLeish, as well as with the "concert" reading of plays which has become popular in recent years.

Like most of Seneca's plays, *Phaedra* derives from an Attic model, in this instance a work by Euripides. Although the general outline of the *Hippolytus* is repeated in Seneca's play, the marked differences of the latter, particularly in the concept of Phaedra's character, have led scholars to conclude that Seneca was more likely following Euripides' earlier play on this subject, which has now been lost.

The plays of Seneca in Latin, in translation, and in imitations were popular during the Renaissance and are regarded as important influences on Elizabethan dramatists, including Shakespeare. Useful comment on Senecan drama and its influence will be found in J. W. Cunliffe, *The Influence of Seneca on Elizabethan Tragedy* (Manchester, 1893); A. D. Godley, "Senecan Tragedy" in *English Literature and the Classics*, ed. G. S. Gordon (Oxford, 1912), pp. 228–247; Léon Hermann, *Le Théâtre de Sénèque* (Paris, 1924); Norman T. Pratt, Jr.,

*Dramatic Suspense in Seneca and in His Greek Precursors* (Princeton, 1939); and Clarence W. Mendel, *Our Seneca* (New Haven, 1941). Verse translations of the plays by F. J. Miller are available in *The Tragedies of Seneca* (Chicago, 1907), later reprinted in *The Complete Roman Drama*, ed. George E. Duckworth, 2 vols. (New York, 1942). Miller has also translated the plays into prose for the Loeb Classical Library, 2 vols. (New York, 1917).

# Phaedra

*Translation by F. J. Miller*

◇  ◇  ◇

## DRAMATIS PERSONAE

HIPPOLYTUS, *son of Theseus and Antiope, an Amazon*
PHAEDRA, *wife of Theseus and stepmother of Hippolytus*
THESEUS, *King of Athens*
NURSE *of Phaedra*
MESSENGER
SLAVES AND ATTENDANTS
CHORUS *of Athenian citizens*

*The scene is laid throughout in the court in front of the royal palace at Athens; and the action is confined to the space of one day.*

Theseus had wed Antiope, the Amazon, and of their union had been born Hippolytus. This youth grew up to love the chase, austere and beautiful, shunning the haunts of men, and scorning the love of women. Theseus had meanwhile slain Antiope, and married Phaedra, Cretan Minos' child.

And now, for four years past, the king has not been seen upon the earth, for, following the mad adventure of his bosom friend, Pirithoüs, he has descended into Tartara, and thence, men think, he never will return.

Deserted by her lord, the hapless Phaedra has conceived a hopeless passion for Hippolytus; for Venus, mindful of that ancient shame, which Phaedra's ancestor, Apollo, had exposed, has sent this madness on her, even as Pasiphaë, her mother, had been cursed with a most mad and fatal malady.

---

Reprinted from *The Tragedies of Seneca* (Chicago, 1907).

## ACT I

HIPPOLYTUS (*in hunting costume, assigning duties and places to his servants and companions of the hunt*).

Up comrades, and the shadowy groves
With nets encircle; swiftly range
The heights of our Cecropian hills;
Scour well those coverts on the slopes
Of Parnes, or in Thria's vale                                    5
Whose chattering streamlet roars along
In rapid course; go climb the hills
Whose peaks are ever white with snows
Of Scythia. Let others go
Where woods with lofty alders stand                             10
In dense array; where pastures lie
Whose springing grass is waked to life
By Zephyr's breath, dew laden. Go,
Where calm Ilissus flows along
The level fields, a sluggish stream,                            15
Whose winding course the barren sands
With niggard water laps. Go ye
Along the leftward-leading way,
Where Marathon her forest glades
Reveals, where nightly with their young                         20
The suckling mothers feed. Do you,
Where, softened by the warming winds
From southern lands, Acharnae melts
His snows, repair; let others seek
Hymettus' rocky slopes, far famed                               25
For honey; others still the glades
Of small Aphidnae. All too long
That region has unharried lain
Where Sunium with its jutting shore
Thrusts out the curving sea.                                    30
If any feels the forest's lure,
Him Phlye calls, where dwells the boar
Now scarred and known by many a wound,
The farmers' fear.
Now free the dogs from straining leash,                         35
That hunt in silence; but the hounds
Of keen Molossian breed hold fast
In check; let the savage Cretans strain

With chaffing necks upon their chains;
The Spartans hold in strongest curb,                          40
With caution bind, for bold their breed,
And eager for the prey.
The time will come when their baying loud
Through the hollow rocks shall echo; now
Let them snuff the air with nostrils keen,                    45
And with lowered muzzles seek the tracks
Of beasts, while yet the dawn is dim,
And while the dewy earth still holds
The marks of treading feet. Let some
On burdened necks the wide nets bear,                         50
And others haste to bring the snares
Of smooth-wrought cords. Let feathers, dyed
With crimson, hedge the timid deer
With terrors vain. Do thou use darts
Of Crete, and thou the heavy spear                            55
By both hands wielded. Thou shall sit
In hiding and with clamors loud
Drive out the frightened beasts; and thou,
When all is done, with curving blade
Shalt break the victims.                                      60
And thou, be with thy worshiper,
O goddess of the chase, whose rule
Extends o'er all the secret haunts
Of earth; whose darts unerring pierce
The flying prey; whose thirst is quenched                     65
By cool Araxes' distant stream,
Or for whose sport the Ister spreads
His frozen waves. Thy hand pursues
Gaetulian lions, Cretan deer;
And now the swiftly fleeing does                              70
With lighter stroke are pierced. To thee
The spotted tigers yield, to thee
The bisons, shaggy backed, and the wild,
Broad-hornéd oxen of the woods.
Whatever feeds upon the plains                                75
In desert pasture lands; whate'er
The needy Garamantian knows,
Whate'er the Arab rich in woods,
Or wild Sarmatian, wandering free
Across the lonely wilderness;                                 80
Whate'er the rugged Pyrenees

Or deep Hyrcanian glades conceal:
All fear thy bow, thou huntress queen.
If any worshiper of thine
Takes to the hunt thy favoring will,                     85
His nets hold fast the struggling prey;
No birds break from his snares; for him
The groaning wagons homeward come
With booty rich; the hounds come back
With muzzles deeply dyed in blood,                       90
And all the rustic throng returns
In shouting triumph home.
But lo, the goddess hears. The hounds
Are baying loud and clear to announce
The start. I'm summoned to the woods.                    95
Here, here I'll hasten where the road
Most quickly leads away.
                              (*Exit.*)
                    _____

PHAEDRA. O mighty Crete, thou mistress of the deep,
    Whose ships uncounted sail through every sea
    Wherever Nereus shows their beaks the way,          100
    E'en to Assyria's shores; why dost thou here
    Compel me thus in woe and tears to live,
    A hostage given to the hated foe,
    And to a foeman wed? Behold my lord,
    Deserting me, his bride, is far away,               105
    And keeps his wonted faith. Through shadows deep
    Of that dark pool which may not be recrossed,
    This doughty follower of a madcap prince
    Has gone, that from the very throne of Dis
    He might seduce and bear away his queen.            110
    With such mad folly linked he went away,
    Restrained by neither fear nor shame. And so,
    In deepest Acheron, illicit love
    This father of Hippolytus desires.
    But other, greater griefs than this oppress         115
    My sorrowing soul; no quiet rest by night,
    No slumber deep comes to dissolve my cares;
    But woe is fed and grows within my heart,
    And there burns hot as Aetna's raging fires.
    My loom stands empty and my listless hands          120
    Drop idly from their tasks. No more I care
    To make my votive offerings to the gods,

Nor, with the Athenian women mingled, dance
Around their sacred shrines, and conscious brands
Toss high in secret rites. I have no heart                    125
With chaste and pious prayers to worship her,
That mighty goddess who was set to guard
This Attic land. My only joy is found
In swift pursuit of fleeing beasts of prey,
My soft hands brandishing the heavy spear.                    130
But what will come of this? Why do I love
The forest glades so madly? Ah, I feel
The fatal malady my mother felt;
For both have learned within the forest depths
To sin in love. O mother, now my heart                        135
Doth ache for thee; for, swept away by sin
Unspeakable, thou boldly didst conceive
A shameful passion for the savage lord
Of the wild herd. Untamable was he,
That stern and lustful leader of the flock;                   140
And yet he loved. But in my passion's need
What god can help me? Where the Daedalus
Who can my love relieve? Should he return
Who shut our monster in the labyrinth,
He could not by his well-known Attic skill                    145
Avail to save me from this dire mischance.
For Venus, filled with deadly hate of us,
The stock of Phoebus, seeks through me to avenge
The chains which fettered her in shame to Mars,
And all our house with direful love she fills.                150
No princess of our race has ever loved
In modest wise, but always monstrously.
NURSE. O wife of Theseus, glorious child of Jove,
Drive from thy modest breast these shameful thoughts.
Put out these flames; and give thyself no hope                155
Of such dire love as this. Whoe'er at first
Has set himself to fight and conquer love,
A safe and easy victory finds. But he,
Who dallies with its evil sweets, too late
Refuses to endure the galling yoke                            160
Which he himself has placed upon his neck.
I know full well how scornful of the truth,
How harsh the swollen pride of princesses,
How it refuses to be bent aright.
Whatever outcome chance allots, I'll bear;                    165

For dawning freedom makes the agéd brave.
To will to live uprightly nor to fall
From virtue's ways is best; but next to this
Is sense of shame, the knowing when to stop
A sinful course. What, pray, will be the end                    170
For thee, poor mistress? Why dost heap thy house
With further infamy? Wouldst thou outsin
Thy mother? For thy impious love is worse
Than her unnatural and monstrous love.
The first you would impute to character,                         175
The last to fate. If, since thy husband sees
No more the realms of earth, thou dost believe
That this thy sin is safe and free from fear,
Thou art in error. Grant that he is held
Imprisoned fast in Lethe's lowest depths,                        180
And must forever feel the bonds of Styx:
Would he, thy sire, who by his spreading sway
Encroaches on the sea, who gives their laws
Unto a hundred peoples, e'er permit
So great a crime as this to lie unknown?                         185
Keen is a parent's watchful care. And yet,
Suppose that by our craft and guile we hide
This crime from him: what of thy mother's sire,
Who floods the earth with his illuming rays?
And what of him who makes the earth to quake,                    190
The bolts of Aetna flashing in his hand,
The father of the gods? And dost thou think
That it can be that thou couldst hide thy sin
From these thy grandsires, all-beholding ones?
But even should the favor of the gods,                           195
Complaisant, hide thy shame from all the world;
Though to thy lust alone should fall that grace
Denied to other crimes: still must thou fear.
What of that ever-present punishment,
The terror of the soul that knows its guilt,                     200
Is stained with crime and fearful of itself?
Some women have with safety sinned, but none
With peace of soul. Then quench these flames, I pray,
Of impious love, and shun this monstrous crime
Which no barbaric land has ever done,                            205
No Getan wandering on his lonely plains,
No savage Taurian, no Scythian.
Expel from thy chaste soul this hideous thing,

And, mindful of thy mother's sin, avoid
Such monstrous unions. Wouldst in marriage give          210
Thyself to son and father? Wouldst thou take
In thine incestuous womb a progeny
So basely mixed? Then go the length of sin:
O'erthrow all nature with thy shameful fires.
Why should the monsters cease? Why empty stands         215
Thy brother's labyrinth? Shall all the world
Be shocked with prodigies, shall nature's laws
Be scorned, whene'er a Cretan woman loves?
PHAEDRA. I know that what thou say'st is true, dear nurse;
But raging passion forces me to take                     220
The path of sin. Full consciously my soul
Goes headlong on its downward way, ofttimes
With backward glance, sane counsel seeking still,
Without avail. So, when the mariner
Would sail his ship against the boisterous waves,       225
His toil is all in vain, and, vanquished quite,
The ship drifts onward with the hurrying tide.
For what can reason do when passion rules,
When love, almighty, dominates the soul?
The wingéd god is lord through all the earth,           230
And with his flames unquenchable the heart
Of Jove himself is burned. The god of war
Has felt his fire; and Vulcan too, that god
Who forges Jove's three-forkéd thunderbolts;
Yea, he, who in the hold of Aetna huge                  235
Is lord of ever-blazing furnaces,
By this small spark is burned. Apollo, too,
Who sends his arrows with unerring aim,
Was pierced by Cupid's still more certain darts.
For equally in heaven and earth the god                 240
Is powerful.
NURSE.          The god! 'Tis vicious lust
That hath his godhead framed; and, that its ends
More fully may be gained, it has assigned
To its unbridled love the specious name,
Divinity! 'Tis Venus' son, in sooth,                    245
Sent wandering through all the earth! He flies
Through empty air and in his boyish hands
His deadly weapon bears! Though least of gods,
He holds the widest sway! Such vain conceits
The love-mad soul adopts, love's goddess feigns,        250

And Cupid's bow. Whoe'er too much enjoys
The smiles of fortune and in ease is lapped,
Is ever seeking unaccustomed joys.
Then that dire comrade of a high estate,
Inordinate desire, comes in. The feast                              255
Of yesterday no longer pleases; now
A home of sane and simple living, food [1]
Of humble sort, are odious. Oh, why
Does this destructive pest so rarely come
To lowly homes, but chooses rather homes                           260
Of luxury? And why does modest love
Beneath the humble roof abide, and bless
With wholesome intercourse the common throng?
Why do the poor restrain their appetites,
Whereas the rich, on empire propped, desire                        265
More than is right. Who wields too much of power
Desires to gain what is beyond his power.
What is befitting to thy high estate
Thou knowest well. Then fitting reverence show
To thy returning husband's sovereignty.                            270
PHAEDRA. The sovereignty of love is over me,
The highest rule of all. My lord's return,
I fear it not; for never more has he,
Who once within the silent depths of night
Has plunged, beheld again the light of day.                        275
NURSE. Trust not the power of Dis; for though his realm
He closely bar, and though the Stygian dog
Keep watch and ward upon the baleful doors,
Theseus can always walk forbidden ways.
PHAEDRA. Perchance he'll give indulgence to my love.               280
NURSE. But he was harsh e'en to a modest wife;
His heavy hand Antiope has known.
But grant that thou canst bend thy angry lord:
Canst bend as well the stubborn soul of him,
Hippolytus, who hates the very name                                285
Of womankind? Inexorable his resolve
To spend his life unwedded. He so shuns
The sacred rites of marriage, thou wouldst know
That he of Amazonian stock was born.
PHAEDRA. Though on the tops of snowy hills he hide,                290
Or swiftly course along the ragged cliffs,
Through forests deep, o'er mountains, 'tis my will

[1] Reading, *cibus.*

To follow him.
NURSE.                    And will he turn again,
And yield himself unto thy sweet caress?
Or will he lay aside his modesty                              295
At thy vile love's behest?  Will he give o'er
His hate of womankind for thee alone,
On whose account, perchance, he hates them all?
PHAEDRA.  Can he not be by any prayers o'ercome?
NURSE.  He's wild.
PHAEDRA.                    Yes, but the beasts are tamed by love.   300
NURSE.  He'll flee.
PHAEDRA.                    Through Ocean's self I'll follow him.
NURSE.  Thy sire remember.
PHAEDRA.                    And my mother too.
NURSE.  Women he hates.
PHAEDRA.                    Then I'll no rival fear.
NURSE.  Thy husband comes.
PHAEDRA.                    With him Pirithoüs!
NURSE.  Thy sire!
PHAEDRA.          To Ariadne he was kind.                       305
NURSE.  O child, by these white locks of age, I pray,
This care-filled heart, these breasts that suckled thee,
Put off this rage; to thine own rescue come.
The greater part of life is will to live.
PHAEDRA.  Shame has not wholly fled my noble soul.             310
I yield: let love, which will not be controlled,
Be conquered.  Nor shalt thou, fair fame, be stained.
This way alone is left, sole hope of woe:
Theseus I'll follow, and by death shun sin.
NURSE.  Oh, check, my child, this wild, impetuous thought;     315
Be calm.  For now I think thee worthy life,
Because thou hast condemned thyself to death.
PHAEDRA.  I am resolved to die, and only seek
The mode of death.  Shall I my spirit free
By twisted rope, or fall upon the sword,                       320
Or shall I leap from yonder citadel?
NURSE.  Shall my old age permit thee thus to die
Self-slain?  Thy deadly, raging purpose stay.
No one may easily come back to life.
PHAEDRA.  No argument can stay the will of one                 325
Who has resolved to die, and ought to die.
Quick, let me arm myself in honor's cause.
NURSE.  Sole comfort of my weary age, my child,

If such unruly passion sways thy heart,
Away with reputation! 'Tis a thing                              330
Which rarely with reality agrees;
It smiles upon the ill-deserving man,
And from the good withholds his meed of praise.
Let us make trial of that stubborn soul.
Mine be the task to approach the savage youth,                  335
And bend his will relentless to our own.

———————————

CHORUS. Thou goddess, child of the foaming sea,
    Thou mother of love, how fierce are the flames,
    And how sharp are the darts of thy petulant boy;
    How deadly of aim his bow.                                  340
    Deep to the heart the poison sinks
    When the veins are imbued with his hidden flame;
    No gaping wound upon the breast
    Does his arrow leave; but far within
    It burns with consuming fire.                               345
    No peace or rest does he give; world wide
    Are his flying weapons sown abroad:
    The shores that see the rising sun,
    And the land that lies at the goal of the west;
    The south where raging Cancer glows,                        350
    And the land of the cold Arcadian Bear
    With its ever-wandering tribes — all know
    And have felt the fires of love.
    The hot blood of youth he rouses to madness,
    The smouldering embers of age he rekindles,                 355
    And even the innocent breasts of maids
    Are stirred by passion unknown.
    He bids the immortals desert the skies
    And dwell on the earth in forms assumed.
    For love, Apollo kept the herds                             360
    Of Thessaly's king, and, his lyre unused,
    He called to his bulls on the gentle pipe.
    How oft has Jove himself put on
    The lower forms of life, who rules
    The sky and the clouds. Now a bird he seems,                365
    With white wings hovering, with voice
    More sweet than the song of the dying swan;
    Now with lowering front, as a wanton bull,
    He offers his back to the sport of maids;
    And soon through his brother's waves he floats,             370

With his hoofs like sturdy oars, and his breast
Stoutly opposing the waves, in fear
For the captured maid he bears.  For love,
The shining goddess of the night
Her dim skies left, and her glittering car                          375
To her brother allotted to guide.  Untrained
In managing the dusky steeds,
Within a shorter circuit now
He learns to direct his course.  Meanwhile
The nights no more their accustomed space                           380
Retained, and the dawn came slowly back,
Since 'neath a heavier burden now
The axle trembled.  Love compelled
Alcmena's son to lay aside
His quiver and the threat'ning spoil                                385
Of that great lion's skin he bore,
And have his fingers set with gems,
His shaggy locks in order dressed.
His limbs were wrapped in cloth of gold,
His feet with yellow sandals bound;                                 390
And with that hand which bore but now
The mighty club, he wound the thread
Which from his mistress' spindle fell.
The sight all Persia saw, and they
Who dwell in Lydia's fertile realm —                                395
The savage lion's skin laid by,
And on those shoulders, once the prop
For heaven's vast dome, a gauzy cloak
Of Tyrian manufacture spread.
Accursed is love, its victims know,                                 400
And all too strong.  In every land,
In the all-encircling briny deep,
In the airy heavens where the bright stars course,
There pitiless love holds sway.
The sea-green band of the Nereids                                   405
Have felt his darts in their deepest waves,
And the waters of ocean cannot quench
Their flames.  The birds know the passion of love,
And mighty bulls, with its fire inflamed,
Wage furious battle, while the herd                                 410
Look on in wonder.  Even stags,
Though timorous of heart, will fight
If for their mates they fear, while loud

Resound the snortings of their wrath.
When with love the striped tigers burn,                    415
The swarthy Indian cowers in fear.
For love the boar whets his deadly tusks
And his huge mouth is white with foam.
The African lions toss their manes
When love inflames their hearts, and the woods             420
Resound with their savage roars.
The monsters of the raging deep,
And those great beasts, the elephants,
Feel the sway of love; since nature's power
Claims everything, and nothing spares.                     425
Hate perishes when love commands,
And ancient feuds yield to his touch.
Why need I more his sway approve,
When even stepdames yield to love?


## ACT II

*(Enter* NURSE *from the palace.)*

CHORUS. Speak, nurse, the news thou bring'st. How fares the
    queen?                                                 430
Do her fierce fires of love know any end?
NURSE. I have no hope that such a malady
    Can be relieved; her maddened passion's flames
    Will endless burn. A hidden, silent fire
    Consumes her, and her raging love, though shut         435
    Within her heart, is by her face betrayed.
    Her eyes dart fire; anon, her sunken gaze
    Avoids the light of day. Her restless soul
    Can find no pleasure long in anything.
    Her aimless love allows her limbs no rest.             440
    Now, as with dying, tottering steps, she goes,
    And scarce can hold her nodding head erect;
    And now lies down to sleep. But, sleepless quite,
    She spends the night in tears. Now does she bid
    Me lift her up, and straight to lay her down;          445
    To loose her locks, and bind them up again.
    In restless mood she constantly demands
    Fresh robes. She has no care for food or health.
    With failing strength she walks, with aimless feet.
    Her old-time strength is gone; no longer shines        450

The ruddy glow of health upon her face.
Care feeds upon her limbs; her trembling steps
Betray her weakness, and the tender grace
Of her once blooming beauty is no more.
Her eyes, which once with Phoebus' brilliance shone,                    455
No longer gleam with their ancestral fires.
Her tears flow ever, and her cheeks are wet
With constant rain; as when, on Taurus' top,
The snows are melted by a warming shower.
But look, the palace doors are opening,                                 460
And she, reclining on her couch of gold,
And sick of soul, refuses one by one
The customary garments of her state.

PHAEDRA. Remove, ye slaves, those bright and gold-wrought
    robes;
Away with Tyrian purple, and the webs                                   465
Of silk whose threads the far-off eastern tribes
From leaves of trees collect. Gird high my robes;
I'll wear no necklace, nor shall snowy pearls,
The gift of Indian seas, weigh down my ears.
No nard from far Assyria shall scent                                    470
My locks; thus loosely tossing let them fall
Around my neck and shoulders; let them stream
Upon the wind, by my swift running stirred.
Upon my left I'll wear a quiver girt,
And in my right hand will I brandish free                               475
A hunting-spear of Thessaly; for thus
The mother of Hippolytus was clad.
So did she lead her hosts from the frozen shores
Of Pontus, when to Attica she came,
From distant Tanaïs or Maeotis' banks,                                  480
Her comely locks down flowing from a knot,
Her side protected by a crescent shield.
Like her would I betake me to the woods.

CHORUS. Cease thy laments, for grief will not avail
The wretched. Rather seek to appease the will                          485
Of that wild virgin goddess of the woods.

NURSE (to DIANA). O queen of forests, thou who dwell'st alone
On mountain tops, and thou who only art
Within their desert haunts adored, convert,
We pray, to better issue these sad fears.                              490
O mighty goddess of the woods and groves,
Bright star of heaven, thou glory of the night,

Whose torch, alternate with the sun, illumes
The sky, thou three-formed Hecate — Oh, smile,
We pray, on these our hopes; the unbending soul 495
Of stern Hippolytus subdue for us.
Teach him to love; our passion's mutual flame
May he endure. May he give ready ear
To our request. His hard and stubborn heart
Do thou make soft to us. Enthral his mind. 500
Though stern of soul, averse to love, and fierce,
May he yet yield himself to Venus' laws.
Bend all thy powers to this. So may thy face
Be ever clear, and through the rifted clouds
Mayst thou sail on with crescent shining bright; 505
So, when thou driv'st thy chariot through the sky,
May no Thessalian mummeries prevail
To draw thee from thy nightly journey down;
And may no shepherd boast himself of thee.
Lo, thou art here in answer to our prayer; 510

(HIPPOLYTUS *is seen approaching.*)

I see Hippolytus himself, alone,
Approaching to perform the yearly rites
To Dian due.

(*To herself.*)

Why dost thou hesitate?
Both time and place are given by fortune's lot.
Use all thy arts. Why do I quake with fear? 515
It is no easy task to do the deed
Enjoined on me. Yet she, who serves a queen,
Must banish from her heart all thought of right;
For sense of shame ill serves a royal will.

(*Enter* HIPPOLYTUS.)

HIPPOLYTUS. Why dost thou hither turn thine agéd feet, 520
O faithful nurse? Why is thy face so sad,
Thy brow so troubled? Truly is my sire
In safety, Phaedra safe, and their two sons.
NURSE. Thou need'st not fear for them; the kingdom stands
In prosperous estate, and all thy house 525
Rejoices in the blessings of the gods.
But Oh, do thou with greater kindness look
Upon thy fortune. For my heart is vexed
And anxious for thy sake; for thou thyself
With grievous sufferings dost bruise thy soul. 530

If fate compels it, one may be forgiven
For wretchedness; but if, of his own will,
A man prefers to live in misery,
Brings tortures on himself, then he deserves
To lose those gifts he knows not how to use.                535
Be mindful of thy youth; relax thy mind.
Lift high the blazing torch on festal nights;
Let Bacchus free thee from thy weighty cares;
Enjoy this time which speeds so swiftly by.
Now is the time when love comes easily,                     540
And smiles on youth. Come, let thy soul rejoice.
Why dost thou lie upon a lonely couch?
Dissolve in pleasures that grim mood of thine,
And snatch the passing joys;[1] let loose the reins.
Forbid that these, the best days of thy life,               545
Should vanish unenjoyed. Its proper hue
Has God allotted to each time of life,
And leads from step to step the age of man.
So joy becomes the young, a face severe
The agéd. Why dost thou restrain thyself,                   550
And strangle at their birth the joys of life?
That crop rewards the farmer's labor most
Which in the young and tender sprouting-time
Runs riot in the fields. With lofty top
That tree will overspread the neighboring grove,            555
Which no begrudging hand cuts back or prunes.
So do our inborn powers a richer fruit
Of praise and glory bear, if liberty,
Unchecked and boundless, feed the noble soul.
Thou, harsh, uncouth, and ignorant of life,                 560
Dost spend thy youth to joy and love unknown.
Think'st thou that this is man's allotted task,
To suffer hardships, curb the rushing steeds,
And fight like savage beasts in bloody war?
When he beheld the boundless greed of death,                565
The mighty father of the world ordained
A means by which the race might be renewed.
Suppose the power of Venus over men
Should cease, who doth supply and still renew
The stream of life, then would this lovely world            570
Become a foul, unsightly thing indeed:
The sea would bear no fish within its waves,

[1] Reading, *luxus*.

The woods no beasts of prey, the air no birds;
But through its empty space the winds alone
Would rove. How various the forms of death                          575
That seize and feed upon our mortal race:
The wrecking sea, the sword, and treachery!
But say that these are lacking: still we fall
Of our own gravity to gloomy Styx.
Suppose our youth should choose a mateless life,                     580
And live in childless state: then all this world
Of teeming life which thou dost see, would live
This generation only, and would fall
In ruins on itself. Then spend thy life
As nature doth direct; frequent the town,                           585
And live in friendly union with thy kind.
HIPPOLYTUS. There is no life so free, so innocent,
Which better cherishes the ancient rites,
Than that which spurns the crowded ways of men
And seeks the silent places of the woods.                           590
His soul no maddening greed of gain inflames
Who on the lofty levels of the hills
His blameless pleasures finds. No fickle breath
Of passing favor frets him here, no sting
Of base ingratitude, no poisonous hate.                             595
He fears no kingdom's laws; nor, in the quest
Of power, does he pursue the phantom shapes
Of fame and wealth. From hope and fear alike
Is he removed. No black and biting spite
With base, malicious tooth preys on him here.                       600
He never hears of those base, shameful things
That spawn amid the city's teeming throngs.
It is not his with guilty heart to quake
At every sound; he need not hide his thoughts
With guileful words; in pride of sinful wealth                      605
He seeks to own no lordly palace propped
Upon a thousand pillars, with its beams
In flaunting arrogance incased with gold.
No streams of blood his pious altars drench;
No hecatombs of snowy bullocks stand                                610
Foredoomed to death, their foreheads sprinkled o'er
With sacred meal; but in the spacious fields,
Beneath the sky, in fearless innocence,
He wanders lord of all. His only guile,
To set the cunning snare for beasts of prey;                        615

And, when o'erspent with labors of the chase,
He soothes his body in the shining stream
Of cool Ilissus.  Now swift Alpheus' banks
He skirts, and now the lofty forest's deep,
Dense places treads, where Lerna, clear and cool,                    620
Pours forth her glimmering streams.
Here twittering birds make all the woods resound,
And through the branches of the ancient beech
The leaves are all a-flutter in the breeze.
How sweet upon some vagrant river's bank,                            625
Or on the verdant turf, to lie at length,
And quaff one's fill of deep, delicious sleep,
Whether in hurrying floods some copious stream
Pours down its waves, or through the vernal flowers
Some murmuring brook sings sweetly as it flows.                      630
The windfall apples of the wood appease
His hunger, while the ripening berries plucked
From wayside thickets grant an easy meal.
He gladly shuns the luxuries of kings.
Let mighty lords from anxious cups of gold                           635
Their nectar quaff; for him how sweet to catch
With naked hand the water of the spring!
More certain slumber soothes him, though his couch
Be hard, if free from care he lay him down.
With guilty soul he seeks no shameful deeds                          640
In nooks remote upon some hidden couch,
Nor timorous hides in labyrinthine cell;
He courts the open air and light of day,
And lives before the conscious eye of heaven.
Such was the life, I think, the ancients lived,                     645
Those primal men who mingled with the gods.
They were not blinded by the love of gold;
No sacred stone divided off the fields
And lotted each his own in judgment there.
Nor yet did vessels rashly plow the seas;                           650
But each his native waters knew alone.
Then cities were not girt with massive walls,
With frequent towers set; no soldier there
To savage arms his hands applied, nor burst
The close-barred gates with huge and heavy stones                   655
From ponderous engines hurled.  As yet the earth
Endured no master's rule, nor felt the sway
Of laboring oxen yoked in common toil;

But all the fields, self-fruitful, fed mankind,
Who took and asked no more. The woods gave wealth,   660
And shady grottoes natural homes supplied.
Unholy greed first broke these peaceful bonds,
And headlong wrath, and lust which sets aflame
The hearts of men. Then came the cruel thirst
For empire; and the weak became the prey   665
Of strong, and might was counted right. At first
Men fought with naked fists, but soon they turned
Rough clubs and stones to use of arms. Not yet
Were cornel spears with slender points of iron,
And long, sharp-pointed swords, and crested helms.   670
Such weapons wrath invented. Warlike Mars
Produced new arts of strife, and forms of death
In countless numbers made. Thence streams of gore
Stained every land, and reddened every sea.
Then crime, o'erleaping every bound, ran wild;   675
Invaded every home. No hideous deed
Was left undone: but brothers by the hand
Of brothers fell, parents by children's hands,
Husbands by wives', and impious mothers killed
Their helpless babes. Stepmothers need no words;   680
The very beasts are kind compared with them.
Of all these evils woman was the cause,
The leader she. She with her wicked arts
Besets the minds of men; and all for her
And her vile, lustful ways, unnumbered towns   685
Lie low in smoking heaps; whole nations rush
To arms; and kingdoms, utterly o'erthrown,
Drag down their ruined peoples in their fall.
Though I should name no other, Aegeus' wife
Would prove all womankind a cursèd race.   690
NURSE. Why blame all women for the crimes of few?
HIPPOLYTUS. I hate them all. I dread and shun and curse
Them all. Whether from reason, instinct, blind
And causeless madness, this I know — I hate.
And sooner shall you fire and water wed;   695
Sooner shall dangerous quicksands friendly turn
And give safe anchorage; and sooner far
Shall Tethys from her utmost western bounds
Bring forth the shining day, and savage wolves
Smile kindly on the timid does, than I,   700
O'ercome, feel ought but hate to womankind.

NURSE. But oft doth love put reins on stubborn souls,
And all their hatred to affection turns.
Behold thy mother's realm of warlike dames;
Yet even they the sway of passion know.                              705
Of this thy birth itself is proof enough.

HIPPOLYTUS. My comfort for my mother's loss is this,
That now I'm free to hate all womankind.

NURSE. As some hard crag, on every side unmoved,
Resists the waves, and dashes backward far                           710
The opposing floods, so he doth spurn my words.
But hither Phaedra comes with hasty step,
Impatient of delay. What fate is hers?
Or to what action doth her madness tend?

       (PHAEDRA *enters and falls fainting to the earth.*)

But see, in sudden fainting fit she falls,                           715
And deathlike pallor overspreads her face.

       (HIPPOLYTUS *hastens to raise her up in his arms.*)

Lift up thy face, speak out, my daughter, see,
Thine own Hippolytus embraces thee.

PHAEDRA (*recovering from her faint*). Who gives me back to
    griefs, and floods again
My soul with heavy care? How well for me                             720
Had I sunk down to death!

HIPPOLYTUS.             But why, poor soul,
Dost thou lament the gift of life restored?

PHAEDRA (*aside*). Come dare, attempt, fulfil thine own command.
Speak out, and fearlessly. Who asks in fear
Suggests a prompt refusal. Even now                                  725
The greater part of my offense is done.
Too late my present modesty. My love,
I know, is base; but if I persevere,
Perchance the marriage torch will hide my sin.
Success makes certain sins respectable.                              730
Come now, begin.

       (*To* HIPPPOLYTUS.)

             Bend lower down thine ear,
I pray; if any comrade be at hand,
Let him depart, that we may speak alone.

HIPPOLYTUS. Behold, the place is free from witnesses.

PHAEDRA. My lips refuse to speak my waiting words;                   735
A mighty force compels my utterance,
A mightier holds it back. Ye heavenly powers,

I call ye all to witness, what I wish —
HIPPOLYTUS. Thy heart desires and cannot tell its wish?
PHAEDRA. Light cares speak out, the weighty have no words. 740
HIPPOLYTUS. Into my ears, my mother, tell thy cares.
PHAEDRA. The name of mother is too proud and high;
My heart dictates some humbler name than that.
Pray call me sister — slave, Hippolytus.
Yes, slave I'd be. I'll bear all servitude; 745
And shouldst thou bid me tread the driven snows,
To walk along high Pindus' frozen peaks,
I'd not refuse; no, not if thou shouldst bid
Me go through fire, and serried ranks of foes,
I would not hesitate to bare my breast 750
Unto the naked swords. Take thou the power
Which was consigned to me. Make me thy slave.
Rule thou the state, and let me subject be.
It is no woman's task to guard this realm
Of many towns. Do thou, who in the flower 755
Of youth rejoicest, rule the citizens
With strong paternal sway. But me receive
Into thy arms, and there protect thy slave
And suppliant. My widowhood relieve.
HIPPOLYTUS. May God on high this omen dark avert! 760
My father will in safety soon return.
PHAEDRA. Not so: the king of that fast-holding realm
And silent Styx has never opened back
The doors of earth to those who once have left
The realms above. Think'st thou that he will loose 765
The ravisher of his couch? Unless, indeed,
Grim Pluto has at last grown mild to love.
HIPPOLYTUS. The righteous gods of heaven will bring him back.
But while the gods still hold our prayers in doubt,
My brothers will I make my pious care, 770
And thee as well. Think not thou art bereft;
For I will fill for thee my father's place.
PHAEDRA (*aside*). Oh, hope of lovers, easily beguiled!
Deceitful love! Has he[1] not said enough?
I'll ply him now with prayers.

(*To* HIPPOLYTUS.)

Oh, pity me. 775
Hear thou the prayers which I must only think.
I long to utter them, but am ashamed.

[1] Reading, *dixit*.

HIPPOLYTUS.  What is thy trouble then?

PHAEDRA.                                              A trouble mine,
Which thou wouldst scarce believe could vex the soul
Of any stepdame.

HIPPOLYTUS.            Speak more openly;                        780
In doubtful words thy meaning thou dost wrap.

PHAEDRA.  My maddened heart with burning love is scorched;
My inmost marrow is devoured with love;
And through my veins and vitals steals the fire,
As when the flames through roomy holds of ships        785
Run darting.

HIPPOLYTUS.      Surely with a modest love
For Theseus thou dost burn.

PHAEDRA.                          Hippolytus,
'Tis thus with me: I love those former looks
Of Theseus, which in early manhood once
He wore, when first a beard began to show                  790
Upon his modest cheeks, what time he saw
The Cretan monster's hidden lurking-place,
And by a thread his labyrinthine way
Retraced.  Oh, what a glorious sight he was!
Soft fillets held in check his flowing locks,              795
And modesty upon his tender face
Glowed blushing red.  His soft-appearing arms
But half concealed his muscles' manly strength.
His face was like thy heavenly Phoebe's face,
Or my Apollo's, or 'twas like thine own.                    800
Like thee, like thee he was when first he pleased
His enemy.  Just so he proudly held
His head erect; still more in thee shines out
That beauty unadorned; in thee I find
Thy father all.  And yet thy mother's stern                805
And lofty beauty has some share in thee;
Her Scythian firmness tempers Grecian grace.
If with thy father thou hadst sailed to Crete,
My sister would have spun the thread for thee
And not for him.  O sister, wheresoe'er                      810
In heaven's starry vault thou shinest, thee,
Oh, thee I call to aid my hapless cause,
So like thine own.  One house has overthrown
Two sisters, thee the father, me the son.

                              (*To* HIPPOLYTUS.)
Behold, as suppliant, fallen to thy knees,                  815

A royal princess kneels. Without a spot
Of sin, unstained and innocent, was I;
And thou alone hast wrought the change in me.
See, at thy feet I kneel and pray, resolved
This day shall end my misery or life.                        820
Oh, pity her who loves thee —
HIPPOLYTUS.                              God in heaven,
Great ruler of all gods, dost thou this sin
So calmly hear, so calmly see?  If now
Thou hurlest not thy bolt with deadly hand,
What shameful cause will ever send it forth?                 825
Let all the sky in shattered ruins fall,
And hide the light of day in murky clouds.
Let stars turn back, and trace again their course
Athwart their proper ways.  And thou, great star
Of stars, thou radiant Sun, let not thine eyes               830
Behold the impious shame of this thy stock;
But hide thy face, and to the darkness flee.
Why is thy hand, O king of gods and men,
Inactive?  Why by forkéd lightning's brands
Is not the world in flames?  Direct thy bolts                835
At me; pierce me.  Let that fierce darting flame
Consume me quite, for mine is all the blame.
I ought to die, for I have favor found
In my stepmother's eyes.

(*To* PHAEDRA.)
                Did I seem one
To thee to do this vile and shameful thing?                  840
Did I seem easy fuel to thy fire,
I only?  Has my virtuous life deserved
Such estimate?  Thou, worse than all thy kind!
Thou woman, who hast in thy heart conceived
A deed more shameful than thy mother's sin,                  845
Whose womb gave monstrous birth; thou worse than she!
She stained herself with vilest lust, and long
Concealed the deed.  But all in vain: at last,
Her two-formed child revealed his mother's crime,
And by his fierce bull-visage proved her guilt.              850
Of such a womb and mother art thou born.
Oh, thrice and four times blesséd is their lot
Whom hate and treachery give o'er and doom
To death.  O father, how I envy thee!
Thy stepdame was the Colchian; but this,                     855

This woman is a greater curse than she.

PHAEDRA. I clearly see the destiny of my house:
We follow ever what we should avoid.
But I have given over self-control;
I'll follow thee through fire, through raging sea,      860
O'er ragged cliffs, through roaring torrents wild —
Wherever thou dost go, in mad pursuit
I shall be borne. Again, O haughty one,
I fall in suppliance and embrace thy knees.

HIPPOLYTUS. Away from my chaste body with thy touch      865
Impure! What more? She falls upon my breast!
I'll draw my sword and smite as she deserves.
See, by her twisted locks, I backward bend
Her shameless head. No blood more worthily
Was ever spilled, O goddess of the bow,      870
Upon thy altars.

PHAEDRA.            Now, Hippolytus,
Thou dost fulfil the fondest wish of mine;
Thou sav'st me from my madness; greater far
Than all my hopes, that by the hands I love,
By thine own hands, I perish ere I sin.      875

HIPPOLYTUS. Then live, be gone! Thou shalt gain naught from
   me.
And this my sword, defiled by thy base touch,
No more shall hang upon my modest side.

            (*He throws his sword from him.*)

What Tanaïs will make me clean again?
Or what Maeotis rushing to the sea,      880
With its barbaric waves? Not Neptune's self,
With all his ocean's waters could avail
To cleanse so foul a stain. O woods! O beasts!

            (*He rushes off into the depths of the forest.*)

NURSE (*in soliloquy, while* PHAEDRA *seems to have fallen in a
   fainting fit*).
Now is her fault discovered. Soul of mine,
Why dost thou stand in dumb amaze? This crime      885
We must throw back upon the man himself,
And charge him with a guilty love, ourselves.
Sin must be hid by sin. The safest way
Is to go straight forward on the course you fear.
Who is to know, since no one saw the deed,      890
Whether we dared, ourselves, or suffered ill?

(*Raising her voice in a loud cry.*)
Help! Help! ye dames of Athens! Faithful band
Of slaves, bring aid! Behold Hippolytus,
With vile adultery, attacks the queen!
He has her in his power! He threatens death!           895
At point of sword he storms her chastity!
There, he has gone in haste, and left behind
His sword in trembling, panic-stricken flight.
This proof of guilt we'll keep. But first restore
The stricken queen to life. Let all remain            900
Just as they are, her locks disheveled, torn,
To show how great a wrong she has endured.
Back to the city bear her now. Revive,
My mistress. Why dost seek to harm thyself
And shun thy comrades' eyes. For be thou sure        905
Not circumstance but will can make impure.

(*Exeunt.*)

CHORUS. He fled away like the storm-blast wild,
    More swift than cloud-compelling winds;
    And swifter than the comet's torch,
    When, driven before the wind, it speeds          910
    With long-drawn, trailing fires.
    Let fame, that boasts of her olden times,
    Compare with thine all ancient charms:
    Beyond compare does thy beauty shine,
    Clear and bright as the full-orbed moon,          915
    When, with waxing hours in splendor joined,
    Night long she speeds her shining car,
    And her ruddy face so brightly gleams,
    That the fires of the lesser stars are dimmed.
    He is fair as the messenger of night,             920
    When he leads the evening shadows in,
    Himself new bathed in the ocean's foam;
    Or when, the darkness put to flight,
    He heralds the dawn — bright Lucifer.
    And thou of the thyrsus, Indian Bacchus,          925
    With the flowing locks of endless youth,
    With thine ivy-clad spear the tigers driving,
    And thy turban set on thy hornéd head:
    Not thus will thy glorious locks outshine
    The unadorned hair of Hippolytus.                 930
    And admire not thy beauty over much,
    For fame has spread the story far,

How Phaedra's sister preferred to thee,
O Bromius, a mortal man.
Ah beauty, a doubtful boon art thou,                            935
The gift of a fleeting hour! How swift
On flying feet thou glidest away!
So flowery meadows of the spring
The summer's burning heat devours,
When midday's raging sun rides high,                            940
And night's brief round is hurried through.
As the lilies languish on their stems,
So pleasing tresses fail the head;
And swiftly is the radiance dimmed
Which gleams from the tender cheeks of youth!                   945
Each day hath its spoil from the lovely form;
For beauty flees and soon is gone.
Who then would trust a gift so frail?
Nay, use its joys, while still thou mayst;
For silent time will soon destroy thee,                         950
And hours to baser hours steal on.
Why seek the desert wilds? Thy form
Is no more safe in pathless ways.
If in the forest's depths thou hide,
When Titan brings the noonday heat,                             955
The saucy Naïds will surround thee,
Who are wont in their clear springs to snare
The lovely youth; and 'gainst thy sleep
The wanton goddesses of groves,
The Dryads, who the roving Pans                                 960
Drive in pursuit, will mischief plot.
Or else that glowing star, whose birth
The old Arcadians beheld,
Will see thee from the spangled sky,
And straight forget to drive her car.                           965
Of late she blushed a fiery red,
And yet no staining cloud obscured
Her shining disk. But we, in fear
For her troubled face, clashed cymbals loud,
Deeming her harried by the charms                               970
Of Thessaly. But for thee alone
Was all her toil; thou wast the cause
Of her long delay; for, seeing thee,
The night's fair goddess checked her course.
If only winter's blasts would beat                              975

Less fiercely on that face of thine;
If less it felt the sun's hot rays,
More bright than Parian marble's gleam
Would it appear. How beautiful
The manly sternness in thy face, 980
Thy brow's dark frowning majesty!
Compare with Phoebus' that fair neck.
His hair o'er his shoulders flowing free,
Unbound by fillet, ornaments
And shelters him. A shaggy brow 985
Becomes thee best; thee, shorter locks,
In tossing disarray. 'Tis thine
The rough and warlike gods to meet
In strife, and by thy mighty strength
To overcome them. Even now, 990
The muscles of a Hercules
Thy youthful arms can match. Thy breast
Is broader than the breast of Mars.
If on a horny-footed steed
Thou'rt pleased to mount, not Castor's self 995
More easily could hold in check
The Spartan Cyllarus.
Take thong in hand; with all thy strength
Discharge the javelin: not so far,
Though they be trained to hurl the dart, 1000
Will Cretans send the slender reed.
Or if it please thee into air,
In Parthian style, to shoot thy darts,
None will descend without its bird,
Fixed deep within the throbbing breast; 1005
From out the very clouds thy prey
Thou wilt regain.
By few has beauty been possessed
(The voice of history proclaims)
Without some loss or suffering. 1010
But thee, unharmed, may God pass by
More merciful, and may thy form,
Now famous for its beauty, show
At last the marks of ugly age.
What crime would woman's fury leave undared? 1015
She plans against this harmless youth some fraud.
Behold her scheme! For by her tumbled hair,
All torn, she seeks sure credence for her tale.

She wets her cheeks with tears; and every art
That woman's shrewdness knows, does she employ.                    1020
(*A man is seen approaching, who proves to be* THESEUS.)
But who is that who comes with grace of kings
Displayed upon his face, his lofty head
Held high in kingly pride? In countenance,
How like the young Pirithoüs he seems,
Were not his cheeks too deadly pale and wan,                       1025
And if his hair fell not in locks unkempt.
Behold, 'tis Theseus' self returned to earth.


# ACT III

THESEUS. At last have I escaped from endless night,
That shadowy realm which close confines the dead.
And now my eyes can scarce endure the light                        1030
Which I have long desired. Eleusin now
Has four times reaped her ripened grain, the gift
Triptolemus bestowed; thrice and again
Has Libra measured equal day and night,
Since dubious battling with an unknown fate                        1035
Has held me in the toils of life and death.
To me, though dead to all things else, one part
Of life remained, the consciousness of ill.
Alcides was the end. When he came down
To bring the dog by force from Tartarus,                           1040
He brought me also to the upper world.
But ah, my wearied frame has lost the strength
It had of old; I walk with faltering steps.
Alas! how great a task it was to reach
The world of light from lower Phlegethon,                          1045
To flee from death and follow Hercules!
     But why this sound of wailing in my ears?
Let someone tell; for agonies of woe
And grief and lamentations sad I meet
Upon the very threshold of my home —                               1050
A fitting welcome to a guest from hell.
NURSE. The queen is obstinately bent on death,
And scorns the strong remonstrance of our tears.
THESEUS. Why should she die, her husband safe returned?
NURSE. That very cause compels her speedy death.                   1055
THESEUS. Thy words are dark and hide some weighty truth.

Speak out and tell what grief weighs down her soul.
NURSE. She tells her grief to none. Some secret woe
  She hides within her heart, and is resolved
  To take her secret with her to the grave.                        1060
  But speed thee to her; there is need of haste.
THESEUS. Unbar the close-shut portals of my house.

  (*The doors are opened and* THESEUS *encounters his wife just within.*)

THESEUS (*to* PHAEDRA). My queen, is't thus thou dost receive
    thy lord,
  And welcome back thy husband long desired?
  Nay, put away the sword from thy right hand,                     1065
  And give me heart again. Reveal to me
  The cause that forces thee to flee from life.
PHAEDRA. Alas, great Theseus, by thy kingly power,
  And by thy children's souls, by thy return,
  And by my ashes, suffer me to die.                               1070
THESEUS. What cause compels thy death?
PHAEDRA.                              The fruit of death
  Would perish if I let its cause be known.
THESEUS. None else shall hear it save myself alone.
PHAEDRA. A chaste wife fears her husband most of all.
THESEUS. Speak out; I'll hide thy secret in my heart.             1075
PHAEDRA. The secret thou wouldst have another guard,
  First guard thyself.
THESEUS.               No chance of death thou'lt find.
PHAEDRA. Death cannot fail the heart that's bent on death.
THESEUS. Confess what sin must be atoned by death.
PHAEDRA. My life.
THESEUS.          Will not my tears avail with thee?              1080
PHAEDRA. That death is best which one's own friends lament.
THESEUS. She still persists in silence. By the lash
  And chains shall her old nurse be forced to tell
  What she will not declare. Put her in chains.
  Now let the lash lay bare her hidden thoughts.                   1085
PHAEDRA. Hold, stay thy hand, for I myself will speak.
THESEUS. Why dost thou turn thy grieving face away,
  And hide the quickly rising shower of tears
  Behind thy robe?
PHAEDRA.          Thee, thee do I invoke,
  O father of the gods, and thee, O Sun,                           1090
  Thou shining glory of the heavenly dome,
  On whom as founder doth our house depend,

I call ye both to witness that I strove
Against his prayers, though sorely tried. To threats
Of death my spirit did not yield; but force                              1095
O'ercame my body. This the shameful stain
Upon my honor which my blood must cleanse.
THESEUS. Come, tell, who hath defiled our honor so?
PHAEDRA. Whom thou wouldst least expect.
THESEUS.                                                    But who is he?
I wait to hear his name.
PHAEDRA.                          This sword shall tell,                 1100
Which in his terror at our loud laments,
The adulterer left, fearing the citizens.
THESEUS. Ah me! What villainy do I behold?
What monstrous deed is this? The royal sword,
Its ivory hilt with tiny signs engraved,                                 1105
Shines out, the glory of the Athenian race.
But he — where has he gone?
PHAEDRA.                              These slaves have seen
How, borne on speeding feet, he fled away.
THESEUS. Oh, holy piety! O thou who reign'st
In heaven, and thou who rulest in the seas,                              1110
Whence came this base infection of our race?
Was he of Grecian birth, or did he spring
From Scythian Taurus or some Colchian stream?
The type reverts to its ancestral stock,
And blood ignoble but repeats its source.                                1115
This is the madness of that savage race,
To scorn all lawful love, and prostitute
At last the long-chaste body to the crowd.
Oh, loathsome race, restrained by no good laws
Which milder climes revere! The very beasts                             1120
Shun love incestuous, and keep the laws
Of nature with instinctive chastity.
Where is that face, that feigned austerity,
That rough and careless garb that sought to ape
The ancient customs? Where that aspect stern,                           1125
That sour severity which age assumes?
O life, two-faced! How thou dost hide thy thoughts!
For fairest faces cover foulest hearts;
The chaste demeanor hides inchastity;
The gentle, boldness; seeming goodness, sin.                            1130
False men approve the truth; the faint of heart
Affect a blustering mood. O thou, of woods

Enamored, savage, rough and virgin pure,
Didst thou reserve thyself for me alone?
On my couch first and with so fell a crime                          1135
Wast thou inclined to try thy manly powers?
Now, now I thank the kindly gods of heaven
That long ago I slew Antiope;
That, when I went below to Stygian caves,
I did not leave thy mother for thy lust.                            1140
Go, get thee far away to unknown lands;
And there, though to her utmost bounds removed,
The earth should hem thee off by ocean's wastes;
Though thou shouldst dwell at the Antipodes;
Though to the frigid northern realms thou go,                       1145
And deep within her farthest caverns hide;
Or, though beyond the reach of winter placed,
And drifting snows, thou leave the boisterous threats
Of frosty Boreas in mad pursuit:
Thou still shalt meet thy fitting punishment.                       1150
Persistent shall I chase thee in thy flight
Through all thy hiding-places. Ways remote,
Hemmed in, secluded, hard and trackless ways,
I'll traverse in pursuit. No obstacle
Shall block my way. Thou know'st whence I return.                   1155
And whither spears cannot be hurled at thee
I'll hurl my prayers. My father of the sea
Once promised me that thrice I might prevail
With him in prayer, and ratified the boon
By oath upon the inviolable Styx.                                   1160

(*To* NEPTUNE.)

Thou ruler of the sea, the boon bestow,
And grant my prayer: let not Hippolytus
Live to behold another sun's bright rays,
But may he go to meet those shades of hell
Enraged at my escape. O father, now                                 1165
I pray that aid which still I deprecate.
This last of thy three boons I would not use,
If I were not beset by grievous ills.
Amidst the depths of hell and dreadful Dis,
Amidst the infernal king's pursuing threats,                        1170
I did not call on thee. But now I claim
Thy promise, father. Why delay thine aid?
Why are thy waves inactive? Let the winds
That drive the blackening clouds bring darkness on;

Snatch stars and sky from sight; pour forth the sea;    1175
Arouse thy watery monsters, and let loose
On him from ocean's depths thy swelling waves.

(*Exit* THESEUS.)

CHORUS.  Great nature, mother of the gods,
  And thou, fire-girt Olympus' lord,
  Who speedest through the flying skies          1180
  The scattered stars, the wandering ways
  Of constellations, and the heavens
  Upon their whirling axes turn'st:
  Why is thy care so great to keep
  The annual highways of the air,                1185
  That now the hoary frosts may strip
  The woods of leaves, and now the trees
  May spread once more their pleasant shade;
  That now the summer's fervent heat
  May ripen Ceres' gift, and soon                1190
  Her strength the Autumn may subdue?
  But why, though thou dost rule so wide,
  Though in thy hand the ponderous worlds
  Are poised, and calmly wheel along
  Their appointed ways, why dost thou shun       1195
  The affairs of men and have no care
  For them?  Art not solicitous
  That good should prosper, and that sin
  Receive its just deserts?  But no:
  Blind Fortune rules the affairs of men,        1200
  Dispensing with unthinking hand
  Her gifts, oft favoring the worst.
  And so the violent oppress
  The innocent; and fraud holds sway
  In highest places.  To the hands               1205
  Of brutish men the rabble most
  Rejoice to trust their government;
  The same they honor and they hate,
  With fickle will.  Sad virtue finds
  Her recompense for righteousness               1210
  All gone away; and poverty,
  Relentless, follows innocence;
  While, deep intrenched in wickedness,
  The adulterer sits secure, and reigns.
  O modesty — an empty name!                     1215
  And worth — a glorious cheat!

But what would yonder messenger announce,
Who comes in haste, with woeful countenance?

## ACT IV

(*Enter* MESSENGER.)

MESSENGER. O slavery, thou hard and bitter lot,
  Why must I voice these woes unspeakable?     1220
THESEUS. Fear not, but boldly tell the worst mischance;
  For mine a heart not unprepared for grief.
MESSENGER. My tongue can find no words to voice its woe.
THESEUS. But speak, what evil fortune still besets
  My shattered house?
MESSENGER.         Hippolytus is dead!     1225
THESEUS. The father knew long since his son had died;
  But now the adulterer has met his end.
  Tell me, I pray, the manner of his death.
MESSENGER. When, fleeing forth, he left the city's walls,
  With maddened speed he hurried on his way,     1230
  And quickly yoked his chargers to his car,
  And curbed them to his will with close-drawn reins.
  And then, with much wild speech, and cursing loud
  His native land, oft calling on his sire,
  He fiercely shook the reins above his steeds;     1235
  When suddenly, far out the vast sea roared,
  And heaved itself to heaven. No wind was there
  To stir the sea, no quarter of the sky
  Broke in upon its peace; the rising waves
  Were by their own peculiar tempest raised     1240
  No blast so great had ever stirred the straits
  Of Sicily, nor had the deep e'er swelled
  With such wild rage before the north wind's breath,
  When high cliffs trembled with the shock of waves,
  And hoary foam smote high Leucate's top.     1245
  The sea then rose into a mighty heap,
  And, big with monstrous birth, was landward borne.
  For no ship's wrecking was this swelling pest
  Intended; landward was its aim. The flood
  Rolled shoreward heavily, something unknown     1250
  Within its laden bosom carrying.
  What land, new born, will lift its head aloft?
  Is some new island of the Cyclades

Arising?  Now the rocky heights are hid,
Held sacred to the Epidaurian god,                          1255
And those high crags well known for Sciron's crime;
No longer can be seen that land whose shores
Are washed by double seas.  While in amaze
We look in fear and wonder, suddenly
The whole sea bellows, and on every side                    1260
The towering cliffs re-echo with the roar;
While all their tops the leaping spray bedews.
The deep spouts forth and vomits up its waves
In alternating streams, like some huge whale
Which roves the ocean, spouting up the floods.              1265
Then did that mound of waters strongly heave
And break itself, and threw upon the shore
A thing more terrible than all our fears.
The sea itself rushed landward, following
That monstrous thing.  I shudder at the thought.            1270
What form and bearing had the monster huge!
A bull it was in form, with dark-green neck
Uplifted high, its lofty front adorned
With verdant mane.  Its ears with shaggy hair
Were rough; its horns with changing color flashed,          1275
Such as the lord of some fierce herd would have,
Both earth and ocean-born.  He vomits flames;
With flames his fierce eyes gleam.  His glossy neck
Great couch-like muscles shows, and as he breathes,
His spreading nostrils quiver with the blast                1280
Of his deep panting.  Breast and dewlap hang
All green with clinging moss; and on his sides
Red lichens cling.  His hinder parts appear
In monstrous shape, and like some scaly fish
His vast and shapeless members drag along;                  1285
As are those monsters of the distant seas
Which swallow ships, and spout[1] them forth again.
The country-side was panic stricken; herds
In frenzied terror scattered through the fields;
Nor did the herdsmen think to follow them.                  1290
The wild beasts in the forest pastures fled
In all directions, and the hunters shook
With deadly fear.  Hippolytus alone
Was not afraid, but curbed his frantic steeds
With close-drawn reins, and with his well-known voice       1295

[1] Reading, *reddit*.

He cheered them on. The road to Argos[1] runs
Precipitous along the broken hills,
On one side bordered by the roaring sea.
Here does that massive monster whet himself
And kindle hot his wrath; then, when he felt          1300
His courage strong within his breast, and when
His power to attempt the strife he had rehearsed,
He charged Hippolytus with headlong course,
The ground scarce touching with his bounding feet;
And, fearful, stopped before the trembling steeds.    1305
But this thy son, with savage countenance,
Stood steadfast, threatening, before the foe.
His features changed not, while he thundered loud:
"This empty terror cannot daunt my soul,
For 'twas my father's task to vanquish bulls."         1310
But straightway, disobedient to the reins,
The horses hurried off the car. And now,
The highway leaving, maddened by their fear,
They plunged along where'er their terror led,
And took their way among the rocky fields.             1315
But he, their driver, as some captain strong
Holds straight his bark upon the boisterous sea,
Lest she oppose her side against the waves,
And by his art escapes the yawning floods;
Not otherwise he guides the whirling car.              1320
For now with tight-drawn reins he curbs his steeds,
And now upon their backs he plies the lash.
But doggedly that monster kept along,
Now running by their side, now leaping straight
Upon them as they came, from every hand               1325
Great fear inspiring. Soon all further flight
Was checked; for that dread, hornéd, ocean beast
With lowering front charged full against their course.
Then, truly, did the horses, wild with fear,
Break loose from all control; and from the yoke        1330
They madly struggled to withdraw their necks,
Their master hurling to their stamping feet.
Headlong among the loosened reins he fell,
His form all tangled in their clinging strands.
The more he struggled to release himself               1335
The tighter those relentless fetters bound.
The steeds perceived what they had done, and now,

[1] Reading, *Argos.*

With empty car, and no one mastering them,
They ran where terror bade.  Just so, of old,
Not recognizing their accustomed load,                        1340
And hot with anger that the car of day
Had been entrusted to a spurious sun,
The steeds of Phoebus hurled young Phaëthon
Far through the airs of heaven in wandering course.
Now far and wide he stains the fields with blood,            1345
His head rebounding from the smitten rocks.
The bramble thickets pluck away his hair,
And that fair face is bruised upon the stones.
His fatal beauty which had been his bane,
Is ruined now by many a wound.  His limbs                     1350
Are dragged along upon the flying wheels.
At last, his bleeding trunk upon a charred
And pointed stake is caught, pierced through the groin;
And for a little, by its master held,
The car stood still.  The horses by that wound               1355
Were held a while, but soon they break delay —
And break their master too.  While on they rush,
The whipping branches cut his dying form,
The rough and thorny brambles tear his flesh,
And every bush retains its part of him.                       1360
Now bands of servants scour those woeful fields,
Those places where Hippolytus was dragged,
And where his bloody trail directs the way;
And sorrowing dogs trace out their master's limbs.
But not as yet has all this careful toil                      1365
Of grieving friends sufficed to gather all.
And has it come to this, that glorious form?
But now the partner of his father's realm,
And his acknowledged heir, illustrious youth,
Who shone refulgent like the stars — behold                  1370
His scattered fragments for the funeral pile
They gather up and heap them on the bier!
THESEUS.  O mother Nature, all too potent thou!
How firmly dost thou hold me by the ties
Of blood!  How thou dost force me to obey                     1375
Thy will!  I wished to slay my guilty son,
While yet he lived; but now I mourn his loss.
MESSENGER.  One may not rightly mourn what he has willed.[1]
THESEUS.  This is indeed the crowning woe, I think,

[1] Reading, *haud quisquam honeste flere, quod voluit, potest.*

When chance fulfils the prayers we should not make. 1380
MESSENGER. If still you hate your son, why weep for him?
THESEUS. Because I slew, not lost my son, I weep.

CHORUS. How on the wheel of circumstance
We mortals whirl! 'Gainst humble folk
Does fate more gently rage, and God 1385
More lightly smites the lightly blest.
A life in dim retirement spent
Insures a peaceful soul; and he
Who in a lowly cottage dwells
May live to tranquil age at last. 1390
The mountain tops that pierce the skies,
Feel all the stormy winds that blow,
Fierce Eurus, Notus, and the threats
Of Boreas, and Corus too,
       Storm bringer.
The vale low lying seldom feels 1395
The thunder's stroke; but Caucasus,
The huge, and the lofty Phrygian groves
Of mother Cybele have felt
The bolts of Jove and Thunderer.
For Jupiter in jealousy 1400
Attacks the heights too near his skies;
But never is the humble roof
Uptorn by jealous heaven's assaults.
Round mighty kings and homes of kings
       He thunders.
The passing hour on doubtful wings 1405
Flits ever; nor may any claim
Swift Fortune's pledge. Behold our king,
Who sees at last the glowing stars
And light of day, the gloom of hell
Behind him left, a sad return 1410
Laments; for this his welcome home
He finds more sorrowful by far
Than dismal, dark Avernus' self.
O Pallas, by the Athenian race
In reverence held, that once again 1415
Thy Theseus sees the light of day,
And has escaped the pools of Styx,
Thou owest naught to greedy Dis;
For still the number of the shades

Within the infernal tyrant's power
   Remains the same.                                                    1420
But why the sounds of wailing that we hear?
And what would Phaedra with her naked sword?


## ACT V

*(Enter* PHAEDRA *with a drawn sword in her hand.)*

THESEUS *(to* PHAEDRA*).* What madness pricks thee on, all wild
   with grief?
What means that sword? or why these loud laments?
Why weepest thou above the hated corpse?                                 1425
PHAEDRA. Me, me, O savage ruler of the deep,
Attack; against me send the monstrous shapes
That breed within the caverns of the sea,
Whatever Tethys in her heart conceals,
And ocean hides within his wandering waves.                              1430
O Theseus, always ill of omen thou!
Oh, never to thy loved ones safe returned,
Since son and father by their death have paid
For thy home-coming. Thou of thine own house
Art the destroyer; ever baneful thou,                                    1435
Whether in love or hatred of thy wives.
     *(Turning to the mangled corpse.)*
Hippolytus, is this thy face I see?
Have I brought thee to this? What Sinis wild,
What pitiless Procrustes mangled thee?
What Cretan bull-man, filling all the cave                               1440
Of Daedalus with his vast bellowings,
Has rent thee thus upon his savage horns?
Ah me! where now is fled thy beauty bright,
Thy eyes, my stars? Dost thou all lifeless lie?
Come back a little while and hear my words.                              1445
'Tis nothing base I speak. With my own hand
I'll make thee full atonement, and will plunge
The avenging sword within my sinful breast,
And so be free from life and guilt at once.
Thee will I follow through Tartarean pools,                              1450
Across the Styx, through streams of liquid fire.
Let me appease the spirit of the dead.
Accept the spoils I offer, take this lock
Torn from my bleeding forehead. 'Twas not right

To join our souls in life; but surely now                    1455
We may by death unite our fates.
(*To herself.*)
Now die,
If thou art undefiled, to appease thy lord;
But if defiled, die for thy lover's sake.
Is't meet that I should live and seek again
My husband's couch, by such foul incest stained?            1460
This wrong was lacking still, that, as if pure,
Thou shouldst enjoy that union, justified.
O death, thou only cure for evil love,
For injured chastity the last resort:
I fly to thee; spread wide thy soothing arms.               1465
Hear me, O Athens; thou, O father, hear,
Thou worse than stepdame: I have falsely sworn.
The crime, which I myself within my heart,
With passion mad, conceived, I basely charged
To him. An empty vengeance hast thou wrought                1470
Upon thy son; for he in chastity,
Through fault of the unchaste, lies there, unstained
And innocent.
(*To* HIPPOLYTUS.)
Regain thine honor now;
Behold my impious breast awaits the stroke
Of justice, and my blood makes sacrifice                    1475
Unto the spirit of a guiltless man.
(*To* THESEUS.)
How thou mayst recompense thy murdered son,
Learn now from me — and seek the Acheron.
(*She falls upon her sword and dies.*)
THESEUS. Ye jaws of wan Avernus, and ye caves
Of Taenara, ye floods of Lethe's stream,                    1480
A soothing balm to hearts o'ercome with grief,
Ye sluggish pools: take ye my impious soul
And plunge me deep in your eternal woes.
Now come, ye savage monsters of the deep,
Whatever Proteus hides within his caves,                    1485
And drown me in your pools, me who rejoice
In crime so hideous. O father, thou
Who ever dost too readily assent
Unto my wrathful prayers, I merit not
An easy death, who on my son have brought                   1490

A death so strange, and scattered through the fields
His mangled limbs; who, while, as austere judge,
I sought to punish evil falsely charged,
Have fallen myself into the pit of crime.
For heaven, hell, and seas have by my sins          1495
Been peopled; now no further lot remains;
Three kingdoms know me now. Was it for this
That I returned? Was heaven's light restored
To me that I might see two funerals,
A double death? That I, bereft of wife              1500
And son, should with one torch upon the pyre
Consume them both? Thou giver of the light
Which has so baleful proved, O, Hercules,
Take back thy boon, and give me up again
To Dis; restore me to the cursèd shades             1505
Whom I escaped. Oh, impious, in vain
I call upon that death I left behind.
Thou bloody man, well skilled in deadly arts,
Who hast contrived unwonted ways of death
And terrible, now deal unto thyself                 1510
The fitting punishment. Let some great pine
Be bent to earth and hurl thee high in air;
Or let me headlong leap from Sciron's cliff.
More dreadful punishments have I beheld,
Which Phlegethon upon the guilty souls              1515
Encircled by his fiery stream inflicts.
What suffering awaits me, and what place,
Full well I know. Make room, ye guilty shades;
On me, me only, let that rock be placed,
The everlasting toil of Sisyphus,                   1520
And let these wearied hands upbear its weight;
Let cooling waters lap and mock my lips;
Let that fell vulture fly from Tityos,
And let my vitals ever living be
For punishment. And thou, Ixion, sire               1525
Of my Pirithoüs, take rest awhile,
And let the wheel that never stops its flight
Bear these my limbs upon its whirling rim.
Now yawn, O earth, and chaos dire, receive,
I pray, receive me to your depths; for thus         1530
'Tis fitting that I journey to the shades.
I go to meet my son. And fear thou not,
Thou king of dead men's souls; I come in peace

To that eternal home, whence ne'er again
Shall I come forth.
              My prayers move not the gods.    1535
But if some impious plea I made to them,
How ready would they be to grant my prayer!
CHORUS. Theseus, thou hast unending time to mourn.
Now pay the funeral honors due thy son,
And bury these poor torn and scattered limbs.    1540
THESEUS. Then hither bring the pitiful remains
Of that dear corpse, and heap together here
That shapeless mass of flesh, those mangled limbs.
Is this Hippolytus? I realize
My depth of crime, for I have murdered thee.    1545
And lest but once and I alone should sin,
A parent, bent to do an impious thing,
My father did I summon to my aid.
Behold, my father's boon do I enjoy.
O childlessness, a bitter loss art thou    1550
For broken age! But come, embrace his limbs,
Whatever of thy hapless son is left,
And clasp them, wretched father, to thy breast.
Arrange in order those dismembered parts,
And to their proper place restore them. Here    1555
His brave right hand should be. Place here the left,
Well trained to curb his horses with the reins.
The marks of his left side I recognize;
And yet how large a part is lacking still
Unto our tears. Be firm, ye trembling hands,    1560
To do the last sad offices of grief;
Be dry, my cheeks, and stay your flowing tears,
While I count o'er the members of my son,
And lay his body out for burial.
What is this shapeless piece, on all sides torn    1565
With many a wound? I know not what it is,
Save that 'tis part of thee. Here lay it down.
Not in its own, but in an empty place.
That face, that once with starry splendor gleamed,
That softened by its grace e'en foemen's eyes,    1570
Has that bright beauty come to this? O fate,
How bitter! Deadly favor of the gods!
And is it thus my son comes back to me
In answer to my prayers? These final rites
Thy father pays, receive, O thou my son,    1575

Who often to thy funeral must be borne.
And now let fires consume these dear remains.
Throw open wide my palace, dark with death,
And let all Athens ring with loud laments.
Do some of you prepare the royal pyre,                    1580
And others seek yet farther in the fields
His scattered parts.

(*Pointing to* PHAEDRA'S *corpse.*)

Let earth on her be spread,
And may it heavy rest upon her head.

◇  ◇  ◇

# STUDY AIDS

ACT I. *Lines 1–97.* Hippolytus' opening speech is composed of a
series of instructions to his men concerning hunting locales and
methods. What kind of theatrical techniques would be required to
realize the elements of spectacle implied in the speech? Can you think
of similar scenes from opera or ballet? Or is this scene essentially un-
stageable, a matter of allusion rather than scenic presentation? Although Hippolytus makes no explicit references to his character traits
in this speech and is not, of course, involved in any dramatic action, is
his character nevertheless revealed to some extent? What is the dramatic connection between this speech and Hippolytus' next (ll. 587ff.)?

*Lines 98–152.* Analyze Phaedra's speech for the various motivations
which she imputes to herself. Which is the most important? Does she
ultimately come to blame her fate on one of these?

*Lines 128–132.* What is Phaedra's explanation for finding joy only
in hunting in the woods? Compare the psychological function of the
woodland imagery in this play with that in the similar situation in the
*Hippolytus.*

*Lines 153–218.* Since Phaedra had not yet referred to her love for
Hippolytus specifically, what can be deduced from the Nurse's evident knowledge of it as revealed in this speech? How are we to interpret this method of revealing vital information to the audience? Is it,
as some scholars maintain, a lapse in dramatic technique, which is the
result of a divorce between dramatic composition and theatrical presentation? Or is it merely an assumption that the audience, hearing or
reading, already know the main outlines of the story? Could they

understand the dialogue very well if they were not already thoroughly familiar with Greek mythology?

Seneca found the dramatic convention of the *confidante* in Euripides. What major alteration in the moral and psychological role of the Nurse as confidante *vis-à-vis* Phaedra is effected by Seneca in this play? Consider the opening lines of the Nurse's speech.

Analyze the Nurse's moral wisdom and psychological insight. Is it sound, comprehensive, relevant to Phaedra's situation?

*Lines 219–241.* Although Phaedra admits that she is conscious of her sin in desiring Hippolytus, does she here or elsewhere indicate that she is making or has made a struggle to overcome her passion?

*Lines 241–267.* How does the Nurse puncture Phaedra's rationalization about the "winged god"? Do the Nurse's strictures against the propensity toward self-indulgence of the rich and powerful seem directed particularly toward the Roman ruling class of Seneca's time, as scholars have suggested, or do they have a general validity?

*Lines 271–305.* Is Phaedra's clever punning on "sovereignty" in her reply to the Nurse indicative of the shrewd intelligence with which she pursues the object of her passion, dismissing rational argument and rationalizing her guilt? Some critics feel that such word-play weakens dramatic effectiveness by substituting verbal cleverness for direct emotional confrontation. Do you think that it diminishes the strength of the scene?

*Lines 310–336.* What justification is there for interpreting Phaedra's threat of suicide as merely a clever device for manipulating the Nurse to do her bidding?

*Lines 337–429.* How well is the miscellany of knowledge of geography, mythology, and zoology integrated with the theme of love's power in this choral ode? Does the zoological imagery, in particular, seem bizarre? Identify the mythological allusions and comment on their evocative power in their present context.

ACT II. *Lines 432–463.* How can you account, from a dramaturgical point of view, for the redundancy of having the Nurse describe in detail Phaedra's condition and then having Phaedra enact these details immediately after? Is it more reasonable to understand this redundancy as a characteristic of closet drama, written without consideration for theatrical presentation — or, on the contrary, as a striving after an extreme theatrical effect, the Nurse's words serving as an introduction for a grand entrance?

*Lines 464–483.* What is revealed about Phaedra's psychological state by her wish to be dressed as Hippolytus' mother? Does it seem to intensify the attraction which she finds in the very sinfulness of her passion? Analyze the ironic ambiguity in the symbolism of the woods as it appears in the lines of Phaedra, the chorus, and the Nurse. Do the forests stand for the same power for each?

*Lines 524–586.* What effect does the Nurse's duplicity have on the tone and cogency of her blandishments of Hippolytus?

*Lines 587–690.* What is the thematic relationship between this speech of Hippolytus and the one with which he opened the play? In his mind the forest life is identified with simplicity and innocence. How does this notion contrast with its meaning for Phaedra? Does Hippolytus' vision of a golden age of man reveal him to be a naive or sentimental idealist? Is there some sense in which his misogyny has its source in his kind of idealism? The notion of a golden age of man in the distant past is a philosophical commonplace of Western thought. Is its expression here well integrated into the theme and characterization of this play, or does it seem to be merely a rhetorical set-piece added for verbal decoration?

Can you explain Hippolytus' reference to stepmothers before he knows about Phaedra's love for him? Must it be read, as some scholars have done, as a topicality relating to Seneca's own times, inserted prematurely and clumsily and with little regard to consistency of characterization? Or does it make some sense in the context of Hippolytus' misogynous tirade?

*Lines 715–721.* Is Phaedra's fainting fit the genuine result of her despair at overhearing Hippolytus' rejection of her, or is it a pretense to trap Hippolytus into holding her in his arms? Can what we already know of Phaedra's character help us to answer this question in the absence of explicit statement in the text? If you were staging the play, how could you effectively communicate to the audience through the action that the faint was a trick?

*Lines 721–906.* Analyze the sources of dramatic irony in the dialogue between Phaedra and Hippolytus. What is the double meaning which informs most of Phaedra's lines and which permits her to intend one meaning whereas Hippolytus perceives a quite different one?

Does Phaedra's comparison of Hippolytus' appearance to that of the young Theseus help to explain her fascination with Hippolytus in a more sympathetic way, or does it rather intensify the incestuous character of her passion?

After Hippolytus finally realizes the meaning and object of Phaedra's passion, is it in keeping with his youthful innocence and idealism that he first takes the blame on himself for having attracted her?

When Phaedra asks Hippolytus to kill her with his drawn sword, is she speaking out of despair or is she attempting another stratagem to seduce him? Although it is the Nurse who devises the scheme to cover up Phaedra's guilt by accusing Hippolytus, why is it really Phaedra to whom the blame for the tragedy must be assigned?

*Lines 907-1027.* How is the ode in praise of Hippolytus' beauty related to the dramatic action of the play at this point? What melancholy aspect of physical beauty furnishes the main theme of the ode?

ACT III. *Lines 1028-1051.* What is Theseus' condition upon his return? What are the theatrical possibilities in his entrance at this point? What makes it so easy to impose a false story upon him? Why does he seem so willing, even eager, to believe the worst about men? Is there a sardonic humor in his comment on the lamentations which are the first sounds he hears upon his return home?

*Lines 1063-1081.* In the exchange between Phaedra and Theseus there occurs a good example of stichomythia. Analyze the verbal dexterity in these alternating lines. Does the rhetorical cleverness intrude upon the dramatic situation and disrupt it? Or does this device reveal with some psychological penetration the self-conscious, studied, and deliberate steps which Phaedra is taking to condemn an innocent person?

*Lines 1109-1177.* Theseus delivers a passionate speech, but one which is carefully structured. What are its principal themes? How are these themes made concrete? Note the epigrammatic and aphoristic lines. In what way are they appropriate to Theseus' character and to the tone of his speech? What qualities and attitudes previously revealed by Hippolytus are now recalled to his disadvantage by Theseus? What is the irony in Theseus' reference to his former wife Antiope?

*Lines 1178-1218.* Is there one character in particular to whom this ode concerning nature's carelessness of man's welfare is relevant?

ACT IV. *Lines 1229-1372.* The Messenger's speech is a *tour de force* of dramatic reporting. Analyze the components of its artistry. How is it organized? What is its tone and how is this achieved? How graphic and concrete is the language? What principle of selection in details is evident? Compare this speech with its counterpart in Euripides and in Racine. What important differences do you note? What is your reaction to the gruesome details of this speech? Is their horror greater or less than the violence commonly depicted on the movie screen? Is their effect heightened or diminished by the fact that they are merely reported rather than represented?

*Lines 1373-1382.* How does Theseus' expression of grief at the Messenger's news prepare for his reactions later?

*Lines 1383-1422.* In extolling the peace of "a life in dim retirement spent" the chorus recalls similar praise of the humble, simple life expressed earlier by the Nurse and Hippolytus. What is the connection between this idealization of one "who in a lowly cottage dwells" and the action of the play?

ACT V. *Lines 1423-1478.* Does Phaedra kill herself because of her despair over having lost Hippolytus, whom she promises to join in the underworld, or because of her shame before her husband? What does she declare to be her motive? With what ironic force does she accuse Theseus of being a hater of his wives, of being always "ill of omen"? Is she trying to shift the guilt for what has happened from herself to him?

Given the turnings of her mind in this final speech, does Phaedra's confession of her false accusation carry any redemptive force?

Euripides has Phaedra die off-stage; but Seneca has her die, as it were, in full view of the audience by falling on her sword. What is gained or lost in dramatic effectiveness in each case?

*Lines 1479-1583.* After Phaedra's death, Theseus in his own longing for death invokes all the terrors and darkness of hell upon himself. What aspect of his recent past history makes this particularly relevant and poignant? Is his condemnation of the gods at the end of this speech justified by the previous action of the play?

The play closes with the macabre spectacle of Theseus piecing together the remains of his son's body. Could such a scene possibly be staged? Do you think a Roman audience would have tolerated it? Would we tolerate it today? on the stage? in the movies? Ignoring the question of its effect, can you relate this concluding scene of total and violent physical dissolution to the theme and structure of the whole play?

After his long lament over Hippolytus and his order for the funeral rites, what is the force of the two lines Theseus speaks over the corpse of Phaedra? Would this brief moment be effective on stage? What is the dramatic and thematic function of ending the play with a reference to Phaedra?

# DISCUSSION TOPICS

1. What is the overall structure of the play in terms of act divisions, choral odes, sequence of scenes?

2. Seneca does not have gods appear on the stage as Euripides does. Does this imply a different attitude toward the relationship of human will and divine power? Try to formulate as precisely as possible the shift in attitude between the two plays. Can such a shift be paralleled in other aspects of Greek and Roman culture?

3. Seneca's verse is heavily allusive. How do the allusions function, generally, in the play? Do they seem to be ornaments stuck on here and there, or do they clearly relate to the dramatic action?

4. The many long, elaborate speeches in Seneca's play usually strike modern ears as too "poetic," rhetorical, or even bombastic. But audiences in the past have relished the "art" of this style with its amplitude of examples, details, and allusions. How can you account for such a shift in taste? How does Seneca compare with the other playwrights in this collection in this respect? Comment on O'Neill's prose as an extreme in the other direction.

5. The eminent contemporary critic Northrop Frye has written: "The truism, the sententious axiom, the proverb, the *topos* or rhetorical commonplace, the irresistibly quotable phrase — such things are the very life blood of poetry." Are "such things" a part of Seneca's style?

6. Seneca's *Phaedra* is marked by several sections of dialogue which appear to have the form of debates about love, passion, human will, and so forth. Find these debates and analyze the moral wisdom they contain. To what extent does debate serve as action in this play? In the light of this feature, would the designation "drama of ideas" be an appropriate one here?

7. Relate the role of violent physical horror in Seneca's play to its general role in Roman culture of the period. Does such horror have a counterpart in our own popular dramatic entertainment? (Consider, for example, the James Bond thrillers.)

8. Turn to the essay "Tragedy and Moralism: Euripides and Seneca" by Norman T. Pratt, in Part Three of this book. Be prepared to summarize Professor Pratt's views and to indicate where and why you agree and/or disagree with them.

# *JEAN RACINE*

◇◇◇◇◇◇◇◇◇◇◇◇◇◇◇◇◇◇◇◇◇◇◇◇◇◇◇◇◇◇◇◇◇◇◇◇◇

JEAN RACINE (1639–1699) was born near Soissons at La Ferté Milon, where his father was a government official. His family was connected with the Jansenists, a religious group sometimes described as "Calvinistic" Catholics. The Jansenists held and taught extremely rigorous views concerning original sin and man's resulting state of utter depravity. They were the object of some persecution because their teachings seemed to support the idea of predestination, which conflicted with the Church's position on the freedom of the will. The Jansenist influence was strong on Racine in his family life and in his schooling. Although his parents died when he was very young, he was brought up by his grandmother, a Jansenist, and he was educated by Jansenists first at a college in Beauvais and later, from 1655 to 1659, at a center near Port-Royal. In addition, however, to absorbing these sombre religious doctrines, he acquired a mastery of Greek and a close familiarity with Euripides, whose influence is readily apparent in several of his plays. To the disappointment of his family, Racine declined to take holy orders and eventually determined upon a career as a dramatist in Paris.

Racine's early attempts in the theatre were not successful, and for a time he withdrew from Paris. But returning in 1663, he managed to win the support of the court and nobility and to establish himself as a successful playwright. In 1667 he began a series of plays which placed him, with Corneille and Molière, among the chief dramatists of his age, and, as it has turned out, of succeeding ages. Beginning with *Andromaque* (1677), the series included: *Britannicus* (1669), *Bérénice* (1670), *Bajazet* (1672), *Mithridate* (1673), *Iphigénie in Aulide* (1674), and *Phèdre* (1677). In 1677 Racine was appointed official historian to the court of Louis XIV, a considerable social elevation for someone of his middle-class background. It was perhaps this appointment, along with unhappy experiences connected with the opening of *Phaedra* and a renewed interest in the Jansenists, which led him to withdraw from the theatre in 1677. Whatever the reasons, he returned to Port-Royal, married, raised a large family, and lived quietly for the remaining years of his life. At the request of Mme. de Maintenon, he returned briefly to playwriting with two distinguished dramas on biblical subjects, *Esther* (1689) and *Athalie* (1691), written for performance at her school for girls at Saint-Cyr.

*Phèdre et Hippolyte*, as the original title read, was first performed on January 1, 1677, at the Hotel de Bourgogne, reputed to be the best theatre in Paris for tragedy. Unlike the other theatres, in which a play was often lost in the over-elaborate scenic effects, the Hotel de Bourgogne was noted for a simplicity of stage design which permitted the full poetic and histrionic realization of the dramatic text. The leading role was played by Racine's mistress, Mlle. de Champmesle, whom he himself coached in the part. But the early performances were marred by the spite Racine had somehow aroused in certain Parisians. A wealthy lady of the nobility, learning of the impending production of *Phaedra*, encouraged an inferior writer, Nicolas Pradon, to write a play on the same subject. She then had it performed at the same time as Racine's work, bought up the seats for both theatres, and arranged that the audience for Racine's play be composed of an unruly, hissing claque. It was shortly after this experience that Racine retired from the theatre and returned to Port-Royal, but not before seeing the play through these difficulties to a more successful reception. *Phaedra* has since come to be regarded by many as the greatest tragedy in French.

A useful biography of Racine is A. F. B. Clark, *Racine* (1939). Background material as well as perceptive comment on Racine's plays can be found in Martin Turnell, *The Classical Moment* (1963). Recent studies of the plays are V. Orgel, *A New View of the Plays of Racine* (1948); Eugène Vinaver, *Racine and Poetic Tragedy*, tr. P. Mansell Jones (1955); and Bernard Weinberg, *The Art of Jean Racine* (1963). R. C. Knight edited *Phaedra* in 1943, and Kenneth Muir has recently translated five of Racine's plays (*Andromache, Brittanicus, Berenice, Phaedra,* and *Athaliah*) into English verse in *Jean Racine* (1960).

◇ ◇ ◇

## Racine's Preface to *Phaedra*[1]

Here is another tragedy the subject of which is taken from Euripides. Although I have followed a route slightly different from that author's in the conduct of the action, I have allowed myself to enrich my play with everything which appeared to me most striking in his. While I owe him only the single idea of the character of Phaedra, I could say that I owe him what I could most reasonably place on the stage. I am not at all surprised that this character was so successful in Euripides' time, and that it has also been so well received in our own century, since it has all the qualities which Aristotle demanded in the heroes of a tragedy and which are proper to arouse pity and terror. Indeed, Phaedra is neither completely guilty nor completely innocent. She is involved, by her destiny and by the wrath of the gods, in an illicit passion of which she is the first to be horrified. She makes every effort to overcome it. She prefers to let herself die rather than to declare it to anyone. And when she is forced to discover it, she speaks of it with a confusion which makes it clear that her crime is more a punishment of the gods than an act of her will.

I have even taken pains to render her a little less odious than in the tragedies of the ancients, where she resolves all by herself to accuse Hippolytus. I felt that this calumny was too low and too foul to put into the mouth of a princess who otherwise has such noble and such virtuous sentiments. This baseness seemed to me more suitable to a nurse who would have more servile inclinations but who nevertheless undertakes this false accusation only in order to save the life and the honor of her mistress. Phaedra gives her consent to it only because she is in such an agitated state that she is beside herself, and a moment later in the action she defends innocence and declares the truth.

Hippolytus is accused in Euripides and Seneca of having actually violated his stepmother: *vim corpus tulit.* But here he is accused only of having had the intention. I wished to spare Theseus a confusion which would have made him less sympathetic to the audience.

As for the character of Hippolytus, I have noticed among the ancients that Euripides is reproached for having presented him as a philosopher free from any imperfection. As a result the death of the

[1] This preface was published with the first edition of the play in 1677. Translation by the editors.

young prince caused more indignation than pity. I felt that I should give him some flaw which would make him somewhat guilty towards his father, without diminishing however the greatness of soul with which he spares Phaedra's honor and allows himself to be oppressed without accusing her. I regard as a "flaw" the passion which he feels, despite himself, for Aricia, who is the daughter and the sister of his father's mortal enemies.

This Aricia is not just a character of my own invention. Virgil says that Hippolytus married her and had a son by her after Aesculapius had brought him back to life. And I have also read in some authors that Hippolytus had married and brought to Italy a young Athenian of high birth who was called Aricia and who had given her name to a small town in Italy.

I cite these authorities because I have been very scrupulously devoted to following the fable. I have even followed the story of Theseus as it is presented in Plutarch.

It is in this historian that I found that what gave occasion for the belief that Theseus descended into the underworld to bring back Proserpine was a journey which the prince had made in Epirus to the source of the Acheron, at the home of a king whose wife Pirithöus wished to carry off and who kept Theseus a prisoner after having killed Pirithöus. So I have tried to preserve the credibility of the story, without losing anything of the ornaments of the fable, which provides in abundance for poetry. And the rumor of Theseus' death, based on this fabled journey, gives Phaedra the opportunity to make a declaration of love, which becomes one of the principal causes of her disaster, and which she would never have dared to make so long as she believed that her husband was alive.

For the rest, I dare not yet assert that this play is indeed the best of my tragedies. I leave it to readers and to time to decide its true worth. What I can assert is that I have not created a play in which virtue is put in a more positive light than in this one. The least faults are severely punished. The mere thought of crime is regarded with as much horror as the crime itself. The weaknesses of love are shown as real weaknesses. The passions are exhibited only in order to show all the disorder of which they are the cause, and vice is painted everywhere in colors which make its hideousness recognized and hated. That is the proper end which everyone who works for the public should bear in mind. And that is what the first tragic poets kept in sight above all else. Their theatre was a school where virtue was taught no less well than in the schools of the philosophers. So Aristotle was willing to give rules for drama; and Socrates, the wisest of philosophers, did not disdain to put his hand to the tragedies of Euripides. It would be very desirable if our works were as solid and as full of useful instruction as those of these poets. That might perhaps be a way of reconciling tragedy with a great number of people, famous for their piety and their doctrine, who have recently condemned it; and who would judge it, without a doubt, more favorably if the authors worried as much about instructing their audiences as about entertaining them, and if they thereby followed the true purpose of tragedy.

# Phaedra

*English Version by Robert Lowell*

❖ ❖ ❖

## CHARACTERS

THESEUS, *son of Aegeus and King of Athens*
PHAEDRA, *wife of Theseus and daughter of Minos and Pasiphaë*
HIPPOLYTUS, *son of Theseus and Antiope, Queen of the Amazons*
ARICIA, *princess of the royal blood of Athens*
OENONE, *nurse of Phaedra*
THERAMENES, *tutor of Hippolytus*
ISMENE, *friend of Aricia*
PANOPE, *waiting-woman of Phaedra*
GUARDS

*The scene is laid in Troezen, a city about forty miles from Athens, on the opposite side of the Gulf of Aegina.*

The story of Racine's *Phaedra* is a Greek myth. Phaedra, the wife of Theseus, the hero and king of Athens, is the daughter of Minos and Pasiphaë, the rulers of Crete. Pasiphaë coupled with a bull, and bore the Minotaur, half bull and half man, who was slain by Theseus in the maze at Crete. Phaedra falls madly in love with her stepson, Hippolytus. She is rejected by him, and falsely accuses him of trying to assault her. Theseus prays to Poseidon, the sea-god, to destroy Hippolytus; Hippolytus is destroyed. Phaedra confesses and kills herself. *Phaedra* is in some ways a miraculous translation and adaptation of Euripides' *Hippolytus*. Racine quite alters and to my mind even surpasses his wonderful original.

---

# ACT I

## Scene 1

HIPPOLYTUS, THERAMENES

HIPPOLYTUS. No no, my friend, we're off! Six months have passed
since Father heard the ocean howl and cast
his galley on the Aegean's skull-white froth.
Listen! The blank sea calls us — off, off, off!
I'll follow Father to the fountainhead                              5
and marsh of hell. We're off. Alive or dead,
I'll find him.
THERAMENES.    Where, my lord? I've sent a host
of veteran seamen up and down the coast;
each village, creek and cove from here to Crete
has been ransacked and questioned by my fleet;                     10
my flagship skirted Hades' rapids, furled
sail there a day, and scoured the underworld.
Have you fresh news? New hopes? One even doubts
if noble Theseus wants his whereabouts
discovered. Does he need his helpers to share                      15
the plunder of his latest love affair;
a shipload of spectators and his son
to watch him ruin his last Amazon —
some creature, taller than a man, whose tanned
and single bosom slithers from his hand,                           20
when he leaps to crush her like a waterfall
of honeysuckle?
HIPPOLYTUS.        You are cynical,
my friend. Your insinuations wrong a king,
sick as myself of his philandering.
His heart is Phaedra's and no rivals dare                          25
to challenge Phaedra's sole possession there.
I sail to find my father. The command
of duty calls me from this stifling land.
THERAMENES. This stifling land? Is that how you deride
this gentle province where you used to ride                        30
the bridle-paths, pursuing happiness?
You cured your orphaned childhood's loneliness
and found a peace here you preferred to all
the blaze of Athens' brawling protocol.

A rage for exploits blinds you. Your disease                          35
is boredom.
HIPPOLYTUS.  Friend, this kingdom lost its peace,
when Father left my mother, for defiled
bull-serviced Pasiphaë's child. The child
of homicidal Minos is our queen!
THERAMENES.  Yes, Phaedra reigns and rules here. I have seen          40
you crouch before her outbursts like a cur.
When she first met you, she refused to stir
until your father drove you out of court.
The news is better now; our friends report
the queen is dying. Will you cross the seas,                          45
desert your party and abandon Greece?
Why flee from Phaedra? Phaedra fears the night
less than she fears the day that strives to light
the universal ennui of her eyes —
this dying woman, who desires to die!                                 50
HIPPOLYTUS.  No, I despise her Cretan vanity,
hysteria and idle cruelty.
I fear Aricia; she alone survives
the blood-feud that destroyed her brothers' lives.
THERAMENES.  Prince, Prince, forgive my laughter. Must you fly       55
beyond the limits of the world and die,
floating in flotsam, friendless, far from help,
and clubbed to death by Tartars in the kelp?
Why arm the shrinking violet with a knife?
Do you hate Aricia, and fear for your life,                           60
Prince?
HIPPOLYTUS.  If I hated her, I'd trust myself
and stay.
THERAMENES.  Shall I explain you to yourself?
Prince, you have ceased to be that hard-mouthed, proud
and pure Hippolytus, who scorned the crowd
of common lovers once and rose above                                 65
your wayward father by despising love.
Now you justify your father, and you feel
love's poison running through you, now you kneel
and breathe the heavy incense, and a god
possesses you and revels in your blood!                              70
Are you in love?
HIPPOLYTUS.          Theramenes, when I call
and cry for help, you push me to the wall.
Why do you plague me, and try to make me fear

the qualities you taught me to revere?
I sucked in prudence with my mother's milk.                    75
Antiope, no harlot draped in silk,
first hardened me. I was my mother's son
and not my father's. When the Amazon,
my mother, was dethroned, my mind approved
her lessons more than ever. I still loved               80
her bristling chastity. Later, you told
stories about my father's deeds that made me hold
back judgment — how he stood for Hercules,
a second Hercules who cleared the Cretan seas
of pirates, throttled Scirron, Cercyon,                 85
Procrustes, Sinnis, and the giant man
of Epidaurus writhing in his gore.
He pierced the maze and killed the Minotaur.
Other things turned my stomach: that long list
of women, all refusing to resist.                       90
Helen, caught up with all her honeyed flesh
from Sparta; Periboea, young and fresh,
already tired of Salinis. A hundred more,
their names forgotten by my father — whore
and virgin, child and mother, all deceived,             95
if their protestations can be believed!
Ariadne declaiming to the rocks,
her sister, Phaedra, kidnapped. Phaedra locks
the gate at last! You know how often I
would weary, fall to nodding and deny                   100
the possibility of hearing the whole
ignoble, dull, insipid boast unroll.
And now I too must fall. The gods have made me creep.
How can I be in love? I have no specious heap
of honors, friend. No mastered monsters drape          105
my shoulders — Theseus' excuse to rape
at will. Suppose I chose a woman. Why
choose an orphan? Aricia is eternally
cut off from marriage, lest she breed
successors to her fierce brothers, and seed            110
the land with treason. Father only grants
her life on one condition. This — he wants
no bridal torch to burn for her. Unwooed
and childless, she must answer for the blood
her brothers shed. How can I marry her,                115
gaily subvert our kingdom's character,

and sail on the high seas of love?

THERAMENES.                   You'll prove
nothing by reason, for you are in love.
Theseus' injustice to Aricia throws
her in the light; your eyes he wished to close     **120**
are open. She dazzles you. Her pitiful
seclusion makes her doubly terrible.
Does this innocent passion freeze your blood?
There's sweetness in it. Is your only good
the dismal famine of your chastity?     **125**
You shun your father's path? Where would you be,
Prince, if Antiope had never burned
chastely for Theseus? Love, my lord, has turned
the head of Hercules, and thousands — fired
the forge of Vulcan! All your uninspired, cold     **130**
moralizing is nothing, Prince. You have changed!
Now no one sees you riding, half-deranged
along the sand-bars, where you drove your horse
and foaming chariot with all your force,
tilting and staggering upright through the surf —     **135**
far from their usual course across the turf.
The woods are quiet. . . . How your eyes hang down!
You often murmur and forget to frown.
All's out, Prince. You're in love, you burn. Flames, flames,
Prince! A dissimulated sickness maims     **140**
the youthful quickness of your daring. Does
lovely Aricia haunt you?

HIPPOLYTUS.              Friend, spare us.
I sail to find my father.

THERAMENES.           Will you see
Phaedra before you go?

HIPPOLYTUS.          I mean to be
here when she comes. Go, tell her. I will do     **145**
my duty. Wait, I see her nurse. What new
troubles torment her?

## Scene 2

HIPPOLYTUS, THERAMENES, OENONE

OENONE. Who has griefs like mine,
my lord? I cannot help the queen in her decline.
Although I sit beside her day and night,

she shuts her eyes and withers in my sight.
An eternal tumult roisters through her head,                    5
panics her sleep, and drags her from her bed.
Just now she fled me at the prime
of day to see the sun for the last time.
She's coming.
HIPPOLYTUS.        So! I'll steal away. My flight
removes a hateful object from her sight.                        10


## Scene 3

### PHAEDRA, OENONE

PHAEDRA. Dearest, we'll go no further. I must rest.
I'll sit here. My emotions shake my breast,
the sunlight throws black bars across my eyes.
My knees give. If I fall, why should I rise,
Nurse? (*She sits down.*)
OENONE.                    Heaven help us! Let me comfort you.     5
PHAEDRA. Tear off these gross, official rings, undo
these royal veils. They drag me to the ground.
Why have you frilled me, laced me, crowned me, and wound
my hair in turrets? All your skill torments
and chokes me. I am crushed by ornaments.                       10
Everything hurts me, and drags me to my knees!
OENONE. Now this, now that, Madam. You never cease
commanding us, then cancelling your commands.
You feel your strength return, summon all hands
to dress you like a bride, then say you choke!                  15
We open all the windows, fetch a cloak,
rush you outdoors. It's no use, you decide
that sunlight kills you, and only want to hide.
PHAEDRA. I feel the heaven's royal radiance cool
and fail, as if it feared my terrible                           20
shame has destroyed its right to shine on men.
I'll never look upon the sun again.
OENONE. Renunciation on renunciation!
Now you slander the source of your creation.
Why do you run to death and tear your hair?                     25
PHAEDRA. Oh God, take me to some sunless forest lair . . .
There hoof-beats raise a dust-cloud, and my eye
follows a horseman outlined on the sky!
OENONE. What's this, my lady?

PHAEDRA.                    I have lost my mind.
Where am I?  O forget my words!  I find                    30
I've lost the habit now of talking sense.
My face is red and guilty — evidence
of treason!  I've betrayed my darkest fears,
Nurse, and my eyes, despite me, fill with tears.
OENONE.  Lady, if you must weep, weep for your silence    35
that filled your days and mine with violence.
Ah deaf to argument and numb to care,
you have no mercy on us.  Spare me, spare
yourself.  Your blood is like polluted water,
fouling a mind desiring its own slaughter.              40
The sun has died and shadows filled the skies
thrice now, since you have closed your eyes;
the day has broken through the night's content
thrice now, since you have tasted nourishment.
Is your salvation from your terrified                    45
conscience this passive, servile suicide?
Lady, your madness harms the gods who gave
you life, betrays your husband.  Who will save
your children?  Your downfall will orphan them,
deprive them of their kingdom, and condemn             50
their lives and future to the discipline
of one who abhors you and all your kin,
a tyrant suckled by an Amazon,
Hippolytus . . .
PHAEDRA.                Oh God!
OENONE.                    You still hate someone;
thank heaven for that, Madam!                          
PHAEDRA.                        You spoke his name!     55
OENONE.  Hippolytus, Hippolytus!  There's hope
in hatred, Lady.  Give your anger rope.
I love your anger.  If the winds of love
and fury stir you, you will live.  Above
your children towers this foreigner, this child        60
of Scythian cannibals, now wild
to ruin the kingdom, master Greece, and choke
the children of the gods beneath his yoke.
Why dawdle?  Why deliberate at length?
Oh, gather up your dissipated strength.                 65
PHAEDRA.  I've lived too long.
OENONE.                    Always, always agonized!
Is your conscience still stunned and paralyzed?

Do you think you have washed your hands in blood?
PHAEDRA. Thank God, my hands are clean still. Would to God
my heart were innocent!
OENONE.        Your heart, your heart!      70
What have you done that tears your soul apart?
PHAEDRA. I've said too much. Oenone, let me die;
by dying I shall escape blasphemy.
OENONE. Search for another hand to close your eyes.
Oh cruel Queen, I see that you despise      75
my sorrow and devotion. I'll die first,
and end the anguish of this service cursed
by your perversity. A thousand roads
always lie open to the killing gods.
I'll choose the nearest. Lady, tell me how      80
Oenone's love has failed you. Will you allow
your nurse to die, your nurse, who gave up all —
nation, parents, children, to serve in thrall?
I saved you from your mother, King Minos' wife!
Will your death pay me for giving up my life?      85
PHAEDRA. What I could tell you, I have told you. Nurse,
only my silence saves me from the curse
of heaven.
OENONE.        How could you tell me anything
worse than watching you dying?
PHAEDRA.            I would bring
my life and rank dishonor. What can I say      90
to save myself, or put off death a day?
OENONE. Ah Lady, I implore you by my tears,
and by your suffering body. Heaven hears,
and knows the truth already. Let me see.
PHAEDRA. Stand up.
OENONE.        Your hesitation's killing me!      95
PHAEDRA. What can I tell you? How the gods reprove me!
OENONE. Speak!
PHAEDRA.        Oh Venus, murdering Venus! love
gored Pasiphaë with the bull.
OENONE.            Forget
your mother! When she died she paid her debt.
PHAEDRA. Oh Ariadne, oh my Sister, lost      100
for love of Theseus on that rocky coast.
OENONE. Lady, what nervous languor makes you rave
against your family; they are in the grave.
PHAEDRA. Remorseless Aphrodite drives me. I,

my race's last and worst love-victim, die.                    105
OENONE. Are you in love?
PHAEDRA.                    I am with love!
OENONE.                              Who
  is he?
PHAEDRA. I'll tell you. Nothing love can do
  could equal . . . Nurse, I am in love. The shame
  kills me. I love the . . . . Do not ask his name.
OENONE. Who?
PHAEDRA.        Nurse, you know my old loathing for the son   110
  of Theseus and the barbarous Amazon?
OENONE. Hippolytus! My God, oh my God!
PHAEDRA.                              You,
  not I, have named him.
OENONE.                    What can you do,
  but die? Your words have turned my blood to ice.
  Oh righteous heavens, must the blasphemies                  115
  of Pasiphaë fall upon her daughter?
  Her Furies strike us down across the water.
  Why did we come here?
PHAEDRA. My evil comes from farther off. In May,
  in brilliant Athens, on my marriage day,                    120
  I turned aside for shelter from the smile
  of Theseus. Death was frowning in an aisle —
  Hippolytus! I saw his face, turned white!
  My lost and dazzled eyes saw only night,
  capricious burnings flickered through my bleak              125
  abandoned flesh. I could not breathe or speak.
  I faced my flaming executioner,
  Aphrodite, my mother's murderer!
  I tried to calm her wrath by flowers and praise,
  I built her a temple, fretted months and days               130
  on decoration. I even hoped to find
  symbols and stays for my distracted mind,
  searching the guts of sacrificial steers.
  Yet when my erring passions, mutineers
  to virtue, offered incense at the shrine                    135
  of love, I failed to silence the malign
  Goddess. Alas, my hungry open mouth,
  thirsting with adoration, tasted drouth —
  Venus resigned her altar to my new lord —
  and even while I was praying, I adored                       140
  Hippolytus above the sacred flame,

now offered to his name I could not name.
I fled him, yet he stormed me in disguise,
and seemed to watch me with his father's eyes.
I even turned against myself, screwed up                    145
my slack courage to fury, and would not stop
shrieking and raging, till half-dead with love
and the hatred of a stepmother, I drove
Hippolytus in exile from the rest
and strenuous wardship of his father's breast.              150
Then I could breathe, Oenone; he was gone;
my lazy, nerveless days meandered on
through dreams and daydreams, like a stately carriage
touring the level landscape of my marriage.
Yet nothing worked. My husband sent me here                 155
to Troezen, far from Athens; once again the dear
face shattered me; I saw Hippolytus
each day, and felt my ancient, venomous
passion tear my body limb from limb;
naked, Venus was clawing down her victim.                   160
What could I do? Each moment, terrified
by loose diseased emotions, now I cried
for death to save my glory and expel
my gloomy frenzy from this world, my hell.
And yet your tears and words bewildered me,                 165
and so endangered my tranquillity,
at last I spoke. Nurse, I shall not repent,
if you will leave me the passive content
of dry silence and solitude.

## Scene 4

PHAEDRA, OENONE, PANOPE

PANOPE. My heart breaks. Would to God, I could refuse
to tell your majesty my evil news.
The King is dead! Listen, the heavens ring
with shouts and lamentations for the King.
PHAEDRA. The King is dead? What's this?
PANOPE.                                        In vain
you beg the gods to send him back again.
Hippolytus has heard the true report,
he is already heading for the port.
PHAEDRA. Oh God!

PANOPE.                    They've heard in Athens.  Everyone          10
   is joining factions — some salute your son,
   others are calling for Hippolytus;
   they want him to reform and harden us —
   even Aricia claims the loyalty
   of a fanatical minority.
   The Prince's captains have recalled their men.          15
   His flag is up, and now he sails again
   for Athens.  Queen, if he appear there now,
   he'll drag the people with him!
OENONE.                         Stop, allow
   the Queen a little respite for her grief.
   She hears you, and will act for our relief.          20


## Scene 5

### PHAEDRA, OENONE

OENONE.  I'd given up persuading you to live;
   death was your refuge, only death could give
   you peace and save your troubled glory.  I
   myself desired to follow you, and die.
   But this catastrophe prescribes new laws:          5
   the king is dead, and for the king who was,
   fate offers you his kingdom.  You have a son;
   he should be king!  If you abandon
   him, he'll be a slave.  The gods, his ancestors,
   will curse and drive you on your fatal course.          10
   Live!  Who'll condemn you if you love and woo
   the Prince?  Your stepson is no kin to you,
   now that your royal husband's death has cut
   and freed you from the throttling marriage-knot.
   Do not torment the Prince with persecution,          15
   and give a leader to the revolution;
   no, win his friendship, bind him to your side.
   Give him this city and its countryside.
   He will renounce the walls of Athens, piled
   stone on stone by Minerva for your child.          20
   Stand with Hippolytus, annihilate
   Aricia's faction, and possess the state!
PHAEDRA.  So be it!  Your superior force has won.

I will live if compassion for my son,
devotion to the Prince, and love of power     25
can give me courage in this fearful hour.

## ACT II

### Scene 1

ARICIA, ISMENE

ARICIA. What's this? The Prince has sent a messenger?
The Prince begs me to wait and meet him here?
The Prince begs! Goose, you've lost your feeble wits!
ISMENE. Lady, be calm. These are the benefits
of Theseus' death: first Prince Hippolytus     5
comes courting favors; soon the populous
cities of Greece will follow — they will eat
out of your hand, Princess, and kiss your feet.
ARICIA. This felon's hand, this slave's! My dear, your news
is only frivolous gossip, I refuse     10
to hope.
ISMENE. Ah Princess, the just powers of hell
have struck. Theseus has joined your brothers!
ARICIA.                                                        Tell
me how he died.
ISMENE.                    Princess, fearful tales
are circulating. Sailors saw his sails,
his infamous black sails, spin round and round     15
in Charybdis' whirlpool; all hands were drowned.
Yet others say on better evidence
that Theseus and Pirithoüs passed the dense
darkness of hell to rape Persephone.
Pirithoüs was murdered by the hound;     20
Theseus, still living, was buried in the ground.
ARICIA. This is an old wives' tale. Only the dead
enter the underworld, and see the bed
of Queen Persephone. What brought him there?
ISMENE. Princess, the King is dead — dead! Everywhere     25
men know and mourn. Already our worshipping
townsmen acclaim Hippolytus for their king;
in her great palace, Phaedra, the self-styled
regent, rages and trembles for her child.

ARICIA. What makes you think the puritanical          30
son of Theseus is human? Will he recall
my sentence and relent?
ISMENE.                         I know he will.
ARICIA. You know nothing about him. He would kill
a woman, rather than be kind to one.
That wolf-cub of a fighting Amazon                    35
hates me above all women. He would walk
from here to hell, rather than hear me talk.
ISMENE. Do you know Hippolytus? Listen to me.
His famous, blasphemous frigidity,
what is it, when you've seen him close at hand?       40
I've watched him like a hawk, and seen him stand
shaking beside you — all his reputation
for hating womenkind bears no relation
to what I saw. He couldn't take his eyes
off you! His eyes speak what his tongue denies.       45
ARICIA. I can't believe you. Your story's absurd!
How greedily I listen to each word!
Ismene, you know me, you know how my heart
was reared on death and always set apart
from what it cherished — can this plaything of        50
the gods and furies feel the peace of love?
What sights I've seen, Ismene! "Heads will roll,"
my brothers told me, "we will rule." I, the sole
survivor of those fabulous kings, who tilled
the soil of Greece, have seen my brothers killed,     55
six brothers murdered! In a single hour,
the tyrant, Theseus, lopped them in their flower.
The monster spared my life, and yet decreed
the torments of this childless life I lead
in exile, where no Greek can look on me;              60
my forced, perpetual virginity
preserves his crown; no son shall bear my name
or blow my brothers' ashes into flame.
Ismene, you know how well his tyranny
favors my temperament and strengthens me              65
to guard the honor of my reputation;
his rigor fortified my inclination.
How could I test his son's civilities?
I'd never even seen him with my eyes!
I'd never seen him. I'd restrained my eye,            70
that giddy nerve, from dwelling thoughtlessly

upon his outward grace and beauty — on mere
embellishments of nature, a veneer
the Prince himself despises and ignores.
My heart loves nobler virtues, and adores 75
in him his father's hard intelligence.
He has his father's daring and a sense
of honor his father lacks. Let me confess,
I love him for his lofty haughtiness
never submitted to a woman's yoke. 80
How could Phaedra's splendid marriage provoke
my jealousy? Have I so little pride,
I'd snatch at a rake's heart, a heart denied
to none — all riddled, opened up to let
thousands pass in like water through a net? 85
To carry sorrows to a heart, alone
untouched by passion, inflexible as stone,
to fasten my dominion on a force
as nervous as a never-harnessed horse —
this stirs me, this enflames me. Devilish Zeus 90
is easier mastered than Hippolytus;
heaven's love-infatuated emperor
confers less glory on his conqueror!
Ismene, I'm afraid. Why should I boast?
His very virtues I admire the most 95
threaten to rise and throw me from the brink
of hope. What girlish folly made me think
Hippolytus could love Aricia?
ISMENE.                              Here
he is. He loves you, Princess. Have no fear.

## Scene 2

### ARICIA, ISMENE, HIPPOLYTUS

HIPPOLYTUS.                    Princess, before
I leave here, I must tell you what's in store
for you in Greece. Alas, my father's dead.
The fierce forebodings that disquieted
my peace are true. Death, only death, could hide 5
his valor from this world he pacified.
The homicidal Fates will not release
the comrade, friend and peer of Hercules.
Princess, I trust your hate will not resent

honors whose justice is self-evident.                          10
A single hope alleviates my grief,
Princess, I hope to offer you relief.
I now revoke a law whose cruelty
has pained my conscience. Princess, you are free
to marry. Oh enjoy this province, whose               15
honest, unhesitating subjects choose
Hippolytus for king. Live free as air,
here, free as I am, much more free!
ARICIA.                                    I dare
not hope. You are too gracious. Can you free
Aricia from your father's stern decree?               20
HIPPOLYTUS. Princess, the Athenian people, torn in two
between myself and Phaedra's son, want you.
ARICIA. Want me, my lord!
HIPPOLYTUS.                        I've no illusions. Lame
Athenian precedents condemn my claim,
because my mother was a foreigner.                    25
But what is that? If my only rival were
my younger brother, his minority
would clear my legal disability.
However, a better claim than his or mine
now favors you, ennobled by the line             30
of great Erectheus. Your direct descent
sets you before my father; he was only lent
this kingdom by adoption. Once the common
Athenian, dazed by Theseus' superhuman
energies, had no longing to exhume               35
the rights that rushed your brothers to their doom.
Now Athens calls you home; the ancient feud
too long has stained the sacred olive wood;
blood festers in the furrows of our soil
to blight its fruits and scorch the farmer's toil.    40
This province suits me, let the vines of Crete
offer my brother a secure retreat.
The rest is yours. All Attica is yours;
I go to win you what your right assures.
ARICIA. Am I awake, my lord? Your sayings seem        45
like weird phantasmagoria in a dream.
How can your sparkling promises be true?
Some god, my lord, some god, has entered you!
How justly you are worshipped in this town;
oh how the truth surpasses your renown!               50

You wish to endow me with your heritage!
I only hoped you would not hate me. This rage
your father felt, how can you put it by
and treat me kindly?
HIPPOLYTUS.                  Princess, is my eye
blind to beauty? Am I a bear, a bull, a boar,                    55
some abortion fathered by the Minotaur?
Some one-eyed Cyclops, able to resist
Aricia's loveliness and still exist?
How can a man stand up against your grace?
ARICIA. My lord, my lord!
HIPPOLYTUS.                  I cannot hide my face,           60
Princess! I'm driven. Why does my violence
so silence reason and intelligence?
Must I be still, and let my adoration
simmer away in silent resignation?
Princess, I've lost all power to restrain                       65
myself. You see a madman, whose insane
pride hated love, and hoped to sit ashore,
watching the galleys founder in the war;
I was Diana's liegeman, dressed in steel.
I hoped to trample love beneath my heel—                     70
alas, the flaming Venus burns me down,
I am the last dependent on her crown.
What left me charred and writhing in her clutch?
A single moment and a single touch.
Six months now, bounding like a wounded stag,                75
I've tried to shake this poisoned dart, and drag
myself to safety from your eyes that blind
when present, and when absent leave behind
volleys of burning arrows in my mind.
Ah Princess, shall I dive into the sea,                        80
or steal the wings of Icarus to flee
love's Midas' touch that turns my world to gold?
Your image drives me stumbling through the cold,
floods my deserted forest caves with light,
darkens the day and dazzles through my night.                 85
I'm grafted to your side by all I see;
all things unite us and imprison me.
I have no courage for the Spartan exercise
that trained my hand and steeled my energies.
Where are my horses? I forget their names.                    90
My triumphs with my chariot at the games

no longer give me strength to mount a horse.
The ocean drives me shuddering from its shores.
Does such a savage conquest make you blush?
My boorish gestures, headlong cries that rush                    95
at you like formless monsters from the sea?
Ah, Princess, hear me! Your serenity
must pardon the distortions of a weak
and new-born lover, forced by you to speak
love's foreign language, words that snarl and yelp . . .         100
I never could have spoken without your help.


## Scene 3

### ARICIA, ISMENE, HIPPOLYTUS, THERAMENES

THERAMENES. I announce the Queen. She comes hurriedly,
    looking for you.
HIPPOLYTUS.            For me!
THERAMENES.                       Don't ask me why;
    she insisted. I promised I'd prevail
    on you to speak with her before you sail.
HIPPOLYTUS. What can she want to hear? What can I say?            5
ARICIA. Wait for her, here! You cannot turn away.
    Forget her malice. Hating her will serve
    no purpose. Wait for her! Her tears deserve
    your pity.
HIPPOLYTUS. You're going, Princess? And I must go
    to Athens, far from you. How shall I know                     10
    if you accept my love?
ARICIA.                    My Lord, pursue
    your gracious promise. Do what you must do,
    make Athens tributary to my rule.
    Nothing you offer is unacceptable,
    yet this empire, so great, so glorious,                       15
    is the least precious of your gifts to us.


## Scene 4

### HIPPOLYTUS, THERAMENES

HIPPOLYTUS. We're ready. Wait, the Queen's here. I need you.
    You must interrupt this tedious interview.
    Hurry down to the ship, then rush back, pale
    and breathless. Say the wind's up and we must sail.

## Scene 5

HIPPOLYTUS, OENONE, PHAEDRA

PHAEDRA (*to* OENONE). He's here! Why does he scowl and look
away from me? What shall I do? What shall I say?
OENONE. Speak for your son, he has no other patron.
PHAEDRA. Why are you so impatient to be gone
from us, my lord? Stay! we will weep together.          5
Pity my son; he too has lost his father.
My own death's near. Rebellion, sick with wrongs,
now like a sea-beast, lifts its slimey prongs,
its muck, its jelly. You alone now stand
to save the state. Who else can understand          10
a mother? I forget. You will not hear
me! An enemy deserves no pity. I fear
your anger. Must my son, your brother, Prince,
be punished for his cruel mother's sins?
HIPPOLYTUS. I've no such thoughts.
PHAEDRA.                           I persecuted you          15
blindly, and now you have good reason to
return my impudence. How could you find
the motivation of this heart and mind
that scourged and tortured you, till you began
to lose the calm composure of a man,          20
and dwindle to a harsh and sullen boy,
a thing of ice, unable to enjoy
the charms of any civilized resource
except the heavy friendship of your horse,
that whirled you far from women, court and throne,          25
to course the savage woods for wolves alone?
You have good reason, yet if pain's a measure,
no one has less deserved your stern displeasure.
My lord, no one has more deserved compassion.
HIPPOLYTUS. Lady, I understand a mother's passion,          30
a mother jealous for her children's rights.
How can she spare a first wife's son? Long nights
of plotting, devious days of quarrelling —
a madhouse! What else can remarriage bring?
Another would have shown equal hostility,          35
pushed her advantage more outrageously.
PHAEDRA. My lord, if you had known how far my love

and yearning have exalted me above
this usual weakness . . . Our afflicting kinship
is ending . . .
HIPPOLYTUS. Madam, the precious minutes slip                    40
by, I fatigue you. Fight against your fears.
Perhaps Poseidon has listened to our tears,
perhaps your husband's still alive. He hears
us, he is surging home — only a short
day's cruise conceals him, as he scuds for port.          45
PHAEDRA. That's folly, my lord. Who has twice visited
black Hades and the river of the dead
and returned? No, the poisonous Acheron
never lets go. Theseus drifts on and on,
a gutted galley on that clotted waste —                        50
he woos, he wins Persephone, the chaste . . .
What am I saying? Theseus is not dead.
He lives in you. He speaks, he's taller by a head.
I see him, touch him, and my heart — a reef . . .
Ah Prince, I wander. Love betrays my grief . . .          55
HIPPOLYTUS. No, no, my father lives. Lady, the blind
furies release him; in your loyal mind,
love's fullness holds him, and he cannot die.
PHAEDRA. I hunger for Theseus. Always in my eye
he wanders, not as he appeared in hell,                        60
lascivious eulogist of any belle
he found there, from the lowest to the Queen;
no, faithful, airy, just a little mean
through virtue, charming all, yet young and new,
as we would paint a god — as I now see you!               65
Your valiant shyness would have graced his speech,
he would have had your stature, eyes, and reach,
Prince, when he flashed across our Cretan waters,
the loved enslaver of King Minos' daughters.
Where were you? How could he conscript the flower         70
of Athens' youth against my father's power,
and ignore you? You were too young, they say;
you should have voyaged as a stowaway.
No dawdling bypath would have saved our bull,
when your just vengeance thundered through its skull.     75
There, light of foot, and certain of your goal,
you would have struck my brother's monstrous soul,
and pierced our maze's slow meanders, led
by Ariadne and her subtle thread.

By Ariadne? Prince, *I* would have fought                              80
for precedence; my every flaming thought,
love-quickened, would have shot you through the dark,
straight as an arrow to your quaking mark.
Could I have waited, panting, perishing,
entrusting your survival to a string,                                 85
like Ariadne, when she skulked behind,
there at the portal, to bemuse her mind
among the solemn cloisters of the porch?
No, Phaedra would have snatched your burning torch,
and lunged before you, reeling like a priest                          90
of Dionysus to distract the beast.
I would have reached the final corridor
a lap before you, and killed the Minotaur!
Lost in the labyrinth, and at your side,
would it have mattered, if I lived or died?                           95
HIPPOLYTUS. What are you saying, Madam? You forget
my father is your husband!
PHAEDRA.                            I have let
you see my grief for Theseus! How could I
forget my honor and my majesty,
Prince?
HIPPOLYTUS. Madam, forgive me! My foolish youth             100
conjectured hideous untruths from your truth.
I cannot face my insolence. Farewell . . .
PHAEDRA. You monster! You understood me too well!
Why do you hang there, speechless, petrified,
polite! My mind whirls. What have I to hide?                 105
Phaedra in all her madness stands before you.
I love you! Fool, I love you, I adore you!
Do not imagine that my mind approved
my first defection, Prince, or that I loved
your youth light-heartedly, and fed my treason              110
with cowardly compliance, till I lost my reason.
I wished to hate you, but the gods corrupt
us; though I never suffered their abrupt
seductions, shattering advances, I
too bear their sensual lightnings in my thigh.              115
I too am dying. I have felt the heat
that drove my mother through the fields of Crete,
the bride of Minos, dying for the full
magnetic April thunders of the bull.
I struggled with my sickness, but I found                   120

no grace or magic to preserve my sound
intelligence and honor from this lust,
plowing my body with its horny thrust.
At first I fled you, and when this fell short
of safety, Prince, I exiled you from court.                    125
Alas, my violence to resist you made
my face inhuman, hateful. I was afraid
to kiss my husband lest I love his son.
I made you fear me (this was easily done);
you loathed me more, I ached for you no less.                  130
Misfortune magnified your loveliness.
I grew so wrung and wasted, men mistook
me for the Sibyl. If you could bear to look
your eyes would tell you. Do you believe my passion
is voluntary? That my obscene confession                       135
is some dark trick, some oily artifice?
I came to beg you not to sacrifice
my son, already uncertain of his life.
Ridiculous, mad embassy, for a wife
who loves her stepson! Prince, I only spoke                    140
about myself! Avenge yourself, invoke
your father; a worse monster threatens you
than any Theseus ever fought and slew.
The wife of Theseus loves Hippolytus!
See, Prince! Look, this monster, ravenous                      145
for her execution, will not flinch.
I want your sword's spasmodic final inch.
OENONE. Madam, put down this weapon. Your distress
attracts the people. Fly these witnesses.
Hurry! Stop kneeling! What a time to pray!                     15ℴ

## Scene 6

### THERAMENES, HIPPOLYTUS

THERAMENES. Is this Phaedra, fleeing, or rather dragged away
sobbing? Where is your sword? Who tore
this empty scabbard from your belt?
HIPPOLYTUS.                                    No more!
Oh let me get away! I face disaster.
Horrors unnerve me. Help! I cannot master                        5
my terror. Phaedra . . . No, I won't expose
her. No! Something I do not dare disclose . . .

THERAMENES. Our ship is ready, but before you leave,
listen! Prince, what we never would believe
has happened: Athens has voted for your brother.    10
The citizens have made him king. His mother
is regent.
HIPPOLYTUS. Phaedra is in power!
THERAMENES. An envoy sent from Athens came this hour
to place the scepter in her hands. Her son
is king.
HIPPOLYTUS. Almighty gods, you know this woman!    15
Is it her spotless virtue you reward?
THERAMENES. I've heard a rumor. Someone swam aboard
a ship off Epirus. He claims the King
is still alive. I've searched. I know the thing
is nonsense.
HIPPOLYTUS. Search! Nothing must be neglected.    20
If the king's dead, I'll rouse the disaffected
people, crown Aricia, and place our lands,
our people, and our lives in worthy hands.


# ACT III

## Scene 1

### PHAEDRA, OENONE

PHAEDRA. Why do my people rush to crown me queen?
Who can even want to see me? They have seen
my downfall. Will their praise deliver me?
Oh bury me at the bottom of the sea!
Nurse, I have said too much! Led on by you,    5
I've said what no one should have listened to.
*He* listened. How could he pretend my drift
was hidden? Something held him, and made him shift
his ground . . . He only wanted to depart
and hide, while I was pouring out my heart.    10
Oh how his blushing multiplied my shame!
Why did you hold me back? You are to blame,
Oenone. But for you, I would have killed
myself. Would he have stood there, iron-willed
and merciless, while I fell upon his sword?    15
He would have snatched it, touched me, and restored

my life! No, no!
OENONE.                    Control yourself! No peace
comes from surrendering to your disease,
Madam. Oh daughter of the kings of Crete,
why are you weeping and fawning at the feet                    20
of this barbarian, less afraid of fate
than of a woman? You must rule the state.
PHAEDRA. Can I, who have no courage to restrain
the insurrection of my passions, reign?
Will the Athenians trust their sovereignty                     25
to me? Love's despotism is crushing me,
I am ruined.
OENONE.        Fly!
PHAEDRA.             How can I leave him?
OENONE. Lady, you have already banished him;
can't you take flight?
PHAEDRA.                  The time for flight has passed.
He knows me now. I rushed beyond the last                      30
limits of modesty, when I confessed.
Hope was no longer blasting through my breast;
I was resigned to hopelessness and death,
and gasping out my last innocent breath,
Oenone, when you forced me back to life.                       35
You thought I was no longer Theseus' wife,
and let me feel that I was free to love.
OENONE. I would have done anything to remove
your danger. Whether I'm guilty or innocent
is all the same to me. Your punishment                         40
should fall on one who tried to kill you, not
on poor Oenone. Lady, you must plot
and sacrifice this monster, whose unjust
abhorrence left you dying in the dust.
Oh humble him, undo him, oh despise                            45
him! Lady, you must see him with my eyes.
PHAEDRA. Oenone, he was nourished in the woods;
he is all shyness and ungracious moods
because the forests left him half-inhuman.
He's never heard love spoken by a woman!                       50
We've gone too far. Oenone, we're unwise;
perhaps the young man's silence was surprise.
OENONE. His mother, the Amazon, was never moved
by men.
PHAEDRA. The boy exists. She must have loved!

OENONE. He has a sullen hatred for our sex. 55
PHAEDRA. Oh, all the better; rivals will not vex
my chances. Your advice is out of season;
now you must serve my frenzy, not my reason!
You tell me love has never touched his heart;
we'll look, we'll find an undefended part. 60
He's turned his bronze prows seaward; look, the wind
already blows like a trumpeter behind
his bulging canvas! The Acropolis
of Athens and its empire shall be his!
Hurry, Oenone, hunt the young man down, 65
blind him with dazzling visions of the crown.
Go tell him I relinquish my command,
I only want the guidance of his hand.
Let him assume these powers that weary me;
he will instruct my son in sovereignty. 70
Perhaps he will adopt my son, and be
the son's and mother's one divinity!
Oenone, rush to him, use every means
to bend and win him; if he fears the Queen's
too proud, he'll listen to her slave. Plead, groan, 75
insist . . . say I am giving him my throne. . . .
No, say I'm dying!

## Scene 2

### PHAEDRA

PHAEDRA. Implacable Aphrodite, now you see
the depths to which your tireless cruelty
has driven Phaedra — here is my bosom;
every thrust and arrow has struck home!
Oh Goddess, if you hunger for renown, 5
rise now, and shoot a worthier victim down!
Conquer the barbarous Hippolytus,
who mocks the graces and the power of Venus,
and gazes on your godhead with disgust.
Avenge me, Venus! See, my cause is just, 10
my cause is yours. Oh bend him to my will! . . .
You're back, Oenone? Does he hate me still?

## Scene 3

PHAEDRA, OENONE

OENONE. Your love is folly, dash it from your soul,
gather your scattered pride and self-control,
Madam! I've seen the royal ship arrive.
Theseus is back, Theseus is still alive!
Thousands of voices thunder from the docks.                5
People are waving flags and climbing rocks.
While I was looking for Hippolytus . . .
PHAEDRA. My husband's living! Must you trouble us
by talking? What am I living for?
He lives, Oenone, let me hear no more                       10
about it.
OENONE.   Why?
PHAEDRA.            I told you, but my fears
were stilled, alas, and smothered by your tears.
Had I died this morning, I might have faced
the gods. I heeded you and die disgraced!
OENONE. You are disgraced!
PHAEDRA.                    Oh Gods of wrath,              15
how far I've travelled on my dangerous path!
I go to meet my husband; at his side
will stand Hippolytus. How shall I hide
my thick adulterous passion for this youth,
who has rejected me, and knows the truth?                  20
Will the stern Prince stand smiling and approve
the labored histrionics of my love
for Theseus, see my lips, still languishing
for his, betray his father and his King?
Will he not draw his sword and strike me dead?             25
Suppose he spares me? What if nothing's said?
Am I a gorgon, or Circe, or the infidel
Medea, stifled by the flames of hell,
yet rising like Aphrodite from the sea,
refreshed and radiant with indecency?                      30
Can I kiss Theseus with dissembled poise?
I think each stone and pillar has a voice.
The very dust rises to disabuse
my husband — to defame me and accuse!
Oenone, I want to die. Death will give                     35

me freedom; oh it's nothing not to live;
death to the unhappy's no catastrophe!
I fear the name that must live after me,
and crush my son until the end of time.
Is his inheritance his mother's crime?                                    40
his right to curse me, when my pollution stains
the blood of heaven bubbling in his veins?
The day will come, alas, the day will come,
when nothing will be left to save him from
the voices of despair. If he should live                                  45
he'll flee his subjects like a fugitive.
OENONE. He has my pity. Who has ever built
firmer foundations to expose her guilt?
But why expose your son? Is your contribution
for his defense to serve the prosecution?                                 50
Suppose you kill yourself? The world will say
you fled your outraged husband in dismay.
Could there be stronger evidence and proof
than Phaedra crushed beneath the horse's hoof
of blasphemous self-destruction to convince                               55
the crowds who'll dance attendance on the Prince?
The crowds will mob your children when they hear
their defamation by a foreigner!
Wouldn't you rather see earth bury us?
Tell me, do you still love Hippolytus?                                    60
PHAEDRA. I see him as a beast, who'd murder us.
OENONE. Madam, let the positions be reversed!
You fear the Prince; you must accuse him first.
Who'll dare assert your story is untrue,
if all the evidence shall speak for you:                                  65
your present grief, your past despair of mind,
the Prince's sword so luckily left behind?
Do you think Theseus will oppose his son's
second exile? He has consented once!
PHAEDRA. How dare I take this murderous, plunging course?                  70
OENONE. I tremble, Lady, I too feel remorse.
If death could rescue you from infamy,
Madam, I too would follow you and die.
Help me by being silent. I will speak
in such a way the King will only seek                                     75
a bloodless exile to assert his rights.
A father is still a father when he smites.
You shudder at this evil sacrifice.

but nothing's evil or too high a price
to save your menaced honor from defeat.                       80
Ah Minos, Minos, you defended Crete
by killing young men! Help us! If the cost
for saving Phaedra is a holocaust
of virtue, Minos, you must sanctify
our undertaking, or watch your daughter die.                  85
I see the King.
PHAEDRA.            I see Hippolytus.


## Scene 4

### PHAEDRA, THESEUS, HIPPOLYTUS, OENONE, THERAMENES

THESEUS. Fate's heard me, Phaedra, and removed the bar
that kept me from your arms.
PHAEDRA.                    Theseus, stop where you are!
Your raptures and endearments are profane.
Your arm must never comfort me again.
You have been wronged, the gods who spared your life          5
have used your absence to disgrace your wife,
unworthy now to please you or come near.
My only refuge is to disappear.


## Scene 5

### THESEUS, HIPPOLYTUS

THESEUS. What a strange welcome! This bewilders me.
My son, what's happened?
HIPPOLYTUS.                 Phaedra holds the key.
Ask Phaedra. If you love me, let me leave
this kingdom. I'm determined to achieve
some action that will show my strength. I fear             5
Phaedra. I am afraid of living here.
THESEUS. My son, you want to leave me?
HIPPOLYTUS.                            I never sought
her grace or favor. Your decision brought
her here from Athens. Your desires prevailed
against my judgment, Father, when you sailed               10
leaving Phaedra and Aricia in my care.
I've done my duty, now I must prepare
for sterner actions, I must test my skill

on monsters far more dangerous to kill
than any wolf or eagle in this wood. 15
Release me, I too must prove my manhood!
Oh Father, you were hardly half my age,
when herds of giants writhed before your rage —
you were already famous as the scourge
of insolence. Our people saw you purge 20
the pirates from the shores of Greece and Thrace,
the harmless merchantman was free to race
the winds, and weary Hercules could pause
from slaughter, knowing you upheld his cause.
The world revered you. I am still unknown; 25
even my mother's deeds surpass my own.
Some tyrants have escaped you; let me meet
with them and throw their bodies at your feet.
I'll drag them from their wolf-holes; if I die,
my death will show I struggled worthily. 30
Oh, Father, raise me from oblivion;
my deeds shall tell the universe I am your son.
THESEUS. What do I see? Oh gods, what horror drives
my queen and children fleeing for their lives
before me? If so little warmth remains, 35
oh why did you release me from my chains?
Why am I hated, and so little loved?
I had a friend, just one. His folly moved
me till I aided his conspiracy
to ravish Queen Persephone. 40
The gods, tormented by our blasphemous
designs, befogged our minds and blinded us —
we invaded Epirus instead of hell.
There a diseased and subtle tyrant fell
upon us as we slept, and while I stood 45
by, helpless, monsters crazed for human blood
consumed Pirithoüs. I myself was chained
fast in a death-deep dungeon. I remained
six months there, then the gods had pity,
and put me in possession of the city. 50
I killed the tyrant; now his body feasts
the famished, pampered bellies of his beasts.
At last, I voyaged home, cast anchor, furled
my sails. When I was rushing to my world —
what am I saying? When my heart and soul 55
were mine again, unable to control

themselves for longing — who receives me?  All run
and shun me, as if I were a skeleton.
Now I myself begin to feel the fear
I inspire.  I wish I were a prisoner                               60
again or dead.  Speak!  Phaedra says my home
was outraged.  Who betrayed me?  Someone come
and tell me.  I have fought for Greece.  Will Greece,
sustained by Theseus, give my enemies
asylum in my household?  Tell me why                              65
I've no avenger?  Is my son a spy?
You will not answer.  I must know my fate.
Suspicion chokes me, while I hesitate
and stand here pleading.  Wait, let no one stir.
Phaedra shall tell me what has troubled her.                      70


## Scene 6

### HIPPOLYTUS

HIPPOLYTUS.  What now?  His anger turns my blood to ice.
Will Phaedra, always uncertain, sacrifice
herself?  What will she tell the King?  How hot
the air's becoming here!  I feel the rot
of love seeping like poison through this house.                    5
I feel the pollution.  I cannot rouse
my former loyalties.  When I try to gather
the necessary strength to face my father,
my mind spins with some dark presentiment . . .
How can such terror touch the innocent?                           10
I LOVE ARICIA!  Father, I confess
my treason to you is my happiness!
I LOVE ARICIA!  Will this bring you joy,
our love you have no power to destroy?


# ACT IV

## Scene 1

### THESEUS, OENONE

THESEUS.  What's this, you tell me he dishonors me,
and has assaulted Phaedra's chastity?
Oh heavy fortune, I no longer know

who loves me, who I am, or where I go.
Who has ever seen such disloyalty 5
after such love?  Such sly audacity?
His youth made no impression on her soul,
so he fell back on force to reach his goal!
I recognize this perjured sword; I gave
him this myself to teach him to be brave! 10
Oh Zeus, are blood-ties no impediment?
Even Phaedra to save him from punishment!
Why did her silence spare this parricide?
OENONE. She hoped to spare a trusting father's pride.
She felt so sickened by your son's attempt, 15
his hot eyes leering at her with contempt,
she had no wish to live.  She read out her will
to me, then lifted up her arm to kill
herself.  I struck the sword out of her hand.
Fainting, she babbled the secret she had planned 20
to bury with her in the grave.  My ears
unwillingly interpreted her tears.
THESEUS. Oh traitor!  I know why he seemed to blanch
and toss with terror like an aspen branch
when Phaedra saw him.  Now I know why he stood 25
back, then embraced me so coldly he froze my blood.
Was Athens the first stage for his obscene
attentions?  Did he dare attack the Queen
before our marriage?
OENONE.              Remember her disgust
and hate then?  She already feared his lust. 30
THESEUS. And when I sailed, this started up again?
OENONE. I've hidden nothing.  Do you want your pain
redoubled?  Phaedra calls me.  Let me go,
and save her.  I have told you what I know.


## Scene 2

### THESEUS, HIPPOLYTUS

THESEUS. My son returns!  Oh God, reserved and cool,
dressed in a casual freedom that could fool
the sharpest.  Is it right his brows should blaze
and dazzle me with virtue's sacred rays?
Are there not signs?  Should not ADULTERER 5
in looping scarlet script be branded there?

HIPPOLYTUS.  What cares becloud your kingly countenance,
   Father!  What is this irritated glance?
   Tell me!  Are you afraid to trust your son?
THESEUS.  How dare you stand here?  May the great Zeus stone          10
   me, if I let my fondness and your birth
   protect you!  Is my strength which rid the earth
   of brigands paralysed?  Am I so sick
   and senile, any coward with a stick
   can strike me?  Am I a schoolboy's target?  Oh God,                15
   am I food for vultures?  Some carrion you must prod
   and poke to see if it's alive or dead?
   Your hands are moist and itching for my bed,
   Coward!  Wasn't begetting you enough
   dishonor to destroy me?  Must I snuff                             20
   your perjured life, my own son's life, and stain
   a thousand glories?  Let the gods restrain
   my fury!  Fly!  live hated and alone —
   there are places where my name may be unknown.
   Go, find them, follow your disastrous star                       25
   through filth; if I discover where you are,
   I'll add another body to the hill
   of vermin I've extinguished by my skill.
   Fly from me, let the grieving storm-winds bear
   your contagion from me.  You corrupt the air.                    30
   I call upon Poseidon.  Help me, Lord
   of Ocean, help your servant!  Once my sword
   heaped crucified assassins on your shore
   and let them burn like beacons.  God, you swore
   my first request would be fulfilled.  My first!                  35
   I never made it.  Even through the worst
   torments of Epirus I held my peace;
   no threat or torture brought me to my knees
   beseeching favors; even then I knew
   some greater project was reserved for you!                       40
   Poseidon, now I kneel.  Avenge me, dash
   my incestuous son against your rocks, and wash
   his dishonor from my household; wave on wave
   of roaring nothingness shall be his grave.
HIPPOLYTUS.  Phaedra accuses me of lawless love!                     45
   Phaedra!  My heart stops, I can hardly move
   my lips and answer.  I have no defense,
   if you condemn me without evidence.
THESEUS.  Oh coward, you were counting on the Queen

to hide your brutal insolence and screen 50
your outrage with her weakness! You forgot
something. You dropped your sword and spoiled your plot.
You should have kept it. Surely you had time
to kill the only witness to your crime!

HIPPOLYTUS. Why do I stand this, and forbear to clear 55
away these lies, and let the truth appear?
I could so easily. Where would you be,
if I spoke out? Respect my loyalty,
Father, respect your own intelligence.
Examine me. What am I? My defense 60
is my whole life. When have I wavered, when
have I pursued the vices of young men?
Father, you have no scaffolding to rig
your charges on. Small crimes precede the big.
Phaedra accused me of attempting rape! 65
Am I some Proteus, who can change his shape?
Nature despises such disparities.
Vice, like virtue, advances by degrees.
Bred by Antiope to manly arms,
I hate the fever of this lust that warms 70
the loins and rots the spirit. I was taught
uprightness by Theramenes. I fought
with wolves, tamed horses, gave my soul to sport,
and shunned the joys of women and the court.
I dislike praise, but those who know me best 75
grant me one virtue — it's that I detest
the very crimes of which I am accused.
How often you yourself have been amused
and puzzled by my love of purity,
pushed to the point of crudeness. By the sea 80
and in the forests, I have filled my heart
with freedom, far from women.

THESEUS.                              When this part
was dropped, could only Phaedra violate
the cold abyss of your immaculate
reptilian soul? How could this funeral urn 85
contain a heart, a living heart, or burn
for any woman but my wife?

HIPPOLYTUS.                         Ah no!
Father, I too have seen my passions blow
into a tempest. Why should I conceal
my true offense? I feel, Father, I feel 90

what other young men feel. I love, I love
Aricia. Father, I love the sister of
your worst enemies. I worship her!
I only feel and breathe and live for her!
THESEUS. You love Aricia? God! No, this is meant          95
to blind my eyes and throw me off the scent.
HIPPOLYTUS. Father, for six months I have done my worst
to kill this passion. You shall be the first
to know . . . You frown still. Nothing can remove
your dark obsession. Father, what will prove          100
my innocence? I swear by earth and sky,
and nature's solemn, shining majesty. . . .
THESEUS. Oaths and religion are the common cant
of all betrayers. If you wish to taunt
me, find a better prop than blasphemy.          105
HIPPOLYTUS. All's blasphemy to eyes that cannot see.
Could even Phaedra bear me such ill will?
THESEUS. Phaedra, Phaedra! Name her again, I'll kill
you! My hand's already on my sword.
HIPPOLYTUS.                                    Explain
my terms of exile. What do you ordain?          110
THESEUS. Sail out across the ocean. Everywhere
on earth and under heaven is too near.
HIPPOLYTUS. Who'll take me in? Oh who will pity me,
and give me bread, if you abandon me?
THESEUS. You'll find fitting companions. Look for friends          115
who honor everything that most offends.
Pimps and jackals who praise adultery
and incest will protect your purity.
HIPPOLYTUS. Adultery! Is it your privilege
to fling this word in my teeth? I've reached the edge          120
of madness . . . No, I'll say no more. Compare
my breeding with Phaedra's. Think and beware . . .
She had a mother . . . No, I must not speak.
THESEUS. You devil, you'll attack the queen still weak
from your assault. How can you stand and face          125
your father? Must I drive you from this place
with my own hand? Run off, or I will flog
you with the flat of my sword like a dog!

## Scene 3

### THESEUS

THESEUS. You go to your inevitable fate,
Child — by the river immortals venerate.
Poseidon gave his word. You cannot fly;
death and the gods march on invisibly.
I loved you once; despite your perfidy,                              5
my bowels writhe inside me. Must you die?
Yes; I am in too deep now to draw back.
What son has placed his father on such a rack?
What father groans for such a monstrous birth?
Oh gods, your thunder throws me to the earth.                        10

## Scene 4

### THESEUS, PHAEDRA

PHAEDRA. Theseus, I heard the deluge of your voice,
and stand here trembling. If there's time for choice,
hold back your hand, still bloodless; spare your race!
I supplicate you, here I kneel for grace.
Oh, Theseus, Theseus, will you drench the earth              5
with your own blood? His virtue, youth and birth
cry out for him. Is he already slain
by you for me — spare me this incestuous pain!
THESEUS. Phaedra, my son's blood has not touched my hand;
and yet I'll be avenged. On sea and land,                           10
spirits, the swift of foot, shall track him down.
Poseidon owes me this. Why do you frown?
PHAEDRA. Poseidon owes you this? What have you done
in anger?
THESEUS.      What! You wish to help my son?
No, stir my anger, back me to the hilt,                             15
call for blacker colors to paint his guilt.
Lash, strike and drive me on! You cannot guess
the nerve and fury of his wickedness.
Phaedra, he slandered your sincerity,
he told me your accusation was a lie.                               20
He swore he loved Aricia, he wants to wed
Aricia. . . .

PHAEDRA.        What, my lord?
THESEUS.                    That's what he said.
Of course, I scorn his shallow artifice.
Help me, Poseidon hear me, sacrifice
my son. I seek the altar. Come! Let us both                    25
kneel down and beg the gods to keep their oath.


## Scene 5

### PHAEDRA

PHAEDRA.  My husband's gone, still rumbling his own name
and fame. He has no inkling of the flame
his words have started. If he hadn't spoken,
I might . . . I was on my feet, I'd broken
loose from Oenone, and had just begun                          5
to say I know not what to save his son.
Who knows how far I would have gone? Remorse,
longing and anguish shook me with such force,
I might have told the truth and suffered death,
before this revelation stopped my breath:                      10
Hippolytus is not insensible,
only insensible to me! His dull
heart chases shadows. He is glad to rest
upon Aricia's adolescent breast!
Oh thin abstraction! When I saw his firm                       15
repugnance spurn my passion like a worm,
I thought he had some magic to withstand
the lure of any woman in the land,
and now I see a schoolgirl leads the boy,
as simply as her puppy or a toy.                               20
Was I about to perish for this sham,
this panting hypocrite? Perhaps I am
the only woman that he could refuse!


## Scene 6

### PHAEDRA, OENONE

PHAEDRA.  Oenone, dearest, have you heard the news?
OENONE.  No, I know nothing, but I am afraid.
How can I follow you? You have betrayed

your life and children. What have you revealed,
Madam?

PHAEDRA. I have a rival in the field, 5
Oenone.

OENONE. What?

PHAEDRA. Oenone, he's in love —
this howling monster, able to disprove
my beauty, mock my passion, scorn each prayer,
and face me like a tiger in its lair —
he's tamed, the beast is harnessed to a cart; 10
Aricia's found an entrance to his heart.

OENONE. Aricia?

PHAEDRA. Nurse, my last calamity
has come. This is the bottom of the sea.
All that preceded this had little force —
the flames of lust, the horrors of remorse, 15
the prim refusal by my grim young master,
were only feeble hints of this disaster.
They love each other! Passion blinded me.
I let them blind me, let them meet and see
each other freely! Was such bounty wrong? 20
Oenone, you have known this all along,
you must have seen their meetings, watched them sneak
off to their forest, playing hide-and-seek!
Alas, such rendezvous are no offence:
innocent nature smiles on innocence, 25
for them each natural impulse was allowed,
each day was summer and without a cloud.
Oenone, nature hated me. I fled
its light, as if a price were on my head.
I shut my eyes and hungered for my end. 30
Death was the only God my vows could bend.
And even while my desolation served
me gall and tears, I knew I was observed;
I never had security or leisure
for honest weeping, but must steal this pleasure. 35
Oh hideous pomp; a monarch only wears
the robes of majesty to hide her tears!

OENONE. How can their folly help them? They will never
enjoy its fruit.

PHAEDRA. Ugh, they will love forever —
even while I am talking, they embrace, 40
they scorn me, they are laughing in my face!

In the teeth of exile, I hear them swear
they will be true forever, everywhere.
Oenone, have pity on my jealous rage;
I'll kill this happiness that jeers at age.                          45
I'll summon Theseus; hate shall answer hate!
I'll drive my husband to annihilate
Aricia — let no trivial punishment,
her instant death, or bloodless banishment . . .
What am I saying? Have I lost my mind?                               50
I am jealous, and call my husband! Bind
me, gag me; I am frothing with desire.
My husband is alive, and I'm on fire!
For whom? Hippolytus. When I have said
his name, blood fills my eyes, my heart stops dead.                  55
Imposture, incest, murder! I have passed
the limits of damnation; now at last,
my lover's lifeblood is my single food;
nothing else cools my murderous thirst for blood.
Yet I live on. I live looked down upon                               60
by my progenitor, the sacred sun,
by Zeus, by Europa, by the universe
of gods and stars, my ancestors. They curse
their daughter. Let me die. In the great night
of Hades, I'll find shelter from their sight.                        65
What am I saying? I've no place to turn:
Minos, my father, holds the judge's urn.
The gods have placed damnation in his hands,
the shades in Hades follow his commands.
Will he not shake and curse his fatal star                           70
that brings his daughter trembling to his bar?
His child by Pasiphaë forced to tell
a thousand sins unclassified in hell?
Father, when you interpret what I speak,
I fear your fortitude will be too weak                               75
to hold the urn. I see you fumbling for
new punishments for crimes unknown before.
You'll be your own child's executioner!
You cannot kill me; look, my murderer
is Venus, who destroyed our family;                                  80
Father, she has already murdered me.
I killed myself — and what is worse I wasted
my life for pleasure I have never tasted.
My love flees me still, and my last gasp,

is for the fleeting flesh I failed to clasp.  85
OENONE. Madam, Madam, cast off this groundless terror!
Is love now an unprecedented error?
You love! What then? You love! Accept your fate.
You're not the first to sail into this strait.
Will chaos overturn the earth and Jove,  90
because a mortal woman is in love?
Such accidents are easy, all too common.
A woman must submit to being woman.
You curse a failure in the source of things.
Venus has feasted on the hearts of kings;  95
even the gods, man's judges, feel desire,
Zeus learned to live with his adulterous fire.
PHAEDRA. Must I still listen, and drink your poisoned breath?
My death redoubled on the edge of death —
I'd fled Hippolytus and I was free  100
till your entreaties stabbed and blinded me,
and dragged me howling to the pit of lust.
Oenone, I was learning to be just.
You fed my malice. Attacking the young Prince
was not enough; you clothed him with my sins.  105
You wished to kill him; he is dying now,
because of you, and Theseus' brutal vow.
You watch my torture; I'm the last ungorged
scrap rotting in this trap your plots have forged.
What binds you to me? Leave me, go, and die,  110
may your punishment be to terrify
all those who ruin princes by their lies,
hints, acquiescence, filth, and blasphemies —
panders who grease the grooves of inclination,
and lure our willing bodies from salvation.  115
Go die, go frighten false flatterers, the worst
friends the gods can give to kings they've cursed!
OENONE (*alone*). I have given all and left all for her service,
almighty Gods! I have been paid my price!

# ACT V

## Scene 1

### HIPPOLYTUS, ARICIA

ARICIA. Take a stand, speak the truth, if you respect
　your father's glory and your life. Protect
　yourself! I'm nothing to you. You consent
　without a struggle to your banishment.
　If you are weary of Aricia, go;                                    5
　at least do something to prevent the blow
　that dooms your honor and existence — both
　at a stroke! Your father must recall his oath;
　there is time still, but if the truth's concealed,
　you offer your accuser a free field.                              10
　Speak to your father!
HIPPOLYTUS.　　　　　　　I've already said
　what's lawful. Shall I point to his soiled bed,
　tell Athens how his marriage was foresworn,
　make Theseus curse the day that he was born?
　My aching heart recoils. I only want                              15
　God and Aricia for my confidants.
　See how I love you; love makes me confide
　in you this horror I have tried to hide
　from my own heart. My faith must not be broken;
　forget, if possible, what I have spoken.                          20
　Ah Princess, if even a whisper slips
　past you, it will perjure your pure lips.
　God's justice is committed to the cause
　of those who love him, and uphold his laws;
　sooner or later, heaven itself will rise                          25
　in wrath and punish Phaedra's blasphemies.
　I must not. If I rip away her mask,
　I'll kill my father. Give me what I ask.
　Do this! Then throw away your chains; it's right
　for you to follow me, and share my flight.                        30
　Fly from this prison; here the vices seethe
　and simmer, virtue has no air to breathe.
　In the confusion of my exile, none
　will even notice that Aricia's gone.

Banished and broken, Princess, I am still                        35
a force in Greece. Your guards obey my will,
powerful intercessors wish us well:
our neighbors, Argos' citadel
is armed, and in Mycenae our allies
will shelter us, if lying Phaedra tries                          40
to harry us from our paternal throne,
and steal our sacred titles for her son.
The gods are ours, they urge us to attack.
Why do you tremble, falter and hold back?
Your interests drive me to this sacrifice.                       45
While I'm on fire, your blood has changed to ice.
Princess, is exile more than you can face?
ARICIA. Exile with you, my lord? What sweeter place
is under heaven? Standing at your side,
I'd let the universe and heaven slide.                           50
You're my one love, my king, but can I hope
for peace and honor, Prince, if I elope
unmarried? This . . . I wasn't questioning
the decency of flying from the king.
Is he my father? Only an abject                                  55
spirit honors tyrants with respect.
You say you love me. Prince, I am afraid.
HIPPOLYTUS. Aricia, you shall never be betrayed;
accept me! Let our love be sanctified,
then flee from your oppressor as my bride.                       60
Bear witness, oh you gods, our love released
by danger, needs no temple or a priest.
It's faith, not ceremonial, that saves.
Here at the city gates, among these graves
the resting places of my ancient line,                           65
there stands a sacred temple and a shrine.
Here, where no mortal ever swore in vain,
here in these shadows, where eternal pain
is ready to engulf the perjurer;
here heaven's scepter quivers to confer                          70
its final sanction; here, my Love, we'll kneel,
and pray the gods to consecrate and seal
our love. Zeus, the father of the world will stand
here as your father and bestow your hand.
Only the pure shall be our witnesses:                            75
Hera, the guarantor of marriages,
Demeter and the virgin Artemis.

ARICIA. The King is coming. Fly. I'll stay and meet
his anger here and cover your retreat.
Hurry. Be off, send me some friend to guide              80
my timid footsteps, husband, to your side.

## Scene 2

### THESEUS, ISMENE, ARICIA

THESEUS. Oh God, illuminate my troubled mind.
Show me the answer I have failed to find.
ARICIA. Go, Ismene, be ready to escape.

## Scene 3

### THESEUS, ARICIA

THESEUS. Princess, you are disturbed. You twist your cape
and blush. The Prince was talking to you. Why
is he running?
ARICIA.                    We've said our last goodbye,
my lord.
THESEUS.        I see the beauty of your eyes
moves even my son, and you have gained a prize          5
no woman hoped for.
ARICIA.                    He hasn't taken on
your hatred for me, though he is your son.
THESEUS. I follow. I can hear the oaths he swore.
He knelt, he wept. He has done this before
and worse. You are deceived.
ARICIA.                    Deceived, my lord?          10
THESEUS. Princess, are you so rich? Can you afford
to hunger for this lover that my queen
rejected? Your betrayer loves my wife.
ARICIA. How can you bear to blacken his pure life?
Is kingship only for the blind and strong,              15
unable to distinguish right from wrong?
What insolent prerogative obscures
a light that shines in every eye but yours?
You have betrayed him to his enemies.
What more, my lord? Repent your blasphemies.           20
Are you not fearful lest the gods so loathe
and hate you they will gratify your oath?

Fear God, my lord, fear God. How many times
he grants men's wishes to expose their crimes.
THESEUS. Love blinds you, Princess, and beclouds your reason.    25
Your outburst cannot cover up his treason.
My trust's in witnesses that cannot lie.
I have seen Phaedra's tears. She tried to die.
ARICIA. Take care, your highness. When your killing hand
drove all the thieves and reptiles from the land,    30
you missed one monster, one was left alive,
one. . . . No, I must not name her, Sire, or strive
to save your helpless son; he wants to spare
your reputation. Let me go. I dare
not stay here. If I stayed I'd be too weak    35
to keep my promise. I'd be forced to speak.


## Scene 4

### THESEUS

THESEUS. What was she saying? I must try to reach
the meaning of her interrupted speech.
Is it a pitfall? A conspiracy?
Are they plotting together to torture me?
Why did I let the rash, wild girl depart?    5
What is this whisper crying in my heart?
A secret pity fills my soul with pain.
I must question Oenone once again.
My guards, summon Oenone to the throne.
Quick, bring her. I must talk with her alone.    10


## Scene 5

### THESEUS, PANOPE

PANOPE. The Queen's deranged, your highness. Some accursed
madness is driving her; some fury stalks
behind her back, possesses her, and talks
its evil through her, and blasphemes the world.
She cursed Oenone. Now Oenone's hurled    5
herself into the ocean, Sire, and drowned.
Why did she do it? No reason can be found.
THESEUS. Oenone's drowned?
PANOPE.                    Her death has brought no peace.

The cries of Phaedra's troubled soul increase.
Now driven by some sinister unrest,                    10
she snatches up her children to her breast,
pets them and weeps, till something makes her scoff
at her affection, and she drives them off.
Her glance is drunken and irregular,
she looks through us and wonders who we are;          15
thrice she has started letters to you, Sire,
thrice tossed the shredded fragments in the fire.
Oh call her to you. Help her!
THESEUS.  The nurse is drowned?  Phaedra wishes to die?
Oh gods!  Summon my son.  Let him defend              20
himself, tell him I'm ready to attend.
I want him!

(*Exit* PANOPE.)

Neptune, hear me, spare my son!
My vengeance was too hastily begun.
Oh why was I so eager to believe
Oenone's accusation?  The gods deceive                25
the victims they are ready to destroy!


*Scene 6*

THESEUS, THERAMENES

THESEUS.  Here is Theramenes.  Where is my boy,
my first-born?  He was yours to guard and keep.
Where is he?  Answer me.  What's this?  You weep?
THERAMENES.  Oh tardy, futile grief, his blood is shed.
My lord, your son, Hippolytus, is dead.               5
THESEUS.  Oh gods have mercy!
THERAMENES.                  I saw him die.  The most
lovely and innocent of men is lost.
THESEUS.  He's dead?  The gods have hurried him away
and killed him? . . . just as I began to pray. . . .
What sudden thunderbolt has struck him down?          10
THERAMENES.  We'd started out, and hardly left the town.
He held the reins; a few feet to his rear,
a single, silent guard held up a spear.
He followed the Mycenae highroad, deep
in thought, reins dangling, as if half asleep;        15
his famous horses, only he could hold,
trudged on with lowered heads, and sometimes rolled

their dull eyes slowly — they seemed to have caught
their master's melancholy, and aped his thought.
Then all at once winds struck us like a fist,                        20
we heard a sudden roaring through the mist;
from underground a voice in agony
answered the prolonged groaning of the sea.
We shook, the horses' manes rose on their heads,
and now against a sky of blacks and reds,                            25
we saw the flat waves hump into a mountain
of green-white water rising like a fountain,
as it reached land and crashed with a last roar
to shatter like a galley on the shore.
Out of its fragments rose a monster, half                            30
dragon, half bull; a mouth that seemed to laugh
drooled venom on its dirty yellow scales
and python belly, forking to three tails.
The shore was shaken like a tuning fork,
ships bounced on the stung sea like bits of cork,                    35
the earth moved, and the sun spun round and round,
a sulphur-colored venom swept the ground.
We fled; each felt his useless courage falter,
and sought asylum at a nearby altar.
Only the Prince remained; he wheeled about,                          40
and hurled a javelin through the monster's snout.
Each kept advancing. Flung from the Prince's arm,
dart after dart struck where the blood was warm.
The monster in its death-throes felt defeat,
and bounded howling to the horses' feet.                             45
There its stretched gullet and its armor broke,
and drenched the chariot with blood and smoke,
and then the horses, terror-struck, stampeded.
Their master's whip and shouting went unheeded,
they dragged his breathless body to the spray.                       50
Their red mouths bit the bloody surf, men say
Poseidon stood beside them, that the god
was stabbing at their bellies with a goad.
Their terror drove them crashing on a cliff,
the chariot crashed in two, they ran as if                           55
the Furies screamed and crackled in their manes,
their fallen hero tangled in the reins,
jounced on the rocks behind them. The sweet light
of heaven never will expunge this sight:
the horses that Hippolytus had tamed,                                60

now dragged him headlong, and their mad hooves maimed
his face past recognition. When he tried
to call them, calling only terrified;
faster and ever faster moved their feet,
his body was a piece of bloody meat.                              65
The cliffs and ocean trembled to our shout,
at last their panic failed, they turned about,
and stopped not far from where those hallowed graves,
the Prince's fathers, overlook the waves.
I ran on breathless, guards were at my back,                     70
my master's blood had left a generous track.
The stones were red, each thistle in the mud
was stuck with bits of hair and skin and blood.
I came upon him, called; he stretched his right
hand to me, blinked his eyes, then closed them tight.            75
"I die," he whispered, "it's the gods' desire.
Friend, stand between Aricia and my sire —
some day enlightened, softened, disabused,
he will lament his son, falsely accused;
then when at last he wishes to appease                           80
my soul, he'll treat my lover well, release
and honor Aricia. . . ." On this word, he died.
Only a broken body testified
he'd lived and loved once. On the sand now lies
something his father will not recognize.                         85
THESEUS. My son, my son! Alas, I stand alone.
Before the gods. I never can atone.
THERAMENES. Meanwhile Aricia, rushing down the path,
    approached us. She was fleeing from your wrath,
    my lord, and wished to make Hippolytus                       90
    her husband in God's eyes. Then nearing us,
    she saw the signs of struggle in the waste,
    she saw (oh what a sight) her love defaced,
    her young love lying lifeless on the sand.
    At first she hardly seemed to understand;                    95
    while staring at the body in the grass,
    she kept on asking where her lover was.
    At last the black and fearful truth broke through
    her desolation! She seemed to curse the blue
    and murdering ocean, as she caught his head                  100
    up in her lap; then fainting lay half dead,
    until Ismene somehow summoned back her breath,
    restored the child to life — or rather death.

I come, great King, to urge my final task,
your dying son's last outcry was to ask     105
mercy for poor Aricia, for his bride.
Now Phaedra comes. She killed him. She has lied.

### Scene 7

THESEUS, PHAEDRA, PANOPE

THESEUS. Ah Phaedra, you have won. He's dead. A man
was killed. Were you watching? His horses ran
him down, and tore his body limb from limb.
Poseidon struck him, Theseus murdered him.
I served you! Tell me why Oenone died?          5
Was it to save you? Is her suicide
a proof of your truth? No, since he's dead, I must
accept your evidence, just or unjust.
I must believe my faith has been abused;
you have accused him; he shall stand accused.    10
He's friendless, even in the world below.
There the shades fear him! Am I forced to know
the truth? Truth cannot bring my son to life
if fathers murder, shall I kill my wife
too? Leave me, Phaedra. Far from you, exiled      15
from Greece, I will lament my murdered child.
I am a murdered gladiator, whirled
in black circles. I want to leave the world,
but my whole life rises to increase my guilt —
all those dazzled, dazzling eyes, my glory built   20
on killing killers. Less known, less magnified,
I might escape, and find a place to hide.
Stand back, Poseidon. I know the gods are hard
to please. I pleased you. This is my reward:
I killed my son. I killed him! Only a God          25
spares enemies, and wants his servants' blood!
PHAEDRA. No, Theseus, I must disobey your prayer.
Listen to me. I'm dying. I declare
Hippolytus was innocent.
THESEUS. Ah Phaedra, on your evidence, I sent      30
him to his death. Do you ask me to forgive
my son's assassin? Can I let you live?
PHAEDRA. My time's too short, your highness. It was I,
who lusted for your son with my hot eye.

The flames of Aphrodite maddened me;                         35
I loathed myself, and yearned outrageously
like a starved wolf to fall upon the sheep.
I wished to hold him to me in my sleep
and dreamt I had him. Then Oenone's tears
troubled my mind; she played upon my fears,      40
until pleading forced me to declare
I loved your son. He scorned me. In despair,
I plotted with my nurse, and our conspiracy
made you believe your son assaulted me.
Oenone's punished; fleeing from my wrath,        45
she drowned herself, and found a too easy path
to death and hell. Perhaps you wonder why
I still survive her, and refuse to die?
Theseus, I stand before you to absolve
your noble son. Sire, only this resolve          50
upheld me, and made me throw down my knife
I've chosen a slower way to end my life —
Medea's poison; chills already dart
along my boiling veins and squeeze my heart.
A cold composure I have never known              55
gives me a moment's poise. I stand alone
and seem to see my outraged husband fade
and waver into death's dissolving shade.
My eyes at last give up their light, and see
the day they've soiled resume its purity.        60
PANOPE. She's dead, my lord.
THESEUS.                         Would God, all memory
of her and me had died with her! Now I
must live. This knowledge that has come too late
must give me strength and help me expiate
my sacrilegious vow. Let's go, I'll pay          65
my son the honors he has earned today.
His father's tears shall mingle with his blood.
My love that did my son so little good
asks mercy from his spirit. I declare
Aricia is my daughter and my heir.               70

❖ ❖ ❖

## STUDY AIDS

**ACT I.** *Scene 1.* Theramenes is Hippolytus' confidant just as Ismene is Aricia's and Oenone is Phaedra's. What is the dramatic function of this expansion of the confidant(e) role beyond its more restricted use in the *Hippolytus*?

Why is Hippolytus embarrassed by Theramenes' reference to the amorous exploits of Theseus?

How is the Troezen-Athens contrast exploited by Racine? In developing Hippolytus' character? In defining the political situation?

How might Theramenes' reference to Hippolytus' riding the bridle paths be considered a foreshadowing? Where else in the play does this kind of foreshadowing occur?

Hippolytus is the first to mention Phaedra's heredity. In what context does he bring it up? Compare this with the other contexts in which it is mentioned, especially by Phaedra herself.

During the dialogue of the opening scene Theseus, Phaedra, and Aricia are introduced. What other significant narrative elements are revealed in this scene? Is all this information conveyed in dramatic terms? Find other scenes in which there is also a heavy burden of exposition. Is it well integrated with the action?

Before Phaedra appears, her psychological state is described in images of day and night, light and darkness (ll. 47-50). Analyze the function of this imagery in the play.

In what tone does Theramenes chide Hippolytus for his "hatred" of Aricia?

How is the Hippolytus-Theseus relationship developed in ll. 81-107? How does Hippolytus' condemnation of Theseus' love affairs help us to better understand Phaedra's predicament?

Is Theramenes' analysis of the passion of love in ll. 117-142 relevant only to Hippolytus' situation, or does it represent attitudes and ideas which prevail in the play as a whole?

*Scene 2.* Note the continuity of scene transitions and the neoclassical convention of never emptying the stage between scenes. How are transitions accomplished in Euripides and Seneca? What might be some of the implications of this convention for scenic design and staging?

*Scene 3.* Analyze Phaedra's speeches for indications of gesture and posture. What physical, emotional, and vocal resources would be required of an actress in this role? Consider ll. 26–28. What is the significance of these hallucinatory lines?

Is Phaedra obsessed with the idea of suicide from the beginning, or does it come to dominate her thinking only as circumstances increase her isolation and despair?

In both Racine and Euripides it is the nurse who confers objective reality on Phaedra's inner torment by pronouncing Hippolytus' name. How is this dramatic device given ironic reinforcement in Racine's play? Why is Phaedra reluctant to put her passion into words? How would doing so change her condition? What are the contrary forces which create such unbearable tension within her?

Phaedra is driven by her own lust, the enmity of the gods, her fatal heredity, and the cruel twist of circumstances. Analyze the relative importance of each of these forces as they act on her throughout Scenes 3, 4, and 5.

*Scene 4.* Define carefully the political problems which arise at the report of Theseus' death.

*Scene 5.* How culpable is Oenone in contriving at the false report of Theseus' death? Does Theseus' presumed death cancel out both the adulterous and incestuous aspects of Phaedra's love? How much are Phaedra's hopes justified by events, and how much are they the function of her tendency to self-deception? To what extent does she project her self-deception onto Oenone?

ACT II. *Scene 1.* Analyze the parallelism between Act II, Scene 1, and Act I, Scene 1. Does the careful symmetry of dramatic organization which pervades the whole play tend to define the balance and opposition of moral and psychological conflict? Or does it appear to be merely a mechanical scheme superimposed on the material by the canons of neo-classical criticism, which demand structural symmetry?

In what significant ways is Aricia very much like Hippolytus?

*Scene 2.* Construct a family tree to clarify the lines of descent to which Hippolytus refers in offering Aricia the rule of Athens.

What kind of lover does Hippolytus reveal himself to be by his protestations to Aricia? How is this related to his cold rebuff of Phaedra which follows?

*Scene 5.* Does Phaedra really come to Hippolytus as an advocate of her son? Is this a devious stratagem of Phaedra's, or is it another example of the power of her self-deception (see ll. 137–140)?

What is the conscious or unconscious strategy in Phaedra's blaming herself for Hippolytus' rough manner? Does Hippolytus suggest that Theseus may still be alive (ll. 43, 56) because he senses the drift of Phaedra's words? Work out the staging of this climactic scene. At what lines should Phaedra touch Hippolytus and how should he react?

Comment on the hallucinatory quality of ll. 59–95. Is Phaedra here bordering on literal madness?

How do ll. 97–99 indicate Phaedra's final struggle to master her passion? What components of her personality have the strongest restraining effect upon her passions?

Analyze the imagery of Phaedra's speech in ll. 103–147. What kinds of images figure here?

ACT III. *Scene 1.* Did Phaedra only feign her threat of suicide with Hippolytus' sword? How justified is she in shifting the blame for her predicament onto Oenone? How cogent is the nurse's defense?

What is one of the major ironies of the action prepared for by l. 56?

*Scene 3.* In the two scenes immediately preceding the announcement that Theseus is alive and is returning, the action is directed toward the Phaedra-Hippolytus-Aricia plot rather than to the possibility of Theseus' return. What is the effect of this structuring of the plot? Is there a sense of a fatal destiny closing in on Phaedra from all sides which mocks at her efforts to order reality in her own way?

Phaedra's speech, ll. 15–46, is divided into two distinct parts: ll. 15–37 and 38–46. What is the relationship between the two? How could the shift in subject be best accomplished through the voice, gestures, and movement of the actress playing Phaedra?

What is the relationship between Oenone's scheme to accuse Hippolytus and the problem raised by Phaedra in the speech analyzed above? How is the malice in the scheme mitigated by the nurse's acknowledgment of remorse and her prayer to Minos?

*Scene 4.* What is the ambiguity in the speech with which Phaedra greets Theseus? How does this speech reflect the tension between Phaedra's sense of right and her moral cowardice?

*Scene 5.* From Theseus' opening speech, does he appear as a rather old man tired out by his latest exploits, or does he seem a vigorous king still able to control a difficult situation? (Consider also Act IV, Scene 2, ll. 12–17.) Why has the scene of his exploits been changed from Hell to Epirus? How is this the result of neo-classical dramatic conventions?

*Scene 6.* How has Hippolytus' guilt over his love for Aricia affected his ability to confront his father?

ACT IV. *Scene 1.* The burden of accusing Hippolytus is placed completely on Oenone by her own design. Does the ambiguity of Phaedra's greeting and her subsequent silence indicate that she is as culpable as Oenone?

*Scene 2.* What restrains Hippolytus from denouncing Phaedra to his father? What arguments does Hippolytus use in his defense? How do these only point up the essential differences in character between father and son and therefore aggravate the conflict rather than resolve it? Is Hippolytus rash, foolish, or simply naive in thinking he can explain his innocence to his father by confessing his love for Aricia? How does Hippolytus make his exit at the end of his scene? Describe his posture, gait, and manner.

*Scene 3.* What is the dramatic function of the sudden shift of mood in Theseus' soliloquy?

*Scenes 4 and 5.* At this point the sub-plot fuses with the main plot. How is this fusion crucial for the revelation of Phaedra's character?

*Scene 6.* Is it typical of Phaedra to indulge in fantasies (ll. 12–37) such as she does about the rendezvous of Hippolytus and Aricia? What do such fantasies reveal about Phaedra? How does her fantasy of freedom and innocence contrast with the real state of affairs? In ll. 66–81 Phaedra refers again to her fatal heredity in loving criminally; but in addition to sinful passion, what must she bear as a result of her kinship to Minos? What is the final irony of Phaedra's view of her own fate as indicated in the closing couplet of this speech? Is there any justice in Phaedra's last attack on Oenone? Or it is wholly a function of her hysterical despair?

ACT V. *Scene 1.* What is the fundamental irony in ll. 23–26?

*Scenes 2–5.* Theseus is the central character in this rapid succession of scenes. Trace the course of his seeking and gaining insight into his tragic error, from the first line of Scene 2 to the last of Scene 5.

*Scene 6.* Compare Racine's handling of the report of Hippolytus' death with Euripides' and Seneca's in terms of the sequence of events, the supernatural agents, the behavior of Hippolytus, and the degree and details of violence.

*Scene 7.* How have the tragic experiences of Theseus led him to a re-evaluation of all his past exploits? How have they re-educated him to realize his own fallibility and the gods' hostility? How does the fact that he gains these insights mitigate his murder-guilt?

What strong contrast with Phaedra's previous manner and tone would you require at the end to reinforce the redeeming qualities of her final speech? Or would you have her end as she began, agonized, uncontrolled, self-dramatizing?

## DISCUSSION TOPICS

1. Find references in the play to the power of heredity in men's lives. On the basis of these references, can you generalize about the role assigned to this force in the play?

2. The Hippolytus-Aricia relationship is Racine's invention. He attempts to justify it in his preface by citing the need for some tragic flaw in Hippolytus' character in order to satisfy neo-classical canons of tragedy. The flaw would be Hippolytus' love for an enemy of his people — a not uncommon theme in seventeenth-century heroic-romantic tragedy. Evaluate the merits of this kind of theorizing as it applies to this play.

3. Provide some plausible dramatic and psychological functions for the Hippolytus-Aricia relationship. Is it the stereotyped conflict between love and honor that would be expected, and perhaps demanded, by Racine's audience? Is there any reason to suppose, especially in the light of Jeffers' later treatment of this subject, that it would be necessary to remove completely any doubts raised by the Greek version concerning homosexual tendencies in Hippolytus? What psychological pattern does this aspect of Hippolytus' character take in O'Neill's play?

4. Is there some sense in which Aricia assumes the role in Racine which Artemis plays in Euripides? Is Aricia an effective foil for Phaedra? Compare her love for Hippolytus with Phaedra's.

5. Of all the imagery, two patterns seem in particular to pervade and dominate the play: day-night, light-darkness; and ship-sea-storm. Find as many examples of such images as you can. In each case explain the relationship of the image to its local context, and then show how the whole group reinforces, and even defines, the major themes of the play.

6. If the Phaedra of Euripides is characterized by her intelligence and moral sense, and the Phaedra of Seneca by her deviousness and lust, for what qualities is Racine's Phaedra notable?

7. Speaking of the writers of the seventeenth century, Martin Turnell concludes in *The Classical Moment*: "The writers are haunted by fear of a concrete threat to society, by the fear that it may sud-

denly be swept away by the excesses of passion; and it was because Racine seemed, to his contemporaries, as indeed he was, a reckless champion of the primacy of passion that his work caused such a scandal."

With reference to the *Phaedra*, how valid was the view of Racine's contemporaries as expressed in the foregoing statement?

8. Ever since its original performance, for which Racine himself directed and rehearsed his own mistress in the title role, this play has been a vehicle for great actresses, of whom Eleonora Duse and Sarah Bernhardt are perhaps the most famous. As a result, the play has often appeared to be sharply focused on the heroine, with the other characters serving chiefly as background. However, the great twentieth-century French directer Jean-Louis Barrault has conceived of it as an "orchestrated" work requiring a specific "voice" (as in opera) and function for each character, no one of whom dominates the action. Argue the merits of these interpretations as they are related to your analysis of the play.

9. If you know French, or at least command a reading knowledge of it, compare several passages from Lowell's translation, especially where the imagery seems particularly vivid, with the original. What kinds of liberties has the translator taken? To what extent has Lowell sometimes turned the merest hint of an image in the original into a striking figure in the translation? (If your French is not strong enough for such a comparison, select another translation of the play, that by Kenneth Muir, for example, and note the differences between the two translations.)

10. Turn to the essay "The Tragedy of Passion: Racine's *Phèdre*" by Henri Peyre, in Part Three of this book. Summarize Professor Peyre's interpretation of the play and indicate where and why you agree and/or disagree with him.

11. Read Racine's preface (p. 111), which in many ways is a statement typical of neo-classical literary theory. What importance do individuals and practices from the distant past have for Racine's views? In what ways is the play made to conform to principles and values external to the play? What, according to Racine, is the proper end or function of tragedy? Do you agree with Racine's defense of tragedy based on its ability to instruct the audience and to inculcate virtue? Is there any other basis for defending drama than its didactic capabilities? How close a correlation do you find between Racine's precepts for a tragedy and his *Phaedra*?

# ROBINSON JEFFERS

ROBINSON JEFFERS (1887–1962) was born in Pittsburgh into a family which was financially able to provide him with a good formal education and intellectually capable of creating a family life conducive to mental stimulation. While abroad with his family as a young boy, Jeffers was instructed by tutors (including his father, who was well-read in theology and classical literature) and in good private schools. Shortly after returning to the United States in 1903, the family settled in California, where the young Jeffers completed his undergraduate work at Occidental College, Los Angeles, taking his degree in 1905. There followed a period of restless inquiry during which time he studied medicine, English, and forestry at several universities. At length he determined to devote his life to poetry, and a legacy in 1912 gave him financial independence and leisure to pursue his craft. In 1913 he married Una Call Kuster, whose influence on his writing he regarded as major, and moved to Carmel, California; here he built a house and the now-famous stone tower in which, overlooking the Pacific and the rugged northern Californian coast, he was to write the volumes of poetry which would win him a large following. Except for infrequent travels, Jeffers lived the remainder of his life in seclusion with his wife and twin sons, amid the lonely splendor of the Monterey coastal mountains.

His first two volumes of poems, *Flagons and Apples* (1912) and *Californians* (1916), were, as he later wrote, "preparatory exercises, to say the best for them," and attracted little notice. But *Tamar and Other Poems* (1925) enlarged and reprinted in 1926 as *Roan Stallion, Tamar and Other Poems*, brought him recognition and acclaim as a major American poet. Jeffers' standing with literary critics and fellow-poets has not, however, remained constantly high. Changes in taste are difficult to account for, but the devaluation in Jeffers' literary stock in recent years is an undisputed fact. It may be that the tone of violence, pessimism, and misanthropy in his work became too insistent or rep-

167

etitious, appearing at last as merely a device wielded for its shock value. Or perhaps Jeffers' manner was too direct and simple, too overtly didactic for a generation delighting in the subtleties and implicit meanings of Pound, Eliot, and Joyce. Whatever the reason, as the body of his work grew from the Depression through World War II, his prestige among critics seemed to decline.

Jeffers did regain critical attention and some praise as a dramatist in the forties. Although some of his longer poems have been adapted for stage presentation, his reputation as a dramatist is based on his two adaptations from Euripides: *Medea* and *The Cretan Woman*. The first, produced in 1947 with Judith Anderson as a vigorously passionate Medea, was a major event in the New York theatrical season. The play subsequently enjoyed a successful tour of other American cities. *The Cretan Woman*, praised by Eric Bentley as "one of the finest of American plays," appeared in 1954 in a volume entitled *Hungerfield and Other Poems*. It had its first stage performance in the same year at the Arena Stage in Washington, D.C., in a production directed by Basil Langdon. Though its success did not equal that of *Medea*, during 1954 it had a successful off-Broadway run at the Provincetown Playhouse in New York.

Book and drama reviews of *The Cretan Woman* can be found in *The Atlantic Monthly*, September 1954, p. 68; *Catholic World*, July 1954, pp. 270–273; *Commonweal*, September 10, 1954, p. 142; *Poetry*, July 1954, pp. 226–231; *Saturday Review of Literature*, January 16 and June 5, 1954, pp. 17 and 142; and in the book review sections of the New York *Herald Tribune*, January 24, 1954, p. 5, and the New York *Times*, January 10, 1954, p. 18. Aside from such reviews and the brief discussion by Gerald C. Weales in *American Drama Since World War II* (New York, 1962), pp. 194–195, and the appreciative comments by Horace Gregory in *The Dying Gladiators* (New York, 1961), p. 19, the play has received little critical attention. For the student wishing to study Jeffers further, three recent books may be mentioned: Radcliffe Squires, *The Loyalties of Robinson Jeffers* (Ann Arbor, Michigan, 1956); Mercedes Monjian, *Robinson Jeffers, A Study in Inhumanism* (Pittsburgh, 1958); and Frederic I. Carpenter, *Robinson Jeffers* (New York, 1962). Other articles and books are listed in *Literary History of the United States*, ed. Robert Spiller and others (New York, 1948), III, 593–595, and its *Supplement*, ed. Richard M. Ludwig (New York, 1959), p. 149; and H. C. Woodbridge, "A Bibliographical Note on Jeffers," *The American Book Collector*, X (September 1959), 15–18. A representative selection from Jeffers' work is *The Selected Poetry of Robinson Jeffers* (New York, 1938).

# The Cretan Woman

## (*Based on the* Hippolytus *of* Euripides)

❖ ❖ ❖

*Scene. In front of the house of* THESEUS *at Troezene. Old masonry; big door, two or three stone steps up to it. Left foreground, stone altar of* APHRODITE. *Wooded hills in the blue background.*

### PERSONS

> CHORUS, *three poor women of the country. Tattered clothes, colorful patches; flowers in hair, or bright ribbons.* SECOND WOMAN *carries a basket,* THIRD WOMAN *a primitive musical instrument, called here a zither.*
>
> SELENE, *Phaedra's waiting-woman; neither young nor old; demurely well dressed according to her station in life.*
>
> PHAEDRA
>
> THE GODDESS APHRODITE
>
> HIPPOLYTUS
>
> ALCYON *and* ANDROS, *friends of Hippolytus*
>
> MESSENGER
>
> THESEUS, *old, powerful, heroic in appearance*
>
> ARMED ATTENDANTS *of Theseus*

(CHORUS — *the three poor women* — *enter from the right, along a curving path that goes near the altar before it reaches the house.*)

FIRST WOMAN. We have never quite starved, thanks to some god or other: but my husband has had no work since New Year's.

SECOND WOMAN. Don't be troubled, darling. You are still young enough to attract a lover from time to time. Some kindly old gentleman . . .

FIRST WOMAN. How you talk!

169

SECOND WOMAN. A piece of fish or a pound of olives, if not a copper coin.

THIRD WOMAN. My husband has plenty of work, and well-paid too; but he drinks every penny. I don't think we could live without these hand-outs from the palace.

(*They are approaching the altar.*)

FIRST WOMAN. We have still a handful of meal in the bin . . . (*She throws her hand to her heart, staring at the altar, and steps backward.*) Oh — hush!

THIRD WOMAN (*staring and retreating*). I feel it too!

FIRST WOMAN. Something divine is here. There was such a dizziness at my heart suddenly . . .

THIRD WOMAN. I feel my eyes dazzle and my knees tremble.

SECOND WOMAN. Did you feel something? It is the great Goddess — Aphrodite — her altar.

FIRST WOMAN (*her hand at her throat*). Walk wide of it! She is angry.
There is a divine anger in this place: like the glaring eyes
Of a wild beast. Yet she is kind, we know . . .

SECOND WOMAN. What I felt — like an earthquake. Something has roused her.

(*They tiptoe at a distance around the altar and approach the door of the house.*)

FIRST WOMAN (*speaking low*). I hope all's well in this great house.
The Goddess doesn't waste wrath on poor people.

THIRD WOMAN. I am still afraid. Terribly. I feel the power . . .

SECOND WOMAN. If this great house ever falls — I wish it no evil — I wish my boy had the looting of it.

FIRST WOMAN. The door is tight shut, and I dare not knock. Make a little music on that zither of yours, Cleone. But softly.

(THIRD WOMAN *plucks the strings of her instrument; a low music is heard. The door opens partially;* SELENE *speaks through the opening.*)

SELENE (*intensely whispers*). Go away. Be quiet.

FIRST WOMAN. Our children are hungry. Have you nothing for us today?

SELENE. Be off. Let my lady sleep.

FIRST WOMAN. Not even a spoiled cake or a stale crust?

SELENE (*slips through the doorway and stands on the threshold, closing the door carefully behind her*). Will you worry me to death?
Be quiet, women.
My lady is ill; she never closed her eyes all night long,
And has just fallen asleep. She has been delirious, I think.

I have been beaten like a fluttering bird, all night and day,
In the storm of her mind.
FIRST WOMAN.                    What is it, a fever?
SELENE. And for three days she has not tasted food.
Oh, I am weary!
SECOND WOMAN. You mean there was food and she wouldn't eat it!
SELENE.                    She is like someone possessed
By an angry god.
THE WOMEN (*startled, look significantly at each other, and back
    toward the altar*). Oh!
FIRST WOMAN. What goddess?
SELENE.                    A divine power — how could I know?
There is a mystery . . .
In the delirium, in all the wild rush of her mind
There is something she avoids, something she hides. Like the mad
    waves of the sea, moulding but hiding
A sunken reef.
FIRST WOMAN. I will tell you. We felt the anger — we all felt it —
of a — certain Divine Person
When we approached this house.
SELENE.                    What Person? (FIRST WOMAN
    *shakes her head, finger to lips, afraid to speak.*) I say what god,
    or what goddess? (FIRST WOMAN *shakes her head;* SECOND WOMAN
    *points stealthily toward the altar.*)
SELENE. There? Aphrodite? That's out. Or it has nothing to do with
    my lady Phaedra.
She is loving and good, and she neglects no divinity.
And faithful to her dear husband, my lord Theseus: almost *too*
    faithful
To be a woman. Oh, what a time I've had
Trying to make her eat, cooking things . . .
SECOND WOMAN (*hungrily*). What kind of things?
SELENE. Little Cretan cakes, for instance. Brown spice, golden honey,
    a whipped egg . . .
SECOND AND THIRD WOMEN. Oh! Oh!
SELENE. I thought perhaps she was homesick for the dear island
Where she was born. That's what they eat there.
She poured the dish on the floor when it came in . . .
SECOND WOMAN. Oh!
SELENE.                    And the slaves had them. Worse than that:
Once she called for raw meat, flesh with the blood, like a northern
    barbarian: she, royal-born,
Of the most highly cultured family in Europe! and naturally

Shrieked when the mere smell . . . (*Listening*) Oh dear! Is she
calling me?
Is she awake?

> (*The door opens as she turns to it.* PHAEDRA *stands in the
> doorway; a beautiful woman wound carelessly in a cloak, hag-
> gard but royal.* SELENE *steps back from her.*)

SELENE. My lady!

> (PHAEDRA *stands bewildered, gazing at the women and the scene.
> Her lips move, but without a voice. Finally she speaks aloud,
> slowly and clearly.*)

PHAEDRA. I will not shame myself. I will not defile this house.
SELENE. What are you saying?
PHAEDRA.                                     I *will* not.
And you, be silent. You are my servant, I think. What's your name?
Selene? My poor Selene.

> (*She gazes from one to other of the women.*)

Who are all these women, Selene? So many and so very many
and such proud faces?
Are you the queens of the East that have come to comfort me?
I will die sooner.
SELENE. You are ill, my lady. You are weak, trembling with fever:
come back, dear,
Into the house.
PHAEDRA (*stepping down from the doorway*). Not at all: I will walk
in my lovely garden: up and down: and feel the warm sun . . .
(*She shudders violently.*)
They say death's bitter cold. Ah? You beautiful haughty queens,
I shall soon know.

> (SELENE *supports her as she moves forward. The women fol-
> low.*)

PHAEDRA (*to herself*). I'll tear it out of me. Tear. *Tear*, you know:
like a barbed spearhead
Out of my bitter heart. (*She shudders.*) Bitter cold: bitter heart:
my bitter longing. The bitter end.
What a queer word!
FIRST WOMAN. She is going straight toward the goddess.
SECOND WOMAN. The altar: see? Like a gray moth
To candle flame. Like a sleepwalker.
FIRST WOMAN. Let us go back to the great door, Cleone,
And see if we can get something.

> (*They return to the door, but often looking back to see what
> happens.* THIRD WOMAN *plays her zither. Presently the door*

*half opens, the basket is passed through it. Meanwhile* PHAEDRA *moves helplessly toward the altar.*)

SELENE (*trying to draw her aside*). This way, my lady: the path is better.

PHAEDRA. Let me alone, woman.
I will pray here: it seems to be a religious place. I cannot well remember . . .
There are so many gods in so many places . . .

SELENE. Do not go near it!

(*She reaches out her arms in vain;* PHAEDRA *blindly moves on. But suddenly jerks and stiffens, throwing her head back.*)

PHAEDRA (*in a strangled voice*). This is the one! (*Retreating*) The awful power
That has me in hand. The goddess of love and longing, cruel, cruel and beautiful. I may as well confess now.
The crime is not great if I will not yield. — It is my husband's son by that Amazon woman.
It is Hippolytus.
I have long loved his beauty: but now the goddess has thrown stark madness
Into my heart: *I want. I want* . . . I will never yield to it.

SELENE. You — are in love with — Hippolytus?

PHAEDRA.                                    If you call it love!
This loathsomeness in me. This disease. This burning shame.
(*Dazed, looks around.*) Why, where have my great queens of the East gone to? (*Laughing*)
They thought I meant it! They thought I didn't know a beggar-woman
From a great queen!

SELENE (*pointing*). They are at their trade yonder. (*Thoughtfully*)
Hippolytus . . .
Is not the kind of young man for any woman to love.

PHAEDRA.                                    What?

SELENE (*with slow emphasis*). He does not care for women.

PHAEDRA. I am glad of that. Why should he waste himself? Cold, proud and pure. — I'm going in, Selene.
Oh, I am tired of the light. I have a cold edge in me
That thinks it is worse than evil; it is ridiculous. — Like all our miseries! — Will you come?
— And of course you understand that this is secret; and we'll never, never, speak of it again. I shall not live long.

SELENE. You are better for having told me, dear. You walk more firmly; you have faced the truth . . .

PHAEDRA.                                 Be silent, will you!
I have not faced the truth but an idiot deception, a great false fire
   in the fog
On a phantom coast. — If decency and common shame were out
   of the question — For I love his father,
My husband Theseus. It is not even *possible* to love two men. I
   know how my heart lighted up
When I came down the plank from the Cretan ship and saw him
   — tall, fierce and tender, there waiting for me,
In the dirty-cluttered Athenian harbor among the sailors — like the
   temple of a god
On a high rock. For I *love* him, you know! Theseus I love. I have
   been fighting myself . . .
He is — not young — if any person he loves should betray him
   . . . When anyone's very young he can slide
From one lust to another, nothing is mortal: but a fierce man of
   war growing grizzle
Under the helmet: I know him: if anyone should betray him even
   in thought,
He'd hate the world. — And when I look at . . . his son . . .
   my eyes
Scald with the stupid tears. — Die . . . ah! No choice. (*Quietly*)
   I am going in to hide myself
From the great eye of the sun; I have only one god
To pray to now. Not Love, not Light, not Fortune. Death, tall and
   silent,
Has a flower in his hand; its name is Forgetfulness.
Its name — we hope — is Peace. (*They approach the door.*) Why,
   look: here are my gay-colored East-queens!
Have you had good fortune, majesties? (SECOND WOMAN *hides the
   basket behind her.*) No: show me. (*It is shown.*) Poor women:
   it is not much. May I take a crust from it?
I do not think I have eaten since dawn.
SELENE. My lady!
PHAEDRA.                 One little crumb. I have been too proud in my
   lifetime:
That's a great sin. But now I will beg of beggars, a bit of bread to
   eat. You are kind, women.
I am truly grateful.
       (*She goes into the house;* SELENE *follows, weeping. The stage
       is gradually growing darker.*)
FIRST WOMAN. The goddess has unraveled her mind. As if she were
   struck by sudden lightning

When she went near the altar.
SECOND WOMAN (*terrified*). The altar! Look!

(*The women cower and shield their eyes.* THE GODDESS APHRO-
DITE *has glided from behind a flowering bush, and leans her
hand on the altar, her spot of light increasing. She is tall and
very beautiful, marble white and marble-polished, but perhaps
pale gold hair. She has a spray of fruit-blossom in her hand,
and plays with it. She speaks as if she were alone, thinking
aloud.*)

APHRODITE. . . . So I have come down to this place,
And will work my will. I am not the least clever of the powers of
  heaven.

(*She smiles, fondling the blossom-spray.*)

I am the goddess the Greeks call Aphrodite; and the Romans will
  call me Venus; the Goddess of Love. I make the orchard-trees
Flower, and bear their sweet fruit. I make the joyful birds to mate
  in the branches. I make the man
Lean to the woman. I make the huge blue tides of the ocean follow
  the moon; I make the multitude
Of the stars in the sky to love each other, and love the earth.
  Without my saving power
They would fly apart into the horror of night. And even the atoms
  of things, the hot whirling atoms,
Would split apart: the whole world would burst apart into smoking
  dust, chaos and darkness; all life
Would gasp and perish. But love supports and preserves them:
  *my saving power.*

This is my altar,
Where men worship me. Sometimes I grant the prayers of those
  that worship me: but those who reject me
I will certainly punish. Not because I am angry: love is my nature:
  the man who rejects love
Will be certainly punished.

There is a young man here,
Hippolytus, the son of Theseus, who rejects love and disdains to
  worship me. Horses, hounds and keen hunting,
And the dear friendship of the young men, his comrades, are all
  he cares for.
(*Bitterly*) A chaste young athlete. He boasts of it:
That he will never make love to a woman nor worship

The Queen of Love. (*Pauses and smiles, admiring the blossom
spray.*) Well . . . I shall have my will of him. The young man
Will be taken care of. It is not right — nor safe — to be insolent
To a great goddess.

                   I am a little sorry for the lady Phaedra, his old
father's young wife,
Who must go down into shame and madness to make his ruin;
and I am sorry for the old hero,
Theseus, his father: but to suffer is man's fate, and they have to
bear it. We gods and goddesses
Must not be very scrupulous; we are forces of nature, vast and
inflexible, and neither mercy
Nor fear can move us. Men and women are the pawns we play
with; we work our games out on a wide chess board,
The great brown-and-green earth. (*She pauses, lifts her head and
smiles frankly at the audience.*) You are gathered here
To see the game?
                Watch, then. I have planted the agony of love in
that woman's flesh, like a poisoned sword
In her beautiful body: and I shall watch unseen, from my altar here,
the sudden accomplishment
Of my planned purpose. The day will be
Today. *This* day. Look: the dark night is passing;
The beautiful feet of dawn come over the mountain, the pale bright
feet sandaled with music,
Driving the gentle stars, like a man frightening
A flock of birds.

    (*Light increases on the sky and background, and comes slowly
downward onto the stage. Pastoral music of flutes, increasing
with the light. Meanwhile the spot of light fades from the altar;
the goddess vanishes. She leaves her blossom-spray on the altar.
The women, who have been crouching by the door of the
house, are seen clearly again. They move like persons awaking
from a night's sleep.*)

FIRST WOMAN (*pushing back her hair*). I had a terrible dream.
SECOND WOMAN. A dream? I too!
FIRST WOMAN. I dreamed that a strong flame burned on the stone . . .
    (*furtively pointing*)
The altar there . . . a white-hot column of fire,
Whirling and smoking: and little men and women were struggling
in it,
Burning alive. Frightful . . .

SECOND WOMAN. I dreamed that a great white cat — a snow-leopard —
With pitiless glaring eyes and fierce claws unsheathed
Crouched on the altar, ready to pounce . . . on me I thought . . .
Oh, how foolish it is to tell our dreams!
They bring bad luck.

THIRD WOMAN. Not mine, dear. I too had a dream, a pleasant
one.

I dreamed that a pure-white dove came down from heaven
And perched on the altar; she had a spray of white apple blossom
In her beak . . . Why, look, look! There it *is!*
Was my dream true?

FIRST WOMAN. No doubt someone left it there in the evening.

(*The door opens, and the women move backward from it.*
HIPPOLYTUS *stands in the doorway, tall and young, dressed for
hunting. He has a short heavy lance in his hand. He moves
forward on to the doorstep, his head held high, looking at the
distant country. Another young man, slender and rather effem-
inate, comes from the door.*)

HIPPOLYTUS. How beautiful the early light is; when the mist rises
from the mountain and the lark sings high. Did you bring the
heavy arrows, Alcyon?

ALCYON. Heavy and light, both quivers, for beasts and birds.
My lord Hippolytus . . .

HIPPOLYTUS. Come, come! We have no lords here.
I am Hippolytus: you are my dear friend Alcyon,
My young hunting companion.

ALCYON. I will remember, sir.

HIPPOLYTUS. And no sirs either. Indeed I think I am half a year
Younger than you are, Alcyon.

ALCYON. That's true.

(*A third young man comes into the doorway. He is burly,
somewhat older than the others, heavy-shouldered and yawning.*)

HIPPOLYTUS (*with a gesture*). Our studious friend,
Andros.

ALCYON. Studious, you call him?

HIPPOLYTUS. Of drinking-songs and merry music. Oh, he's a student.
What got you up so early, Andros?

ANDROS. The cock crowing: the tall bird that hates sleep. (*He rubs
his eyes sleepily.*)
We'll eat him, I hope, this evening.

HIPPOLYTUS (*laying his arm affectionately around* ALCYON's *shoulders*).

What shall we do with our day, Andros? Do we hunt again?
The country people say that a great wild boar
Rages in the wood yonder.

ANDROS.                                    All right, all right: I'll risk anything.
I am still drunk . . . with sleep.

HIPPOLYTUS.                                    Or shall we race
Our horses along the shore, where the careful waves
Comb the sand clean and smooth?

ANDROS. Just as you like. But what's happened to you?
Are you in love, Hippolytus? I never knew you
To lack decision.

HIPPOLYTUS. We'll hunt, then. (*He smiles at* ALCYON, *turns back to*
ANDROS.) I love my friends, Andros . . .
If they are brave and beautiful.

ANDROS. That's good. But pretty girls too,
And tenderly smiling women are worth considering. There is a kind
of an altar over there (*Pointing*)
You ought to pray to.

HIPPOLYTUS. I? No. I will worship the great Goddess of Love
. . . At a great distance. (*He makes a gay gesture of salutation.*)
All hail! Hail, Aphrodite! — The truth is:
I am a little cold toward the divinities
That are worshipped at night, with grotesque antics; the Goddess
of Witchcraft and the Goddess of Love . . .
Such a pair! Seriously, Andros:
The world is full of breeders: a couple in every bush: disgusting.
      As for me, I'll spend my passion
On wild boars and wild horses.

THIRD WOMAN.                              I see the blossom spray
Move on the altar!

SECOND WOMAN. I see the glaring eyes . . .

FIRST WOMAN. I see the fire of her anger . . .

HIPPOLYTUS. What are the women singing, Alcyon? (*Pointing*)
Those poor patched women?

ALCYON. Some uncomfortable old ballad, no doubt.
They are too far away: I can hear the voices
But not the words.

      (SELENE *comes around the corner of the house, wringing her*
      *hands.*)

SELENE. I don't know what to do! I know well enough: I must obey
      my lady's will. But I'm terribly afraid . . .

      (*She approaches the young men from behind them. They are*
      *looking at the beggar women.*)

ANDROS. Those three? They come to the house every day with their little basket; they make a music
And beg for food.

ALCYON (*to* SELENE, *seeing her behind his shoulder*). What is it?

SELENE. I have a message for my lord Hippolytus.

HIPPOLYTUS (*turns and looks down at her; speaks impatiently*). Well, What?

SELENE. From my lady Phaedra . . .
It is private, sir.

HIPPOLYTUS. Speak your message: these are my friends.

SELENE. I should have said
Secret. She is dying, sir.

HIPPOLYTUS. What!

SELENE. I think so.

HIPPOLYTUS. I am sorry that she is ill. Will you go down to the stable, my friends? I'll see you presently,
Or send for you.

ALCYON (*to* ANDROS, *as they go off together*). Bad news comes suddenly!

ANDROS. The mornings are unlucky, boy. We ought to sleep longer.

(*Exeunt.*)

HIPPOLYTUS. I knew that your lady had been ill, Selene: I never thought . . .

SELENE. It was last night sir.
She lay like one in a trance, perfectly motionless, drugged with her sorrow, not even breathing . . .

HIPPOLYTUS. What sorrow?

SELENE. I cannot tell you. (*A pause*) Suddenly — it was near dawn — she started up
With a moan like a scream. She stood like a dim white pillar in the dark room, saying "I can't die
And I can't live. Why should I bear this pain forever in silence?"
It was pitiful, sir.

HIPPOLYTUS. Certainly. But what can I do?

SELENE. She made me comb her bright hair, "to look well," she said, "When I am cold. For I am the daughter of a great man, and the wife
Of a great man." And now for hours
She has walked back and forth, back and forth, moaning. This is the restless agony that comes when death
Is at the door.

(PHAEDRA *comes into the doorway; pale, calm, self-possessed; clothed like a queen. They do not see her yet.*)

SELENE. She spoke your name once or twice.
Your father is away from home, and in his absence
You are head of the house.
HIPPOLYTUS. My father will be back tomorrow, I believe.
PHAEDRA. I do not know
Whether I have to die. I shall soon know.
SELENE. Oh, my lady . . .
PHAEDRA. You may go in, Selene.
I shall not need you. (SELENE *hesitates;* PHAEDRA *comes down and
stands on the lowest step. Speaks imperiously*) Go in!
With the other servants.
(SELENE, *wringing her hands, returns as she has come; but stops
and stands watching by the house corner.*)
HIPPOLYTUS. You have been ill, Phaedra.
PHAEDRA. I have been patient, Hippolytus.
I think we must bear our fates, and accept
What the gods send. They send sickness or health, evil or good,
passionate longing
Or the power to resist it. We have to do
What the gods choose.
HIPPOLYTUS. Not entirely, Phaedra.
We have to *suffer* what they choose: but we control our own wills
and acts
For good or evil.
PHAEDRA. But if one becomes *insane*, Hippolytus? The gods
send madness too. Madness, you know.
And we have to submit. (*Smiling suddenly*) What a bore these
philosophies are, my dear! Good and evil! We're not school-
children —
Though fairly young still.
HIPPOLYTUS. I am very glad, Phaedra,
That you are not so ill as your woman said. She pretended
You had a dying message for me.
PHAEDRA. Why. Yes. I have. I nearly
Forgot. And I am truly very near to death. It is not well with me
. . . (*Pressing her hand between her breasts*)
In here. (*A pause*) I am your father's wife, Hippolytus: I love you.
I love you very deeply.
It is my duty. — How high and angrily you turn away from me!
That haughty thrust of the chin. I've always noticed
This coldness in you: it grieved me.
HIPPOLYTUS. You are quite wrong. I am not demonstrative perhaps
. . . I have affections

Like other men; or perhaps more than others — and I am very glad
that my father chose
So good and beautiful . . .

PHAEDRA. Let us not speak any more of your father: this concerns *me.*
I only want you
To be kind to me — as I would be to you . . . (*She breaks off.*)
I think so much of my childhood lately,
In the high sacred island, in my father's palace,
Beautiful Crete: we used to play a game there called hide-'n'-seek:
there was room there: one of my sisters
Got lost in the endless echoing corridors, the famous Labyrinth:
we hunted her for hours, we could hear her crying
Pitifully, far off . . . Hunt *me,* Hippolytus!
You are a great hunter, it is your life,
Hunting wild beasts in the black woods: can't you hear me crying?
I am lost, I am lost, I am crying
Pitifully . . .

HIPPOLYTUS. I am bound to honor you: I cannot understand you
clearly.

PHAEDRA. You cannot understand?
No, you can't understand. You know the secret ways of the deer
on the mountain; you know where the wolves run;
You know on what rock over what hidden water deep in wet
woods the spotted lynx
Watches, and her wild topaz eyes
Burn like twin fires in the green twilight, flaming for blood: — but
what a woman wants . . .
No, you can't understand. You think I have something monstrous
hidden in my mind. It is not true.
Kindness I want. Only kindness: Is that a monster? Why do you
hate me, Hippolytus?
All cold, all angry.

(*He turns sharply away from her and turns back.*)

HIPPOLYTUS.      You are mistaken in that, Phaedra. I have felt
kindness . . . I will confess it:
In my manner I loved you. The way you moved, and your mind
and soul. I have thanked God that my nature
Is not . . . *inclined* toward women: or I might have loved you
Beyond what's right. Oh, I could conquer it: we know how to rule
ourselves, we have self-control; we are not leaves
Blown by the wind!
But it might have been painful.

PHAEDRA.      So I am to suffer all the pain,

And you go free! — The battle-captain of those grim warrior-
women, the breastless Amazons,
Was your mother: your father conquered her with his sword and
his spear, he clubbed her down and she hated him . . .
And he raped her. *You* were born of that horror: no wonder
You distrust love! — Listen to me. I am a civilized person, Hippoly-
tus, in exile here
Among savages: the fierce little cutthroat tribes of Greece, feudists
and killers. Lovers of tragedy! — We Cretans
Love light and laughter. We like things refined and brilliant; bright
games, gay music, brave colors. We have girl-acrobats
Who ride wild bulls, diving over the horns, blithe on the snout of
death: *our* courage, that hates no person.
— I tell you, Hippolytus, there are two heads of civilization on
earth: Egypt and Crete: but holy Egypt
Is so old, so old, stone-stiff and pious
In the petrified desert: we Cretans
Can be passionate still. We have hot blood, we love beauty, we
hate bigotry.
We know that good and evil and virtue and sin — are words, tired
words: but *love* is more beautiful than sunrise
Or the heart of a rose: the love of man and woman can be more
beautiful than the great-throated nightingale
Her heartbreak song: when all the leaves of the trees hang still to
hear it, and the stars in hushed heaven
Hold their breath and lean lower. — Ours could be. *Our* love could
be.

(*The three women have come near them to listen.*)

HIPPOLYTUS. I say keep your tongue carefully.
If you have evil thoughts do not speak them. (*Pointing*) These
peering creatures have ears
Under their hair.
PHAEDRA (*staring with dazed eyes at the women*). There are people
here? Why — *who cares?* — not I. Listen, women:
I have put all my life on this little hope — and I think I am losing
it —
I am no doubt a dead woman talking to you: Theseus will kill me
If this man will not — but I am not ashamed of this little hope, I
will not hide it, I will sing it aloud
From the tops of the houses . . .
HIPPOLYTUS. Have you gone mad?

(SELENE, *who has been watching, runs to her.*)

FIRST WOMAN.                     We are your friends, my lady.
What wrong is done you?
PHAEDRA (*to* HIPPOLYTUS, *ignoring the women*). Mad — if you like —
     more or less — But not so mad as a rabid dog in the dog-days,
     in the white of summer,
     Slavering and snapping . . . And not so mad as my mother who
     went insane with love of a black bull,
     That snuffling horror: — I know well enough
     All the shames of my race; the slaves used to whisper in the dark
     arches . . . There is a goddess, Hippolytus,
     A terrible one: she rides me . . .
SELENE (*catching her arm, terrified for her*). Hush! Hush!
PHAEDRA.                          Merciless, with quirt and spur . . .
     She is like a leopard
     That has leaped on a deer: the great hooked claws drag through
     the tender flesh: the young doe staggers
     Under that weight of pain, sobbing and running — Forgive me: I
     do not want to seem pitiful —
     She is called the Goddess of Love, that merciless one — I cannot
     help myself — forgive me . . . (*Sobs, hiding her face from him.*)
SELENE. My lady! For God's sake, hush!
HIPPOLYTUS. Let her go on, woman. Let her speak it all out, all her
     stark madness:
     And I shall be proved innocent. There are witnesses . . .
     Now: and if the woman wants to destroy herself, let her do so.
     My patience has reached an end.
PHAEDRA. *Be careful!* You are not perfectly sure of being proved
     innocent, Hippolytus.
     A black thought crossed my mind — like a vulture
     Across a window — but I'm not mean enough —
     Oh, be at rest, fear nothing. I have degraded myself already
     Beyond all bounds.
SELENE (*her arm around her*). Come into the house, dear. My darling
     . . . my precious . . . (PHAEDRA *shakes her off.*)
PHAEDRA. Keep off me, will you! (*Raises her head proudly*) As I
     was saying, this goddess —
     I was speaking of one of the powers of Heaven, I think? Some
     divine one . . . My mind goes black suddenly
     From time to time . . . (*She draws her hand over her eyes.*) This
     goddess, the Cyprian, the sweetly smiling white Aphrodite —
     She was born of the sea, and the sea's treachery
     Is in her blood: she has broken my little boat — no more of that!
     — she has the sea's sucking whirlpool

In her white body: *all* women have: it wants . . . it wants . . .
As for me:
I am a little mad, as you say. — You breed horses, Hippolytus?
HIPPOLYTUS (*turning from her*). Observe her, women.
And if you are called in witness, report it. She is clearly insane; not
responsible; not to be blamed.
As if some raging alien spirit overpowered her: demon or goddess:
Outside her own pure heart. You know the taint in the blood —
curse, if you call it so —
On the royal family of rich Crete —
PHAEDRA.                                          This man so hates me
That he digs up my father and my mother and my ancestors! (*To*
HIPPOLYTUS) You have a good lance there:
That boar-spear with the great metal head, your toy that you play
with: will you do me a kindness, fellow?
You say you are not unfriendly to me — Stick it into me! (*She
kneels, tears at the cloth on her breast.*)
Here! Here I say. Slake your hate and my love!
HIPPOLYTUS (*gravely, with pity*). You see her, women?
PHAEDRA (*still kneels, her body and head arched backward*). You'd
better strike: I am growing dangerous.
I am growing to be a poison . . . Oh, my dear, my dear, have pity
on me! I am not hateful yet.
My skin is white, I think, and my mind still clean, and my body
stainless: at least
It is not ugly: my women have sometimes called me beautiful.
Slaves' flattery: ah? Well, not much worse
Than a deer in the woods, or one of those wildcats
You hunt so avidly . . .
This arm seems round and smooth, and the throat's fair enough;
and the clear shoulders: I have no blemish I know of . . .
I am the humblest person alive, Hippolytus,
Here, praying to you.
HIPPOLYTUS (*relenting*). Let me say this, Phaedra,
And then be silent forever: it is true you are very beautiful; and I
could love you . . . in spite of nature . . .
But not of honor. That holds me.
PHAEDRA (*embraces his knees*). I am so thirsty for you, Hippolytus!
I am burning alive. Forget your father: forget your honor and
mine, what do they matter? Forget
Your impediment of nature. I have put life and death on this throw
of the dice: and degraded myself . . .

I am not insane. I have loved you a long while. I have degraded
   myself . . .
Take this degraded body here kneeling to you. Do what you like:
   love it or kill it. Oh . . .
Lift it up: love it! (*She embraces his knees.*)
HIPPOLYTUS. Shameless: take your hands from me. Stand up, will you!
   It is not my intention
To be made publicly ridiculous. (*To* SELENE) You there! Uncoil
   your madwoman: she wearies me.
Nurse her into the house.
PHAEDRA (*standing up*). I do not need
Anyone's help. And I am not a weeper, either. I've played my life
   and lost, and here's death —
Without a tear. — Very well: go back then:
And hunt your beasts. Ride with your laughing boys. Run your
   fleet horses. It is possible some pointed thing
Will fly after you.
HIPPOLYTUS (*turning to go*). There is nothing so unclean as madness.
   (*Turning back to* SELENE) Watch your mistress carefully:
Not to do herself harm. (*He goes toward the rear.*)
PHAEDRA. Me? Let him watch his own disaster!
ANDROS (*comes from the trees in the distance; stops at sight of* HIP-
   POLYTUS). Oh, are you coming?
We waited long for you: horse, hound and man too. Is the lady
   really so ill?
HIPPOLYTUS (*shaking his head, joining him*). Very ill, very ill.
Ask me no questions, Andros: the best is silence.
I am sorry for her. — Are Alcyon and the others there?
ANDROS. Fussing with dog leashes. . . .
   (*They go out together.*)
   (*Meanwhile* PHAEDRA *has fallen on the door steps, in spite of*
   SELENE *supporting her. The women stand watching.*)
FIRST WOMAN. This is the worst thing that can happen to a woman:
   when love meets contempt.
   (PHAEDRA's *body jerks as under a whiplash. She half raises her-
   self.*)
PHAEDRA. Contempt. I know: contempt —
Is for the fallen. Not alone I will fall.
SECOND WOMAN. To give gold for sawdust, and love for light ashes —
   Is woman's fate. To give her dear fragrance for a dog-bite . . .
PHAEDRA (*sitting on the step*). He said: "Keep your hands off me."

(*Looking at her hands*) Rejected: you pale things: I will send
rougher hands
Than these poor lilies. (*She relapses on the step, face down, sobbing.*) Ah, darkness, darkness, darkness . . .
SELENE. Hush, child. Oh, hush . . .
THIRD WOMAN. While the young man goes laughing with his companions.
PHAEDRA. He will not last long! — What are *you?* Spirits tormenting
me?
There was a kind of hypocrisy about my passion before. I could
see through it more or less.
Now it's deep, thick . . . I have quite lost myself. (*Looks down
at herself. Feels herself with her hands.*) This thing: this pitiful
flesh: is this Phaedra,
The daughter of the wise ruler of famous Crete?
Or a scorned whore? (*Stroking her hand down her arm.*) Oh,
here's something. (*She takes off her bracelet and flings it.*)
Break it in three pieces.
THE WOMEN (*pick up the heavy bracelet, show it to each other*).
Gold, gold. We are rich!

(*A man running dashes onto the stage, speaks breathlessly.*)

MESSENGER. He sent me ahead. I ran faster than the horses.
I heard the wind of their breath blowing behind me.
Is all well here?

(*The women gape at him in frightened silence.* PHAEDRA *in her
black meditation ignores him.*)

PHAEDRA (*her hands tearing at each other*). A refused whore!

(*She gathers herself; stands up, cool and self-possessed.*)

What did you say? Certainly all is well here. And my lord Theseus
Is well, I hope?
MESSENGER (*who did not see her at first*). Oh — Very well, Madam:
but much troubled
By the tone of the oracle.
PHAEDRA (*calmly*). The oracle — I remember. He went to consult it.
MESSENGER. And it answered . . .
PHAEDRA. You needn't tell me, Messenger. My lord will tell me.
MESSENGER.                              It answered strangely.
It said that his house was burning, he must hasten home!
PHAEDRA (*easily*). Did it so? Very interesting.
But you can see there's no fire here: no sort of trouble.
Take the man into the house, Selene. Let him eat and drink.

MESSENGER. No, no. My thanks, Madam. I must race back
  To say all's well. (*He goes.*)
PHAEDRA (*instantly dismissing him from her mind, relapsing into black
  meditation*). A scorned importunate whore: refused
  And despised: kneeling, hugging his thighs: let her be hanged.
  —And how his young men will laugh!
  Between the minstrel's song and the juggler's tricks,
  Over the wine.
FIRST WOMAN. Truly his house was burning, and the god knew it.
  But that fire's out.
PHAEDRA.                 Is it out? A worse burns then.
  A deadlier fire.
SELENE.                 No: on the kindly hearth:
  The warm life of the house.
PHAEDRA.                 From the hearth to the roof-beams
  This red fire leaps.
SELENE. No. No. No! Women: Will you hear me? I pray you listen
  to me.
  You are friendly to my dear mistress: you take her bounty: I think
  you love her: promise me on oath, women,
  Never to speak of what you have seen and heard here, neither to
  my lord Theseus nor any other:
  Your husbands, your children: not to any acquaintance: never to
  whisper it. For gossip and scandalous tongues are worse
  Than fire in the roof.
THE WOMEN.                 I promise. Oh, I swear it.
SELENE. My mistress is pure and good: you know that.
  Our silence will make her well. This wound will heal,
  This black storm will blow over.
PHAEDRA.                 Fool!
SECOND WOMAN. Truly it will, Phaedra! For time, that eats up our
  pleasures,
  Also mends pain.
FIIRST WOMAN.          A man crossing the mountain
  Feels the cold like a knife
  Severing his bones; he sees black abysses
  Infinitely far down;
  And here the jagged rock-heads, the death-white
  Teeth of snow on the rock.
  He shudders in the knife-keen wind.
  It is death, he thinks.
PHAEDRA.                 I do not *think:* I *know*
  That death is here at hand: but not a clean death.

SECOND WOMAN. From the wide plain looking backward, from the
rich plain
The traveler: his mountain
Hangs like a hyacinth bell,
Purple on the pale sky:
The peaks of the rock are like a flower's petals
And the color joyful . . .

PHAEDRA. I am preparing a thing that will *not* be joyful.

FIRST WOMAN. Would God that I knew the joy
Of driving through pleasant valleys in a green land,
As Theseus does: the horses lean on the yoke,
They snort the storm of their breath:
On one side of the way is clear water welling
Cold under willows; behind me white dust
Floats in the sun like a flag;
On the other side of the way is perhaps a hill
Clothed with green vineyard,
The little wax-yellow flowers and the curling tendrils
Like a girl's hair: on high the temple of a god
Lifts honey-colored marble above green leaves.
Happy are the hours there . . .

PHAEDRA.                              The woman sees happiness.
But as for me, I see shame, I see corpses.

SECOND WOMAN. The girls and young men go up
Singing together, carrying the lamb and the golden corn,
The broad green leaves and the grape clusters,
To the beauty of the god in the blue-veiled autumn . . .

PHAEDRA. I say, be quiet! — How can I endure myself?
He knew me for what I am, and he did rightly
When he despised me. False to the bone. I think too much,
And lose myself among the pictures my mind makes. The core of
me — the — what they call heart —
Hidden and I cannot find it. I feel my mind swooping, I feel the
awful storms of brute instinct,
And between — nothing. — But this I know: I will not betray him.
I will not be false. — As for you, women, I pray you — when
Theseus comes —
Be silent. Cover up my folly. Have mercy on me. Let my name
be remembered
As one who was chaste and faithful, never looking aside from her
one man, and died young,
For no particular reason . . .

SELENE (*frightened*). He is coming now, my lady! Listen: they are
here.

We must be ready, we must smile and be quiet: that's woman's
happiness.

PHAEDRA. Woman's . . . happiness!

SELENE. I pray you, my lady!

PHAEDRA. Let him come.

FIRST WOMAN (*to* PHAEDRA). Silence is God's best gift.

(THESEUS, *with armed attendants, comes rapidly forward.*)

SECOND WOMAN. I will be silent . . .

SELENE. Lock up your lips, women!

THESEUS (*looking at the house; to his nearest attendant*). The house
has no damage at all; nor the roof either.

No smoke; no wailing. What did that priestess mean? (*Suspiciously*)

Why are you crowding the door, women?

> (*They move aside, in silence.* THESEUS *sees* PHAEDRA, *sitting on
> the step, staring at him.*)

Is it well with you, Phaedra?

> (*She stares at him, without moving.*)

SELENE (*stammering with nervousness*). She has been a little ill. I
brought her out for the sun . . .

It is no great disorder, my lord: your absence

Has made her sad.

THESEUS. I galloped home at the full stretch of the horses, my charioteer

Whipping and shouting: for the oracle

Sang that my house was fired. What has happened?

SELENE. Nothing, sir.

THESEUS. Why does she not speak then?

SELENE. Nothing whatever, sir —

Except my lady's small illness.

PHAEDRA (*standing up, clear and bitter*). She lies, Theseus.

THESEUS. What?

PHAEDRA.        Evil *has* happened.

The worst and shamefullest.

SELENE (*rapidly*). She is full of fever, my lord: her mind wanders
and boggles like a lost bird . . .

PHAEDRA. What a desperate liar! — But it is not her fault: I'll not let
any servant of mine

Be whipped for *me.* I say the woman is an open liar; but trying to
protect me
From your just wrath. My lord, a common sweating peasant weary
at the plow
Would not endure it.

SELENE.                        Her delirium of fever . . .

PHAEDRA.                                              Silent, you!
Pray to God in your heart.

THESEUS. I am not a patient man. I hate the female herd, that chatters
like monkeys
And never speaks.

PHAEDRA.        Without chattering, my lord: nothing shrill, no outcry:
Coldly and clearly: — Your bed is defiled and your house broken.
If I should bear a child,
It will not be yours.

(THESEUS *draws his short sword half way from the scabbard,
and slams it back again; staggering with rage.*)

THESEUS. Go on. Speak.

PHAEDRA.                        This defiled body
Is waiting for you to scour it with sudden death.

THESEUS. Go on. Speak more.

PHAEDRA.                        Its woman-weakness met violence
In the bed of shame.

THESEUS. So you say. They all say that. — Who was the man?

PHAEDRA. It is true, my lord.
See on my throat the marks of his strangling hands.

THESEUS. I do not see them. (*Shouts*) Who?

PHAEDRA. A man well known to you.
Now give me death, Theseus.

THESEUS. Presently perhaps. Who was it? (*No answer*) Who?

PHAEDRA. I will not tell you.

THESEUS.                        White fool —
Will you drive me mad?

PHAEDRA. No. *He* was mad, I think. *I* will be silent.
I will not drive you mad: you'd run stark raving
If I answered you.

THESEUS. You'll answer, you'll answer. You cheap toy — broken
trinket — mud-trampled rose-petal —
I have to kill a swine: *what* swine?

PHAEDRA. You have killed too many men, Theseus, famous for blood.
Your hands stink of it.
I noticed that.

THESEUS (*shouting*). Who was it?

PHAEDRA.          No matter how well you wash them, Theseus.
— I'd sent my woman away
Because her breathing made a noise in the night. I was alone,
Naked in bed, half asleep: the door moved on its well-oiled hinges,
    and that young man
Stood in the room.

THESEUS (*black with rage, controlling himself*). Patience. Patience.

PHAEDRA. I saw him well: there was a night-lamp:
And he told me his name. He said that something deadly had
    happened, and he had to speak to me.
I knew him well, Theseus; I perfectly trusted him;
I let him come near the bed. When your wrath cools
I'll speak his name. It is one you trust. He held a knife at my
    throat —
And . . . did . . . his will. I was too weak and cowardly to cry to
the slaves. I pled with him.
I wept and pled: saying, "Though my life and honor are nothing to
    you,
Will you dishonor your father Theseus, whose wife I am?"

THESEUS (*shouting*). Agh! — No. — What were you saying?
What did you say, Phaedra?

PHAEDRA. That my prayer was vain. He was like a beast, like a wild
    beast.
(*Coldly*) That is his nature.

THESEUS (*drawing his sword*). You dirty leavings. — You say that my
    son Hippolytus —

PHAEDRA. I will not send the father against the son.
I never named him.

THESEUS. — took you by force? Raped you? Oh, lying fool —
Tell me something true once!

SELENE (*screams suddenly*). Ai! (*Sobs*) Oh, oh . . .

PHAEDRA (*coldly watching her*). These women know it.
They will probably lie, to cover it.

THESEUS. Who caught you at it? Who? That woman? (*Indicating*
    SELENE)
You'd not tell but for that.

PHAEDRA. No one. They slept. But I being mad with grief and my
    life is death —
I told them.

FIRST WOMAN. We saw her making lamentation, sir.
This morning. Weeping and crying.

THESEUS.                              You repented — ah?

You tempted him, you perverted him, handled him, slavered on
  him —
And you repented. (*Pause*) I don't believe it.
Somebody caught you at it: you wept for *that*. (*Covering his eyes*)
  — My own loved son.

FIRST WOMAN. Oh, she is not to blame, sir, not to blame; guiltless. It
  was her misfortune
But not her crime.

THESEUS.              Call it *misfortune* do you, foul-mouth?
  You prim-tongued fool! Misfortune! God help me hold myself!
I want to go stabbing, stabbing, stabbing . . . (*To his nearest atten-
  dant*) Bring him in!

ATTENDANT. What, sir?

THESEUS. Bring him in. He is either hunting or about the place somewhere . . .

                    (PHAEDRA *smiles a little.*)

THESEUS (*grimly self-controlled*). I will not enter my house
Until I've cleaned it.

ATTENDANT. We'll find him, sir. (*He and another go out.*)

THESEUS. Take men with you. Bind him if he resists.
But wound him not.

ANOTHER ATTENDANT (*an old man*). Take heed, my lord, not to judge
  rashly. We know
That all women are liars.

THESEUS. Not to their own hurt.

OLD ATTENDANT. Even to their own hurt, my lord.
And your son, we know, dislikes women . . .

THESEUS. Therefore he did it.
Pure hatred. Pure evil.

PHAEDRA (*almost brightly*). How many people have you killed in all
  your life, Theseus? Three hundred?
With your own hand?
That's what they call a hero. That's what they call a great man.
  Kill, kill, and kill:
They put up statues. But spare your son, Theseus,
Though he is vicious: a beast, an evil beast: you twisted his name
  out of me . . .

THESEUS (*ignores her; sheathes his sword; his eyes rove about the
  scene; fasten on* THIRD WOMAN). You with the zither.
You patched thing. Make music.

THIRD WOMAN. Me, sir? It is vile music, sir, dog's music —
And we are so broken with the woe of this house . . .

THESEUS (*both hands on his temples, his body tense and writhing*).
Play!
PHAEDRA. It will not heal your wound, Theseus.
Only blood heals . . . *your* wounds.
THESEUS. It will pass the interval. You have half an hour, I believe,
of life yet.
Before your breath stops.
PHAEDRA (*smiling*). But I *wish* to die, Theseus!

(THIRD WOMAN *begins to play*.)

SECOND WOMAN. I am terrified . . .

(*She sings — or rather speaks, but with consciousness of the
music*.)

What is best for a man?
For our human half-darkness under the stars
Is full of evil; grief after grief comes in,
Like wolves leaping the fold-wall . . .
FIRST WOMAN. Silence is best.
SECOND WOMAN. Grief after grief,
Like waves flooding the sea-wall: but wealth could stop them.
A golden dyke: a rich man can buy security . . .
FIRST WOMAN. Then why do the great kings die by violence?
SECOND WOMAN. Pure love is best.
Let pure love be my heaven, and fair love my fortress . . .
FIRST WOMAN. But if you love someone, death comes and takes him.
THIRD WOMAN (*striking the zither strings with her hand, breaking off
the music*). Then death is best!
FIRST WOMAN.                          Death is good in his time.
Silence is best.
THIRD WOMAN. An old old song, my lord. It doesn't make sense —
And I can't help it.
PHAEDRA. See how you've calmed him, women! He has bitten his
lips through, the beard's blood-lined,
Black-red on the grim gray. Why — it's the gnashing muzzle of a
wild boar! Perhaps Hippolytus
Would like to hunt it! — I warned you, Theseus,
Music will never soothe: you didn't even hear them. What your
wound wants for cure is somebody's blood.
Sword's joy: a turn of the wrist —
And the flashing red river.
THESEUS. I have been thinking so. (*He moves threateningly toward
her*.)

PHAEDRA. The joy of stabbing . . .

> (*He comes to her, hand on sword-hilt.*)

— Me? No! Not me, Theseus! (*She shrinks backward from him.*)
Not me! You are grim, dearest, but you are just. All men have said
That you are just . . . (*She kneels to him.*)

THESEUS. What a harlot's face you have!

PHAEDRA. Now my life hangs on a hair — consider yet,
Would I — or any woman — willingly embroil myself with a young
man well known
Averse from women? Think what you like of me — dearest, don't
strike! —
I am not such a fool. Hippolytus is that sex — higher or lower, I
know not, but strange —
That loves its own . . .

THESEUS. I'll ask him when he comes. I see you have considered him.

PHAEDRA. Not till you forced me to!

THESEUS. It doesn't matter. You'll not be alive when he comes. As
you say:
It will be a great pleasure. I know that my son Hippolytus
Is pure and true.

PHAEDRA (*standing up*). Very well. I beg no more. How they'll laugh
in Athens!
How they'll whisper it here: "That poor Cretan woman!
The son wronged her and the father killed her, though innocent.
That's what she gets for marrying a deadly Greek!"
I have a strange horror of that gray blade, Theseus: but here's my
throat. I am not a coward.

THESEUS (*sighing*). You have a few minutes yet: I'll hear him first.
I am just, as you say.
I have lived with some honor and respect. I have led the people
and been true to my friends, and done — they tell me —
Valiantly once or twice. I have been thought of as a man who
could — at least —
Guard his own gear . . . But old age comes, old age comes,
And flies defile us. — Presently you will hear such a slapping of
flies around here — but not Hippolytus,
Not for your weight in lies . . . Oh Phaedra, Phaedra!
This is a dream, not truth. You will wake up and say: "What was
I saying?
It was a dream." . . . I know you are not false — when I first saw
you — those wide-open shieldless eyes
Full of trust, brave little circles of tender sky — and the soft mouth
that knew not

Whether to laugh or weep, and did both at once — I loved you,
   Phaedra, forever.
You were like a small child: a beautiful courageous child . . . (*He
   lifts his head to listen.*) Are they coming now? Tell them it's
   over.
It was a dream. — But truly, if my son hurt you . . .
He shall not live.

> (HIPPOLYTUS *enters. He moves freely and with confidence.
> But the two guards, walking slightly behind him on each side,
> look like jailers rather than attendants.*)

PHAEDRA (*clearly and carefully*). Do you still despise me, Hippolytus?
HIPPOLYTUS (*ignoring her*). You have come home, Father: I am glad
   of that.
But why in anger? — At least your honest idiots, the axemen here,
Seem to believe so . . . Apparently they are right for once. I see
   the black
Vein on your brow . . .
THESEUS (*eyes him gravely in silence; turns to* PHAEDRA). Is this the
   man?
PHAEDRA. No.
THESEUS. What do you mean — no? That you lied? (*Trembling
   with anger again*)
And now confess it? I will put the matter more plainly:
Is this the man who rode you last night?
HIPPOLYTUS. Are you raving mad, Father!
THESEUS. *Someone* is going to die. Not you, perhaps.
PHAEDRA (*to* THESEUS). I have some nerves of decency still: though
   you don't think so. I will not talk your sword
Into the belly of your son.
THESEUS (*his hand on the hilt*). Into your own then?
PHAEDRA (*calmly*). I am such a coward, Theseus. If I hadn't been a
   coward
I'd have screamed and got help: but he was over me
Like a wild beast. Don't strike, dear! It was he: yes: Hippolytus.
   Don't strike!
THESEUS. Do they say I am not a patient man?
Fools! Cold as stone. (*To* HIPPOLYTUS) Why were you not hunt-
   ing today?
HIPPOLYTUS. She lies, Father: that's clear enough:
Either out of insanity or shaking terror. Shut her up: and tell me
   clearly what monstrous thing
I am accused of.

THESEUS. A crime. You are my son, God help me. A crime
that only iron-in-the-guts
Cures. — Why were you not hunting today?
HIPPOLYTUS. Because I did not choose to. I was somewhat . . . de-
jected.
I was at the stable: some of the young men went . . .
THESEUS. Dejected?
HIPPOLYTUS. Sad; tired; sorrowful . . .
THESEUS. Oh! Your exertions
In the night tired you? (*Moaning with rage*) Oh, Oh . . . You
. . . blond pillar of righteousness! Filth: filth: filth!
God strike you dead!
HIPPOLYTUS. God is more just, I hope
Than you are. This is blind nonsense. Have you ever known me
To follow women? As for being . . . tired: a person whom I
once loved and honored had done
A shameful thing. It grieved me.
THESEUS. What person?
HIPPOLYTUS. I cannot tell you, Father: I am not a tale-bearer.
The thing failed, and is finished.
PHAEDRA. Do you think it is *finished*, Hippolytus? *Love* has an end:
but deep hate has no floor,
It falls forever. — I say that he had neither shame nor mercy,
Theseus.
He choked me with his claws while his body soiled me.
You take it quietly. It is true you are growing old, Theseus.
THESEUS. Shut your mouth.
PHAEDRA. It is right for a violent man to be very careful
Before he acts.
HIPPOLYTUS (*to* PHAEDRA). I understand you now: clearly. There is
not one hair of difference between the extremes
Of love and hate. They are the same thing, one identical fury. —
This woman is insane, Father.
She is unspeakably false.
PHAEDRA (*quietly and sadly*). I loved you once, Hippolytus.
HIPPOLYTUS. Yes? *I will tell him.*
PHAEDRA. And you, pitiless,
Came in and robbed me! I pray you, Theseus, to kill me now. You
are a man of blood, as all know.
They say shame dies in the grave. But as for the young man, al-
though he is evil, and has earned sudden darkness:
He is your son, remember.
THESEUS (*scowling with doubt, looking from one to the other, like a*

*tormented bull*). The worse. But something holds my hand . . .

PHAEDRA. He was right, then. He said,
"My father is an old man and will hardly care."

THESEUS (*sword in hand*). Ah . . .

(*He takes a step toward* HIPPOLYTUS, *but turns to look when* ALCYON *cries out.*)

ALCYON (*has entered in wild haste, cries loudly*). What are they doing to you, Hippolytus?

HIPPOLYTUS. Nothing . . . A little matter of life and death, my dear. And honor, as they say — if anything like that is left in this foul pit. You cannot help me. But wait, for these women may.

ALCYON (*struggling to come near him, but held back by the guards*). I'll serve you with my life or my death: that much I know.

HIPPOLYTUS (*smiles at him, then speaks to the women*). Women: you were here this morning, when . . . (*Pointing*) she there Displayed her shame. I was sorry for it. But now you can bear true witness. The woman made a shrill noise, Pitiful and indecent . . . no more of that. Did she say at any time she had suffered violence? From me or anyone?

(*They stand silent, gaping at him.*)

THESEUS. Answer!

FIRST WOMAN (*after a moment*). Silence is best.

THESEUS. You gaudy dummies, who bribed you? (*To* ATTENDANT) Bring whips!

SECOND WOMAN (*to* HIPPOLYTUS). She begged you to kill her, sir.

HIPPOLYTUS. Did she accuse me of anything?

SECOND WOMAN. She said, "hard-hearted" —

PHAEDRA. He had come to my bed like a wild beast in rut: I said, *hard-hearted!* Tell him the truth, women, the truth at last: that I said He had destroyed me — that I said he had come . . .

THESEUS. Silent! Let *them* talk.

PHAEDRA. You then, Selene! You know well Whether he had me or not, by force and violence, In the awful night.

SELENE.                And from that moment You have never ceased weeping. Oh, it was cruel! Oh, it was monstrous! I'd gladly cut out his eyes With my own hand.

THESEUS (*gravely, moving toward his son*). You have heard your death sung, Hippolytus.

ALCYON (*screaming*). It is a lie! Stop! She lies. She'll say anything
To please her mistress . . .
SECOND WOMAN. What the woman says is true, sir,
God's frightful truth. Although I begged her to cover it up with
silence — there is no crime in silence . . .
FIRST WOMAN. It is all true.
ALCYON (*screaming*). Stop! Kill her: kill Phaedra: *she* is the one . . .
(*Meanwhile* THESEUS *has come slowly and fatally to* HIPPO-
LYTUS.)
HIPPOLYTUS (*holding out his hand to ward off the sword; speaking
quietly*). They're making a fool of you, Father. — It is bitter to
be killed innocent, by women's lies.
THESEUS. You model of chastity!
(*He shifts his sword with skilled suddenness, drives it under
the breastbone, from below upward.*)
HIPPOLYTUS (*bending forward and falling*). Fool. Oh . . .
(*Shocked silence; then* PHAEDRA'S *clear voice.*)
PHAEDRA. Do you still despise me, Hippolytus?
HIPPOLYTUS (*struggling for breath*). Stand off . . . Give me room
to die in . . . (*He raises his head and shoulders from the ground:
a gasping shout*) Yes! I despise you. (*Turns painfully in silence;
looks up at* THESEUS *and says tenderly*) My poor father. (*He
dies.*)
PHAEDRA (*like a bewildered child, quietly, her hand to her mouth*).
But I love him, Theseus!
ALCYON (*struggling with a guard*). Let me pass. Let me pass, fellow.
Let me at him.
THE GUARD. Watch out: he has a knife . . . (*A yelp of pain*) Ow!
ANOTHER GUARD (*behind* ALCYON, *brutal and unexcited*). Kill: huh?
(*He stabs him from behind;* ALCYON *drops silently.*) Woman-
boy, huh? Lie down.
(*No one gives attention to this by-play.* THESEUS *stands look-
ing down at his son.*)
PHAEDRA. But I'd have died for you, Hippolytus! Gladly have died
for you. I fought myself —
I tried to save you . . .
He was your best, old man: and so you have killed him. The best
youth in all Greece, beautiful Hippolytus,
Is slain for *me*. I lied, you understand: he was clear: he was pure
as crystal: and any fool but you, Theseus,
Would have perceived it. I ran mad for love of him; I prayed to
him, I pursued him, I hugged his knees —

Here, before these women, in the eyes of the morning —
And he refused me. He loved me perhaps a little: but he was pure
And honorable: so I had you kill him.
It was you I hated, Theseus: an old gray manslayer; an old gray
wolf, stinking of blood, destroyer
Of generations. For fifty years you have been killing the sons of
men — *and now your own son.*

THESEUS (*looks vaguely up at her*). Pray you, be quiet . . . (*He
looks down again*).

PHAEDRA. You understand you have killed him, Theseus?
Your son is dead: he will never rise again.
Your beautiful son. *You* killed him. Now *me*, I hope.

(*His face is contorted; he shudders; finally looks up.*)

THESEUS. You yap at me like a sick hound, and I cannot hear you.

PHAEDRA. I see that you understand though, Theseus. (*A pause*)
Dull, and a man of blood, easy to fool . . . (*A pause*)
Your lovely son. (*A pause*) Hold all the agony you can. Stuff it
into your heart. *Mine's* full. (*A pause*) Still silent?
You will soon burst, Theseus. (*A pause*) Perhaps you will kill
yourself. (*A pause*) Me first, you know.

THESEUS (*looks at her; rubs his eyes*). I have some blood in them . . .
Dull, and a man of blood . . . Some god came into me;
Some evil god. (*He looks down again.*)

PHAEDRA. How cowardly it is in men, to say
That a god did it! *You* did it. (*A pause*) And *I* . . . deluded you.
(*A pause*) Surely you can do it again? For me? (*She comes near
him, pulling open the clothing at her breast.*) See: deep! (*He
gives her no attention.*)
Not yet? — I am almost a little sorry for us. — I wish the long
black ship that brought me here
Had split on the sharp reef in the raging storm. I wish my bones
were churning unfleshed forever,
White in black water, out of the sun, wide-washed, far-apart, scat-
tered; and slime-running seaweed —
Those cold black leaves — grew where my blood runs — where my
heart beats — here in the ribs — here —
Where your red sword should rest soon. — You were so beautiful,
Hippolytus, you were so beautiful!
I sought you as a brown moth seeks the bright flame: or as the
young darkness
Loves the evening star: or a starved beast his prey. I was that
beast. On my knees I hunted you.
You have died: who can live? (*She has approached the steps, and*

*now goes up into the doorway; gazes back at the body.*) I loved
you so.

THESEUS. The woman makes a great noise
And it means nothing.

PHAEDRA. Are you beginning at last to understand? Are you beginning
To *feel* now, Theseus?

THESEUS (*on one knee by the body; shakes his head in bewilderment*).
I loved him . . .

PHAEDRA (*pityingly*). I know. I counted on it.
How wretched I should be if I alone wept! — Stay there and watch
him for me, Selene,
And tell me all that he does: his groans, words, grief, outcries and
so forth —
And whether he goes wild or not. Watch very carefully:
For he — my husband — is a great man, powerful and pitiable; the
glory of Athens and Greece,
Famous into far Asia: and I have almost come to the Greek opin-
ion: that there is nothing
Nobler than a great man in his mortal grief. Or . . . (*She begins
to weep*) a loved beautiful youth . . .
Suddenly slain. Oh . . . (*She raises her head, speaks proudly*)
These are the agonies that men remember forever; imperishable
jewels of the age; and their mighty spirits
In spite of God live on. As for me — me too perhaps they'll re-
member — to spit on.
I can't say that I care. As for you, Theseus — (*She smiles brightly
at him, speaks slowly and lovingly*)
Come soon, dear. What else can you do? Weep, and then come.

(*She stands a moment, gazing, and goes into the house.*
THESEUS *ignores her, crawling beside his son's body. Violently
trembling he touches the body; shakes his head stupidly.
Touches it again.*)

FIRST WOMAN. He will not dare to touch the face.

SECOND WOMAN. He has touched the face.

THIRD WOMAN. He never will dare to kiss it.

FIRST WOMAN. When his mind comes back to him,
Suddenly he will give a great cry,
And spring at us with his sword . . .

SECOND WOMAN. Do you think so!

THIRD WOMAN.                                        And kill us all.

(*They, with* SELENE, *withdraw from him in terror, still watching. The guards have already stood back, drilled and impassive.*

*The body of* ALCYON *is concealed behind them.* THESEUS *is alone with his dead son.*)

FIRST WOMAN. He is gazing at him. He has touched his throat.

SECOND WOMAN. He is fondling the bright hair. He is fondling . . .

THIRD WOMAN. He kissed the face!

FIRST WOMAN. He is stroking the cheeks and the bright hair . . .

THESEUS (*leaping up*). Quick, you dogs! Help me!
   I saw him breathe. The color is creeping back
   Into his lips. Bring water and wine and a great linen bandage —
   Oh! Did I hurt you?
   You'll live, you'll live! (*He half raises the body; lets it down
   again; kneels by it.*)

FIRST WOMAN (*after a pause*). The man you have struck *never* lives,
   Theseus.

THESEUS. O God of the Sea: *my* God,
   My foster-father, God of the high and shining and leaping Sea: you
   promised me
   You'd answer three prayers of mine, whatever they were. I pray
   you all three at once:
   Make my son live! *Make my son live. Make my son live.*

FIRST WOMAN. You would have to pray to the God of Death, Theseus,
   Not to the Sea. He has no power in this matter.

SECOND WOMAN. And as to Death: those gray stone lips
   Have never answered a prayer. His ears are stone: men never pray
   to him. His cold gray hands implacably
   Hold what they take.

   (*A scream is heard from the house: running feet and voices.*)

CONFUSED CRIES IN THE HOUSE. Ai! Oh! Oh! Help me. Lift her
   higher, loose the cord! A knife, a knife!

   (THESEUS, *kneeling by the body, seems not to hear them.*)

SECOND WOMAN. What new horror has happened!

SELENE (*screams*). My dearest! Ai! My baby! (*She runs into the
   house.*)

FIRST WOMAN (*pointing at* THESEUS). Look, women!
   He has kissed the wound!

   (*A burst of lamentation — keening — is heard from the house.*)

SECOND WOMAN. Listen: do you hear them?

FIRST WOMAN.                           Someone has died in the house.

THIRD WOMAN. Death in the house: death here. (*She strikes her
   zither and joins in the musical lamentation.*)

SELENE (*comes from the doorway, stands on the top step; cries
   loudly*). Theseus! Theseus!

My lady is dead. My lady Phaedra has died. She hanged herself.
She knotted the hard cord around her white throat . . . (*Weeps,
covering her face.*) Oh, Oh, Oh . . .
THESEUS (*slowly stands up; shakes his head like a hurt bull*). Be silent,
yelpers.
You howlers in the doorways — (*Shouting*) be silent!
(*He looks all about the scene, except at his son's body.*)
I am not so stupid as you believe. I wish my mother had strangled
me
In the night I was born! I wish the sun had gone blind that morn-
ing. I wish that Aethra my mother
Had pointed her breasts with poison before she suckled me, before
I began to be a slayer of men
And a woman's fool. I say there is no pleasure in it; it is not de-
lightful
To be old, mocked and a fool. I say that liars have swindled me
out of reason, like a poor old peasant
Duped in the market; they have diddled him out of his land and
his cows and his very teeth — and there they go laughing
And hang themselves. Why did she laugh like that? What did she
mean? I will never draw sword again.
I wish it had turned in my hand and stabbed me, in my first fight:
but now let it stick in the sheath, blackened
With dear dear blood. My enemies will come and mock me, old
and disarmed: I shall say, "Where is my son
To speak to them between the tall stones? Where is my son Hip-
polytus
To take my part?" He will lie still, he will not come, he will not
answer. There is a darkness:
And those who enter it have no voice any more; and their hands
and feet
Will not move any more; and the dear flesh falls from the rotting
bones, and the beauty is ugliness;
The brave cold eyes are humbled, the bodies stink. I wish I had
died for them!
They were like two stars in heaven: when the high clouds break
open, and a warm wind
Blows in the dark: but I was easily fooled . . .
And my hand leaped. They were nearly the same age; they were
brave and beautiful. I should have helped her
In her deep trouble.
And all this noise was nothing — froth and a noise — a little noise
in the night. The two I loved

Are gone: that's all. I stand
Between two gods; and my north is grief and my south is wailing
and the children laugh at me.
She was in trouble and I did not help her. Indeed I never under-
stood her; she was too beautiful for me.
Her mind moved like a bird.
And now I have to go down all alone in blood, having lived in it,
alone to death,
Having loved deeply. As to — my dear, dear son . . .

    (*He looks down at the body, gives an animal cry of pain,
flings himself on the body. The scene begins to darken.*)

FIRST WOMAN. A mighty man, like a beaten dog or a shot bird,
Crawls in the dust.
The worst wounds that we suffer we inflict on ourselves.

SECOND WOMAN. Hippolytus was happy.
He had his youth, he did no evil, suddenly he died.
The pity of these things has broken my heart.

    (*The scene has darkened to deep twilight. Clear female laugh-
ter is heard from the altar of* APHRODITE. *Light shines increas-
ingly on the altar; the goddess appears there. All gaze at her;
except* THESEUS *by the body of his son.*)

APHRODITE (*laughing*). We are not extremely sorry for the woes of
men.
We laugh in heaven.
We that walk on Olympus and the steep sky,
And under our feet the lightning barks like a dog:
What we desire, we do. (*She smiles.*) I am the power of Love.

    (*She stands smiling and considering.*)

In future days men will become so powerful
That they seem to control the heavens and the earth,
They seem to understand the stars and all science —
Let them beware. Something is lurking hidden.
There is always a knife in the flowers. There is always a lion just
beyond the firelight.

    (*Her light dims out and she vanishes. The scene is all dark.*)

❖ ❖ ❖

## STUDY AIDS

*Page 169.* Sets and props, costumes, sound effects, and the gestures and movements of the actors are as much a part of drama on-stage as the spoken lines. Like many modern dramatists, Jeffers gives rather explicit stage and casting directions in his play. What is the purpose in having the chorus composed of poor women begging for food?

*Pages 170–171.* How do the chorus and Selene develop atmosphere in the play? How would you define this atmosphere? How is it appropriate to or effective for the entrance of Phaedra?

*Page 170.* As the chorus nears the altar of Aphrodite, the First Woman likens the "divine anger" which she senses to "the glaring eyes/ Of a wild beast." What is the force of this simile? On what other occasions do animal images relating to Aphrodite and the force which she represents appear? How do they develop the theme of love? The Second Woman likens her awareness of the goddess to an earthquake. Explain the force of this comparison. What other images linking natural forces and disasters to love can you find in the play?

*Page 170.* The Second Woman says that she wishes the house of Theseus no evil, but that should it fall, she hopes her boy might have "the looting of it." What is the effect of these words? Do they suggest a view of human nature which receives some amplification throughout the play? Does such an attitude help to explain the women's refusal to support Hippolytus in the crucial interview with Theseus? How?

*Page 170.* Selene explains to the chorus that her lady is ill. We later learn that the "illness" is related to her passion for Hippolytus. What other instances can you find in which Phaedra's love is spoken of as a disease?

*Page 171.* Comment on the strength of Selene's statement: "Like the mad waves of the sea, moulding but hiding/ A sunken reef." Is this figure simply "poetic" and decorative, or does it function as genuine revelation of the character of Phaedra?

What do the gestures which Jeffers requires from the chorus in response to Selene's question "What Person?" add to the scene?

*Page 171.* What is the function of the hunger of the chorus and its interest in the food which Phaedra has refused? Why does Jeffers include the detail about Phaedra's calling for raw meat "like a northern barbarian"?

*Page 172.* Why does Phaedra not seem to recognize the chorus and call the women "beautiful haughty queens"? She later (p. 173) indicates that she had recognized them all along. Is this a reflection of her distraught state? Is it an early indication of her proneness to turn her own suffering outward and to involve others in it?

*Page 172.* Comment on Phaedra's comparison of her passion for Hippolytus to "a barbed spearhead." What other examples can you find in the play in which love is compared to a weapon or to some instrument capable of inflicting pain?

The Second Woman likens Phaedra's approach to Aphrodite's altar to a moth's attraction to a flame. Is this comparison too trite, too much of a cliché, to be effective here? Or does it have enough in common with other figures defining love in this play to justify it and give it interest and freshness? This same simile occurs at one other point in the play: where? What is the force, if any, of the repetition?

*Page 173.* Phaedra describes the "goddess of love and longing" as "cruel" and "beautiful." To what extent are both of these qualities of love objectified in the characters and action of the play?

One of the many changes Jeffers has effected in his adaptation of Euripides is his treatment of Hippolytus as a homosexual. What importance does this change have for the play? Does it relate to the question of human will and fate? Does it make Hippolytus' spurning of Phaedra more credible than in Euripides? Does it make Phaedra's infatuation for him too improbable? Might the very improbability of a love-relation between them help to underscore the irrationality of Phaedra's passion?

*Page 174.* What interpretation should be placed upon Phaedra's expression of love and respect for Theseus, especially in light of her cruel treatment of him later in the play? Does she seem too inconsistent to be credible? Might it be argued that the revelation of the inconsistent or contradictory character of human nature is actually a theme of the play? What important information do we gain about Theseus from Phaedra's musings? Why does she dwell on Theseus' age?

*Page 174.* Phaedra says that she will pray to Death, who "has a flower in his hand." What other deity is associated with or symbolized by a flower in the play? Is there some dramatic force in this similarity?

What significance, if any, is to be attached to Phaedra's begging a crust from the member of the chorus?

*Pages 175–176.* Comment on the effectiveness of the use of the spray of fruit-blossom as indicated by the stage direction. How has Jeffers prepared the audience for Aphrodite's appearance? Analyze Aphrodite's long speech. Into what major divisions does it fall? What is the function of each? In her enumeration of her various functions and influences in the universe, how important is the love of man and woman? How do her remarks bear on the theme of love as developed in the play? Aphrodite explains her animosity for Hippolytus and expresses passing regret for the fate of Phaedra. What has Jeffers gained, if anything, by having this information divulged at this point? Compare his handling of such expository material with Euripides' prologue in the *Hippolytus.* According to the goddess, what is the fate of man? Where else does such an idea occur in the play? To what extent might the events of the play be seen as an *implicit* statement of this theme?

*Pages 176–177.* After the disappearance of Aphrodite, each member of the chorus describes the dream she has had. What is the symbolic force of each of the dreams? How do they recall or reinforce images developed earlier? Is there some significance in the contrasting, even contradictory, characteristics of these dreams?

*Pages 177ff.* How do Hippolytus' demeanor and statements confirm or add to earlier statements about him? Is there any significance in his rather informal conduct with his companions and his interest in the "poor patched women" of the chorus? How do these qualities contrast with Phaedra's attitudes? Do they win audience sympathy for him? How?

*Page 180.* What value is there in Hippolytus' mentioning to Selene that Theseus is expected to return the next day?

*Pages 180ff.* How does the discussion between Phaedra and Hippolytus concerning human will and destiny relate to the play? Is it largely philosophical window-dressing and not really germane, or is it a matter of genuine relevance? Explain the distinction which Hippolytus draws between human suffering and acting.

During this discussion, Phaedra alludes to her sister who became lost in the Labyrinth. Of what significance is Phaedra's family background in this play? Is the hereditary influence developed as a significant factor?

*Pages 181–182.* Love has been described in a number of ways during the play. What further perspectives on love are given in Phaedra's speech?

*Pages 182ff.* How do Phaedra's speeches here recall and reinforce earlier images connected with love?

*Page 183.* What is the "black thought" that crosses Phaedra's mind? Why does Phaedra liken it to a vulture? What is gained by mentioning it at this point?

*Page 184.* Phaedra's speech beginning "This man . . ." recalls images of weaponry found earlier in the play. Note the phallic connotations which her lines carry here.

*Page 186.* Why does Phaedra fling her bracelet down? Why does she offer it to the begging women of the chorus?

*Page 186.* How does the revelation from the oracle concerning the burning of Theseus' house tie in with images of love stated earlier?

*Pages 187–188.* What is the function of the women's two versions of the traveler crossing the mountain? Is there some thematic relevance in the two differing versions of the same subject?

*Page 188.* Comment on the function of the speeches by the First and Second Women beginning "Would God that I knew the joy" and "The girls and young men go up."

*Pages 189ff.* What is Phaedra's motivation for lying to Theseus about Hippolytus? Is she retaliating for his rebuff? Are her actions inexplicable without the notion that Aphrodite forces them upon her?

*Pages 189ff.* Comment on the effectiveness of Phaedra's hint-by-hint revelation to Theseus of Hippolytus as her victimizer. How may Theseus' rapid vacillation between belief and disbelief be accounted for? Has it some thematic relevance to the idea of man's rational control of himself and his destiny?

*Page 190.* Earlier in the play, Phaedra spoke of her love for Theseus. Why does she treat him so sadistically at this point? Does her attack on him as a man of blood and violence seem relevant or extraneous to this play and to her character?

*Page 193.* What is the relevance of the exchange among the members of the chorus beginning "What is best for a man"?

*Page 194.* Phaedra reminds Theseus that Hippolytus "is that sex . . ./ That loves its own." Does the known fact of Hippolytus' homosexuality make Phaedra's allegation of rape and Theseus' acceptance of it too incredible and thereby weaken the scene?

*Page 195.* What do the details of Theseus' recollection of his first sight of Phaedra add to our attitude toward Phaedra? toward Theseus? In what way do they underscore the plights of these two figures?

Phaedra's line "Do you still despise me, Hippolytus?" is repeated once again. When? What is the force of its repetition?

*Pages 195–196.* Hippolytus refuses to tell his father the facts concerning Phaedra's approach to him. Why? Does his silence at this
point seem adequately motivated? How do Euripides and Racine
handle this situation as compared with Jeffers?

*Pages 196–197.* Consider the following stage direction: "Scowling
with doubt, looking from one to the other, like a tormented bull."
How does this view of Theseus' indecision relate to issues raised in this
play?

*Page 197.* Why do the women of the chorus not reveal the facts
about Phaedra's approach to Hippolytus? Has Jeffers made their silence more credible than did Euripides?

*Page 198.* What is gained by having Theseus kill Hippolytus on-
stage in full view of the audience?

*Page 198.* Rushing to kill Theseus, Alcyon is himself slain. At this
point the following stage directions appear: "No one gives attention
to this by-play. Theseus stands looking down at his son." What is
the impact of these directions?

*Page 199.* Phaedra explains to her husband that she has tricked him
into killing his son because of her hatred of Theseus and her desire
to punish him for his bloody career. Do these motives seem con-
vincing? Do these attitudes seem dramatically appropriate to Phaedra's character as displayed in the play?

*Page 202.* In Theseus' final speech his moving lament for his innocent son is easily understood and accepted. Is his compassionate and
tolerant understanding of Phaedra as easily acceptable? Is it credible,
for example, that Theseus has been able to learn enough of the facts
of the situation to lead him to this view of a woman whom he has
recently characterized as having the face of a harlot and who has
tricked him into slaughtering his own son?

*Page 203.* Comment on the impact of the appearance of Aphrodite amid the scene of death on-stage. What is her attitude? How
and what does it contribute to the theme of the play? How effective
are the concluding lines of her speech beginning "In future days men
will become so powerful"? Howard Nemerov has written that he
wished that this "blatantly unnecessary 'message for today' could be
left out of Aphrodite's final speech." Do you agree that it destroys
the mood of the play? Do the remarks seem a justifiable implication
of the meaning of the play? Do they pick up threads of imagery
importance in the play?

## DISCUSSION TOPICS

1. Analyze the action of the play, indicating the points of initial disturbance of stability, crisis, and catastrophe. Do the major events seem causally connected? Do they build to climaxes, or do the climaxes, as one critic has observed, simply happen? Is compression a feature of the action of this play? If so, how has it been achieved? Is the action more tightly organized than in the *Hippolytus*?

2. Define the principal themes and discuss their embodiment in the play. How closely correlated are action and meaning? Do thematic statements grow out of the events of the play, or do they appear to have been superimposed upon the action?

3. Some readers and viewers regard this play as intensely pessimistic. Do you share such a view? What comment upon human volition does the play make?

4. Comment on the principal characters. How are their personalities projected? Which figure is most fully realized?

5. Discuss *The Cretan Woman* as poetic drama. How would you describe the principal features of its language?

6. Review the images relating to love. What, if anything, do they have in common? How do they relate to or support the meaning of the play?

7. Comment on Jeffers' use of the chorus. What are its functions? Is it more organic here than in the *Hippolytus*? in Seneca's *Phaedra*? Is it less "choric" than in Euripides' play?

8. What is the function of the goddess in this play? How is her appearance at the close similar to and different from that of Artemis in the *Hippolytus*?

9. Comment on other important similarities and dissimilarities between Jeffers' treatment of the Hippolytus-Phaedra material and that of Euripides, Seneca, and Racine.

10. Discuss the problems which you might encounter in staging this play. (The reviews listed in the introduction will be of interest in this regard.)

11. Consult the reviews of *Hungerfield and Other Poems* by Dudley Fitts in the New York *Times* and by Selden Rodman in *Poetry* (see introduction). Where do you agree and disagree with these writers concerning *The Cretan Woman*?

# EUGENE O'NEILL

◇◇◇◇◇◇◇◇◇◇◇◇◇◇◇◇◇◇◇◇◇◇◇◇◇◇◇◇◇◇◇◇◇◇◇◇

EUGENE O'NEILL (1888–1953) was born the son of a successful actor, James O'Neill, from whom perhaps he early acquired the interest in the theatre which was to grow into his life's work. During his first seven years he traveled about the country on road tours with his family. From 1896 to 1906 he attended various private schools. Failing to complete his first year at Princeton, he began to read widely in the great book of the world, knocking about here and there, trying his hand at various jobs. He worked for a time in a mail order house in New York, served with his father's theatrical troupe, did some gold prospecting, went to sea as an ordinary seaman, and lived the life of a derelict in the waterfront slums of several seaports. During these years he no doubt was storing his mind with a variety of experiences and a broad knowledge and understanding of human nature. But he was also impairing his health, and at length he was forced to spend months convalescing in a tuberculosis sanitarium.

Yet he was to turn this period of enforced calm to good account, for he read widely in dramatic literature and began to write plays himself. In 1914, with the financial backing of his father, he published his first volume of plays, *Thirst and Other One-Act Plays*. In 1914–15 he studied playwriting under Professor George Pierce Baker at Harvard. The following year was a particularly important one in his development as a dramatist, for he then began his long association with the Provincetown Players, who successfully produced *Bound East for Cardiff* during the summer of 1916. Having found a career into which he could channel his great energies, he worked hard and successfully. Although neither personal happiness nor consistent critical approbation was a feature of O'Neill's career, his work brought him wealth, three Pulitzer awards, and, in 1936, the Nobel Prize for Literature. Recent successful productions of his plays, particularly *A Long Day's Journey into Night* and the revival of *Strange Interlude*, attest to the continuing relevance and interest of his work.

Among his many plays, *Desire Under the Elms* remains one of those most able to sustain profitable re-reading and re-viewing. Its first performance was given on November 11, 1924, by the Province-town Players at the Greenwich Village Theatre, New York. Early in the following year the play moved to the Earl Carroll Theatre, where it had two hundred and eight performances. The theme of incest, the frankness of the dialogue, and the overt display of passion by Abbie and Eben brought cries of outrage and attempts by the guardians of the public virtue to bar its further performance and to arrest the members of its cast. But in the years since, the play has been viewed more tolerantly and more intelligently, and it has come to be regarded as one of O'Neill's most memorable and satisfying works. It has been translated into many languages and has been pro-duced in a number of European countries. Perhaps part of its con-tinuing appeal is the "fusion of the archetype with the particular," which Clifford Leech finds "is splendidly achieved in *Desire Under the Elms*." For it is a drama of timeless perplexities in the relations of father and son, mother and son, man and woman; of human beings haunted by desperate needs, real and imagined; of hate and love, greed and sacrifice; of wisdom gained, but only through great suffer-ing; in short, a drama of some major permanent concerns of the hu-man spirit, here renewed with fresh implications in the particularities of the New England setting, speech, and characters. Many, no doubt, would agree with Brooks Atkinson, who wrote concerning a revival of the play in 1952, "When the final accounts are tallied, *Desire Under the Elms* may turn out to be the greatest play written by an American."

The bibliography relating to O'Neill is extensive. Bibliographical aids are Jackson R. Bryer, "Forty Years of O'Neill Criticism. A Selected Bibliography," *Modern Drama*, IV (September 1961), 192–216; Jordan Y. Miller, *Eugene O'Neill and the American Critic. A Summary and Bibliographical Checklist* (Hamden, Conn., 1962); and *O'Neill and His Plays*, ed. Oscar Cargill and others (New York, 1961), a particularly useful work with a wealth of bibliographical information and a generous sampling of comments about and by O'Neill. The December 1960 issue of *Modern Drama* is devoted to O'Neill. A recent collection of critical essays is *O'Neill*, ed. John Gassner (Englewood Cliffs, N.J., 1964). The most recent biography is that by Arthur and Barbara Gelb, *O'Neill* (New York, 1962). Most of the major plays are included in *The Plays of Eugene O'Neill*, 3 vols. (New York, 1951).

# Desire Under the Elms

❖ ❖ ❖

## CHARACTERS

EPHRAIM CABOT

SIMEON  
PETER  } *His sons*  
EBEN

ABBIE PUTNAM

*Young Girl, Two Farmers, The Fiddler, A Sheriff, and other folk from the neighboring farms.*

The action of the entire play takes place in, and immediately outside of, the Cabot farmhouse in New England, in the year 1850. The south end of the house faces front to a stone wall with a wooden gate at center opening on a country road. The house is in good condition but in need of paint. Its walls are a sickly grayish, the green of the shutters faded. Two enormous elms are on each side of the house. They bend their trailing branches down over the roof. They appear to protect and at the same time subdue. There is a sinister maternity in their aspect, a crushing, jealous absorption. They have developed from their intimate contact with the life of man in the house an appalling humaneness. They brood oppressively over the house. They are like exhausted women resting their sagging breasts and hands and hair on its roof, and when it rains their tears trickle down monotonously and rot on the shingles. There is a path running from the gate around the right corner of the house to the front door. A narrow porch is on this side. The end wall facing us has two windows in its upper story, two larger ones on the floor below. The two upper are those of the father's bedroom and that of the brothers. On the left, ground floor, is the kitchen — on the right, the parlor, the shades of which are always drawn down.

## PART ONE · SCENE ONE

*Exterior of the farmhouse. It is sunset of a day at the beginning of summer in the year 1850. There is no wind and everything is still. The sky above the roof is suffused with deep colors, the green of the elms glows, but the house is in shadow, seeming pale and washed out by contrast.*

*A door opens and* EBEN CABOT *comes to the end of the porch and stands looking down the road to the right. He has a large bell in his hand and this he swings mechanically, awakening a deafening clangor. Then he puts his hands on his hips and stares up at the sky. He sighs with a puzzled awe and blurts out with halting appreciation.*

EBEN. God! Purty! (*His eyes fall and he stares about him frowningly. He is twenty-five, tall and sinewy. His face is well-formed, good-looking, but its expression is resentful and defensive. His defiant, dark eyes remind one of a wild animal's in captivity. Each day is a cage in which he finds himself trapped but inwardly unsubdued. There is a fierce repressed vitality about him. He has black hair, mustache, a thin curly trace of beard. He is dressed in rough farm clothes.*

*He spits on the ground with intense disgust, turns and goes back into the house.*

SIMEON *and* PETER *come in from their work in the fields. They are tall men, much older than their half-brother [*SIMEON *is thirty-nine and* PETER *thirty-seven], built on a squarer, simpler model, fleshier in body, more bovine and homelier in face, shrewder and more practical. Their shoulders stoop a bit from years of farm work. They clump heavily along in their clumsy thick-soled boots caked with earth. Their clothes, their faces, hands, bare arms and throats are earth-stained. They smell of earth. They stand together for a moment in front of the house and, as if with the one impulse, stare dumbly up at the sky, leaning on their hoes. Their faces have a compressed, unresigned expression. As they look upward, this softens.*)

SIMEON (*grudgingly*). Purty.

PETER. Ay-eh.

SIMEON (*suddenly*). Eighteen year ago.

PETER. What?

SIMEON. Jenn. My woman. She died.

PETER. I'd fergot.

SIMEON. I rec'lect — now an' agin. Makes it lonesome. She'd hair long's a hoss' tail — an' yaller like gold!

PETER. Waal — she's gone. (*This with indifferent finality — then after a pause*) They's gold in the West, Sim.

SIMEON (*still under the influence of sunset — vaguely*). In the sky?

PETER. Waal — in a manner o' speakin' — thar's the promise. (*Growing excited*) Gold in the sky — in the West — Golden Gate — Californi-a! — Goldest West! — fields o' gold!

SIMEON (*excited in his turn*). Fortunes layin' just atop o' the ground waitin' t' be picked! Solomon's mines, they says! (*For a moment they continue looking up at the sky — then their eyes drop.*)

PETER (*with sardonic bitterness*). Here — it's stones atop o' the ground — stones atop o' stones — makin' stone walls — year atop o' year — him 'n' yew 'n' me 'n' then Eben — makin' stone walls fur him to fence us in!

SIMEON. We've wuked. Give our strength. Give our years. Plowed 'em under in the ground, — (*he stamps rebelliously*) — rottin' — makin' soil for his crops! (*A pause*) Waal — the farm pays good for hereabouts.

PETER. If we plowed in Californi-a, they'd be lumps o' gold in the furrow!

SIMEON. Californi-a's t'other side o' earth, a'most. We got t' calc'late —

PETER (*after a pause*). 'Twould be hard fur me, too, to give up what we've 'arned here by our sweat. (*A pause.* EBEN *sticks his head out of the dining-room window, listening.*)

SIMEON. Ay-eh. (*A pause*) Mebbe — he'll die soon.

PETER (*doubtfully*). Mebbe.

SIMEON. Mebbe — fur all we knows — he's dead now.

PETER. Ye'd need proof.

SIMEON. He's been gone two months — with no word.

PETER. Left us in the fields an evenin' like this. Hitched up an' druv off into the West. That's plum onnateral. He hain't never been off this farm 'ceptin' t' the village in thirty year or more, not since he married Eben's maw. (*A pause. Shrewdly*) I calc'late we might git him declared crazy by the court.

SIMEON. He skinned 'em too slick. He got the best o' all on 'em.

They'd never b'lieve him crazy. (*A pause*) We got t' wait — till he's under ground.

EBEN (*with a sardonic chuckle*). Honor thy father! (*They turn, startled, and stare at him. He grins, then scowls.*) I pray he's died. (*They stare at him. He continues matter-of-factly*) Supper's ready.

SIMEON *and* PETER (*together*). Ay-eh.

EBEN (*gazing up at the sky*). Sun's downin' purty.

SIMEON *and* PETER (*together*). Ay-eh. They's gold in the West.

EBEN. Ay-eh. (*Pointing*) Yonder atop o' the hill pasture, ye mean?

SIMEON *and* PETER (*together*). In Californi-a!

EBEN. Hunh? (*Stares at them indifferently for a second, then drawls*) Waal — supper's gittin' cold. (*He turns back into kitchen.*)

SIMEON (*startled — smacks his lips*). I air hungry!

PETER (*sniffing*). I smells bacon!

SIMEON (*with hungry appreciation*). Bacon's good!

PETER (*in same tone*). Bacon's bacon! (*They turn, shouldering each other, their bodies bumping and rubbing together as they hurry clumsily to their food, like two friendly oxen toward their evening meal. They disappear around the right corner of house and can be heard entering the door.*)

CURTAIN

## SCENE TWO

*The color fades from the sky. Twilight begins. The interior of the kitchen is now visible. A pine table is at center, a cookstove in the right rear corner, four rough wooden chairs, a tallow candle on the table. In the middle of the rear wall is fastened a big advertising poster with a ship in full sail and the word "California" in big letters. Kitchen utensils hang from nails. Everything is neat and in order but the atmosphere is of a men's camp kitchen rather than that of a home.*

*Places for three are laid.* EBEN *takes boiled potatoes and bacon from the stove and puts them on the table, also a loaf of bread and a crock of water.* SIMEON *and* PETER *shoulder in, slump down in their chairs without a word.* EBEN *joins them. The three eat in silence for a moment, the two elder as naturally unrestrained as beasts of the field,* EBEN *picking at his food without appetite, glancing at them with a tolerant dislike.*

SIMEON (*suddenly turns to* EBEN). Looky here! Ye'd oughtn't t' said that, Eben.

PETER. 'Twa'n't righteous.

EBEN. What?

SIMEON. Ye prayed he'd died.

EBEN. Waal — don't yew pray it? (*A pause.*)

PETER. He's our Paw.

EBEN (*violently*). Not mine!

SIMEON (*dryly*). Ye'd not let no one else say that about yer Maw! Ha! (*He gives one abrupt sardonic guffaw.* PETER *grins.*)

EBEN (*very pale*). I meant — I hain't his'n — I hain't like him — he hain't me!

PETER (*dryly*). Wait till ye've growed his age!

EBEN (*intensely*). I'm Maw — every drop o' blood! (*A pause. They stare at him with indifferent curiosity.*)

PETER (*reminiscently*). She was good t' Sim 'n' me. A good step-maw's scurse.

SIMEON. She was good t' everyone.

EBEN (*greatly moved, gets to his feet and makes an awkward bow to each of them — stammering*). I be thankful t' ye. I'm her — her heir. (*He sits down in confusion.*)

PETER (*after a pause — judicially*). She was good even t' him.

EBEN (*fiercely*). An' fur thanks he killed her!

SIMEON (*after a pause*). No one never kills nobody. It's allus somethin'. That's the murderer.

EBEN. Didn't he slave Maw t' death?

PETER. He's slaved himself t' death. He's slaved Sim 'n' me 'n' yew t' death — on'y none o' us hain't died — yit.

SIMEON. It's somethin' — drivin' him — t' drive us!

EBEN (*vengefully*). Waal — I hold him t' jedgment! (*Then scornfully*) Somethin'! What's somethin'?

SIMEON. Dunno.

EBEN (*sardonically*). What's drivin' yew to Californi-a, mebbe? (*They look at him in surprise.*) Oh, I've heerd ye! (*Then, after a pause*) But ye'll never go t' the gold fields!

PETER (*assertively*). Mebbe!

EBEN. Whar'll ye git the money?

PETER. We kin walk. It's an a'mighty ways — Californi-a — but if yew was t' put all the steps we've walked on this farm end t' end we'd be in the moon!

EBEN. The Injuns'll skulp ye on the plains.

SIMEON (*with grim humor*). We'll mebbe make 'em pay a hair fur a hair!

EBEN (*decisively*). But t'ain't that. Ye won't never go because ye'll wait here fur yer share o' the farm, thinkin' allus he'll die soon.

SIMEON (*after a pause*). We've a right.

PETER. Two-thirds belongs t'us.

EBEN (*jumping to his feet*). Ye've no right! She wa'n't yewr Maw! It was her farm! Didn't he steal it from her? She's dead. It's my farm.

SIMEON (*sardonically*). Tell that t' Paw — when he comes! I'll bet ye a dollar he'll laugh — fur once in his life. Ha! (*He laughs himself in one single mirthless bark.*)

PETER (*amused in turn, echoes his brother*). Ha!

SIMEON (*after a pause*). What've ye got held agin us, Eben? Year arter year it's skulked in yer eye — somethin'.

PETER. Ay-eh.

EBEN. Ay-eh. They's somethin'. (*Suddenly exploding*) Why didn't ye never stand between him 'n' my Maw when he was slavin' her to her grave — t' pay her back fur the kindness she done t' yew? (*There is a long pause. They stare at him in surprise.*)

SIMEON. Waal — the stock'd got t' be watered.

PETER. 'R they was woodin' t' do.

SIMEON. 'R plowin'.

PETER. 'R hayin'.

SIMEON. 'R spreadin' manure.

PETER. 'R weedin'.

SIMEON. 'R prunin'.

PETER. 'R milkin'.

EBEN (*breaking in harshly*). An' makin' walls — stone atop o' stone — makin' walls till yer heart's a stone ye heft up out o' the way o' growth onto a stone wall t' wall in yer heart!

SIMEON (*matter-of-factly*). We never had no time t' meddle.

PETER (*to* EBEN). Yew was fifteen afore yer Maw died — an' big fur yer age. Why didn't ye never do nothin'?

EBEN (*harshly*). They was chores t' do, wa'n't they? (*A pause — then slowly*) It was on'y arter she died I come to think o' it. Me cookin' — doin' her work — that made me know her, suffer her sufferin' — she'd come back t' help — come back t' bile potatoes — come back t' fry bacon — come back t' bake biscuits — come back all cramped up t' shake the fire, an' carry ashes, her eyes weepin' an' bloody with smoke an' cinders same's they used t' be. She still comes back — stands by the stove thar in the evenin' — she can't find it nateral sleepin' an' restin' in peace. She can't git used t' bein' free — even in her grave.

SIMEON. She never complained none.

EBEN. She'd got too tired. She'd got too used t' bein' too tired. That was what he done. (*With vengeful passion*) An' sooner'r later, I'll meddle. I'll say the thin's I didn't say then t' him! I'll yell 'em at the top o' my lungs. I'll see t' it my Maw gits some rest an' sleep in her grave! (*He sits down again, relapsing into a brooding silence. They look at him with a queer indifferent curiosity.*)

PETER (*after a pause*). Whar in tarnation d'ye s'pose he went, Sim?

SIMEON. Dunno. He druv off in the buggy, all spick an' span, with the mare all breshed an' shiny, druv off clackin' his tongue an' wavin' his whip. I remember it right well. I was finishin' plowin', it was spring an' May an' sunset, an' gold in the West, an' he druv off into it. I yells "Whar ye goin', Paw?" an' he hauls up by the stone wall a jiffy. His old snake's eyes was glitterin' in the sun like he'd been drinkin' a jugful an' he says with a mule's grin: "Don't ye run away till I come back!"

PETER. Wonder if he knowed we was wantin' fur Californi-a?

SIMEON. Mebbe. I didn't say nothin' and he says, lookin' kinder queer an' sick: "I been hearin' the hens cluckin' an' the roosters crowin' all the durn day. I been listenin' t' the cows lowin' an' everythin' else kickin' up till I can't stand it no more. It's spring an' I'm feelin' damned," he says. "Damned like an old bare hickory tree fit on'y fur burnin'," he says. An' then I calc'late I must've looked a mite hopeful, fur he adds real spry and vicious: "But don't git no fool idee I'm dead. I've sworn t' live a hundred an' I'll do it, if on'y t' spite yer sinful greed! An' now I'm ridin' out t' learn God's message t' me in the spring, like the prophets done. An' yew git back t' yer plowin'," he says. An' he druv off singin' a hymn. I thought he was drunk — 'r I'd stopped him goin'.

EBEN (*scornfully*). No, ye wouldn't! Ye're scared o' him. He's stronger — inside — than both o' ye put together!

PETER (*sardonically*). An' yew — be yew Samson?

EBEN. I'm gittin' stronger. I kin feel it growin' in me — growin' an' growin' — till it'll bust out —! (*He gets up and puts on his coat and a hat. They watch him, gradually breaking into grins.* EBEN *avoids their eyes sheepishly.*) I'm goin' out fur a spell — up the road.

PETER. T' the village?

SIMEON. T' see Minnie?

EBEN (*defiantly*). Ay-eh!

PETER (*jeeringly*). The Scarlet Woman!

SIMEON. Lust — that's what's growin' in ye!

EBEN. Waal — she's purty!

PETER. She's been purty fur twenty year!

SIMEON. A new coat o' paint'l make a heifer out of forty.

EBEN. She hain't forty!

PETER. If she hain't, she's teeterin' on the edge.

EBEN (*desperately*). What d'yew know —

PETER. All they is . . . Sim knew her — an' then me arter —

SIMEON. An' Paw kin tell yew somethin' too! He was fust!

EBEN. D'ye mean t' say he . . . ?

SIMEON (*with a grin*). Ay-eh! We air his heirs in everythin'!

EBEN (*intensely*). That's more to it! That grows on it! It'll bust soon!
(*Then violently*) I'll go smash my fist in her face! (*He pulls open
the door in rear violently.*)

SIMEON (*with a wink at* PETER — *drawlingly*). Mebbe — but the
night's wa'm — purty — by the time ye git thar mebbe ye'll kiss her
instead!

PETER. Sart'n he will! (*They both roar with coarse laughter.* EBEN
*rushes out and slams the door — then the outside front door —
comes around the corner of the house and stands still by the gate,
staring up at the sky.*)

SIMEON (*looking after him*). Like his Paw.

PETER. Dead spit an' image!

SIMEON. Dog'll eat dog!

PETER. Ay-eh. (*Pause. With yearning*) Mebbe a year from now we'll
be in Californi-a.

SIMEON. Ay-eh. (*A pause. Both yawn.*) Let's git t'bed. (*He blows
out the candle. They go out door in rear.* EBEN *stretches his arms
up to the sky — rebelliously.*)

EBEN. Waal — thar's a star, an' somewhar's they's him, an' here's me,
an' thar's Min up the road — in the same night. What if I does kiss
her? She's like t'night, she's soft 'n' wa'm, her eyes kin wink like a
star, her mouth's wa'm, her arms're wa'm, she smells like a wa'm
plowed field, she's purty . . . Ay-eh! By God A'mighty she's
purty, an' I don't give a damn how many sins she's sinned afore
mine or who she's sinned 'em with, my sin's as purty as any one on
'em! (*He strides off down the road to the left.*)

## SCENE THREE

*It is the pitch darkness just before dawn.* EBEN *comes in from the
left and goes around to the porch, feeling his way, chuckling bitterly and cursing half-aloud to himself.*

EBEN. The cussed old miser! (*He can be heard going in the front
door. There is a pause as he goes upstairs, then a loud knock on the
bedroom door of the brothers.*) Wake up!

SIMEON (*startedly*). Who's thar?

EBEN (*pushing open the door and coming in, a lighted candle in his hand. The bedroom of the brothers is revealed. Its ceiling is the sloping roof. They can stand upright only close to the center dividing wall of the upstairs.* SIMEON *and* PETER *are in a double bed, front.* EBEN's *cot is to the rear.* EBEN *has a mixture of silly grin and vicious scowl on his face*). I be!

PETER (*angrily*). What in hell's-fire . . . ?

EBEN. I got news fur ye! Ha! (*He gives one abrupt sardonic guffaw.*)

SIMEON (*angrily*). Couldn't ye hold it 'til we'd got our sleep?

EBEN. It's nigh sunup. (*Then explosively*) He's gone an' married agen!

SIMEON *and* PETER (*explosively*). Paw?

EBEN. Got himself hitched to a female 'bout thirty-five — an' purty, they says . . .

SIMEON (*aghast*). It's a durn lie!

PETER. Who says?

SIMEON. They been stringin' ye!

EBEN. Think I'm a dunce, do ye? The hull village says. The preacher from New Dover, he brung the news — told it t'our preacher — New Dover, that's whar the old loon got himself hitched — that's whar the woman lived —

PETER (*no longer doubting — stunned*). Waal . . . !

SIMEON (*the same*). Waal . . . !

EBEN (*sitting down on a bed — with vicious hatred*). Ain't he a devil out o' hell? It's jest t' spite us — the damned old mule!

PETER (*after a pause*). Everythin'll go t' her now.

SIMEON. Ay-eh. (*A pause — dully*) Waal — if it's done —

PETER. It's done us. (*Pause — then persuasively*) They's gold in the fields o' Californi-a, Sim. No good a-stayin' here now.

SIMEON. Jest what I was a-thinkin'. (*Then with decision*) S'well fust's last! Let's light out and git this mornin'.

PETER. Suits me.

EBEN. Ye must like walkin'.

SIMEON (*sardonically*). If ye'd grow wings on us we'd fly thar!

EBEN. Ye'd like ridin' better — on a boat, wouldn't ye? (*Fumbles in his pocket and takes out a crumpled sheet of foolscap.*) Waal, if ye sign this ye kin ride on a boat. I've had it writ out an' ready in case ye'd ever go. It says fur three hundred dollars t' each ye agree yewr shares o' the farm is sold t' me. (*They look suspiciously at the paper. A pause.*)

SIMEON (*wonderingly*). But if he's hitched agen —

PETER. An' whar'd yew git that sum o' money, anyways?

EBEN (*cunningly*). I know whar it's hid. I been waitin' — Maw told me. She knew whar it lay fur years, but she was waitin . . It's her'n — the money he hoarded from her farm an' hid from Maw. It's my money by rights now.

PETER. Whar's it hid?

EBEN (*cunningly*). Whar yew won't never find it without me. Maw spied on him — 'r she'd never knowed. (*A pause. They look at him suspiciously, and he at them.*) Waal, is it fa'r trade?

SIMEON. Dunno.

PETER. Dunno.

SIMEON (*looking at window*). Sky's grayin'.

PETER. Ye better start the fire, Eben.

SIMEON. An' fix some vittles.

EBEN. Ay-eh. (*Then with a forced jocular heartiness*) I'll git ye a good one. If ye're startin' t' hoof it t' Californi-a ye'll need somethin' that'll stick t' yer ribs. (*He turns to the door, adding meaningly*) But ye kin ride on a boat if ye'll swap. (*He stops at the door and pauses. They stare at him.*)

SIMEON (*suspiciously*). Whar was ye all night?

EBEN (*defiantly*). Up t' Min's. (*Then slowly*) Walkin' thar, fust I felt 's if I'd kiss her; then I got a-thinkin' o' what ye'd said o' him an' her an' I says, I'll bust her nose fur that! Then I got t' the village an' heerd the news an' I got madder'n hell an' run all the way t' Min's not knowin' what I'd do — (*He pauses—then sheepishly but more defiantly*) Waal — when I seen her, I didn't hit her — nor I didn't kiss her nuther — I begun t' beller like a calf an' cuss at the same time, I was so durn mad — an' she got scared — an' I jest grabbed holt an' tuk her! (*Proudly*) Yes, sirree! I tuk her. She may've been his'n — an' your'n, too — but she's mine now!

SIMEON (*dryly*). In love, air yew?

EBEN (*with lofty scorn*). Love! I don't take no stock in sech slop!

PETER (*winking at* SIMEON). Mebbe Eben's aimin' t' marry, too.

SIMEON. Min'd make a true faithful he'pmeet! (*They snicker.*)

EBEN. What do I care fur her — 'ceptin' she's round an' wa'm? The p'int is she was his'n — an' now she b'longs t' me! (*He goes to the door — then turns — rebelliously*) An' Min hain't sech a bad un. They's worse'n Min in the world, I'll bet ye! Wait'll we see this cow the Old Man's hitched t'! She'll beat Min, I got a notion! (*He starts to go out.*)

SIMEON (*suddenly*). Mebbe ye'll try t' make her your'n, too?

PETER. Ha! (*He gives a sardonic laugh of relish at this idea.*)

EBEN (*spitting with disgust*). Her — here — sleepin' with him — stealin' my Maw's farm! I'd as soon pet a skunk 'r kiss a snake!

(*He goes out. The two stare after him suspiciously. A pause. They listen to his steps receding.*)

PETER. He's startin' the fire.

SIMEON. I'd like t' ride t' Californi-a — but —

PETER. Min might o' put some scheme in his head.

SIMEON. Mebbe it's all a lie 'bout Paw marryin'. We'd best wait an' see the bride.

PETER. An' don't sign nothin' till we does!

SIMEON. Nor till we've tested it's good money! (*Then with a grin*) But if Paw's hitched we'd be sellin' Eben somethin' we'd never git nohow!

PETER. We'll wait an' see. (*Then with sudden vindictive anger*) An' till he comes, let's yew 'n' me not wuk a lick, let Eben tend to thin's if he's a mind t', let's us jest sleep an' eat an' drink likker, an' let the hull damned farm go t' blazes!

SIMEON (*excitedly*). By God, we've 'arned a rest! We'll play rich fur a change. I hain't a-going to stir outa bed till breakfast's ready.

PETER. An' on the table!

SIMEON (*after a pause — thoughtfully*). What d'ye calc'late she'll be like — our new Maw? Like Eben thinks?

PETER. More'n' likely.

SIMEON (*vindictively*). Waal — I hope she's a she-devil that'll make him wish he was dead an' livin' in the pit o' hell fur comfort!

PETER (*fervently*). Amen!

SIMEON (*imitating his father's voice*). "I'm ridin' out t' learn God's message t' me in the spring like the prophets done," he says. I'll bet right then an' thar he knew plumb well he was goin' whorin', the stinkin' old hypocrite!

## SCENE FOUR

*Same as Scene Two — shows the interior of the kitchen with a lighted candle on table. It is gray dawn outside.* SIMEON *and* PETER *are just finishing their breakfast.* EBEN *sits before his plate of untouched food, brooding frowningly.*

PETER (*glancing at him rather irritably*). Lookin' glum don't help none.

SIMEON (*sarcastically*). Sorrowin' over his lust o' the flesh!

PETER (*with a grin*). Was she yer fust?

EBEN (*angrily*). None o' yer business. (*A pause*) I was thinkin' o' him. I got a notion he's gittin' near — I kin feel him comin' on like yew kin feel malaria chill afore it takes ye.

PETER. It's too early yet.

SIMEON. Dunno. He'd like t' catch us nappin' — jest t' have somethin' t' hoss us 'round over.

PETER (*mechanically gets to his feet.* SIMEON *does the same*). Waal — let's git t' wuk. (*They both plod mechanically toward the door before they realize. Then they stop short.*)

SIMEON (*grinning*). Ye're a cussed fool, Pete — and I be wuss! Let him see we hain't wukin'! We don't give a durn!

PETER (*as they go back to the table*). Not a damned durn! It'll serve t' show him we're done with him. (*They sit down again.* EBEN *stares from one to the other with surprise.*)

SIMEON (*grins at him*). We're aimin' t' start bein' lilies o' the field.

PETER. Nary a toil 'r spin 'r lick o' wuk do we put in!

SIMEON. Ye're sole owner — till he comes — that's what ye wanted. Waal, ye got t' be sole hand, too.

PETER. The cows air bellerin'. Ye better hustle at the milkin'.

EBEN (*with excited joy*). Ye mean ye'll sign the paper?

SIMEON (*dryly*). Mebbe.

PETER. Mebbe.

SIMEON. We're considerin'. (*Peremptorily*) Ye better git t' wuk.

EBEN (*with queer excitement*). It's Maw's farm agen! It's my farm! Them's my cows! I'll milk my durn fingers off fur cows o' mine! (*He goes out door in rear, they stare after him indifferently.*)

SIMEON. Like his Paw.

PETER. Dead spit 'n' image!

SIMEON. Waal — let dog eat dog! (EBEN *comes out of front door and around the corner of the house. The sky is beginning to grow flushed with sunrise.* EBEN *stops by the gate and stares around him with glowing, possessive eyes. He takes in the whole farm with his embracing glance of desire.*)

EBEN. It's purty! It's damned purty! It's mine! (*He suddenly throws his head back boldly and glares with hard, defiant eyes at the sky.*) Mine, d'ye hear? Mine! (*He turns and walks quickly off left, rear, toward the barn. The two brothers light their pipes.*)

SIMEON (*putting his muddy boots up on the table, tilting back his chair, and puffing defiantly*). Waal — this air solid comfort — fur once.

PETER. Ay-eh. (*He follows suit. A pause. Unconsciously they both sigh.*)

SIMEON (*suddenly*). He never was much o' a hand at milkin', Eben wa'n't.

PETER (*with a snort*). His hands air like hoofs! (*A pause.*)

SIMEON. Reach down the jug thar! Let's take a swaller. I'm feelin' kind o' low.

PETER. Good idee! (*He does so — gets two glasses — they pour out drinks of whiskey.*) Here's t' the gold in Californi-a!

SIMEON. An' luck t' find it! (*They drink — puff resolutely — sigh — take their feet down from the table.*)

PETER. Likker don't pear t' sot right.

SIMEON. We hain't used t' it this early. (*A pause. They become very restless.*)

PETER. Gittin' close in this kitchen.

SIMEON (*with immense relief*). Let's git a breath o' air. (*They arise briskly and go out rear — appear around house and stop by the gate. They stare up at the sky with a numbed appreciation.*)

PETER. Purty!

SIMEON. Ay-eh. Gold's t' the East now.

PETER. Sun's startin' with us fur the Golden West.

SIMEON (*staring around the farm, his compressed face tightened, unable to conceal his emotion*). Waal — it's our last mornin' — mebbe.

PETER (*the same*). Ay-eh.

SIMEON (*stamps his foot on the earth and addresses it desperately*). Waal — ye've thirty year o' me buried in ye — spread out over ye — blood an' bone an' sweat — rotted away — fertilizin' ye — richin' yer soul — prime manure, by God, that's what I been t' ye!

PETER. Ay-eh! An' me!

SIMEON. An' yew, Peter. (*He sighs — then spits.*) Waal — no use'n cryin' over spilt milk.

PETER. They's gold in the West — an' freedom, mebbe. We been slaves t' stone walls here.

SIMEON (*defiantly*). We hain't nobody's slaves from this out — nor no thin's slaves nuther. (*A pause — restlessly*) Speakin' o' milk, wonder how Eben's managin'?

PETER. I s'pose he's managin'.

SIMEON. Mebbe we'd ought t' help — this once.

PETER. Mebbe. The cows knows us.

SIMEON. An' likes us. They don't know him much.

PETER. An' the hosses, an' pigs, an' chickens. They don't know him much.

SIMEON. They knows us like brothers — an' likes us! (*Proudly*) Hain't we raised 'em t' be fust-rate, number one prize stock?

PETER. We hain't — not no more.

SIMEON (*dully*). I was fergittin'. (*Then resignedly*) Waal, let's go help Eben a spell an' git waked up.

PETER. Suits me. (*They are starting off down left, rear, for the barn when* EBEN *appears from there hurrying toward them, his face excited.*)

EBEN (*breathlessly*). Waal — har they be! The old mule an' the bride! I seen 'em from the barn down below at the turnin'.

PETER. How could ye tell that far?

EBEN. Hain't I as far-sight as he's near-sight? Don't I know the mare 'n' buggy, an' two people settin' in it? Who else . . . ? An' I tell ye I kin feel 'em a-comin', too! (*He squirms as if he had the itch.*)

PETER (*beginning to be angry*). Waal — let him do his own unhitchin'!

SIMEON (*angry in his turn*). Let's hustle in an' git our bundles an' be a-goin' as he's a-comin'. I don't want never t' step inside the door agen arter he's back. (*They both start back around the corner of the house.* EBEN *follows them.*)

EBEN (*anxiously*). Will ye sign it afore ye go?

PETER. Let's see the color o' the old skinflint's money an' we'll sign. (*They disappear left. The two brothers clump upstairs to get their bundles.* EBEN *appears in the kitchen, runs to window, peers out, comes back and pulls up a strip of flooring in under stove, takes out a canvas bag and puts it on table, then he sets the floorboard back in place. The two brothers appear a moment after. They carry old carpet bags.*)

EBEN (*puts his hand on bag guardingly*). Have ye signed?

SIMEON (*shows paper in his hand*). Ay-eh. (*Greedily*) Be that the money?

EBEN (*opens bag and pours out pile of twenty-dollar gold pieces*). Twenty-dollar pieces — thirty on 'em. Count 'em. (*Peter does so, arranging them in stacks of five, biting one or two to test them.*)

PETER. Six hundred. (*He puts them in bag and puts it inside his shirt carefully.*)

SIMEON (*handing paper to* EBEN). Har ye be.

EBEN (*after a glance, folds it carefully and hides it under his shirt — gratefully*). Thank yew.

PETER. Thank yew fur the ride.

SIMEON. We'll send ye a lump o' gold fur Christmas. (*A pause.* EBEN *stares at them and they at him.*)

PETER (*awkwardly*). Waal — we're a-goin'.

SIMEON. Comin' out t' the yard?

EBEN. No. I'm waitin' in here a spell. (*Another silence. The brothers edge awkwardly to door in rear — then turn and stand.*)

SIMEON. Waal — good-by.

PETER. Good-by.

EBEN. Good-by. (*They go out. He sits down at the table, faces the stove and pulls out the paper. He looks from it to the stove. His face, lighted up by the shaft of sunlight from the window, has an expression of trance. His lips move. The two brothers come out to the gate.*)

PETER (*looking off toward barn*). Thar he be — unhitchin'.

SIMEON (*with a chuckle*). I'll bet ye he's riled!

PETER. An' thar she be.

SIMEON. Let's wait 'n' see what our new Maw looks like.

PETER (*with a grin*). An' give him our partin' cuss!

SIMEON (*grinning*). I feel like raisin' fun. I feel light in my head an' feet.

PETER. Me, too. I feel like laffin' till I'd split up the middle.

SIMEON. Reckon it's the likker?

PETER. No. My feet feel itchin' t' walk an' walk — an' jump high over thin's — an'. . . .

SIMEON. Dance? (*A pause.*)

PETER (*puzzled*). It's plumb onnateral.

SIMEON (*a light coming over his face*). I calc'late it's 'cause school's out. It's holiday. Fur once we're free!

PETER (*dazedly*). Free?

SIMEON. The halter's broke — the harness is busted — the fence bars is down — the stone walls air crumblin' an' tumblin'! We'll be kickin' up an' tearin' away down the road!

PETER (*drawing a deep breath — oratorically*). Anybody that wants this stinkin' old rock-pile of a farm kin hev it. T'ain't our'n, no sirree!

SIMEON (*takes the gate off its hinges and puts it under his arm*). We harby 'bolishes shet gates, an' open gates, an' all gates, by thunder!

PETER. We'll take it with us fur luck an' let 'er sail free down some river.

SIMEON (*as a sound of voices comes from left, rear*). Har they comes! (*The two brothers congeal into two stiff, grim-visaged statues.* EPHRAIM CABOT *and* ABBIE PUTNAM *come in.* CABOT *is seventy-five, tall and gaunt, with great, wiry, concentrated power, but stoop-shouldered from toil. His face is as hard as if it were hewn out of a boulder, yet there is a weakness in it, a petty pride in its own narrow strength. His eyes are small, close together, and extremely near-sighted, blinking continually in the effort to focus on objects, their stare having a straining, ingrowing quality. He is dressed in his dismal black Sunday suit.* ABBIE *is thirty-five, buxom, full of vitality. Her round face is pretty but marred by its rather gross sensuality. There is strength and obstinacy in her jaw, a hard de-*

*termination in her eyes, and about her whole personality the same unsettled, untamed, desperate quality which is so apparent in* EBEN.)

CABOT (*as they enter — a queer strangled emotion in his dry cracking voice*). Har we be t' hum, Abbie.

ABBIE (*with lust for the word*). Hum! (*Her eyes gloating on the house without seeming to see the two stiff figures at the gate.*) It's purty — purty! I can't b'lieve it's r'ally mine.

CABOT (*sharply*). Yewr'n? Mine! (*He stares at her penetratingly. She stares back. He adds relentingly*) Our'n — mebbe! It was lonesome too long. I was growin' old in the spring. A hum's got t' hev a woman.

ABBIE (*her voice taking possession*). A woman's got t' hev a hum!

CABOT (*nodding uncertainly*). Ay-eh. (*Then irritably*) Whar be they? Ain't thar nobody about — 'r wukin' — 'r nothin'?

ABBIE (*sees the brothers. She returns their stare of cold appraising contempt with interest — slowly*). Thar's two men loafin' at the gate an' starin' at me like a couple o' strayed hogs.

CABOT (*straining his eyes*). I kin see 'em — but I can't make out. . . .

SIMEON. It's Simeon.

PETER. It's Peter.

CABOT (*exploding*). Why hain't ye wukin'?

SIMEON (*dryly*). We're waitin' t' welcome ye hum — yew an' the bride!

CABOT (*confusedly*). Huh? Waal — this be yer new Maw, boys. (*She stares at them and they at her.*)

SIMEON (*turns away and spits contemptuously*). I see her!

PETER (*spits also*). An' I see her!

ABBIE (*with the conqueror's conscious superiority*). I'll go in an' look at *my* house. (*She goes slowly around to porch.*)

SIMEON (*with a snort*). Her house!

PETER (*calls after her*). Ye'll find Eben inside. Ye better not tell him it's *yewr* house.

ABBIE (*mouthing the name*). Eben. (*Then quietly*) I'll tell Eben.

CABOT (*with a contemptuous sneer*). Ye needn't heed Eben. Eben's a dumb fool — like his Maw — soft an' simple!

SIMEON (*with his sardonic burst of laughter*). Ha! Eben's a chip o' yew — spit 'n' image — hard 'n' bitter's a hickory tree! Dog'll eat dog. He'll eat ye yet, old man!

CABOT (*commandingly*). Ye git t' wuk!

SIMEON (*as* ABBIE *disappears in house—winks at* PETER *and says tauntingly*). So that thar's our new Maw, be it? Whar in hell did ye dig her up? (*He and* PETER *laugh.*)

PETER. Ha! Ye'd better turn her in the pen with the other sows. (*They laugh uproariously, slapping their thighs.*)

CABOT (*so amazed at their effrontery that he stutters in confusion*). Simeon! Peter! What's come over ye? Air ye drunk?

SIMEON. We're free, old man—free o' yew an' the hull damned farm! (*They grow more and more hilarious and excited.*)

PETER. An' we're startin' out fur the gold fields o' Californi-a!

SIMEON. Ye kin take this place an' burn it!

PETER. An' bury it—fur all we cares!

SIMEON. We're free, old man! (*He cuts a caper.*)

PETER. Free! (*He gives a kick in the air.*)

SIMEON (*in a frenzy*). Whoop!

PETER. Whoop! (*They do an absurd Indian war dance about the old man who is petrified between rage and the fear that they are insane.*)

SIMEON. We're free as Injuns! Lucky we don't skulp ye!

PETER. An' burn yer barn an' kill the stock!

SIMEON. An' rape yer new woman! Whoop! (*He and* PETER *stop their dance, holding their sides, rocking with wild laughter.*)

CABOT (*edging away*). Lust fur gold—fur the sinful, easy gold o' Californi-a! It's made ye mad!

SIMEON (*tauntingly*). Wouldn't ye like us to send ye back some sinful gold, ye old sinner?

PETER. They's gold besides what's in Californi-a! (*He retreats back beyond the vision of the old man and takes the bag of money and flaunts it in the air above his head, laughing.*)

SIMEON. And sinfuller, too!

PETER. We'll be voyagin' on the sea! Whoop! (*He leaps up and down.*)

SIMEON. Livin' free! Whoop! (*He leaps in turn.*)

CABOT (*suddenly roaring with rage*). My cuss on ye!

SIMEON. Take our'n in trade fur it! Whoop!

CABOT. I'll hev ye both chained up in the asylum!

PETER. Ye old skinflint! Good-by!

SIMEON. Ye old blood sucker! Good-by!

CABOT. Go afore I . . . !

PETER. Whoop! (*He picks a stone from the road.* SIMEON *does the same.*)

SIMEON. Maw'll be in the parlor.

PETER. Ay-eh! One! Two!

CABOT (*frightened*). What air ye . . . ?

PETER. Three! (*They both throw, the stones hitting the parlor window with a crash of glass, tearing the shade.*)

SIMEON. Whoop!

PETER. Whoop!

CABOT (*in a fury now, rushing toward them*). If I kin lay hands on ye — I'll break yer bones fur ye! (*But they beat a capering retreat before him,* SIMEON *with the gate still under his arm.* CABOT *comes back, panting with impotent rage. Their voices as they go off take up the song of the gold-seekers to the old tune of* "Oh, Susannah!"

> "I jumped aboard the Liza ship,
> And traveled on the sea,
> And every time I thought of home
> I wished it wasn't me!
> Oh! Californi-a,
> That's the land fur me!
> I'm off to Californi-a!
> With my wash bowl on my knee."

(*In the meantime, the window of the upper bedroom on right is raised and* ABBIE *sticks her head out. She looks down at* CABOT — *with a sigh of relief.*)

ABBIE. Waal — that's the last o' them two, hain't it? (*He doesn't answer. Then in possessive tones*) This here's a nice bedroom, Ephraim. It's a r'al nice bed. Is it my room, Ephraim?

CABOT (*grimly — without looking up*). Our'n! (*She cannot control a grimace of aversion and pulls back her head slowly and shuts the window. A sudden horrible thought seems to enter* CABOT'S *head.*) They been up to somethin'! Mebbe — mebbe they've pizened the stock — 'r somethin'! (*He almost runs off down toward the barn. A moment later the kitchen door is slowly pushed open and* ABBIE *enters. For a moment she stands looking at* EBEN. *He does not notice her at first. Her eyes take him in penetratingly with a calculating appraisal of his strength as against hers. But under this her desire is dimly awakened by his youth and good looks. Suddenly he becomes conscious of her presence and looks up. Their eyes meet. He leaps to his feet, glowering at her speechlessly.*)

ABBIE (*in her most seductive tones which she uses all through this scene*). Be you — Eben? I'm Abbie — (*She laughs.*) I mean, I'm yer new Maw.

EBEN (*viciously*). No, damn ye!

ABBIE (*as if she hadn't heard — with a queer smile*). Yer Paw's spoke a lot o' yew. . . .

EBEN. Ha!

ABBIE. Ye mustn't mind him. He's an old man. (*A long pause. They stare at each other.*) I don't want t' pretend playin' Maw t' ye,

Eben. (*Admiringly*) Ye're too big an' too strong fur that. I want
t' be frens with ye. Mebbe with me fur a fren ye'd find ye'd like
livin' here better. I kin make it easy fur ye with him, mebbe.
(*With a scornful sense of power*) I calc'late I kin git him t' do
most anythin' fur me.

EBEN (*with bitter scorn*). Ha! (*They stare again,* EBEN *obscurely
moved, physically attracted to her — in forced stilted tones*) Yew
kin go t' the devil!

ABBIE (*calmly*). If cussin' me does ye good, cuss all ye've a mind t'.
I'm all prepared t' have ye again me — at fust. I don't blame ye
nuther. I'd feel the same at any stranger comin' t' take my Maw's
place. (*He shudders. She is watching him carefully.*) Yew must've
cared a lot fur yewr Maw, didn't ye? My Maw died afore I'd
growed. I don't remember her none. (*A pause*) But yew won't
hate me long, Eben. I'm not the wust in the world — an' yew an'
me've got a lot in common. I kin tell that by lookin' at ye. Waal
— I've had a hard life, too — oceans o' trouble an' nuthin' but wuk
fur reward. I was a orphan early an' had t' wuk fur others in
other folks' hums. Then I married an' he turned out a drunken
spreer an' so he had to wuk fur others an' me too agen in other
folks' hums, an' the baby died, an' my husband got sick an' died too,
an' I was glad sayin' now I'm free fur once, on'y I diskivered right
away all I was free fur was t' wuk agen in other folks' hums, doin'
other folks' wuk till I'd most give up hope o' ever doin' my own
wuk in my own hum, an' then your Paw come. . . . (CABOT *appears returning from the barn. He comes to the gate and looks
down the road the brothers have gone. A faint strain of their retreating voices is heard: "Oh, Californi-a! That's the place for me."
He stands glowering, his fists clenched, his face grim with rage.*)

EBEN (*fighting against his growing attraction and sympathy —
harshly*). An' bought yew — like a harlot! (*She is stung and flushes
angrily. She has been sincerely moved by the recital of her troubles. He adds furiously*) An' the price he's payin' ye — this farm
— was my Maw's, damn ye! — an' mine now!

ABBIE (*with a cool laugh of confidence*). Yewr'n? We'll see 'bout
that! (*Then strongly*) Waal — what if I did need a hum? What
else'd I marry an old man like him fur?

EBEN (*maliciously*). I'll tell him ye said that!

ABBIE (*smiling*). I'll say ye're lyin' a-purpose — an' he'll drive ye off
the place!

EBEN. Ye devil!

ABBIE (*defying him*). This be my farm — this be my hum — this be
my kitchen — !

EBEN (*furiously, as if he were going to attack her*). Shut up, damn
ye!

ABBIE (*walks up to him — a queer coarse expression of desire in her
face and body — slowly*). An' upstairs — that be my bedroom —
an' my bed! (*He stares into her eyes, terribly confused and torn.
She adds softly*) I hain't bad nor mean — 'ceptin' fur an enemy —
but I got t' fight fur what's due me out o' life, if I ever 'spect t' git
it. (*Then putting her hand on his arm — seductively*) Let's yew
'n' me be frens, Eben.

EBEN (*stupidly — as if hypnotized*). Ay-eh. (*Then furiously flinging
off her arm*) No, ye durned old witch! I hate ye! (*He rushes out
the door.*)

ABBIE (*looks after him smiling satisfiedly — then half to herself,
mouthing the word*). Eben's nice. (*She looks at the table, proudly*)
I'll wash up *my* dishes now. (EBEN *appears outside, slamming the
door behind him. He comes around corner, stops on seeing his
father, and stands staring at him with hate.*)

CABOT (*raising his arms to heaven in the fury he can no longer control*). Lord God o' Hosts, smite the undutiful sons with Thy wust
cuss!

EBEN (*breaking in violently*). Yew 'n' yewr God! Allus cussin' folks
— allus naggin' 'em!

CABOT (*oblivious to him — summoningly*). God o' the old! God o'
the lonesome!

EBEN (*mockingly*). Naggin' His sheep t' sin! T' hell with yewr God!
(CABOT *turns. He and* EBEN *glower at each other.*)

CABOT (*harshly*). So it's yew. I might've knowed it. (*Shaking his
finger threateningly at him*) Blasphemin' fool! (*Then quickly*)
Why hain't ye t' wuk?

EBEN. Why hain't yew? They've went. I can't wuk it all alone.

CABOT (*contemptuously*). Nor noways! I'm wuth ten o' ye yit, old's
I be! Ye'll never be more'n half a man! (*Then, matter-of-factly*)
Waal — let's git t' the barn. (*They go. A last faint note of the
"Californi-a" song is heard from the distance.* ABBIE *is washing her
dishes.*)

CURTAIN

PART TWO · SCENE ONE

*The exterior of the farmhouse, as in Part One — a hot Sunday after-noon two months later.* ABBIE, *dressed in her best, is discovered sitting in a rocker at the end of the porch. She rocks listlessly, enervated by the heat, staring in front of her with bored, half-closed eyes.* EBEN *sticks his head out of his bedroom window. He looks around furtively and tries to see — or hear — if anyone is on the porch, but although he has been careful to make no noise,* ABBIE *has sensed his movement. She stops rocking, her face grows animated and eager, she waits attentively.* EBEN *seems to feel her presence, he scowls back his thoughts of her and spits with exaggerated disdain — then withdraws back into the room.* ABBIE *waits, holding her breath as she listens with passionate eagerness for every sound within the house.*
EBEN *comes out. Their eyes meet. His falter, he is confused, he turns away and slams the door resentfully. At this gesture,* ABBIE *laughs tantalizingly, amused but at the same time piqued and irritated. He scowls, strides off the porch to the path and starts to walk past her to the road with a grand swagger of ignoring her existence. He is dressed in his store suit, spruced up, his face shines from soap and water.* ABBIE *leans forward on her chair, her eyes hard and angry now, and, as he passes her, gives a sneering, taunting chuckle.*

EBEN (*stung — turns on her furiously*). What air yew cacklin' 'bout?
ABBIE (*triumphant*). Yew!
EBEN. What about me?
ABBIE. Ye look all slicked up like a prize bull.
EBEN (*with a sneer*). Waal — ye hain't so durned purty yerself, be ye? (*They stare into each other's eyes, his held by hers in spite of himself, hers glowingly possessive. Their physical attraction be-comes a palpable force quivering in the hot air.*)
ABBIE (*softly*). Ye don't mean that, Eben. Ye may think ye mean it, mebbe, but ye don't. Ye can't. It's agin nature, Eben. Ye been fightin' yer nature ever since the day I come — tryin' t' tell yerself I hain't purty t'ye. (*She laughs a low humid laugh without taking her eyes from his. A pause — her body squirms desirously — she murmurs languorously.*) Hain't the sun strong an' hot? Ye kin feel it burnin' into the earth — Nature — makin' thin's grow — bigger 'n' bigger — burnin' inside ye — makin' ye want t' grow —

into somethin' else — till ye're jined with it — an' it's your'n — but
it owns ye, too — an' makes ye grow bigger — like a tree — like
them elums — (*She laughs again softly, holding his eyes.
He takes
a step toward her, compelled against his will.*) Nature'll beat ye,
Eben. Ye might's well own up t' it fust 's last.

EBEN (*trying to break from her spell — confusedly*). If Paw'd hear
ye goin' on. . . . (*Resentfully*) But ye've made such a damned
idjit out o' the old devil . . . ! (ABBIE *laughs.*)

ABBIE. Waal — hain't it easier fur yew with him changed softer?

EBEN (*defiantly*). No. I'm fightin' him — fightin' yew — fightin' fur
Maw's rights t' her hum! (*This breaks her spell for him. He glow-
ers at her.*) An' I'm onto ye. Ye hain't foolin' me a mite. Ye're
aimin' t' swaller up everythin' an' make it your'n. Waal, you'll find
I'm a heap sight bigger hunk nor yew kin chew! (*He turns from
her with a sneer.*)

ABBIE (*trying to regain her ascendancy — seductively*). Eben!

EBEN. Leave me be! (*He starts to walk away.*)

ABBIE (*more commandingly*). Eben!

EBEN (*stops — resentfully*). What d'ye want?

ABBIE (*trying to conceal a growing excitement*). Whar air ye goin'?

EBEN (*with malicious nonchalance*). Oh — up the road a spell.

ABBIE. T' the village?

EBEN (*airily*). Mebbe.

ABBIE (*excitedly*). T' see that Min, I s'pose?

EBEN. Mebbe.

ABBIE (*weakly*). What d'ye want t' waste time on her fur?

EBEN (*revenging himself now — grinning at her*). Ye can't beat Nature, didn't ye say? (*He laughs and again starts to walk away.*)

ABBIE (*bursting out*). An ugly old hake!

EBEN (*with a tantalizing sneer*). She's purtier'n yew be!

ABBIE. That every wuthless drunk in the country has. . . .

EBEN (*tauntingly*). Mebbe — but she's better'n yew. She owns up
fa'r 'n' squar' t' her doin's.

ABBIE (*furiously*). Don't ye dare compare. . . .

EBEN. She don't go sneakin' an' stealin' — what's mine.

ABBIE (*savagely seizing on his weak point*). Your'n? Yew mean —
my farm?

EBEN. I mean the farm yew sold yerself fur like any other old whore
— my farm!

ABBIE (*stung — fiercely*). Ye'll never live t' see the day when even a
stinkin' weed on it 'll belong t' ye! (*Then in a scream*) Git out o'
my sight! Go on t' yer slut — disgracin' yer Paw 'n' me! I'll git
yer Paw t' horsewhip ye off the place if I want t'! Ye're only

livin' here 'cause I tolerate ye! Git along! I hate the sight o' ye!
(*She stops, panting and glaring at him.*)

EBEN (*returning her glance in kind*). An' I hate the sight o' yew!
(*He turns and strides off up the road. She follows his retreating
figure with concentrated hate. Old* CABOT *appears coming up from
the barn. The hard, grim expression of his face has changed. He
seems in some queer way softened, mellowed. His eyes have taken
on a strange, incongruous dreamy quality. Yet there is no hint of
physical weakness about him — rather he looks more robust and
younger.* ABBIE *sees him and turns away quickly with unconcealed
aversion. He comes slowly up to her.*)

CABOT (*mildly*). War yew an' Eben quarrelin' agen?

ABBIE (*shortly*). No.

CABOT. Ye was talkin' a'mighty loud. (*He sits down on the edge of
porch.*)

ABBIE (*snappishly*). If ye heerd us they hain't no need askin' questions.

CABOT. I didn't hear what ye said.

ABBIE (*relieved*). Waal — it wa'n't nothin' t' speak on.

CABOT (*after a pause*). Eben's queer.

ABBIE (*bitterly*). He's the dead spit 'n' image o' yew!

CABOT (*queerly interested*). D'ye think so, Abbie? (*After a pause,
ruminatingly*) Me 'n' Eben's allus fit 'n' fit. I never could b'ar him
noways. He's so thunderin' soft — like his Maw.

ABBIE (*scornfully*). Ay-eh! 'Bout as soft as yew be!

CABOT (*as if he hadn't heard*). Mebbe I been too hard on him.

ABBIE (*jeeringly*). Waal — ye're gittin' soft now — soft as slop! That's
what Eben was sayin'.

CABOT (*his face instantly grim and ominous*). Eben was sayin'? Waal,
he'd best not do nothin' t' try me 'r he'll soon diskiver. . . . (*A
pause. She keeps her face turned away. His gradually softens. He
stares up at the sky.*) Purty, hain't it?

ABBIE (*crossly*). I don't see nothin' purty.

CABOT. The sky. Feels like a wa'm field up thar.

ABBIE (*sarcastically*). Air yew aimin' t' buy up over the farm too?
(*She snickers contemptuously.*)

CABOT (*strangely*). I'd like t' own my place up thar. (*A pause*) I'm
gittin' old, Abbie. I'm gittin' ripe on the bough. (*A pause. She
stares at him mystified. He goes on.*) It's allus lonesome cold in
the house — even when it's bilin' hot outside. Hain't yew noticed?

ABBIE. No.

CABOT. It's wa'm down t' the barn — nice smellin' an' warm — with
the cows. (*A pause*) Cows is queer.

ABBIE. Like yew?

CABOT. Like Eben. (*A pause*) I'm gittin' t' feel resigned t' Eben —
jest as I got t' feel 'bout his Maw. I'm gittin' t' learn to b'ar his
softness — jest like her'n. I calc'late I c'd a'most take t' him — if he
wa'n't sech a dumb fool! (*A pause*) I s'pose it's old age a-creepin'
in my bones.

ABBIE (*indifferently*). Waal — ye hain't dead yet.

CABOT (*roused*). No, I hain't, yew bet — not by a hell of a sight —
I'm sound 'n' tough as hickory! (*Then moodily*) But arter three
score and ten the Lord warns ye t' prepare. (*A pause*) That's why
Eben's come in my head. Now that his cussed sinful brothers is
gone their path t' hell, they's no one left but Eben.

ABBIE (*resentfully*). They's me, hain't they? (*Agitatedly*) What's all
this sudden likin' ye've tuk to Eben? Why don't ye say nothin'
'bout me? Hain't I yer lawful wife?

CABOT (*simply*). Ay-eh. Ye be. (*A pause — he stares at her desirously — his eyes grow avid — then with a sudden movement he
seizes her hands and squeezes them, declaiming in a queer camp
meeting preacher's tempo*) Yew air my Rose o' Sharon! Behold,
yew air fair; yer eyes air doves; yer lips air like scarlet; yer two
breasts air like two fawns; yer navel be like a round goblet; yer
belly be like a heap o' wheat. . . . (*He covers her hand with
kisses. She does not seem to notice. She stares before her with
hard angry eyes.*)

ABBIE (*jerking her hands away — harshly*). So ye're plannin' t' leave
the farm t' Eben, air ye?

CABOT (*dazedly*). Leave. . . . ? (*Then with resentful obstinacy*) I
hain't a-givin' it t' no one!

ABBIE (*remorselessly*). Ye can't take it with ye.

CABOT (*thinks a moment — then reluctantly*). No, I calc'late not.
(*After a pause — with a strange passion*) But if I could, I would,
by the Etarnal! 'R if I could, in my dyin' hour, I'd set it afire an'
watch it burn — this house an' every ear o' corn an' every tree
down t' the last blade o' hay! I'd sit an' know it was all a-dying
with me an' no one else'd ever own what was mine, what I'd made
out o' nothin' with my own sweat 'n' blood! (*A pause — then he
adds with a queer affection*) 'Ceptin' the cows. Them I'd turn free.

ABBIE (*harshly*). An' me?

CABOT (*with a queer smile*). Ye'd be turned free, too.

ABBIE (*furiously*). So that's the thanks I git fur marryin' ye — t' have
ye change kind to Eben who hates ye, an' talk o' turnin' me out in
the road.

CABOT (*hastily*). Abbie! Ye know I wa'n't. . . .

ABBIE (*vengefully*). Just let me tell ye a thing or two 'bout Eben! Whar's he gone? T' see that harlot, Min! I tried fur t' stop him. Disgracin' yew an' me — on the Sabbath, too!

CABOT (*rather guiltily*). He's a sinner — nateral-born. It's lust eatin' his heart.

ABBIE (*enraged beyond endurance — wildly vindictive*). An' his lust fur me! Kin ye find excuses fur that?

CABOT (*stares at her — after a dead pause*). Lust — fur yew?

ABBIE (*defiantly*). He was tryin' t' make love t' me — when ye heerd us quarrelin'.

CABOT (*stares at her — then a terrible expression of rage comes over his face — he springs to his feet shaking all over*). By the A'mighty God I'll end him!

ABBIE (*frightened now for* EBEN). No! Don't ye!

CABOT (*violently*). I'll git the shotgun an' blow his soft brains t' the top o' them elums!

ABBIE (*throwing her arms around him*). No, Ephraim!

CABOT (*pushing her away violently*). I will, by God!

ABBIE (*in a quieting tone*). Listen, Ephraim. 'Twa'n't nothin' bad — on'y a boy's foolin' — 'twa'n't meant serious — jest jokin' an' teasin' . . . .

CABOT. Then why did ye say — lust?

ABBIE. It must hev sounded wusser'n I meant. An' I was mad at thinkin' — ye'd leave him the farm.

CABOT (*quieter but still grim and cruel*). Waal then, I'll horsewhip him off the place if that much'll content ye.

ABBIE (*reaching out and taking his hand*). No. Don't think o' me! Ye mustn't drive him off. 'Tain't sensible. Who'll ye get to help ye on the farm? They's no one hereabouts.

CABOT (*considers this — then nodding his appreciation*). Ye got a head on ye. (*Then irritably*) Waal, let him stay. (*He sits down on the edge of the porch. She sits beside him. He murmurs contemptuously*) I oughtn't t' git riled so — at that 'ere fool calf. (*A pause*) But har's the p'int. What son o' mine'll keep on here t' the farm — when the Lord does call me? Simeon an' Peter air gone t' hell — an' Eben's follerin' 'em.

ABBIE. They's me.

CABOT. Ye're on'y a woman.

ABBIE. I'm yewr wife.

CABOT. That hain't me. A son is me — my blood — mine. Mine ought t' git mine. An' then it's still mine — even though I be six foot under. D'ye see?

ABBIE (*giving him a look of hatred*). Ay-eh. I see. (*She becomes very thoughtful, her face growing shrewd, her eyes studying* CABOT *craftily.*)

CABOT. I'm gittin' old—ripe on the bough. (*Then with a sudden forced reassurance*) Not but what I hain't a hard nut t' crack even yet—an' fur many a year t' come! By the Etarnal, I kin break most o' the young fellers' backs at any kind o' work any day o' the year!

ABBIE (*suddenly*). Mebbe the Lord'll give *us* a son.

CABOT (*turns and stares at her eagerly*). Ye mean—a son—t' me 'n' yew?

ABBIE (*with a cajoling smile*). Ye're a strong man yet, hain't ye? 'Tain't noways impossible, be it? We know that. Why d'ye stare so? Hain't ye never thought o' that afore? I been thinkin' o' it all along. Ay-eh—an' I been prayin' it'd happen, too.

CABOT (*his face growing full of joyous pride and a sort of religious ecstasy*). Ye been prayin', Abbie?—fur a son?—t' us?

ABBIE. Ay-eh. (*With a grim resolution*) I want a son now.

CABOT (*excitedly clutching both of her hands in his*). It'd be the blessin' o' God, Abbie—the blessin' o' God A'mighty on me—in my old age—in my lonesomeness! They hain't nothin' I wouldn't do fur ye then, Abbie. Ye'd hev on'y t' ask it—anythin' ye'd a mind t'!

ABBIE (*interrupting*). Would ye will the farm t' me then—t' me an' it . . . ?

CABOT (*vehemently*). I'd do anythin' ye axed, I tell ye! I swar it! May I be everlastin' damned t' hell if I wouldn't! (*He sinks to his knees pulling her down with him. He trembles all over with the fervor of his hopes.*) Pray t' the Lord agen, Abbie. It's the Sabbath! I'll jine ye! Two prayers air better nor one. "An' God hearkened unto Rachel"! An' God hearkened unto Abbie! Pray, Abbie! Pray fur him to hearken! (*He bows his head, mumbling. She pretends to do likewise but gives him a side glance of scorn and triumph.*)

## SCENE TWO

*About eight in the evening. The interior of the two bedrooms on the top floor is shown.* EBEN *is sitting on the side of his bed in the room on the left. On account of the heat he has taken off everything but his undershirt and pants. His feet are bare. He faces front, brooding moodily, his chin propped on his hands, a desperate expression on his face.*

*In the other room* CABOT *and* ABBIE *are sitting side by side on the*

edge of their bed, an old four-poster with feather mattress. He is
in his night shirt, she in her nightdress. He is still in the queer,
excited mood into which the notion of a son has thrown him. Both
rooms are lighted dimly and flickeringly by tallow candles.

CABOT. The farm needs a son.

ABBIE. I need a son.

CABOT. Ay-eh. Sometimes ye air the farm an' sometimes the farm be
yew. That's why I clove t' ye in my lonesomeness. (*A pause. He
pounds his knee with his fist.*) Me an' the farm has got t' beget a
son!

ABBIE. Ye'd best go t' sleep. Ye're gittin' thin's all mixed.

CABOT (*with an impatient gesture*). No, I hain't. My mind's clear's a
well. Ye don't know me, that's it. (*He stares hopelessly at the
floor.*)

ABBIE (*indifferently*). Mebbe. (*In the next room* EBEN *gets up and
paces up and down distractedly.* ABBIE *hears him. Her eyes fasten
on the intervening wall with concentrated attention.* EBEN *stops and
stares. Their hot glances seem to meet through the wall. Unconsciously he stretches out his arms for her and she half rises. Then
aware, he mutters a curse at himself and flings himself face downward on the bed, his clenched fists above his head, his face buried
in the pillow.* ABBIE *relaxes with a faint sigh but her eyes remain
fixed on the wall; she listens with all her attention for some movement from* EBEN.)

CABOT (*suddenly raises his head and looks at her — scornfully*). Will
ye ever know me — 'r will any man 'r woman? (*Shaking his head*)
No. I calc'late 't wa'n't t' be. (*He turns away.* ABBIE *looks at the
wall. Then, evidently unable to keep silent about his thoughts,
without looking at his wife, he puts out his hand and clutches her
knee. She starts violently, looks at him, sees he is not watching
her, concentrates again on the wall and pays no attention to what
he says.*) Listen, Abbie. When I come here fifty odd year ago —
I was jest twenty an' the strongest an' hardest ye ever seen — ten
times as strong an' fifty times as hard as Eben. Waal — this place
was nothin' but fields o' stones. Folks laughed when I tuk it. They
couldn't know what I knowed. When ye kin make corn sprout out
o' stones, God's livin' in yew! They wa'n't strong enuf fur that!
They reckoned God was easy. They laughed. They don't laugh no
more. Some died hereabouts. Some went West an' died. They're
all under ground — fur follerin' arter an easy God. God hain't easy.
(*He shakes his head slowly.*) An' I growed hard. Folks kept allus
sayin' he's a hard man like 'twas sinful t' be hard, so's at last I said
back at 'em: Waal then, by thunder, ye'll git me hard an' see how

ye like it! (*Then suddenly*) But I give in t' weakness once. 'Twas arter I'd been here two year. I got weak — despairful — they was so many stones. They was a party leavin', givin' up, goin' West. I jined 'em. We tracked on 'n' on. We come t' broad medders, plains, whar the soil was black an' rich as gold. Nary a stone. Easy. Ye'd on'y to plow an' sow an' then set an' smoke yer pipe an' watch thin's grow. I could o' been a rich man — but somethin' in me fit me an fit me — the voice o' God sayin': "This hain't wuth nothin' t' Me. Git ye back t' hum!" I got afeerd o' that voice an' I lit out back t' hum here, leavin' my claim an' crops t' whoever'd a mind t' take 'em. Ay-eh. I actoolly give up what was rightful mine! God's hard, not easy! God's in the stones! Build my church on a rock — out o' stones an' I'll be in them! That's what He meant t' Peter! (*He sighs heavily — a pause.*) Stones. I picked 'em up an' piled 'em into walls. Ye kin read the years o' my life in them walls, every day a hefted stone, climbin' over the hills up and down, fencin' in the fields that was mine, whar I'd made thin's grow out o' nothin' — like the will o' God, like the servant o' His hand. It wa'n't easy. It was hard an' He made me hard fur it. (*He pauses.*) All the time I kept gittin' lonesomer. I tuk a wife. She bore Simeon an' Peter. She was a good woman. She wuked hard. We was married twenty year. She never knowed me. She helped but she never knowed what she was helpin'. I was allus lonesome. She died. After that it wa'n't so lonesome fur a spell. (*A pause*) I lost count o' the years. I had no time t' fool away countin' 'em. Sim an' Peter helped. The farm growed. It was all mine! When I thought o' that I didn't feel lonesome. (*A pause*) But ye can't hitch yer mind t' one thin' day an' night. I tuk another wife — Eben's Maw. Her folks was contestin' me at law over my deeds t' the farm — my farm! That's why Eben keeps a-talkin' his fool talk o' this bein' his Maw's farm. She bore Eben. She was purty — but soft. She tried t' be hard. She couldn't. She never knowed me nor nothin'. It was lonesomer 'n hell with her. After a matter o' sixteen odd years she died. (*A pause*) I lived with the boys. They hated me 'cause I was hard. I hated them 'cause they was soft. They coveted the farm without knowin' what it meant. It made me bitter 'n wormwood. It aged me — them coveting what I'd made fur mine. Then this spring the call come — the voice o' God cryin' in my wilderness, in my lonesomeness — t' go out an' seek an' find! (*Turning to her with strange passion*) I sought ye an' I found ye! Yew air my Rose o' Sharon' Yer eyes air like. . . . (*She has turned a blank face, resentful eyes to his. He stares at her for a moment — then harshly*) Air ye any the wiser fur all I've told ye?

ABBIE (*confusedly*). Mebbe.

CABOT (*pushing her away from him — angrily*). Ye don't know nothin' — nor never will. If ye don't hev a son t' redeem ye. . . . (*This in a tone of cold threat.*)

ABBIE (*resentfully*). I've prayed, hain't I?

CABOT (*bitterly*). Pray agen — fur understandin'!

ABBIE (*a veiled threat in her tone*). Ye'll have a son out o' me, I promise ye.

CABOT. How kin ye promise?

ABBIE. I got second-sight mebbe. I kin foretell. (*She gives a queer smile.*)

CABOT. I believe ye have. Ye give me the chills sometimes. (*He shivers.*) It's cold in this house. It's oneasy. They's thin's pokin' about in the dark — in the corners. (*He pulls on his trousers, tucking in his night shirt, and pulls on his boots.*)

ABBIE (*surprised*). Whar air ye goin'?

CABOT (*queerly*). Down whar it's restful — whar it's warm — down t' the barn. (*Bitterly*) I kin talk t' the cows. They know. They know the farm an' me. They'll give me peace. (*He turns to go out the door.*)

ABBIE (*a bit frightenedly.*) Air ye ailin' tonight, Ephraim?

CABOT. Growin'. Growin' ripe on the bough. (*He turns and goes, his boots clumping down the stairs.* EBEN *sits up with a start, listening.* ABBIE *is conscious of his movement and stares at the wall.* CABOT *comes out of the house around the corner and stands by the gate, blinking at the sky. He stretches up his hands in a tortured gesture.*) God A'mighty, call from the dark! (*He listens as if expecting an answer. Then his arms drop, he shakes his head and plods off toward the barn.* EBEN *and* ABBIE *stare at each other through the wall.* EBEN *sighs heavily and* ABBIE *echoes it. Both become terribly nervous, uneasy. Finally* ABBIE *gets up and listens, her ear to the wall. He acts as if he saw every move she was making, he becomes resolutely still. She seems driven into a decision — goes out the door in rear determinedly. His eyes follow her. Then as the door of his room is opened softly, he turns away, waits in an attitude of strained fixity.* ABBIE *stands for a second staring at him, her eyes burning with desire. Then with a little cry she runs over and throws her arms about his neck, she pulls his head back and covers his mouth with kisses. At first, he submits dumbly; then he puts his arms about her neck and returns her kisses, but finally, suddenly aware of his hatred, he hurls her away from him, springing to his feet. They stand speechless and breathless, panting like two animals.*)

ABBIE (*at last — painfully*). Ye shouldn't, Eben — ye shouldn't — I'd make ye happy!

EBEN (*harshly*). I don't want t' be happy — from yew!

ABBIE (*helplessly*). Ye do, Eben! Ye do! Why d'ye lie?

EBEN (*viciously*). I don't take t' ye, I tell ye! I hate the sight o' ye!

ABBIE (*with an uncertain troubled laugh*). Waal, I kissed ye anyways — an' ye kissed back — yer lips was burnin' — ye can't lie 'bout that! (*Intensely*) If ye don't care, why did ye kiss me back — why was yer lips burnin'?

EBEN (*wiping his mouth*). It was like pizen on 'em. (*Then tauntingly*) When I kissed ye back, mebbe I thought 'twas someone else.

ABBIE (*wildly*). Min?

EBEN. Mebbe.

ABBIE (*torturedly*). Did ye go t' see her? Did ye r'ally go? I thought ye mightn't. Is that why ye throwed me off jest now?

EBEN (*sneeringly*). What if it be?

ABBIE (*raging*). Then ye're a dog, Eben Cabot!

EBEN (*threateningly*). Ye can't talk that way t' me!

ABBIE (*with a shrill laugh*). Can't I? Did ye think I was in love with ye — a weak thin' like yew? Not much, I on'y wanted ye fur a purpose o' my own — an' I'll hev ye fur it yet 'cause I'm stronger'n yew be!

EBEN (*resentfully*). I knowed well it was on'y part o' yer plan t' swaller everythin'!

ABBIE (*tauntingly*). Mebbe!

EBEN (*furious*). Git out o' my room!

ABBIE. This air my room an' ye're on'y hired help!

EBEN (*threateningly*). Git out afore I murder ye!

ABBIE (*quite confident now*). I hain't a mite afeerd. Ye want me, don't ye? Yes, ye do! An' yer Paw's son'll never kill what he wants! Look at yer eyes! They's lust fur me in 'em, burnin' 'em up! Look at yer lips now! They're tremblin' an' longin' t' kiss me, an' yer teeth t' bite! (*He is watching her now with a horrible fascination. She laughs a crazy triumphant laugh*) I'm a-goin' t' make all o' this hum my hum! They's one room hain't mine yet, but it's a-goin' t' be tonight. I'm a-goin' down now an' light up! (*She makes him a mocking bow.*) Won't ye come courtin' me in the best parlor, Mister Cabot?

EBEN (*staring at her—horribly confused—dully*). Don't ye dare! It hain't been opened since Maw died an' was laid out thar! Don't ye . . . ! (*But her eyes are fixed on his so burningly that his will seems to wither before hers. He stands swaying toward her helplessly.*)

ABBIE (*holding his eyes and putting all her will into her words as she backs out the door*). I'll expect ye afore long, Eben.

EBEN (*stares after her for a while, walking toward the door. A light appears in the parlor window. He murmurs*). In the parlor? (*This seems to arouse connotations for he comes back and puts on his white shirt, collar, half ties the tie mechanically, puts on coat, takes his hat, stands barefooted looking about him in bewilderment, mutters wonderingly*.) Maw! Whar air yew? (*Then goes slowly toward the door in rear.*)

## SCENE THREE

*A few minutes later. The interior of the parlor is shown. A grim, repressed room like a tomb in which the family has been interred alive.* ABBIE *sits on the edge of the horsehair sofa. She has lighted all the candles and the room is revealed in all its preserved ugliness. A change has come over the woman. She looks awed and frightened now, ready to run away.*

*The door is opened, and* EBEN *appears. His face wears an expression of obsessed confusion. He stands staring at her, his arms hanging disjointedly from his shoulders, his feet bare, his hat in his hand.*

ABBIE (*after a pause — with a nervous, formal politeness*). Won't ye set?

EBEN (*dully*). Ay-eh. (*Mechanically he places his hat carefully on the floor near the door and sits stiffly beside her on the edge of the sofa. A pause. They both remain rigid, looking straight ahead with eyes full of fear.*)

ABBIE. When I fust come in — in the dark — they seemed somethin' here.

EBEN (*simply*). Maw.

ABBIE. I kin still feel — somethin'. . . .

EBEN. It's Maw.

ABBIE. At fust I was feered o' it. I wanted t' yell an' run. Now — since yew come — seems like it's growin' soft an' kind t' me. (*Addressing the air — queerly*) Thank yew.

EBEN. Maw allus loved me.

ABBIE. Mebbe it knows I love yew, too. Mebbe that makes it kind t' me.

EBEN (*dully*). I dunno. I should think she'd hate ye.

ABBIE (*with certainty*). No. I kin feel it don't — not no more.

EBEN. Hate ye fur stealin' her place — here in her hum — settin' in her parlor whar she was laid — (*He suddenly stops, staring stupidly before him.*)

ABBIE. What is it, Eben?

EBEN (*in a whisper*). Seems like Maw didn't want me t' remind ye.

ABBIE (*excitedly*). I knowed, Eben! It's kind t' me! It don't b'ar me no grudges fur what I never knowed an' couldn't help!

EBEN. Maw b'ars him a grudge.

ABBIE. Waal, so does all o' us.

EBEN. Ay-eh. (*With passion*) I does, by God!

ABBIE (*taking one of his hands in hers and patting it*). Thar! Don't git riled thinkin' o' him. Think o' yer Maw who's kind t' us. Tell me about yer Maw, Eben.

EBEN. They hain't nothin' much. She was kind. She was good.

ABBIE (*putting one arm over his shoulder. He does not seem to notice —passionately*). I'll be kind an' good t' ye!

EBEN. Sometimes she used t' sing fur me.

ABBIE. I'll sing fur ye!

EBEN. This was her hum. This was her farm.

ABBIE. This is my hum! This is my farm!

EBEN. He married her t' steal 'em. She was soft an' easy. He couldn't 'preciate her.

ABBIE. He can't 'preciate me!

EBEN. He murdered her with his hardness.

ABBIE. He's murderin' me!

EBEN. She died. (*A pause*) Sometimes she used to sing fur me. (*He bursts into a fit of sobbing.*)

ABBIE (*both her arms around him — with wild passion*). I'll sing fur ye! I'll die fur ye! (*In spite of her overwhelming desire for him, there is a sincere maternal love in her manner and voice — a horribly frank mixture of lust and mother love.*) Don't cry, Eben! I'll take yer Maw's place! I'll be everythin' she was t' ye! Let me kiss ye, Eben! (*She pulls his head around. He makes a bewildered pretense of resistance. She is tender.*) Don't be afeered! I'll kiss ye pure, Eben — same's if I was a Maw t' ye — an' ye kin kiss me back 's if yew was my son — my boy — sayin' good-night t' me! Kiss me, Eben. (*They kiss in restrained fashion. Then suddenly wild passion overcomes her. She kisses him lustfully again and again and he flings his arms about her and returns her kisses. Suddenly, as in the bedroom, he frees himself from her violently and springs to his feet. He is trembling all over, in a strange state of terror.* ABBIE *strains her arms toward him with fierce pleading.*) Don't ye leave me, Eben! Can't ye see it hain't enuf — lovin' ye like a Maw — can't ye see it's got t' be that an' more — much more

—a hundred times more—fur me t' be happy—fur yew t' be happy?

EBEN (*to the presence he feels in the room*). Maw! Maw! What d'ye want? What air ye tellin' me?

ABBIE. She's tellin' ye t' love me. She knows I love ye an' I'll be good t' ye. Can't ye feel it? Don't ye know? She's tellin' ye t' love me, Eben!

EBEN. Ay-eh. I feel—mebbe she—but—I can't figger out—why —when ye've stole her place—here in her hum—in the parlor whar she was—

ABBIE (*fiercely*). She knows I love ye!

EBEN (*his face suddenly lighting up with a fierce, triumphant grin*). I see it! I sees why. It's her vengeance on him—so's she kin rest quiet in her grave!

ABBIE (*wildly*). Vengeance o' God on the hull o' us! What d'we give a durn? I love ye, Eben! God knows I love ye! (*She stretches out her arms for him.*)

EBEN (*throws himself on his knees beside the sofa and grabs her in his arms—releasing all his pent-up passion*). An' I love yew, Abbie!— now I kin say it! I been dyin' fur want o' ye—every hour since ye come! I love ye! (*Their lips meet in a fierce, bruising kiss.*)

## SCENE FOUR

*Exterior of the farmhouse. It is just dawn. The front door at right is opened and* EBEN *comes out and walks around to the gate. He is dressed in his working clothes. He seems changed. His face wears a bold and confident expression, he is grinning to himself with evident satisfaction. As he gets near the gate, the window of the parlor is heard opening and the shutters are flung back and* ABBIE *sticks her head out. Her hair tumbles over her shoulders in disarray, her face is flushed, she looks at* EBEN *with tender, languorous eyes and calls softly.*

ABBIE. Eben. (*As he turns—playfully*) Jest one more kiss afore ye go. I'm goin' to miss ye fearful all day.

EBEN. An' me yew, ye kin bet! (*He goes to her. They kiss several times. He draws away, laughingly.*) Thar. That's enuf, hain't it? Ye won't hev none left fur next time.

ABBIE. I got a million o' 'em left fur yew! (*Then a bit anxiously*) D'ye r'ally love me, Eben?

EBEN (*emphatically*). I like ye better'n any gal I ever knowed! That's gospel!

ABBIE. Likin' hain't lovin'.

EBEN. Waal then — I love ye. Now air yew satisfied?

ABBIE. Ay-eh, I be. (*She smiles at him adoringly.*)

EBEN. I better git t' the barn. The old critter's liable t' suspicion an' come sneakin' up.

ABBIE (*with a confident laugh*). Let him! I kin allus pull the wool over his eyes. I'm goin' t' leave the shutters open and let in the sun 'n' air. This room's been dead long enuf. Now it's goin' t' be my room!

EBEN (*frowning*). Ay-eh.

ABBIE (*hastily*). I meant — our room.

EBEN. Ay-eh.

ABBIE. We made it our'n last night, didn't we? We give it life — our lovin' did. (*A pause.*)

EBEN (*with a strange look*). Maw's gone back t' her grave. She kin sleep now.

ABBIE. May she rest in peace! (*Then tenderly rebuking*) Ye oughtn't t' talk o' sad thin's — this mornin'.

EBEN. It jest come up in my mind o' itself.

ABBIE. Don't let it. (*He doesn't answer. She yawns.*) Waal, I'm a-goin' t' steal a wink o' sleep. I'll tell the Old Man I hain't feelin' pert. Let him git his own vittles.

EBEN. I see him comin' from the barn. Ye better look smart an' git upstairs.

ABBIE. Ay-eh. Good-by. Don't ferget me. (*She throws him a kiss. He grins — then squares his shoulders and awaits his father confidently.* CABOT *walks slowly up from the left, staring up at the sky with a vague face.*)

EBEN (*jovially*). Mornin', Paw. Star-gazin' in daylight?

CABOT. Purty, hain't it?

EBEN (*looking around him possessively*). It's a durned purty farm.

CABOT. I mean the sky.

EBEN (*grinning*). How d'ye know? Them eyes o' your'n can't see that fur. (*This tickles his humor and he slaps his thigh and laughs.*) Ho-ho! That's a good un!

CABOT (*grimly sarcastic*). Ye're feelin' right chipper, hain't ye? Whar'd ye steal the likker?

EBEN (*good-naturedly*). 'Tain't likker. Jest life. (*Suddenly holding out his hand — soberly*) Yew 'n' me is quits. Let's shake hands.

CABOT (*suspiciously*). What's come over ye?

EBEN. Then don't. Mebbe it's jest as well. (*A moment's pause*)

What's come over me? (*Queerly*) Didn't ye feel her passin' — goin'
back t' her grave?

CABOT (*dully*). Who?

EBEN. Maw. She kin rest now an' sleep content. She's quits with ye.

CABOT (*confusedly*). I rested. I slept good — down with the cows.
They know how t' sleep. They're teachin' me.

EBEN (*suddenly jovial again*). Good fur the cows! Waal — ye better
git t' work.

CABOT (*grimly amused*). Air yew bossin' me, ye calf?

EBEN (*beginning to laugh*). Ay-eh! I'm bossin' yew! Ha-ha-ha! See
how ye like it! Ha-ha-ha! I'm the prize rooster o' this roost. Ha-
ha-ha! (*He goes off toward the barn laughing.*)

CABOT (*looks after him with scornful pity*). Soft-headed. Like his
Maw. Dead spit 'n' image. No hope in him! (*He spits with con-
temptuous disgust.*) A born fool! (*Then matter-of-factly*) Waal
— I'm gittin' peckish. (*He goes toward door.*)

CURTAIN


PART THREE · SCENE ONE

*A night in late spring the following year. The kitchen and the two
bedrooms upstairs are shown. The two bedrooms are dimly lighted
by a tallow candle in each.* EBEN *is sitting on the side of the bed in
his room, his chin propped on his fists, his face a study of the
struggle he is making to understand his conflicting emotions. The
noisy laughter and music from below where a kitchen dance is in
progress annoy and distract him. He scowls at the floor.*

*In the next room a cradle stands beside the double bed.*

*In the kitchen all is festivity. The stove has been taken down to
give more room to the dancers. The chairs, with wooden benches
added, have been pushed back against the walls. On these are
seated, squeezed in tight against one another, farmers and their
wives and their young folks of both sexes from the neighboring
farms. They are all chattering and laughing loudly. They evidently have some secret joke in common. There is no end of
winking, of nudging, of meaning nods of the head toward* CABOT
*who, in a state of extreme hilarious excitement increased by the
amount he has drunk, is standing near the rear door where there is
a small keg of whisky and serving drinks to all the men. In the left
corner, front, dividing the attention with her husband,* ABBIE *is sitting
in a rocking chair, a shawl wrapped about her shoulders. She is very*

*pale, her face is thin and drawn, her eyes are fixed anxiously on the
open door in rear as if waiting for someone.
The musician is tuning up his fiddle, seated in the far right corner.
He is a lanky young fellow with a long, weak face. His pale eyes
blink incessantly and he grins about him slyly with a greedy malice.*

ABBIE (*suddenly turning to a young girl on her right*). Whar's Eben?

YOUNG GIRL (*eyeing her scornfully*). I dunno, Mrs. Cabot. I hain't
seen Eben in ages. (*Meaningly*) Seems like he's spent most o' his
time t' hum since yew come.

ABBIE (*vaguely*). I tuk his Maw's place.

YOUNG GIRL. Ay-eh. So I've heerd. (*She turns away to retail this bit
of gossip to her mother sitting next to her.* ABBIE *turns to her left
to a big stoutish middle-aged man whose flushed face and starting
eyes show the amount of "likker" he has consumed.*)

ABBIE. Ye hain't seen Eben, hev ye?

MAN. No, I hain't. (*Then he adds with a wink*) If yew hain't, who
would?

ABBIE. He's the best dancer in the county. He'd ought t' come an'
dance.

MAN (*with a wink*). Mebbe he's doin' the dutiful an' walkin' the kid
t' sleep. It's a boy, hain't it?

ABBIE (*nodding vaguely*). Ay-eh — born two weeks back — purty's a
picter.

MAN. They all is — t' their Maws. (*Then in a whisper, with a nudge
and a leer*) Listen, Abbie — if ye ever git tired o' Eben, remember
me! Don't fergit now! (*He looks at her uncomprehending face
for a second — then grunts disgustedly.*) Waal — guess I'll likker
agin. (*He goes over and joins* CABOT *who is arguing noisily with an
old farmer over cows. They all drink.*)

ABBIE (*this time appealing to nobody in particular*). Wonder what
Eben's a-doin'? (*Her remark is repeated down the line with many
a guffaw and titter until it reaches the fiddler. He fastens his blinking eyes on* ABBIE.)

FIDDLER (*raising his voice*). Bet I kin tell ye, Abbie, what Eben's
doin'! He's down t' the church offerin' up prayers o' thanksgivin'.
(*They all titter expectantly.*)

A MAN. What fur? (*Another titter.*)

FIDDLER. 'Cause unto him a — (*He hesitates just long enough*) brother
is born! (*A roar of laughter. They all look from* ABBIE *to* CABOT.
*She is oblivious, staring at the door.* CABOT, *although he hasn't heard
the words, is irritated by the laughter and steps forward, glaring
about him. There is an immediate silence.*)

CABOT. What're ye all bleatin' about — like a flock o' goats? Why don't ye dance, damn ye? I axed ye here t' dance — t' eat, drink an' be merry — an' thar ye set cacklin' like a lot o' wet hens with the pip! Ye've swilled my likker an' guzzled my vittles like hogs, hain't ye? Then dance fur me, can't ye? That's fa'r an' squar', hain't it? (*A grumble of resentment goes around but they are all evidently in too much awe of him to express it openly.*)

FIDDLER (*slyly*). We're waitin' fur Eben. (*A suppressed laugh.*)

CABOT (*with a fierce exultation*). T'hell with Eben! Eben's done fur now! I got a new son! (*His mood switching with drunken suddenness*) But ye needn't t' laugh at Eben, none o' ye! He's my blood, if he be a dumb fool. He's better nor any o' yew! He kin do a day's work a'most up t' what I kin — an' that'd put any o' yew pore critters t' shame!

FIDDLER. An' he kin do a good night's work, too! (*A roar of laughter.*)

CABOT. Laugh, ye damn fools! Ye're right jist the same, Fiddler. He kin work day an' night too, like I kin, if need be!

OLD FARMER (*from behind the keg where he is weaving drunkenly back and forth — with great simplicity*). They hain't many t' touch ye, Ephraim — a son at seventy-six. That's a hard man fur ye! I be on'y sixty-eight an' I couldn't do it. (*A roar of laughter in which* CABOT *joins uproariously.*)

CABOT (*slapping him on the back*). I'm sorry fur ye, Hi. I'd never suspicion sech weakness from a boy like yew!

OLD FARMER. An' I never reckoned yew had it in ye nuther, Ephraim. (*There is another laugh.*)

CABOT (*suddenly grim*). I got a lot in me — a hell of a lot — folks don't know on. (*Turning to the fiddler*) Fiddle 'er up, durn ye! Give 'em somethin' t' dance t'! What air ye, an ornament? Hain't this a celebration? Then grease yer elbow an' go it!

FIDDLER (*seizes a drink which the* OLD FARMER *holds out to him and drowns it*). Here goes! (*He starts to fiddle "Lady of the Lake."* Four young fellows and four girls form in two lines and dance a square dance. The* FIDDLER *shouts directions for the different movements, keeping his words in the rhythm of the music and interspersing them with jocular personal remarks to the dancers themselves. The people seated along the walls stamp their feet and clap their hands in unison.* CABOT *is especially active in this respect. Only* ABBIE *remains apathetic, staring at the door as if she were alone in a silent room.*)

FIDDLER. Swing your partner t' the right! That's it, Jim! Give her a b'ar hug! Her Maw hain't lookin'. (*Laughter*) Change partners!

That suits ye, don't it, Essie, now ye got Reub afore ye? Look at
her redden up, will ye? Waal, life is short an' so's love, as the feller
says. (*Laughter.*)

CABOT (*excitedly, stamping his foot*). Go it, boys! Go it, gals!

FIDDLER (*with a wink at the others*). Ye're the spryest seventy-six ever
I sees, Ephraim! Now if ye'd on'y good eye-sight . . . ! (*Suppressed laughter. He gives* CABOT *no chance to retort but roars*)
Promenade! Ye're walkin' like a bride down the aisle, Sarah! Waal,
while they's life they's allus hope, I've heerd tell. Swing your part-
ner to the left! Gosh A'mighty, look at Johnny Cook high-steppin'! They hain't goin' t' be much strength left fur howin' in the
corn lot t'morrow. (*Laughter.*)

CABOT. Go it! Go it! (*Then suddenly, unable to restrain himself any
longer, he prances into the midst of the dancers, scattering them,
waving his arms about wildly.*) Ye're all hoofs! Git out o' my
road! Give me room! I'll show ye dancin'. Ye're all too soft! (*He
pushes them roughly away. They crowd back toward the walls,
muttering, looking at him resentfully.*)

FIDDLER (*jeeringly*). Go it, Ephraim! Go it! (*He starts "Pop, Goes
the Weasel," increasing the tempo with every verse until at the
end he is fiddling crazily as fast as he can go.*)

CABOT (*starts to dance, which he does very well and with tremendous
vigor. Then he begins to improvise, cuts incredibly grotesque
capers, leaping up and cracking his heels together, prancing around
in a circle with body bent in an Indian war dance, then suddenly
straightening up and kicking as high as he can with both legs. He
is like a monkey on a string. And all the while he intersperses his
antics with shouts and derisive comments.*) Whoop! Here's dancin'
fur ye! Whoop! See that! Seventy-six, if I'm a day! Hard as iron
yet! Beatin' the young 'uns like I allus done! Look at me! I'd invite
ye t' dance on my hundredth birthday on'y ye'll all be dead by
then. Ye're a sickly generation! Yer hearts air pink, not red! Yer
veins is full o' mud an' water! I be the on'y man in the county!
Whoop! See that! I'm a Injun! I've killed Injuns in the West afore
ye was born — an' skulped 'em too! They's a arrer wound on my
backside I c'd show ye! The hull tribe chased me. I outrun 'em all
— with the arrer stuck in me! An' I tuk vengeance on 'em. Ten
eyes fur an eye, that was my motter! Whoop! Look at me! I kin
kick the ceilin' off the room! Whoop!

FIDDLER (*stops playing — exhaustedly*). God A'mighty, I got enuf. Ye
got the devil's strength in ye.

CABOT (*delightedly*). Did I beat yew, too? Wa'al, ye played smart.
Hev a swig. (*He pours whisky for himself and* FIDDLER. *They*

*drink. The others watch* CABOT *silently with cold, hostile eyes. There is a dead pause. The* FIDDLER *rests.* CABOT *leans against the keg, panting, glaring around him confusedly. In the room above,* EBEN *gets to his feet and tiptoes out the door in rear, appearing a moment later in the other bedroom. He moves silently, even frightenedly, toward the cradle and stands there looking down at the baby. His face is as vague as his reactions are confused, but there is a trace of tenderness, of interested discovery. At the same moment that he reaches the cradle,* ABBIE *seems to sense something. She gets up weakly and goes to* CABOT.)

ABBIE. I'm goin' up t' the baby.

CABOT (*with real solicitation*). Air ye able fur the stairs? D'ye want me t' help ye, Abbie?

ABBIE. No. I'm able. I'll be down agen soon.

CABOT. Don't ye git wore out! He needs ye, remember — our son does! (*He grins affectionately, patting her on the back. She shrinks from his touch.*)

ABBIE (*dully*). Don't — tech me. I'm goin' — up. (*She goes.* CABOT *looks after her. A whisper goes around the room.* CABOT *turns. It ceases. He wipes his forehead streaming with sweat. He is breathing pantingly.*)

CABOT. I'm a-goin' out t' git fresh air. I'm feelin' a mite dizzy. Fiddle up thar! Dance, all o' ye! Here's likker fur them as wants it. Enjoy yerselves. I'll be back. (*He goes, closing the door behind him.*)

FIDDLER (*sarcastically*). Don't hurry none on our account! (*A suppressed laugh. He imitates* ABBIE) Whar's Eben? (*More laughter.*)

A WOMAN (*loudly*). What's happened in this house is plain as the nose on yer face! (ABBIE *appears in the doorway upstairs and stands looking in surprise and adoration at* EBEN *who does not see her.*)

A MAN. Ssshh! He's li'ble t' be listenin' at the door. That'd be like him. (*Their voices die to an intensive whispering. Their faces are concentrated on this gossip. A noise as of dead leaves in the wind comes from the room.* CABOT *has come out from the porch and stands by the gate, leaning on it, staring at the sky blinkingly.* ABBIE *comes across the room silently.* EBEN *does not notice her until quite near.*)

EBEN (*starting*). Abbie!

ABBIE. Ssshh! (*She throws her arms around him. They kiss — then bend over the cradle together.*) Ain't he purty? — dead spit 'n' image o' yew!

EBEN (*pleased*). Air he? I can't tell none.

ABBIE. E-zactly like!

EBEN (*frowningly*). I don't like this. I don't like lettin' on what's mine's his'n. I been doin' that all my life. I'm gittin' t' the end o' b'arin' it!

ABBIE (*putting her finger on his lips*). We're doin' the best we kin. We got t' wait. Somethin's bound t' happen. (*She puts her arms around him.*) I got t' go back.

EBEN. I'm goin' out. I can't b'ar it with the fiddle playin' an' the laughin'.

ABBIE. Don't git feelin' low. I love ye, Eben. Kiss me. (*He kisses her. They remain in each other's arms.*)

CABOT (*at the gate, confusedly*). Even the music can't drive it out — somethin'. Ye kin feel it droppin' off the elums, climbin' up the roof, sneakin' down the chimney, pokin' in the corners! They's no peace in houses, they's no rest livin' with folks. Somethin's always livin' with ye. (*With a deep sigh*) I'll go t' the barn an' rest a spell. (*He goes wearily toward the barn.*)

FIDDLER (*tuning up*). Let's celebrate the old skunk gittin' fooled! We kin have some fun now he's went. (*He starts to fiddle "Turkey in the Straw." There is real merriment now. The young folks get up to dance.*)

SCENE TWO

*A half hour later — Exterior —* EBEN *is standing by the gate looking up at the sky, an expression of dumb pain bewildered by itself on his face.* CABOT *appears, returning from the barn, walking wearily, his eyes on the ground. He sees* EBEN *and his whole mood immediately changes. He becomes excited, a cruel, triumphant grin comes to his lips, he strides up and slaps* EBEN *on the back. From within comes the whining of the fiddle and the noise of stamping feet and laughing voices.*

CABOT. So har ye be!

EBEN (*startled, stares at him with hatred for a moment — then dully*). Ay-eh.

CABOT (*surveying him jeeringly*). Why hain't ye been in t' dance? They was all axin' fur ye.

EBEN. Let 'em ax!

CABOT. They's a hull passel o' purty gals.

EBEN. T' hell with 'em!

CABOT. Ye'd ought t' be marryin' one o' 'em soon.

EBEN. I hain't marryin' no one.

CABOT. Ye might 'arn a share o' a farm that way.

EBEN (*with a sneer*). Like yew did, ye mean? I hain't that kind.

CABOT (*stung*). Ye lie! 'Twas yer Maw's folks aimed t' steal my farm from me.

EBEN. Other folks don't say so. (*After a pause — defiantly*) An' I got a farm, anyways!

CABOT (*derisively*). Whar?

EBEN (*stamps a foot on the ground*). Har!

CABOT (*throws his head back and laughs coarsely*). Ho-ho! Ye hev, hev ye? Waal, that's a good un!

EBEN (*controlling himself — grimly*). Ye'll see!

CABOT (*stares at him suspiciously, trying to make him out — a pause — then with scornful confidence*). Ay-eh. I'll see. So'll ye. It's ye that's blind — blind as a mole underground. (EBEN *suddenly laughs, one short sardonic bark: "Ha." A pause.* CABOT *peers at him with renewed suspicion.*) What air ye hawin' 'bout? (EBEN *turns away without answering.* CABOT *grows angry.*) God A'mighty, yew air a dumb dunce! They's nothin' in that thick skull o' your'n but noise — like a empty keg it be! (EBEN *doesn't seem to hear.* CABOT'S *rage grows.*) Yewr farm! God A'mighty! If ye wa'n't a born donkey ye'd know ye'll never own stick nor stone on it, specially now arter him bein' born. It's his'n, I tell ye — his'n arter I die — but I'll live a hundred jest t' fool ye all — an' he'll be growed then — yewr age a'most! (EBEN *laughs again his sardonic "Ha." This drives* CABOT *into a fury.*) Ha? Ye think ye kin git 'round that someways, do ye? Waal, it'll be her'n, too — Abbie's — ye won't git 'round her — she knows yer tricks — she'll be too much fur ye — she wants the farm her'n — she was afeerd o' ye — she told me ye was sneakin' 'round tryin' t' make love t' her t' git her on yer side . . . ye . . . ye mad fool, ye! (*He raises his clenched fists threateningly.*)

EBEN (*is confronting him, choking with rage*). Ye lie, ye old skunk! Abbie never said no sech thing!

CABOT (*suddenly triumphant when he sees how shaken* EBEN *is*). She did. An' I says, I'll blow his brains t' the top o' them elums — an' she says no, that hain't sense, who'll ye git t' help ye on the farm in his place — an' then she says yew'n me ought t' have a son — I know we kin, she says — an' I says, if we do, ye kin have anythin' I've got ye've a mind t'. An' she says, I wants Eben cut off so's this farm'll be mine when ye die! (*With terrible gloating*) An' that's what's happened, hain't it? An' the farm's her'n! An' the dust o' the road — that's you'rn! Ha! Now who's hawin'?

EBEN (*has been listening, petrified with grief and rage — suddenly laughs wildly and brokenly*). Ha-ha-ha! So that's her sneakin' game — all along! — like I suspicioned at fust — t' swaller it all — an' me, too . . . ! (*Madly*) I'll murder her! (*He springs toward the porch but* CABOT *is quicker and gets in between.*)

CABOT. No, ye don't!

EBEN. Git out o' my road! (*He tries to throw* CABOT *aside. They grapple in what becomes immediately a murderous struggle. The old man's concentrated strength is too much for* EBEN. CABOT *gets one hand on his throat and presses him back across the stone wall. At the same moment,* ABBIE *comes out on the porch. With a stifled cry she runs toward them.*)

ABBIE. Eben! Ephraim! (*She tugs at the hand on* EBEN's *throat.*) Let go, Ephraim! Ye're chokin' him!

CABOT (*removes his hand and flings* EBEN *sideways full length on the grass, gasping and choking. With a cry,* ABBIE *kneels beside him, trying to take his head on her lap, but he pushes her away.* CABOT *stands looking down with fierce triumph*). Ye needn't t've fret, Abbie, I wa'n't aimin' t' kill him. He hain't wuth hangin' fur — not by a hell of a sight! (*More and more triumphantly*) Seventy-six an' him not thirty yit — an' look whar he be fur thinkin' his Paw was easy! No, by God, I hain't easy! An' him upstairs, I'll raise him t' be like me! (*He turns to leave them.*) I'm goin' in an' dance! — sing an' celebrate! (*He walks to the porch — then turns with a great grin.*) I don't calc'late it's left in him, but if he gits pesky, Abbie, ye jest sing out. I'll come a-runnin' an' by the Etarnal, I'll put him across my knee an' birch him! Ha-ha-ha! (*He goes into the house laughing. A moment later his loud "whoop" is heard.*)

ABBIE (*tenderly*). Eben. Air ye hurt? (*She tries to kiss him but he pushes her violently away and struggles to a sitting position.*)

EBEN (*gaspingly*). T' hell — with ye!

ABBIE (*not believing her ears*). It's me, Eben — Abbie — don't ye know me?

EBEN (*glowering at her with hatred*). Ay-eh — I know ye — now! (*He suddenly breaks down, sobbing weakly.*)

ABBIE (*fearfully*). Eben — what's happened t' ye — why did ye look at me 's if ye hated me?

EBEN (*violently, between sobs and gasps*). I do hate ye! Ye're a whore — a damn trickin' whore!

ABBIE (*shrinking back horrified*). Eben! Ye don't know what ye're sayin'!

EBEN (*scrambling to his feet and following her — accusingly*). Ye're nothin' but a stinkin' passel o' lies! Ye've been lyin' t' me every

word ye spoke, day an' night, since we fust — done it. Ye've kept
sayin' ye loved me. . . .

ABBIE (*frantically*). I do love ye! (*She takes his hands but he flings
hers away.*)

EBEN (*unheeding*). Ye've made a fool o' me — a sick, dumb fool —
a-purpose! Ye've been on'y playin' yer sneakin', stealin' game all
along — gittin' me t' lie with ye so's ye'd hev a son he'd think was
his'n, an' makin' him promise he'd give ye the farm and let me
eat dust, if ye did git him a son! (*Staring at her with anguished,
bewildered eyes*) They must be a devil livin' in ye! T'ain't human
t' be as bad as that be!

ABBIE (*stunned — dully*). He told yew . . . ?

EBEN. Hain't it true? It hain't no good in yew lyin'.

ABBIE (*pleadingly*). Eben, listen — ye must listen — it was long ago
— afore we done nothin' — yew was scornin' me — goin' t' see Min
—when I was lovin' ye — an' I said it t' him t' git vengeance on
ye!

EBEN (*unheedingly. With tortured passion*). I wish ye was dead! I
wish I was dead along with ye afore this come! (*Ragingly*) But I'll
git my vengeance too! I'll pray Maw t' come back t' help me — t'
put her cuss on yew an' him!

ABBIE (*brokenly*). Don't ye, Eben! Don't ye! (*She throws herself
on her knees before him, weeping.*) I didn't mean t' do bad t' ye!
Fergive me, won't ye?

EBEN (*not seeming to hear her — fiercely*). I'll git squar' with the old
skunk — an' yew! I'll tell him the truth 'bout the son he's so proud
o'! Then I'll leave ye here t' pizen each other — with Maw comin'
out o' her grave at nights — an' I'll go t' the gold fields o' Californi-a whar Sim an' Peter be!

ABBIE (*terrified*). Ye won't — leave me? Ye can't!

EBEN (*with fierce determination*). I'm a-goin', I tell ye! I'll git rich
thar an' come back an' fight him fur the farm he stole — an' I'll
kick ye both out in the road — t' beg an' sleep in the woods — an'
yer son along with ye — t' starve an' die! (*He is hysterical at the
end.*)

ABBIE (*with a shudder — humbly*). He's yewr son, too, Eben.

EBEN (*torturedly*). I wish he never was born! I wish he'd die this
minit! I wish I'd never sot eyes on him! It's him — yew havin' him
— a-purpose t' steal — that's changed everythin'!

ABBIE (*gently*). Did ye believe I loved ye — afore he come?

EBEN. Ay-eh — like a dumb ox!

ABBIE. An' ye don't believe no more?

EBEN. B'lieve a lyin' thief! Ha!

ABBIE (*shudders — then humbly*). An' did ye r'ally love me afore?

EBEN (*brokenly*). Ay-eh — an' ye was trickin' me!

ABBIE. An' ye don't love me now!

EBEN (*violently*). I hate ye, I tell ye!

ABBIE. An' ye're truly goin' West — goin' t' leave me — all account o' him being born?

EBEN. I'm a-goin' in the mornin' — or may God strike me t' hell!

ABBIE (*after a pause — with a dreadful cold intensity — slowly*). If that's what his comin's done t' me — killin' yewr love — takin' yew away — my on'y joy — the on'y joy I ever knowed — like heaven t' me — purtier'n heaven — then I hate him, too, even if I be his Maw!

EBEN (*bitterly*). Lies! Ye love him! He'll steal the farm fur ye! (*Brokenly*) But t'ain't the farm so much — not no more — it's yew foolin' me — gittin' me t' love ye — lyin' yew loved me — jest t' git a son t' steal!

ABBIE (*distractedly*). He won't steal! I'd kill him fust! I do love ye! I'll prove t' ye . . . !

EBEN (*harshly*). T'ain't no use lyin' no more. I'm deaf t' ye! (*He turns away.*) I hain't seein' ye agen. Good-by!

ABBIE (*pale with anguish*). Hain't ye even goin' t' kiss me — not once — arter all we loved?

EBEN (*in a hard voice*). I hain't wantin' t' kiss ye never agen! I'm wantin' t' forgit I ever sot eyes on ye!

ABBIE. Eben! — ye mustn't — wait a spell — I want t' tell ye. . . .

EBEN. I'm a-goin' in t' git drunk. I'm a-goin' t' dance.

ABBIE (*clinging to his arm — with passionate earnestness*). If I could make it — 's if he'd never come up between us — if I could prove t' ye I wa'n't schemin' t' steal from ye — so's everythin' could be jest the same with us, lovin' each other jest the same, kissin' an' happy the same's we've been happy afore he come — if I could do it — ye'd love me agen, wouldn't ye? Ye'd kiss me agen? Ye wouldn't never leave me, would ye?

EBEN (*moved*). I calc'late not. (*Then shaking her hand off his arm — with a bitter smile*) But ye hain't God, be ye?

ABBIE (*exultantly*). Remember ye've promised! (*Then with strange intensity*) Mebbe I kin take back one thin' God does!

EBEN (*peering at her*). Ye're gittin' cracked, hain't ye? (*Then going towards door*) I'm a-goin' t' dance.

ABBIE (*calls after him intensely*). I'll prove t' ye! I'll prove I love ye better'n. . . . (*He goes in the door, not seeming to hear. She remains standing where she is, looking after him — then she finishes desperately*) Better'n everythin' else in the world!

## SCENE THREE

*Just before dawn in the morning — shows the kitchen and* CABOT'S
*bedroom. In the kitchen, by the light of a tallow candle on the
table,* EBEN *is sitting, his chin propped on his hands, his drawn face
blank and expressionless. His carpetbag is on the floor beside him.
In the bedroom, dimly lighted by a small whale-oil lamp,* CABOT *lies
asleep.* ABBIE *is bending over the cradle, listening, her face full of
terror yet with an undercurrent of desperate triumph. Suddenly,
she breaks down and sobs, appears about to throw herself on her
knees beside the cradle; but the old man turns restlessly, groaning
in his sleep, and she controls herself, and, shrinking away from the
cradle with a gesture of horror, backs swiftly toward the door in
rear and goes out. A moment later she comes into the kitchen and,
running to* EBEN, *flings her arms about his neck and kisses him
wildly. He hardens himself, he remains unmoved and cold, he keeps
his eyes straight ahead.*

ABBIE (*hysterically*). I done it, Eben! I told ye I'd do it! I've proved
I love ye — better'n everythin' — so's ye can't never doubt me no
more!

EBEN (*dully*). Whatever ye done, it hain't no good now.

ABBIE (*wildly*). Don't ye say that! Kiss me, Eben, won't ye? I need
ye t' kiss me arter what I done! I need ye t' say ye love me!

EBEN (*kisses her without emotion — dully*). That's fur good-by. I'm
a-goin' soon.

ABBIE. No! No! Ye won't go — not now!

EBEN (*going on with his own thoughts*). I been a-thinkin' — an' I
hain't goin' t' tell Paw nothin'. I'll leave Maw t' take vengeance on
ye. If I told him, the old skunk'd jest be stinkin' mean enuf to take
it out on that baby. (*His voice showing emotion in spite of him*)
An' I don't want nothin' bad t' happen t' him. He hain't t' blame
fur yew. (*He adds with a certain queer pride*) An' he looks like
me! An' by God, he's mine! An' some day I'll be a-comin' back
an' . . . !

ABBIE (*too absorbed in her own thoughts to listen to him — pleadingly*). They's no cause fur ye t' go now — they's no sense — it's
all the same's it was — they's nothin' come b'tween us now — arter
what I done!

EBEN (*something in her voice arouses him. He stares at her a bit
frightenedly*). Ye look mad, Abbie. What did ye do?

ABBIE. I — I killed him, Eben.

EBEN (*amazed*). Ye killed him?

ABBIE (*dully*). Ay-eh.

EBEN (*recovering from his astonishment — savagely*). An' serves him right! But we got t' do somethin' quick t' make it look 's if the old skunk'd killed himself when he was drunk. We kin prove by 'em all how drunk he got.

ABBIE (*wildly*). No! No! Not him! (*Laughing distractedly*) But that's what I ought t' done, hain't it? I oughter killed him instead! Why didn't ye tell me?

EBEN (*appalled*). Instead? What d'ye mean?

ABBIE. Not him.

EBEN (*his face grown ghastly*). Not — not that baby!

ABBIE (*dully*). Ay-eh!

EBEN (*falls to his knees as if he'd been struck — his voice trembling with horror*). Oh, God A'mighty! A'mighty God! Maw, whar was ye, why didn't ye stop her?

ABBIE (*simply*). She went back t' her grave that night we fust done it, remember? I hain't felt her about since. (*A pause.* EBEN *hides his head in his hands, trembling all over as if he had the ague. She goes on dully*) I left the piller over his little face. Then he killed himself. He stopped breathin'. (*She begins to weep softly.*)

EBEN (*rage beginning to mingle with grief*). He looked like me. He was mine, damn ye!

ABBIE (*slowly and brokenly*). I didn't want t' do it. I hated myself fur doin' it. I loved him. He was so purty — dead spit 'n' image o' yew. But I loved yew more — an' yew was goin' away — far off whar I'd never see ye agen, never kiss ye, never feel ye pressed agin me agen — an' ye said ye hated me fur havin' him — ye said ye hated him an' wished he was dead — ye said if it hadn't been fur him comin' it'd be the same's afore between us.

EBEN (*unable to endure this, springs to his feet in a fury, threatening her, his twitching fingers seeming to reach out for her throat*). Ye lie! I never said — I never dreamed ye'd — I'd cut off my head afore I'd hurt his finger!

ABBIE (*piteously, sinking on her knees*). Eben, don't ye look at me like that — hatin' me — not after what I done fur ye — fur us — so's we could be happy agen —

EBEN (*furiously now*). Shut up, or I'll kill ye! I see yer game now — the same old sneakin' trick — ye're aimin' t' blame me fur the murder ye done!

ABBIE (*moaning — putting her hands over her ears*). Don't ye, Eben! Don't ye! (*She grasps his legs.*)

EBEN (*his mood suddenly changing to horror, shrinks away from her*). Don't ye tech me! Ye're pizen! How could ye — t' murder a pore little critter — Ye must've swapped yer soul t' hell! (*Suddenly raging*) Ha! I kin see why ye done it! Not the lies ye jest told — but 'cause ye wanted t' steal agen — steal the last thin' ye'd left me — my part o' him — no, the hull o' him — ye saw he looked like me — ye knowed he was all mine — an' ye couldn't b'ar it — I know ye! Ye killed him fur bein' mine! (*All this has driven him almost insane. He makes a rush past her for the door — then turns — shaking both fists at her, violently*) But I'll take vengeance now! I'll git the Sheriff! I'll tell him everythin'! Then I'll sing "I'm off to Californi-a!" an' go — gold — Golden Gate — gold sun — fields o' gold in the West! (*This last he half shouts, half croons incoherently, suddenly breaking off passionately*) I'm a-goin' fur the Sheriff t' come an' git ye! I want ye tuk away, locked up from me! I can't stand t' luk at ye! Murderer an' thief 'r not, ye still tempt me! I'll give ye up t' the Sheriff! (*He turns and runs out, around the corner of house, panting and sobbing, and breaks into a swerving sprint down the road.*)

ABBIE (*struggling to her feet, runs to the door, calling after him*). I love ye, Eben! I love ye! (*She stops at the door weakly, swaying, about to fall.*) I don't care what ye do — if ye'll on'y love me agen — (*She falls limply to the floor in a faint.*)

## SCENE FOUR

*About an hour later. Same as Scene Three. Shows the kitchen and* CABOT's *bedroom. It is after dawn. The sky is brilliant with the sunrise. In the kitchen,* ABBIE *sits at the table, her body limp and exhausted, her head bowed down over her arms, her face hidden. Upstairs,* CABOT *is still asleep but awakes with a start. He looks toward the window and gives a snort of surprise and irritation — throws back the covers and begins hurriedly pulling on his clothes. Without looking behind him, he begins talking to* ABBIE *whom he supposes beside him.*

CABOT. Thunder 'n' lightnin', Abbie! I hain't slept this late in fifty year! Looks 's if the sun was full riz a'most. Must've been the dancin' an' likker. Must be gittin' old. I hope Eben's t' wuk. Ye might've tuk the trouble t' rouse me, Abbie. (*He turns — sees no one there — surprised*) Waal — whar air she? Gittin' vittles, I calc'late. (*He tiptoes to the cradle and peers down — proudly*) Mornin', sonny. Purty's a picter! Sleepin' sound. He don't beller all night like most o' 'em. (*He goes quietly out the door in rear — a few moments later enters kitchen — sees* ABBIE — *with satisfaction*) So thar ye be. Ye got any vittles cooked?

ABBIE (*without moving*). No.

CABOT (*coming to her, almost sympathetically*). Ye feelin' sick?

ABBIE. No.

CABOT (*pats her on shoulder. She shudders*). Ye'd best lie down a spell. (*Half jocularly*) Yer son'll be needin' ye soon. He'd ought t' wake up with a gnashin' appetite, the sound way he's sleepin'.

ABBIE (*shudders — then in a dead voice*). He hain't never goin' t' wake up.

CABOT (*jokingly*). Takes after me this mornin'. I hain't slept so late in . . .

ABBIE. He's dead.

CABOT (*stares at her — bewilderedly*). What. . . .

ABBIE. I killed him.

CABOT (*stepping back from her — aghast*). Air ye drunk — 'r crazy — 'r . . . !

ABBIE (*suddenly lifts her head and turns on him — wildly*). I killed him, I tell ye! I smothered him. Go up an' see if ye don't b'lieve me! (CABOT *stares at her a second, then bolts out the rear door, can be heard bounding up the stairs, and rushes into the bedroom and over to the cradle.* ABBIE *has sunk back lifelessly into her former position.* CABOT *puts his hand down on the body in the crib. An expression of fear and horror comes over his face.*)

CABOT (*shrinking away — trembling*). God A'mighty! God A'mighty. (*He stumbles out the door — in a short while returns to the kitchen — comes to* ABBIE, *the stunned expression still on his face — hoarsely*) Why did ye do it? Why? (*As she doesn't answer, he grabs her violently by the shoulder and shakes her.*) I ax ye why ye done it! Ye'd better tell me 'r . . . !

ABBIE (*gives him a furious push which sends him staggering back and springs to her feet — with wild rage and hatred*). Don't ye dare tech me! What right hev ye t' question me 'bout him? He wa'n't yewr son! Think I'd have a son by yew? I'd die fust! I hate the sight o' ye an' allus did! It's yew I should've murdered, if I'd had good sense! I hate ye! I love Eben. I did from the fust. An' he was Eben's son — mine an' Eben's — not your'n!

CABOT (*stands looking at her dazedly — a pause — finding his words with an effort — dully*). That was it — what I felt — pokin' round the corners — while ye lied — holdin' yerself from me — sayin' ye'd a'ready conceived — (*He lapses into crushed silence — then with a strange emotion*) He's dead, sart'n. I felt his heart. Pore little critter! (*He blinks back one tear, wiping his sleeve across his nose.*)

ABBIE (*hysterically*). Don't ye! Don't ye! (*She sobs unrestrainedly.*)

CABOT (*with a concentrated effort that stiffens his body into a rigid line and hardens his face into a stony mask — through his teeth to himself*). I got t' be — like a stone — a rock o' jedgment! (*A pause. He gets complete control over himself — harshly*) If he was Eben's, I be glad he air gone! An' mebbe I suspicioned it all along. I felt they was somethin' onnateral — somewhars — the house got so lonesome — an' cold — drivin' me down t' the barn — t' the beasts o' the field. . . . Ay-eh. I must've suspicioned — somethin'. Ye didn't fool me — not altogether, leastways — I'm too old a bird — growin' ripe on the bough. . . . (*He becomes aware he is wandering, straightens again, looks at* ABBIE *with a cruel grin.*) So ye'd liked t' hev murdered me 'stead o' him, would ye? Waal, I'll live to a hundred! I'll live t' see ye hung! I'll deliver ye up t' the jedgment o' God an' the law! I'll git the Sheriff now. (*Starts for the door.*)

ABBIE (*dully*). Ye needn't. Eben's gone fur him.

CABOT (*amazed*). Eben — gone fur the Sheriff?

ABBIE. Ay-eh.

CABOT. T' inform agen ye?

ABBIE. Ay-eh.

CABOT (*considers this — a pause — then in a hard voice*). Waal, I'm thankful fur him savin' me the trouble. I'll git t' wuk. (*He goes to the door — then turns — in a voice full of strange emotion*) He'd ought t' been my son, Abbie. Ye'd ought t' loved me. I'm a man. If ye'd loved me, I'd never told no Sheriff on ye no matter what ye did, if they was t' brile me alive!

ABBIE (*defensively*). They's more to it nor yew know, makes him tell.

CABOT (*dryly*). Fur yewr sake, I hope they be. (*He goes out — comes around to the gate — stares up at the sky. His control relaxes. For a moment he is old and weary. He murmurs despairingly*) God A'mighty, I be lonesomer'n ever! (*He hears running footsteps from the left, immediately is himself again.* EBEN *runs in, panting exhaustedly, wild-eyed and mad looking. He lurches through the gate.* CABOT *grabs him by the shoulder.* EBEN *stares at him dumbly.*) Did ye tell the Sheriff?

EBEN (*nodding stupidly*). Ay-eh.

CABOT (*gives him a push away that sends him sprawling — laughing with withering contempt*). Good fur ye! A prime chip o' yer Maw ye be! (*He goes toward the barn, laughing harshly.* EBEN

*scrambles to his feet. Suddenly* CABOT *turns — grimly threatening)*
Git off this farm when the Sheriff takes her — or, by God, he'll
have t' come back an' git me fur murder, too! (*He stalks off.*
EBEN *does not appear to have heard him. He runs to the door and
comes into the kitchen.* ABBIE *looks up with a cry of anguished
joy.* EBEN *stumbles over and throws himself on his knees beside her
— sobbing brokenly.*)

EBEN. Fergive me!

ABBIE (*happily*). Eben! (*She kisses him and pulls his head over
against her breast.*)

EBEN. I love ye! Fergive me!

ABBIE (*ecstatically*). I'd fergive ye all the sins in hell fur sayin' that!
(*She kisses his head, pressing it to her with a fierce passion of possession.*)

EBEN (*brokenly*). But I told the Sheriff. He's comin' fur ye!

ABBIE. I kin b'ar what happens t' me — now!

EBEN. I woke him up. I told him. He says, wait 'til I git dressed. I
was waiting. I got to thinkin' o' yew. I got to thinkin' how I'd
loved ye. It hurt like somethin' was bustin' in my chest an' head.
I got t' cryin'. I knowed sudden I loved ye yet, an' allus would
love ye!

ABBIE (*caressing his hair — tenderly*). My boy, hain't ye?

EBEN. I begun t' run back. I cut across the fields an' through the
woods. I thought ye might have time t' run away — with me —
an' . . .

ABBIE (*shaking her head*). I got t' take my punishment — t' pay fur
my sin.

EBEN. Then I want t' share it with ye.

ABBIE. Ye didn't do nothin'.

EBEN. I put it in yer head. I wisht he was dead! I as much as urged
ye t' do it!

ABBIE. No. It was me alone!

EBEN. I'm as guilty as yew be! He was the child o' our sin.

ABBIE (*lifting her head as if defying God*). I don't repent that sin! I
hain't askin' God t' fergive that!

EBEN. Nor me — but it led up t' the other — an' the murder ye did,
ye did 'count o' me — an' it's my murder, too, I'll tell the Sheriff
— an' if ye deny it, I'll say we planned it t'gether — an' they'll all
b'lieve me, fur they suspicion everythin' we've done, an' it'll seem
likely an' true to 'em. An' it is true — way down. I did help ye —
somehow.

ABBIE (*laying her head on his — sobbing*). No! I don't want yew t'
suffer!

EBEN. I got t' pay fur my part o' the sin! An' I'd suffer wuss leavin' ye, goin' West, thinkin' o' ye day an' night, bein' out when yew was in — (*Lowering his voice*) 'r bein' alive when yew was dead. (*A pause*) I want t' share with ye, Abbie — prison 'r death 'r hell 'r anythin'! (*He looks into her eyes and forces a trembling smile.*) If I'm sharin' with ye, I won't feel lonesome, leastways.

ABBIE (*weakly*). Eben! I won't let ye! I can't let ye!

EBEN (*kissing her — tenderly*). Ye can't he'p yerself. I got ye beat fur once!

ABBIE (*forcing a smile — adoringly*). I hain't beat — s'long's I got ye!

EBEN (*hears the sound of feet outside*). Ssshh! Listen! They've come t' take us!

ABBIE. No, it's him. Don't give him no chance to fight ye, Eben. Don't say nothin' — no matter what he says. An' I won't neither. (*It is* CABOT. *He comes up from the barn in a great state of excitement and strides into the house and then into the kitchen.* EBEN *is kneeling beside* ABBIE, *his arm around her, hers around him. They stare straight ahead.*)

CABOT (*stares at them, his face hard. A long pause — vindictively*). Ye make a slick pair o' murderin' turtle doves! Ye'd ought t' be both hung on the same limb an' left thar t' swing in the breeze an' rot — a warnin' t' old fools like me t' b'ar their lonesomeness alone — an' fur young fools like ye t' hobble their lust. (*A pause. The excitement returns to his face, his eyes snap, he looks a bit crazy.*) I couldn't work today. I couldn't take no interest. T' hell with the farm! I'm leavin' it! I've turned the cows an' other stock loose! I've druv 'em into the woods whar they kin be free! By freein' 'em, I'm freein' myself! I'm quittin' here today! I'll set fire t' house an' barn an' watch 'em burn, an' I'll leave yer Maw t' haunt the ashes, an' I'll will the fields back t' God, so that nothin' human kin never touch 'em! I'll be a-goin' to Californi-a — t' jine Simeon an' Peter — true sons o' mine if they be dumb fools — an' the Cabots'll find Solomon's Mines t'gether! (*He suddenly cuts a mad caper.*) Whoop! What was the song they sung? "Oh, Californi-a! That's the land fur me." (*He sings this — then gets on his knees by the floor-board under which the money was hid.*) An' I'll sail thar on one o' the finest clippers I kin find! I've got the money! Pity ye didn't know whar this was hidden so's ye could steal. . . . (*He has pulled up the board. He stares — feels — stares again. A pause of dead silence. He slowly turns, slumping into a sitting position on the floor, his eyes like those of a dead fish, his face the sickly green of an attack of nausea. He swallows painfully several times — forces a weak smile at last.*) So — ye did steal it!

EBEN (*emotionlessly*). I swapped it t' Sim an' Peter fur their share o' the farm — t' pay their passage t' Californi-a.

CABOT (*with one sardonic*) Ha! (*He begins to recover. Gets slowly to his feet — strangely*) I calc'late God give it to 'em — not yew! God's hard, not easy! Mebbe they's easy in the West but it hain't God's gold. It hain't fur me. I kin hear His voice warnin' me agen t' be hard an' stay on my farm. I kin see his hand usin' Eben t' steal t' keep me from weakness. I kin feel I be in the palm o' His hand, His fingers guidin' me. (*A pause — then he mutters sadly*) It's a-goin' t' be lonesomer now than ever it war afore — an' I'm gittin' old, Lord — ripe on the bough. . . . (*Then stiffening*) Waal — what d'ye want? God's lonesome, hain't He? God's hard an' lonesome! (*A pause. The* SHERIFF *with two men comes up the road from the left. They move cautiously to the door. The* SHERIFF *knocks on it with the butt of his pistol.*)

SHERIFF. Open in the name o' the law! (*They start.*)

CABOT. They've come fur ye. (*He goes to the rear door.*) Come in, Jim! (*The three men enter.* CABOT *meets them in doorway.*) Jest a minit, Jim. I got 'em safe here. (*The* SHERIFF *nods. He and his companions remain in the doorway.*)

EBEN (*suddenly calls*). I lied this mornin', Jim. I helped her to do it. Ye kin take me, too.

ABBIE (*brokenly*). No!

CABOT. Take 'em both. (*He comes forward — stares at* EBEN *with a trace of grudging admiration.*) Purty good — fur yew! Waal, I got t' round up the stock. Good-by.

EBEN. Good-by.

ABBIE. Good-by. (CABOT *turns and strides past the men — comes out and around the corner of the house, his shoulders squared, his face stony, and stalks grimly toward the barn. In the meantime the* SHERIFF *and men have come into the room.*)

SHERIFF (*embarrassedly*). Wall — we'd best start.

ABBIE. Wait. (*Turns to* EBEN.) I love ye, Eben.

EBEN. I love ye, Abbie. (*They kiss. The three men grin and shuffle embarrassedly.* EBEN *takes* ABBIE's *hand. They go out the door in rear, the men following, and come from the house, walking hand in hand to the gate.* EBEN *stops there and points to the sunrise sky.*) Sun's a-rizin'. Purty, hain't it?

ABBIE. Ay-eh. (*They both stand for a moment looking up raptly in attitudes strangely aloof and devout.*)

SHERIFF (*looking around at the farm enviously — to his companion*). It's a jim-dandy farm, no denyin'. Wished I owned it!

CURTAIN

◇ ◇ ◇

STUDY AIDS

PART I. In the setting for this play, what is the symbolic force, if any, of the "two enormous elms" which stand at each side of the house? How is their "sinister maternity" a relevant concern? Does their standing "like exhausted women" suggest a reference to the two exhausted women influential in the play?

*Scene One.* O'Neill clearly contrasts Eben with his two brothers. Why, then, are they given similar responses to the sunset? What is gained by beginning the play at sunset?

Gold — in the sunset, the hair of Simeon's wife, the wealth in the West, and so forth — is an important term in this scene and in the play. Does one meaning tend to dominate the other connotations of gold? If so, which one? To what degree does gold absorb the interests of the characters in the rest of the play?

Simeon and Peter are described as having bovine faces; as they proceed to their dinner, they shoulder each other, hurrying clumsily to their food "like two friendly oxen toward their evening meal." Throughout the play, animal images occur frequently. Note them and comment on their force. What is the relationship between them and human nature as it is presented in the play?

*Scene Two.* In expressing his hatred for Cabot, Eben takes pride in being like his mother and unlike his father. Later Simeon and Peter remark that he is the "dead spit an' image" of his father. In what important ways are Eben and Cabot alike?

Comment on Simeon's statement: "No one never kills nobody. It's allus somethin'. That's the murderer." What are the implications of these words? Do they suggest that there are forces at work in human affairs which men can neither understand nor control? Does such a notion find embodiment elsewhere in the play?

What irony is involved in Eben's criticizing his brothers for "makin' walls till yer heart's a stone"?

Is there symbolic meaning in the fact that the father and the three sons share Min's favors? Might it suggest their basic similarity? Does it offer any special insight into Eben, particularly in view of his intense devotion to his mother and his rivalry with his father?

*Scene Three.* Eben speaks of Min as if she were one of his possessions. Where else do "my" and "mine" figure importantly in the play? Does the frequency of such claims to ownership suggest that intense possessiveness is a major theme?

After Eben has told his brothers about their father's third wife, Simeon asks Eben: "Mebbe ye'll try t' make her your'n, too?" What is the effect of such anticipations of events to come? Can you find other instances of foreshadowing in this play? Comment on the preparations made in Scenes One through Three for the appearance of Cabot. How has O'Neill built up interest and tension concerning his return?

Is there something ironic in Simeon and Peter's failure to enjoy their liberation from the routine of farm chores? Might their offer to help Eben suggest a dissatisfaction with the realization of a "desire" and foreshadow later disappointments for other characters?

*Scene Four.* What is significant about the qualities which O'Neill pictures in Abbie? How does her very first speech relate her to the central attitudes of the other characters?

Note the stage direction which calls for Peter to retreat "back beyond the vision of the old man" and to flaunt the bag of money in the air above his head. In two other instances (Pts. II, Sc. 4, and III, Sc. 1) Cabot's impaired vision is mentioned. Is it symbolic?

What is achieved by having Simeon and Peter break the windows of the parlor? Does this action relate to any pattern of development associated with that room and with the spirit of Eben's mother which haunts it?

What does Abbie reveal about herself in talking with Eben? Much of her long speech to him is expository. How natural does it seem for her to bring forth such information at this point? That is, has O'Neill found some immediate reason or occasion for her to speak in this way? How does what we learn about her help to make our attitude toward her more complex?

Review Part I and generalize on its function in the total structure of the play. What traits in the participants have been emphasized? What immediate and potential conflicts among the characters have been presented or anticipated? Comment on O'Neill's skill in handling the problem of exposition.

PART II. What is the structural relationship of Part II to Part I? To what extent does the action develop out of the dramatic situation defined in Part I?

Part II calls for a special utilization of the interior of the house. With the exterior walls of the rooms removed, their interiors are simultaneously revealed to the audience. Comment on the effects of juxtaposition made possible by such staging in Scene Two and later in Scene One of Part III.

*Scene Two.* What is the function of Cabot's long speech to Abbie? What new insights into his character does it offer? How do these insights enrich the play? Cabot questions: "Will ye ever know me — 'r will any man 'r woman?" How well does he know himself? How well does he know others? Is there something about him which precludes the sympathetic understanding he craves from others? If so, what is it? Comment on his religious views. Does his religion offer him a rationalization and a sanction for his conduct? How is Eben's invoking and obeying the spirit of his mother similar to Cabot's religious beliefs? To what extent is Eben's devotion to his mother a mask for personal greed? Might it also be regarded as a manifestation of an Oedipal barrier to a normal life? Comment on Cabot's speech: "It's cold in this house. It's oneasy. They's thin's pokin' about in the dark — in the corners." Is such a speech largely for the creation of atmosphere? Might it also suggest some sense of guilt on Cabot's part? Why does Cabot spend the night in the barn?

*Scene Three.* Comment on the details describing the parlor. Why should it have been preserved unused in memory of Cabot's wife? Why should it appear like a tomb? Why is it so ugly? Comment on Abbie's motives for moving to the parlor. What motives and needs converge in the adultery of Abbie and Eben? How is Abbie's maternalism simultaneously a means to win Eben and a revelation of her personal need?

PART III. Comment on the relationship of Part III to Part II. What carry-over is there? What new developments occur and what is their relationship to those in Part II? What details from Part I are recalled?

*Scene One.* What is there about Cabot's conduct with his guests which reveals both the fact and the cause of his isolation? Why does Cabot fail to catch the heavy innuendoes from his guests concerning his new son and Eben? Is there some symbolic value in his frantic dancing which earns him only exhaustion and contempt? What significance attaches to his retreat to the barn after his dancing?

*Scene Two.* What is the function of the fight between Cabot and Eben? Might it have been omitted with no real loss to the play? Does it seem to come as a culmination of a psychological theme involving Eben and his father? Is there something symbolically appropriate in the details concerning the stone wall in the following stage direction: "Cabot gets one hand on his [Eben's] throat and presses

him back across the stone wall"? How is it ironic that Cabot takes
pride in his victory? What is achieved by having Cabot win the
fight? What new attitude does Eben reveal in his belief that Abbie
has been using him?

   *Scene Three.* What important change in the character of Abbie
has been shown during Scenes One through Three? How is this
change reflected? How is it related to her ability to murder her own
child? Does the murder come from a sincere, however misguided,
attempt to express her love for Eben, or is it another instance of a
character driven uncontrollably by another "desire"? Is it, perhaps,
both?

   *Scene Four.* What significant transformations have both Abbie
and Eben undergone by the end of the play? What new awarenesses
have they achieved? How do they differ from Cabot in this respect?
Comment on these three figures as tragic figures. What distinction
do Abbie and Eben make between their "sins" of adultery and of
murder? Why are they willing to repent for the latter? How does
the transformation of Abbie and Eben relate to (1) their willingness
to undergo punishment, and (2) Cabot's telling Abbie, "If ye'd loved
me, I'd never told no Sheriff on ye no matter what ye did, if they
was t' brile me alive!"?

   What are the implications of Cabot's discovery that his hidden
gold has been taken? Is it more than a means of condemning him
to a lonely, hard life of work on the farm? Might it also suggest
his unnoticed loss of other kinds of treasure or his lifelong reliance
on non-existent or worthless values?

   What is the effect of Abbie and Eben's appreciation of the beauty
of the sunrise? How does it add poignancy to the scene? Is there
some symbolic force in concluding the play at the dawning of a new
day? If so, what is it?

   What is ironical about the concluding lines by the Sheriff?

## DISCUSSION TOPICS

   1. Discuss O'Neill's adaptation of the Phaedra-Hippolytus story
in *Desire Under the Elms.* What important similarities and differences do you note between O'Neill's use of this ancient story and
that of the other dramatists in this collection?

   2. O'Neill is quite specific about the details of the setting for his
play. How important is the rocky New England farm to the action
of the play and the lives of the characters? Is it chiefly backdrop,
or does it exert a real influence? How, in addition to the physical

properties of the staging, does O'Neill build up a sense of the setting?

3. Comment on the language of this play. What is gained by using the New England dialect? How consistently is it observed? In Seneca's *Phaedra* one finds language which is elaborate and highly ornamented. How does the language of O'Neill's play differ? Does it seem adequate to the burden of the ideas?

4. Alan Downer interprets the theme of the play as "variations on the first word of the title." What "desires" are developed in the play? To what extent are they natural, obsessive, or irrational? Is there some common quality shared in the pursuit of these desires which suggests a view of man and his place in the universe?

5. Do you find other important themes in the play besides that noted by Downer? What are they? How, specifically, are they developed?

6. What view of human nature does the play support or develop? Does it seem that human beings are victims of forces, inside as well as outside themselves, which they can neither understand nor control? One writer has spoken of "the painful nihilism" of the play. Does this seem an apt or accurate phrase to be used in connection with it?

7. Religion is an important aspect of the play. It seems to give Cabot a sense of the rightness in his actions. Eben treats his dead mother as if she were a religious figure — invoking her curse upon his enemies, sensing her presence, and so on. Discuss the impact of these two "religions." Might they be regarded as pathological?

8. Discuss the play in terms of its psychological meaning. Might the play also be regarded as having a moral or ethical meaning?

9. Comment on the three principal characters. Are they over-simplified, two-dimensional figures? Do they have complexity? Do you think O'Neill succeeds in creating in Cabot a believable character, or does he make him into a melodramatic villain?

10. Adultery, family hatreds, and murder are sensational subjects in themselves. Do they serve any larger purpose here than securing the attention of the audience?

11. Turn to the essay "Myth as Tragic Structure in *Desire Under the Elms*" by Edgar F. Racey, Jr., in Part Three of this book. What insights into the play does it give you? Where do you agree and/or disagree with Mr. Racey? Why?

12. Consult and be prepared to comment upon the strengths and weaknesses of Sophus K. Winther's study of the play "*Desire Under the Elms*: A Modern Tragedy," *Modern Drama*, III (December 1961), 326–332.

# PART THREE

# Comment

# The King of the Wood

*Sir James George Frazer*

§ 1. *Diana and Virbius.* — Who does not know Turner's picture of the Golden Bough? The scene, suffused with the golden glow of imagination in which the divine mind of Turner steeped and transfigured even the fairest natural landscape, is a dream-like vision of the little woodland lake of Nemi — "Diana's Mirror," as it was called by the ancients. No one who has seen that calm water, lapped in a green hollow of the Alban hills, can ever forget it. The two characteristic Italian villages which slumber on its banks, and the equally Italian palace whose terraced gardens descend steeply to the lake, hardly break the stillness and even the solitariness of the scene. Diana herself might still linger by this lonely shore, still haunt these woodlands wild.

In antiquity this sylvan landscape was the scene of a strange and recurring tragedy. On the northern shore of the lake, right under the precipitous cliffs on which the modern village of Nemi is perched, stood the sacred grove and sanctuary of Diana Nemorensis, or Diana of the Wood. The lake and the grove were sometimes known as the lake and grove of Aricia. But the town of Aricia (the modern La Riccia) was situated about three miles off, at the foot of the Alban Mount, and separated by a steep descent from the lake, which lies in a small crater-like hollow on the mountain side. In this sacred grove there grew a certain tree round which at any time of the day, and probably far into the night, a grim figure might be seen to prowl. In his hand he carried a drawn sword, and he kept peering warily about him as if at every instant he expected to be set upon by an enemy. He was a priest and a murderer; and the man for whom he looked was sooner or later to murder him and hold the priesthood in his stead. Such was the rule of the sanctuary. A candidate for the priesthood could only succeed to office by slaying the priest, and having slain him, he retained office till he was himself slain by a stronger or a craftier.

The post which he held by this precarious tenure carried with it the title of king; but surely no crowned head ever lay uneasier, or was visited by more evil dreams, than his. For year in, year out, in summer and winter, in fair weather and in foul, he had to keep his lonely watch, and whenever he snatched a troubled slumber it was at the peril of his life. The least relaxation of his vigilance, the smallest abatement of his strength of limb or skill of fence, put him in jeopardy; grey hairs might seal his death-warrant. To gentle and pious pilgrims at the shrine the sight of him might well seem to darken the fair landscape, as when a cloud suddenly blots the sun on a bright day. The dreamy blue of Italian skies, the dappled shade of summer woods, and the sparkle of waves in the sun, can have accorded but ill with that stern and sinister figure. Rather we picture to ourselves the scene as it may have been witnessed by a belated wayfarer on one of those wild autumn nights when the dead leaves are falling thick, and the winds seem to sing the dirge of the dying year. It is a sombre picture, set to melancholy music — the background of forest showing black and jagged against a lowering and stormy sky, the sighing of the wind in the branches, the rustle of the withered leaves under foot, the lapping of the cold water on the shore, and in the foreground, pacing to and fro, now in twilight and now in gloom, a dark figure with a glitter of steel at the shoulder whenever the pale moon, riding clear of the cloud-rack, peers down at him through the matted boughs.

The strange rule of this priesthood has no parallel in classical antiquity, and cannot be explained from it. To find an explanation we must go farther afield. No one will probably deny that such a custom savours of a barbarous age, and, surviving into imperial times, stands out in striking isolation from the polished Italian society of the day, like a primaeval rock rising from a smooth-shaven lawn. It is the very rudeness and barbarity of the custom which allow us a hope of explaining it. For recent researches into the early history of man have revealed the essential similarity with which, under many superficial differences, the human mind has elaborated its first crude philosophy of life. Accordingly, if we can show that a barbarous custom, like that of the priesthood of Nemi, has existed elsewhere; if we can detect the motives which led to its institution; if we can prove that these motives have operated widely, perhaps universally, in human society, producing in varied circumstances a variety of institutions specifically different but generically alike; if we can show, lastly, that these very motives, with some of their derivative institutions, were actually at work in classical antiquity; then we may fairly infer that at a remoter age the same motives gave birth to the priesthood of Nemi. Such an inference, in default of direct evidence as to how the priesthood did actually arise, can never amount to demonstration. But it will be more or less probable according to the degree of completeness with which it fulfils the conditions I have indicated. The object of this book is, by meeting these conditions, to offer a fairly probable explanation of the priesthood of Nemi.

I begin by setting forth the few facts and legends which have come down to us on the subject. According to one story the worship of Diana at Nemi was instituted by Orestes, who, after killing Thoas, King of the Tauric Chersonese (the Crimea), fled with his sister to Italy, bringing with him the image of the Tauric Diana hidden in a faggot of sticks. After his death his bones were transported from Aricia to Rome and buried in front of the temple of Saturn, on the Capitoline slope, beside the temple of Concord. The bloody ritual which legend ascribed to the Tauric Diana is familiar to classical readers; it is said that every stranger who landed on the shore was sacrificed on her altar. But transported to Italy, the rite assumed a milder form. Within the sanctuary at Nemi grew a certain tree of which no branch might be broken. Only a runaway slave was allowed to break off, if he could, one of its boughs. Success in the attempt entitled him to fight the priest in single combat, and if he slew him he reigned in his stead with the title of King of the Wood (*Rex Nemorensis*). According to the public opinion of the ancients the fateful branch was that Golden Bough which, at the Sibyl's bidding, Aeneas plucked before he essayed the perilous journey to the world of the dead. The flight of the slave represented, it was said, the flight of Orestes; his combat with the priest was a reminiscence of the human sacrifices once offered to the Tauric Diana. This rule of succession by the sword was observed down to imperial times; for amongst his other freaks Caligula, thinking that the priest of Nemi had held office too long, hired a more stalwart ruffian to slay him; and a Greek traveller, who visited Italy in the age of the Antonines, remarks that down to his time the priesthood was still the prize of victory in a single combat.

Of the worship of Diana at Nemi some leading features can still be made out. From the votive offerings which have been found on the site, it appears that she was conceived of especially as a huntress, and further as blessing men and women with offspring, and granting expectant mothers an easy delivery. Again, fire seems to have played a foremost part in her ritual. For during her annual festival, held on the thirteenth of August, at the hottest time of the year, her grove shone with a multitude of torches, whose ruddy glare was reflected by the lake; and throughout the length and breadth of Italy the day was kept with holy rites at every domestic hearth. Bronze statuettes found in her precinct represent the goddess herself holding a torch in her raised right hand; and women whose prayers had been heard by her came crowned with wreaths and bearing lighted torches to the sanctuary in fulfilment of their vows. Some one unknown dedicated a perpetually burning lamp in a little shrine at Nemi for the safety of the Emperor Claudius and his family. The terra-cotta lamps which have been discovered in the grove may perhaps have served a like purpose for humbler persons. If so, the analogy of the custom to the Catholic practice of dedicating holy candles in churches would be obvious. Further, the title of Vesta borne by Diana at Nemi points clearly to the maintenance of a perpetual holy fire in her sanctuary. A large circular basement at the north-east corner of the temple, raised on three steps and bearing traces of a mosaic pavement, probably supported a round temple of Diana in her character of Vesta, like the round temple of Vesta in the Roman Forum. Here the sacred fire would seem to have been tended by Vestal Virgins, for the head of a Vestal in terra-cotta was found on the spot, and the worship of a perpetual fire, cared for by holy maidens, appears to have been common in Latium from the earliest to the latest times. Further, at the annual festival of the goddess, hunting dogs were crowned and wild beasts were not molested; young people went through a purificatory ceremony in her honour; wine was brought forth, and the feast consisted of a kid, cakes served piping hot on plates of leaves, and apples still hanging in clusters on the boughs.

But Diana did not reign alone in her grove at Nemi. Two lesser divinities shared her forest sanctuary. One was Egeria, the nymph of the clear water which, bubbling from the basaltic rocks, used to fall in graceful cascades into the lake at the place called Le Mole, because here were established the mills of the modern village of Nemi. The purling of the stream as it ran over the pebbles is mentioned by Ovid, who tells us that he had often drunk of its water. Women with child used to sacrifice to Egeria, because she was believed, like Diana, to be able to grant them an easy delivery. Tradition ran that the nymph had been the wife or mistress of the wise king Numa, that he had consorted with her in the secrecy of the sacred grove, and that the laws which he gave the Romans had been inspired by communion with her divinity. Plutarch compares the legend with other tales of the loves of goddesses for mortal men, such as the love of Cybele and the Moon for the fair youths Attis and Endymion. According to some, the trysting-place of the lovers

was not in the woods of Nemi but in a grove outside the dripping
Porta Capena at Rome, where another sacred spring of Egeria gushed
from a dark cavern. Every day the Roman Vestals fetched water
from this spring to wash the temple of Vesta, carrying it in earthen-
ware pitchers on their heads. In Juvenal's time the natural rock had
been encased in marble, and the hallowed spot was profaned by
gangs of poor Jews, who were suffered to squat, like gypsies, in the
grove. We may suppose that the spring which fell into the lake of
Nemi was the true original Egeria, and that when the first settlers
moved down from the Alban hills to the banks of the Tiber they
brought the nymph with them and found a new home for her in a
grove outside the gates. The remains of baths which have been discovered within the sacred precinct, together with many terra-cotta
models of various parts of the human body, suggest that the waters
of Egeria were used to heal the sick, who may have signified their
hopes or testified their gratitude by dedicating likenesses of the
diseased members to the goddess, in accordance with a custom which
is still observed in many parts of Europe. To this day it would seem
that the spring retains medicinal virtues.

The other of the minor deities at Nemi was Virbius. Legend had
it that Virbius was the young Greek hero Hippolytus, chaste and
fair, who learned the art of venery from the centaur Chiron, and
spent all his days in the greenwood chasing wild beasts with the
virgin huntress Artemis (the Greek counterpart of Diana) for his
only comrade. Proud of her divine society, he spurned the love of
women, and this proved his bane. For Aphrodite, stung by his scorn,
inspired his stepmother Phaedra with love of him; and when he
disdained her wicked advances she falsely accused him to his father
Theseus. The slander was believed, and Theseus prayed to his sire
Poseidon to avenge the imagined wrong. So while Hippolytus drove
in a chariot by the shore of the Saronic Gulf, the sea-god sent a
fierce bull forth from the waves. The terrified horses bolted, threw
Hippolytus from the chariot, and dragged him at their hoofs to
death. But Diana, for the love she bore Hippolytus, persuaded the
leech Aesculapius to bring her fair young hunter back to life by his
simples. Jupiter, indignant that a mortal man should return from the
gates of death, thrust down the meddling leech himself to Hades.
But Diana hid her favourite from the angry god in a thick cloud,
disguised his features by adding years to his life, and then bore him
far away to the dells of Nemi, where she entrusted him to the
nymph Egeria, to live there, unknown and solitary, under the name
of Virbius, in the depth of the Italian forest. There he reigned a king,
and there he dedicated a precinct to Diana. He had a comely son,

Virbius, who, undaunted by his father's fate, drove a team of fiery steeds to join the Latins in the war against Aeneas and the Trojans. Virbius was worshipped as a god not only at Nemi but elsewhere; for in Campania we hear of a special priest devoted to his service. Horses were excluded from the Arician grove and sanctuary because horses had killed Hippolytus. It was unlawful to touch his image. Some thought that he was the sun. "But the truth is," says Servius, "that he is a deity associated with Diana, as Attis is associated with the Mother of the Gods, and Erichthonius with Minerva, and Adonis with Venus." What the nature of that association was we shall enquire presently. Here it is worth observing that in his long and chequered career this mythical personage has displayed a remarkable tenacity of life. For we can hardly doubt that the Saint Hippolytus of the Roman calendar, who was dragged by horses to death on the thirteenth of August, Diana's own day, is no other than the Greek hero of the same name, who, after dying twice over as a heathen sinner, has been happily resuscitated as a Christian saint.

It needs no elaborate demonstration to convince us that the stories told to account for Diana's worship at Nemi are unhistorical. Clearly they belong to that large class of myths which are made up to explain the origin of a religious ritual and have no other foundation than the resemblance, real or imaginary, which may be traced between it and some foreign ritual. The incongruity of these Nemi myths is indeed transparent, since the foundation of the worship is traced now to Orestes and now to Hippolytus, according as this or that feature of the ritual has to be accounted for. The real value of such tales is that they serve to illustrate the nature of the worship by providing a standard with which to compare it; and further, that they bear witness indirectly to its venerable age by showing that the true origin was lost in the mists of a fabulous antiquity. In the latter respect these Nemi legends are probably more to be trusted than the apparently historical tradition, vouched for by Cato the Elder, that the sacred grove was dedicated to Diana by a certain Egerius Baebius or Laevius of Tusculum, a Latin dictator, on behalf of the peoples of Tusculum, Aricia, Lanuvium, Laurentum, Cora, Tibur, Pometia, and Ardea. This tradition indeed speaks for the great age of the sanctuary, since it seems to date its foundation sometime before 495 B.C., the year in which Pometia was sacked by the Romans and disappears from history. But we cannot suppose that so barbarous a rule as that of the Arician priesthood was deliberately instituted by a league of civilised communities, such as the Latin cities undoubtedly were. It must have been handed down from a time beyond the memory of man, when Italy was still in a far ruder state than any known to us in the historical period. The credit of the tradition is rather shaken than confirmed by another story which ascribes the foundation of the sanctuary to a certain Manius Egerius, who gave rise to the saying, "There are many Manii at Aricia." This proverb some explained by alleging that Manius Egerius was the ancestor of a long and distinguished line, whereas others thought it meant that there were many ugly and deformed people at Aricia, and they derived the name Manius from *Mania*, a bogey or bugbear to frighten children. A Roman satirist uses the name Manius as typical of the beggars who lay in wait for pilgrims on the Arician slopes. These differences of opinion, together with the discrepancy between Manius Egerius of Aricia and Egerius Laevius of Tusculum, as well as the resemblance of both names to the mythical Egeria, excite our suspicion. Yet the tradition recorded by Cato seems too circumstantial, and its sponsor too respectable, to allow us to dismiss it as an idle fiction. Rather we may suppose that it refers to some ancient restoration or reconstruction of the sanctuary, which was actually carried out by the confederate states. At any rate it testifies to a belief that the grove had been from early times a common place of worship for many of the oldest cities of the country, if not for the whole Latin confederacy.

§ 2. *Artemis and Hippolytus.* — I have said that the Arician legends of Orestes and Hippolytus, though worthless as history, have a certain value in so far as they may help us to understand the worship at Nemi better by comparing it with the ritual and myths of other sanctuaries. We must ask ourselves, Why did the author of these legends pitch upon Orestes and Hippolytus in order to explain Virbius and the King of the Wood? In regard to Orestes, the answer is obvious. He and the image of the Tauric Diana, which could only be appeased with human blood, were dragged in to render intelligible the murderous rule of succession to the Arician priesthood. In regard to Hippolytus the case is not so plain. The manner of his death suggests readily enough a reason for the exclusion of horses from the grove; but this by itself seems hardly enough to account for the identification. We must try to probe deeper by examining the worship as well as the legend or myth of Hippolytus.

He had a famous sanctuary at his ancestral home of Troezen, situated on that beautiful, almost landlocked bay, where groves of oranges and lemons, with tall cypresses soaring like dark spires above the garden of Hesperides, now clothe the strip of fertile shore at the foot of the rugged mountains. Across the blue water of the tranquil bay, which it shelters from the open sea, rises Poseidon's sacred island, its peaks veiled in the sombre green of the pines. On this fair coast Hippolytus was worshipped. Within his sanctuary stood a temple with an ancient image. His service was performed by a priest who held office for life; every year a sacrificial festival was held in his honour; and his untimely fate was yearly mourned, with weeping and doleful chants, by unwedded maids. Youths and maidens dedicated locks of their hair in his temple before marriage. His grave existed at Troezen, though the people would not show it. It has been suggested, with great plausibility, that in the handsome Hippolytus, beloved of Artemis, cut off in his youthful prime, and yearly mourned by damsels, we have one of those mortal lovers of a goddess who appear so often in ancient religion, and of whom Adonis is the most familiar type. The rivalry of Artemis and Phaedra for the affection of Hippolytus reproduces, it is said, under different names, the rivalry of Aphrodite and Proserpine for the love of Adonis, for Phaedra is merely a double of Aphrodite. The theory probably does no injustice either to Hippolytus or to Artemis. For Artemis was originally a great goddess of fertility, and, on the principles of early religion, she who fertilises nature must herself be fertile, and to be that she must necessarily have a male consort. On this view, Hippolytus was the consort of Artemis at Troezen, and the shorn tresses offered to him by the Troezenian youths and maidens before marriage were designed to strengthen his union with the goddess, and so to promote the fruitfulness of the earth, of cattle, and of mankind. It is some confirmation of this view that within the precinct of Hippolytus at Troezen there were worshipped two female powers named Damia and Auxesia, whose connexion with the fertility of the ground is unquestionable. When Epidaurus suffered from a dearth, the people, in obedience to an oracle, carved images of Damia and Auxesia out of sacred olive wood, and no sooner had they done so and set them up than the earth bore fruit again. Moreover, at Troezen itself, and apparently within the precinct of Hippolytus, a curious festival of stone-throwing was held in honour of these maidens, as the Troezenians called them; and it is easy to show that similar customs have been practised in many lands for the express purpose of ensuring good crops. In the story of the tragic death of the youthful Hippolytus we may discern an analogy with similar tales of other fair but mortal youths who paid with their lives for the brief rapture of the love of an immortal goddess. These hapless lovers were probably not always mere myths, and the legends which traced their spilt blood in the purple bloom of the violet, the scarlet stain of the anemone, or the crimson flush of the rose were no idle poetic emblems of youth and beauty fleeting as the summer flowers. Such fables contain a deeper philosophy of the relation of the life of man to the life of nature — a sad philosophy which gave birth to a tragic practice. What that philosophy and that practice were, we shall learn later on.

§ 3. *Recapitulation.* — We can now perhaps understand why the ancients identified Hippolytus, the consort of Artemis, with Virbius, who, according to Servius, stood to Diana as Adonis to Venus, or Attis to the Mother of the Gods. For Diana, like Artemis, was a goddess of fertility in general, and of childbirth in particular. As such she, like her Greek counterpart, needed a male partner. That partner, if Servius is right, was Virbius. In his character of the founder of the sacred grove and first king of Nemi, Virbius is clearly the mythical predecessor or archetype of the line of priests who served Diana under the title of Kings of the Wood, and who came, like him, one after the other, to a violent end. It is natural, therefore, to conjecture that they stood to the goddess of the grove in the same relation in which Virbius stood to her; in short, that the mortal King of the Wood had for his queen the woodland Diana herself. If the sacred tree which he guarded with his life was supposed, as seems probable, to be her special embodiment, her priest may not only have worshipped it as his goddess but embraced it as his wife. There is at least nothing absurd in the supposition, since even in the time of Pliny a noble Roman used thus to treat a beautiful beech-tree in another sacred grove of Diana on the Alban hills. He embraced it, he kissed it, he lay under its shadow, he poured wine on its trunk. Apparently he took the tree for the goddess. The custom of physically marrying men and women to trees is still practised in India and other parts of the East. Why should it not have obtained in ancient Latium?

Reviewing the evidence as a whole, we may conclude that the worship of Diana in her sacred grove at Nemi was of great importance and immemorial antiquity; that she was revered as the goddess of woodlands and of wild creatures, probably also of domestic cattle and of the fruits of the earth; that she was believed to bless men and women with offspring and to aid mothers in childbed; that her holy fire, tended by chaste virgins, burned perpetually in a round temple within the precinct; that associated with her was a water-nymph Egeria who discharged one of Diana's own functions by succouring women in travail, and who was popularly supposed to have mated with an old Roman king in the sacred grove; further, that Diana of the Wood herself had a male companion Virbius by name, who was to her what Adonis was to Venus, or Attis to Cybele;

and, lastly, that this mythical Virbius was represented in historical times by a line of priests known as Kings of the Wood, who regularly perished by the swords of their successors, and whose lives were in a manner bound up with a certain tree in the grove, because so long as that tree was uninjured they were safe from attack.

# Euripides' Phaedra and Hippolytus

## Richmond Lattimore

PHAEDRA, the wife of Theseus, fell in love with Hippolytus, who was Theseus' son by an earlier liaison with an Amazon woman. This love was communicated to Hippolytus, who rejected it. Phaedra then killed herself and left a note which said that Hippolytus had attacked her. Theseus believed that this was true. He banished his son from the country, and also prayed to Poseidon, asking him to kill Hippolytus. As the young man was departing a monstrous bull came out of the sea and made his horses bolt. Hippolytus was dragged to his death, but before he died Artemis revealed the truth and father and son were reconciled. Hippolytus was worshiped as a hero or a young god after his death.

This is the simple outline of the story out of which Sophocles made a tragedy, and Euripides made two, one of which has survived. The story has been retold, imitated, or adapted by Seneca, Racine, d'Annunzio, O'Neill, Jeffers, and doubtless many others. If we isolate what seems to be the center of the plot, that is, the temptation of a young man by the wife of a man to whom he owes loyalty, his refusal, the calumny of the wife against him which is believed, then the story appears as a particular instance of what we might call a pattern story which (like the story of the foundling or of brother and sister lost and reunited) has numerous independent variants and seems to be one of those forms of fiction which grow naturally out of men's minds and human experience. The best known parallel outside of Greek is the story in *Genesis* (39) where the nameless wife of Potiphar, Joseph's patron, begged Joseph to make love to her, and when he would not she said he had tried to force her and caused him to be thrown into prison. But there are plenty of parallels in the Greek. Homer tells of Bellerophon who at the court of Proetus was solicited by his host's wife, and when he refused her she told her husband of

---

"Phaedra and Hippolytus" reprinted from *Arion*, I, No. 3 (1962), 5–18, by permission of the editors of *Arion*.

Bellerophon's designs on her, and Proetus, unwilling to kill his guest with his own hands, sent him to a friend abroad carrying, in a sealed letter, instructions for his own death (Il. 6.145–211). Homer calls the wife of Proetus Antaea, but others knew her as Stheneboea, and Euripides wrote a tragedy, now lost, which went by that name and used that story. Then there was Astydameia, sometimes called Hippolyta, the wife of Acastus, who when Peleus was the king's suppliant and guest tried to seduce him and when he refused reversed the story in the customary way so that Acastus, believing, stole Peleus' sword and left him alone on the mountain to be killed by wild beasts, or by centaurs (Nem. 5). Pindar told this story and Euripides may have used it in his lost Peleus. Not to go on too long, there was also Tennes, son of Cycnus, traduced like Hippolytus by his amorous stepmother, and put in a box by his father and set adrift at sea (Paus. 10.14.2). Euripides seems to have written a play called Tennes.

We emerge, then, with the story of the young man traduced as a pattern of Greek tragedy, or that legendary material out of which the Greeks made their tragedies, and to this pattern the story of Hippolytus, Phaedra, and Theseus belongs. Sometimes the most striking dramatic effects are wrought when the familiar modes of fiction are made to yield unfamiliar results. In King Lear we have a familiar figure of coldness disguised as love and love disguised as coldness. Of course it is going to be the cool-spoken Cordelia who loves Lear, and the truth must come out and they must be reconciled, and so they are — but too late to do any good, and the happy ending proper to such a morality is mocked and mutilated. Oedipus is the foundling-story, at the end of which the lost child will be recognized and find his own home and people. You will find out who you are and who your parents are, says Teiresias to Oedipus, and you will wish you never had (Sophocles, Oed. Tyr. 413–428). It is the perversion of this blithe type of romance, so happily illustrated in The Winter's Tale and The Importance of Being Earnest, that gives Oedipus its gruesome and ironic force. To the surprise of the story itself, now grown familiar, is added the surprise of making this story come out the way such stories ought not to come out.

And something like this has happened to Hippolytus, both in the story given to Euripides, which does not go quite the way of the pattern story, and in what Euripides did with the story he was given.

Joseph was thrown into prison, but that was where he began those prophetic exercises which brought him to power and made him a great man. When Bellerophon reached his destination, the king who was requested to murder him passed him on, sending him out on deadly errands, and Bellerophon disappointed him and killed monster after monster until he ended with the hand of the princess and half the kingdom. Chiron rescued Peleus who went on to become a hero and a potent king and married the daughter of the sea. The traduced hero like the foundling meets his trials on the way to success, and emerges triumphant because the gods look after their own darlings. But they did not look after Hippolytus. He died.

And what of the lady in the case? Bellerophon in some versions, not the earliest, returned to murder Stheneboea, and Peleus, also in later versions only, butchered Hippolyta for her sins. Are these later embroideries which aim to balance the reward of the virtuous with the punishment of the wicked? We do not know. The false temptress seems early to be not much more than a prop to push the hero off on his brilliant way, not interesting in herself, and her subsequent fate is a matter of indifference. Only in our Hippolytus story does she kill herself.

And these two facts, that the hero does not come through and that the lady buys belief at the price of her own life, change the action of the play from romance to tragedy, and, because action and character are interdependent, they change the characters too.

Phaedra is the easiest, so let us begin with her. She is far more than the mere stock character who sends the hero off to his perils and glories. We can dismiss the wife of Potiphar, though Thomas Mann did not, and say we know all about *her*, but we cannot do that with Euripides' heroines, Phaedra or, if we had that play, Stheneboea. Euripides, as we know, wrote an earlier version, which seems to have given offence, for, says the critic who wrote the preliminary notice in our manuscripts, what was improper and shocking in the first play has been corrected in this one. What gave offence was, for one thing, a scene in which Phaedra made her proposition to Hippolytus in person, but we may choose to suppose that this was not all, that the entire character of Phaedra which supported this action and made it credible, provoked distaste and lost him the prize. Here he has set about to rehabilitate Phaedra, or to make his audience sympathize with her, and whether or not he has succeeded will be a question each reader or listener will have to decide for himself. Let us see, at least, what he has done.

First, Aphrodite herself speaks the prologue, and announces the outcome of the play, the *that* of it not the *how*, and explains that *she* has made Phaedra fall in love with Hippolytus, that Phaedra is keeping it secret and like to die, but she is a necessary instrument for the young man's punishment. We can think what we like about Aphrodite and what she meant to Euripides and we shall have to come back to all that later, but for the dramatic purpose of the prologue we must suspend belief, admit Aphrodite is what she says she is and that what she tells us is so, and therefore Phaedra, resisting love, is beaten from the start. Second, Euripides seems to have gone out of his way to emphasize her youth. She is not a mature woman or a hardened campaigner. The nurse talks to her as if she were a baby. She could be older than Hippolytus, but, since Greek girls often married at 14 or less, she could easily be younger and still have two children. Euripides is content to make us see her as young. (This is of course a shading in sympathy, an aesthetic point, not a moral one, since an eighteen-year-old stepmother who acts like Phaedra is morally no better than a thirty-eight year old, merely, to some, less repulsive.) Also, she is sick, in body as in mind. *Nosos* is her keyword, for she has been starving herself for days, meaning to die before she can have what she wants or not have it. Weakened in every way, she lets the nurse extract, first her secret, then permission to go and do what she can (charms, witchcraft, persuasion?) with Hippolytus; she does not, as in the earlier play, go to him herself.

All this is a mere jumble of data about Phaedra, as stated by Euripides, not, I would repeat, to justify the defamation and instigated murder of a young man by a stepmother who has tried to seduce him, so much as to show that the stepmother who did this was not a monster. Sufficient reason would be that monsters make dull theatre. It takes us somewhat farther, though, if we ask just how much she intended to do to punish Hippolytus, and in what belief.

When Phaedra let the nurse go off on her errand, vaguely described as "to make everybody happy," Phaedra stayed behind while the chorus sang in sympathy, until she overheard the outburst of the young man against the nurse's proposition. We do not know how this scene was staged. Hippolytus and the nurse may have spoken loudly from behind the backdrop, unseen, while Phaedra listened at the door, or more probably the pair burst out through the door, violently talking, while Phaedra huddled away in shame. Did she and Hippolytus ever look each other in the face, did she leave the stage while he was still talking? We do not know, but however this scene was meant, written, and staged, Phaedra had cause for fear. The nurse had sworn Hippolytus to silence before she said anything to him. Now he hinted that he might break that silence. "Do not, my child, disown your sworn oath," said the nurse, and Hippolytus answered in the famous line which Euripides' tormentors never allowed him to forget, "My tongue swore, but my heart remains unsworn" (611–12). Hippolytus paid for that piece of sophistry with his life. For he did not, later, when accused by his father of the rape of the dead Phaedra, tell the truth, even in the most trying circumstances (if he had told the truth he would not have been believed), though he was not above throwing out a couple of good broad hints. What he meant or is meant to have meant is, I think, merely, "You have trapped me with a technicality and I can say nothing, and it is not fair" but he (and Euripides) could not resist putting it in a more pointed and terrifying way. If he meant "you can't hold me with an oath like this" then, before he was through with his too long speech, he saw that honor was going to make him keep his promise (656–60). "I see my duty, madam, and that saves you. If I were not caught by oaths sworn to the gods, which I must not break, I could not have kept it from my father. Now, since I must, I shall stay out of this house while Theseus remains abroad, and I will shut my mouth and say nothing." This he means and this he does. Whether Phaedra heard this last or was listening, or not, it was said too late; the first fatal sentence made her sure that Hippolytus would break his oath, and her thoughts are plain as she speaks to the nurse (688–93). "Now I must think and think quickly. That creature in his rage will tell his father of the wrong *you* made me do, and he will tell grandfather Pittheus all about it and make the whole country ring with scandalous stories. Damn you, go away." This to the nurse; she begs the other women to keep her secret, and they swear by Artemis to do so. Now she will kill herself but so doing she will hurt Hippolytus too. There follows the scene where her body is discovered, with the suicide note.

Her motives are complex, but they do not cancel each other. Foremost, of course, is sheer rage at the self-satisfied young man who has not only turned her down when she was not sure she was offering herself at all but insulted the whole world of women as well. But that is not all. She is a foreign princess, from Crete; her people will be sneered at by these Athenians and Troezenians. Her boys will be disinherited as of a suspect mother, and this bastard, by-blow of an early affair of her husband, will inherit the throne and mock them all. She has been made a fool of; well, she will make a fool of him. Does she foresee his death? Probably not; she says not a word of it. This does not excuse her much. Every playgoer knew that Theseus was of the old line of heroes, honorable and just but terrible in his just angers, the sort of man to strike Hippolytus dead on the spot if he believed Phaedra's story. And Phaedra means that he shall believe it.

Such, then, is Phaedra: treacherous, mean, even murderous under provocation. And yet not, in the end, treacherous, mean or murderous. So Euripides means us to understand, for he has made her three

bitterest enemies pay tribute to her honor. Aphrodite says in the
beginning (47): "Phaedra is honorable, but there is no hope for her."
Hippolytus says in his defence — limited by oath (1032–35):

> Whether, in fear of something, she took her own life,
> I do not know, and am not allowed to say more.
> She could not quite be virtuous, and yet she was.
> So we, who could be virtuous, have been ill used.

Artemis speaks to Theseus (1300–01) of "your wife's mad passion,
or, somehow, her nobility." The hint of an unresolved puzzle about
Phaedra lurks throughout; drama does not have to be finished off in
a precise arrangement of logically coherent contracts, so long as we
believe. Phaedra acted dishonorably because of her own nature yet
acted against her own nature, which was honorable. Can we resolve
further?

Perhaps. With her secret out, Phaedra turned to the women about
her, confiding (377–423, much abridged):

> I think that lives go wrong not because people
> decide to go wrong; no, rather look at it like this:
> we understand the better way and recognize it
> but do not work it out. . . .
> Now I, when I found I felt as I did
> I tried first to keep silent and cover my sickness up.
> Then next, I determined to be strong
> and by force of will to overcome my stupid weakness.
> Third and last, when I was making no headway
> against love, I decided I had to die.
> For I hope, when I do well, that it is plain to all,
> and when I do shame, that I shall not have the world to witness.
> So, dear friends, I must die,
> because I must never be known to have shamed my husband and my
> children, so they may flourish, free to say and do what they please in
> glorious Athens; or, if not, it will not be their mother's fault.

Taking these lines or some of them as the true index of Phaedra's
nature, some critics have very reasonably concluded that she is, indeed, no villainess, but a rather pitiful little Athenian wife who is
concerned beyond anything else with respectability and putting the
best face on things. From four of the lines above this conclusion is
certainly just but it is a final conclusion only if the lines are fully
*in character*, and I am not sure they are.

We remember that when Phaedra first appears she is feverish and
delirious, answers no questions but babbles of woods and waters and
her longing for these. Then, recovering, she speaks reasonably in

answer to the nurse's questioning but is still overwrought, fiercely reticent and ashamed. Once the admission is torn from her, she embarks on the long discourse (58 lines) which I abridged above, explaining in language mostly cool and even, her experience and the reasons for her attitude and purposes. Now it is a sort of dramatic trope or habit of structure (for Euripides and Sophocles) in this period to present, early in the drama, the heroine first strongly emotional and wrought upon and heard in lyric or anapaestic verse: then, in temperate blank verse annotating or explaining her emotion of the previous scene in a long speech, whose burden might be summarized thus: "Women and friends, I am sorry to have made such an exhibit of myself before you, but I have reasons to be so overwrought. Listen and I will tell you" (*Medea: Alcestis,* modified: returned to in *Helen:* Sophocles, *Electra, Trachiniae*). Part of the speaker's bearing here is the generalization of this particular case — this is the sort of thing we women have to put up with, say Deianeira and Medea — a resultant flattening of the heroine's individual features. Deianeira and Medea speak about the routine of courtship and marriage, but their own experience has been anything but routine, and the effect for Medea is that she temporarily loses her vital character of barbarous Colchian witch or minor goddess fetched by her own magic from the end of the world, to enact the lines of Woman or Everywoman (*Medea* 248–49). "Men say of *us* that we sit safe at home and live a life secure, while they carry the spear and fight." These lines seem not part of the heroine Medea, but rather Euripides on women; and so "I think we understand the better way but do not work it out" — this does not show so much what Phaedra was like, but rather represents the poet taking issue with Socrates' proposition that virtue is knowledge and nobody does wrong when he knows better. It is hard to draw the line, and this speech of Phaedra's is by no means all out of character: mixed with the generalizing moralities are outbursts that come from inside the living person, as (413–18):

> I hate those women, virtuous by reputation,
> whose secret lives are full of guilt;
> o queen and mistress, Aphrodite of the waters,
> how can they look those whom they sleep with in the face,
> how can they not shiver at the darkness which has been
> accessory; how not fear the walls of the rooms, that they may speak?

This is Phaedra indeed, but she is concerned with more than the conventions of respectability. Still, it is not all of Phaedra. After all, she was not a typical young Athenian wife of good family, but a princess from Crete, a Dorian or at least a non-Athenian, and so raised, perhaps, by standards which would be most unconventional in Athens. This other side comes out in Phaedra's first scene, where her fevered murmurings are answered by the nurse (198–238):

— Lift my weight, straighten my head.
I am weak, dear friends. My strength is unstrung.
Hold me up, my maids, by the firm curve
of my arms. The veil is a weight. Take it away.
Let my hair stream free on my shoulders.

— There child. Stop tossing about
so crossly.
Keep still, be brave, and the sickness
will not trouble you so.
Mortals always have pain and suffering.

— If I could only lean and drink
from a running spring clear water!
Or in the trees, in the long meadow
grass, lie down and rest.

— Hush dear, what are you saying?
There are people here. Don't speak
so loud. You're almost raving.

— Take me away from here, to the hills.
I want to go to the forest, to the pines
where the hunting hounds
shadow the spotted deer. Oh gods
how I long to hallo the dogs on
and hold close along my blond blown curls
the northern spear, barbed weapon, poise it
and make my cast.

— Dear dear this is wild. What does it mean?
What has riding to hounds to do with you?
This craving for spring water, what is it?
Here by the walls is a fresh bank
and a spring. We can get you a drink from there.

— Artemis, queen of the sea, lady
of lakes, of riding and the thunder of hoof beats,
how I long to be where you are, in the plains,
riding blood horses, breaking them.

— More madness, crazy words, why?
Just now your longing was for hill country, the chase,
and now again for the sand flats, beyond
the breakers, and horses to ride.
Here is a puzzle for diviners. Who knows

what god rides you on a wild rein,
dear child, and stampedes your reason?

Phaedra longs for the woods and the sands, the strenuous life which in fact Hippolytus leads, and critics who have dealt with this scene from the ancient annotator on down have concluded that she longs for this life and these places because she longs for Hippolytus. The implication, if you leave it at that, as the critics constantly do, is that this is all that the lines mean, that this most vivid and imaginative scene in the play contrives no more than a disguise for a love which, intense as it is, is of a quite ordinary sort. I wish to avoid assaults on straw men but when or if this interpretation is held, it is wrong. A character in drama who is not deliberately playing the hypocrite — and Phaedra with her conventional manners burned away by fever is speaking from the bare mind — should be heard as one who speaks the truth. Here she says not one word about Hippolytus, does not long for him to be brought away from his forests and into her bedchamber. There is not a line of sex in the scene. She really does wish she could run and ride; she is not a usual Athenian matron. I have thought Euripides means to characterize her as a girl from Crete, and he does frequently though not consistently emphasize national characteristics. It is important that Medea is not a Greek wife. She is from Colchis, not that Euripides knew much about Colchis or knew it accurately, but the point is that she is a wild barbarian lost and fighting among Greeks, and then again when the purpose serves she will speak not as a barbarian at all but merely as a wife forlorn in an unfair convention of marriage. Phaedra speaking of marriage does not speak as a Cretan but Phaedra longing to run and ride may be doing so. Spartan girls, unlike Athenians, were brought up to a tradition of athletic sports and athletic costumes, and one Euripidean character wonders, affronted, whether girls who showed their legs like that and wrestled with the boys could ever be virtuous even if they wanted to be (*Andromache* 595–600). Euripides, well aware of the Spartan customs, may also have known and taken for granted that his audience would know that Crete was Dorian, that Spartan institutions were much like the Cretan and said by some to have been imported to Sparta from Crete. If that is so, Phaedra is not only a foreigner but a foreigner misunderstood, one dwelling in a country strange to her ways, a displaced person in a predicament congenial to Euripides' invention. It is true that she is attended by a figure who properly belongs only in Athens or in one of the cities Euripides would have thought of as conventionally Greek, the nurse, who in Athens looked after a girl when she was a baby and a child and followed her to her new home when she married. This character is then out of place, but Medea (as does Deianeira) has such a nurse too, more incongruous for a Colchian princess than a Cretan one. Euripides is rather careless in these matters. The play's the thing; and for the play's purposes Phaedra here needs someone to misunderstand her, which this nurse does to perfection with "if you're thirsty, I can find you a drink of water, why go all the way to the woods?" I do not insist on the Cretan coloring. Euripides may not mean us to assume that she was trained to be an athlete and to roam the wilderness. What I do insist on is that she craves to do so. If we put together the following speech with this one, the careful and conscious account of her malady with the uninhibited babbling of delirium caused by that malady, then we see Phaedra and her two lives: the one she has got, fretful and brooding, pampered, sedentary, confined between walls; and the one she wants, free, wild, galloping headlong through the woods and over the sand and flinging herself down to drink without a cup from running streams. Why does she love Hippolytus? People fall in love with the wrong people, or the right ones, principally for their own sake, or Euripides would say because Aphrodite makes them, but if we need more reasons, then it is as true to say that Phaedra loves Hippolytus because he lives and stands for the wild and innocent and strenuous life which she wants and cannot have, and is thought crazy for wanting it, as to say that she longs for wild places because they suggest Hippolytus and if she were there she might be with him.

Which brings us to that young man. The play falls into two halves: the first is the tragedy of Phaedra, the second is the tragedy of Hippolytus. But they are interdependent and neither is complete without the other.

Remembering our pattern story, we will see at once what is the indispensable characteristic of the young hero. He must be virtuous. Hippolytus fills the bill. He is virtuous with a muscular, somewhat belligerent, and utterly self-righteous virtue which makes his critics wonder how in spite of all Phaedra could love him, since we cannot, though we give him full marks.

Agreeing as I do in general with this opinion, I do not wish any more than others to leave it at that. The Prig's Tragedy is not as moving a subject as Euripides wished to make or, somehow, did make, the subject of his play. I do not think the poet, then, intended to create the at times repellent character (at least to modern tastes) which he has created. He failed then in part, but only I think in part, and we can still ask what he was trying to do and how far he succeeded in doing it.

Hippolytus repels us through the starchy rhetoric and phony arguments he uses in his defence before Theseus; in the scene with the nurse because he not only spurns Phaedra but insults her, and because of her all women, wishing they, or sex, could be dispensed with entirely; in the scene of his destruction reported by the messenger, when, dragged and battered and in agony and terror, he cannot even call for help without saying (1242): "Who will come and rescue *me, the best of all men?*" In the Theseus scene he has been accused, accurately, of addressing his father as if he were a public meeting. Well, but his father *is* a public meeting. This is the one person in the world who can break him or save him. The evidence against him is damning, and he is debarred by oath and his own honor from speaking the truth, thus forced back on those arguments from probability which may impress an audience of dilettantes but convince nobody. So he, and the chorus, and we, all knowing the truth, can only watch, helpless, the inevitable drive of Theseus' rage. Euripides' dramaturgy has formed a bitter, breathless scene, but his execution has spoiled it a little because, as so often, he is under the spell of his own virtuosity and does not know where to stop, so the "plain unschooled speech" comes out too obviously varnished. In his protest to the nurse he makes himself ridiculous by his wish that we could deposit money in the temples and buy the seed of children there instead of having to make them as we do. The poet has hurt his hero by forcing him to speak for the poet's own fustian fancy. But under it all lies the strong desperate mood of the play, the wish for the impossible voiced at one time or another by every character in it except Aphrodite (who is having her way). Only one figure of this mood is the Prig's progress, the wish, even the demand, that everybody else in the world shall be as good as he thinks he is. This spoils it somewhat, but even under the disastrous "me, the best of men" we feel a sense of outrage which Hippolytus would be inhuman not to feel. Everything is unfair, and he knows it. Unfairness is the inverse of the impossible wish.

Bastard son of an Amazon forced by Theseus, Hippolytus stood queerly among the Athenian nobles, neither quite Athenian nor quite a noble, but naturally noble, reflecting some of fifth century Greece's wistful admiration of the noble savage, the blissfully uncomplicated barbarian. Only in part: he must also be, no savage, but accomplished in every way, the star of Athens. Out of his strange position Hippolytus has found his way to a life that suited him completely, one utterly immersed in athletics and hunting, blissfully uncomplex, modestly useful, free from society except for the company of a few friends and free from the love of women except for Artemis. Like Ion in the beginning of *Ion* we find him a truly happy young man who has so far escaped all responsibility and is placidly doing only what he wants most to do. "I only hope I can live all my life as I have begun it" (87) are his last words as he deposits his wreath to Artemis. Of course, it does *not* last: the world catches up with him and wrecks his peace.

Racine in his version found all this well enough, but felt that such a character was too philosophical and his sufferings would arouse indignation rather than pity; therefore he, Racine, has presumed to give him an amiable weakness, through his sweetheart, Aricie. Now if Aricie represents Diana of Aricia and Diana is Artemis, I think Racine was right in a way he probably did not suspect, for surely Hippolytus was in love with Artemis. I do not mean that Artemis represents, actually is, the life he loves, for this is true, but that is not what I mean by love. Rather in the full sense Hippolytus loves Artemis as a woman, the voice and fragrance and presence of her and her invisible companionship, which is all that is given him and all that he asks or hopes for. But now he must be entangled with a woman of flesh and blood, the one woman in the world he cannot have and who must not have him, but *also*, and here is the irony, though he does not want her, the nearest thing to Artemis this side of paradise, a woman who could have shared his favorite pleasures and kept him company as well as simply keeping his house. *Medea* gave us one mode of tragedy in marriage, two hostile natures fastened together by accidents of love and need but each inwardly disliking and despising the other. *Hippolytus* conversely gives two ideally suited natures forced apart by circumstance. Or at least, that is one way to put it. The terms are too romantic for fifth century Athens and the interpretation goes beyond Euripides, but the materials for this interpretation were all put by Euripides in his play.

Circumstances, I said, keep these two apart, but it is more than circumstance (*Tyche*) which forces them into hatred and mutual death, it is the whole way of the world and the nature of the world of which their own natures are a part. This way, which one might call love, is here enacted by two goddesses, Aphrodite and Artemis. It is part of the whole structure of the play that these, again, who are here so different and opposed, are elsewhere so often confused, because they are two aspects and faces of the same goddess who is only the eternal constantly recurring figure of the lovely and beloved young woman, variable as Plato's Heavenly Aphrodite and Vulgar Aphrodite, or Sacred and Profane Love. Critics have complained that

Euripides is not clear in his concepts, that Aphrodite in particular is both an immortal person with a human personality, vain and silly and spiteful, and also an impersonal force, the whole reproductive process and urge of nature. This doubtless, I think, is exactly what Euripides meant. One knows very well that floods, blizzards and hurricanes have no personality, that we cannot reason with them and so it is useless to be angry with them and at the same time we cannot when caught help seeing them as maliciously and spitefully aiming at *us*. Here Aphrodite appears not in a theological tract but as a person in a play. She is still divine and we know what she stands for. Artemis is not so clear. She represents, I think, something which the Greeks never isolated and defined, must have felt but did not articulately understand, the sheer pleasure of straining muscles until they ache and running until breath goes (even Pindar commiserates his wrestlers for "toil," congratulates them on success which redeems it and makes it worth while); and Artemis is other things too, the green woods themselves, and lonely places, the harsh and sterile side of pleasure. But also she too is a person in a play: one who cannot stop Aphrodite but resents her and will get her own back, who pities Phaedra and scolds Theseus and then forgives him, who rewards Hippolytus' devotion with the disinterested shadow of love.

Between the two they wreck everything. Things as they are go wrong. Everything is unfair. We can think of Yeats' lines:

> And God-appointed Berkeley, that proved all things a dream,
> That this pragmatical, preposterous pig of a world, its farrow that so
>    solid seem,
> Must vanish on the instant if the mind but change its theme.

The mood of hate for the world despite or because of love for its individual people is very strong in this play, expressed in the constant wish for impossibilities, the sense of outrage, the longing for escape. "My own horses, whom I fed" (1240, 1355–56) complains Hippolytus: or to Zeus (1363–67): "I was the most pious man on earth and you've killed me. Why?" "Why do you not go hide in the hells of the earth for shame," says Artemis to Theseus, "or take wings like a bird and fly away in the air, to escape?" (1290–93) It doesn't make sense, of course: Artemis merely speaks the insistent mood of the drama, and as she does so reminds us of Theseus' line when he discovered Phaedra dead (828): "You were gone suddenly out of my hands, like a bird." So too the women of the chorus, involved only as spectators, long to turn into birds and escape to the ends of the ocean, the inaccessible cliffs and the sea caves.

That the world is more wrong than right is the statement of pes-

simism, and Euripides often seems to be a pessimist, but to summarize
this play as such a statement would be wrong. This is a particular
action done by particular people. Other actions which follow the
pattern story of the young man traduced see these same gods or
others like them guiding their hero through to the end where the
falsified truth is made plain again and the injuries of accidents made
good. Euripides wrote some of these actions as plays, but that did
not make him an optimist. Here the pattern story ends badly and the
gods must see that everything is done for the worst. Theseus in his
first rage and before Hippolytus appeared cursed his son to death,
then forgot it or did not believe Poseidon's promise meant anything;
and was content with a sentence of exile, but Poseidon heard and,
though he did not like to, carried out the sentence. But though the
gods control the springs of action they do not move puppets. Phaedra
and Hippolytus are caught in circumstances, but their own nature
is part of these circumstances, in Phaedra the vanity and lust which,
for all her good qualities, answers Aphrodite, in Hippolytus the
chilly and selfish righteousness, or maybe nothing worse than immaturity, which answers Artemis. Nor again is drama, however realistic,
a mere piece of reality of such and such dimensions transposed, in
full, into words and action. There is no room in this play for a full
Theseus, only enough to fill the stock part of outraged father and
headlong angry king; and so too the gods of the *Hippolytus* appear
not as full theological studies but only as characters in the play sufficient to their part in realizing the action. That, and to establish the
play as a solemn progress at the beginning, in Aphrodite's stiffly
formal prologue: and to fasten it to its base in the cult of contemporary life, in Artemis' farewell (1423–30):

> For you, dear wretch, to atone for your injuries
> I shall give you high honors in the city
> of Troezen: for girls unwedded, near their marriage time
> shall cut their hair short in your memory. You shall have
> the tribute of their tears through time forevermore.
> There will be music made and songs of you, to make
> the virgins think of you, and Phaedra's love
> for you shall not be forgotten and a thing of silence.

# ❖ ❖ ❖ Tragedy and Moralism: Euripides and Seneca

## *Norman T. Pratt, Jr.*

A COMPARISON of the dramas written on the theme of Phaedra and Hippolytus by the Greek Euripides and the Roman Seneca will be used here to indicate some differences of orientation between the two major types of tragic drama surviving from antiquity.[1] This essay presents a basis of differentiation, not a study of the plays in full detail. By the same process we shall try to throw some light upon a major transition in the course of European tragedy, at the point where the classical Greek dramatic tradition ends, and the trends of the "modern" period, including Shakespeare, begin to emerge.

In recent years it has become the literary fashion to emphasize the ritual origin of Greek tragedy and, often, to analyze its form and to interpret the meaning in ritualistic terms. It is, to be sure, one of the few things which we can come close to knowing about the origin of Greek tragic drama that one of its sources was ritual song performed in worship of Dionysus. Dionysus, whom we often think of as the god of wine (Roman Bacchus) was actually a fertility divinity linked with nature's reproductive power and with the cycle of life and death among living things, and conceived of in male terms. Most specifically, he was associated with the life cycle of the vine: its pro-

---

[1] For the reader unfamiliar with this material, the following items are essential: Euripides, *Hippolytus*, trans. David Grene, in *The Complete Greek Tragedies* (Chicago, 1959), III, 163–221; Seneca, *Hippolytus*, trans. F. J. Miller, in *Seneca's Tragedies* (Loeb Classical Library — London, 1917), I, 321–423; Seneca, *On Anger*, trans. J. W. Basore, in *Seneca, Moral Essays* (Loeb Classical Library — London, 1928), I, 107–65; H. D. F. Kitto, *Greek Tragedy: A Literary Study*, Anchor Book, pp. 210–18. I am indebted to Professor Kitto's ideas about the Euripidean *Hippolytus*.

---

duction of harvest, the death-like pruning of its vegetation after harvest, and its reproduction at the advent of the new season.

There is very much that we do not know about all this; the skein of available evidence is scanty and tangled. But it seems clear enough from data concerning such fertility rites and from the evidence of the plays themselves that Greek tragic drama received from ritual — like the ritual of Dionysus — a conception of nature: nature as a complex of forces which bring health or disease to plants and animals. One purpose of such ritual was to effect a reconciliation between individual living things or social organisms and the powers of nature: to avert the destructive impurities, to achieve life-nourishing purity.

The strong tendency in recent work on Greek tragedy, to approach these dramatic creations as founded on and conditioned by ritual, has contributed considerable illumination — as well as much distortion when carried to extremes. For example, Francis Fergusson's influential analysis of *Oedipus the King*[2] is built upon the following ideas: "The Cambridge School of Classical Anthropologists has shown in great detail that the form of Greek tragedy follows the form of a very ancient ritual, that of the *Enniautos-Daimon*, or seasonal god." "It is this tragic rhythm of action which is the substance or spiritual content of the play, and the clue to its extraordinarily comprehensive form."

It would be unjust to be captious about this method, for it has succeeded in revealing implications and dimensions which are fresh discoveries, and in reminding readers that we are dealing not only with a great literary tradition, but also with dramatic creations which are rooted in communal ritual. However — to give a very familiar and generally discredited example — serious distortion results from viewing Oedipus as a ritual scapegoat through whom the impurities of the city are exorcised. It is one dimension of the drama that impurity and abnormality in the family of Laius have brought upon Thebes a taint which must be removed — this must be recognized if we are to understand the role of Apollo the purifier in the drama — but at the end of the tragedy we are left, not with a purified Thebes, but with a suffering tragic hero and the mystery of his experience. The point must be made that there is a great difference in level of intellectual maturity between the plays themselves and the ritualistic concepts by which the "Cambridge anthropologists" and their followers analyze the texts. The fifth-century dramatist shows himself to have been far more sophisticated than this kind of analysis represents him to be. Another major danger is that the imprint of ritual thus tends to become a kind of mechanistic factor

[2] *The Idea of a Theater*, Anchor Book, pp. 38–39, 31.

which presses the drama into a formal mold. The creative function of the dramatist is seriously slighted.

Even so, a strong ritualistic motivation is apparent in the texts. A ritualistic concept is found in the orientation of these tragedies toward the issues involved in the relations between man and the powers controlling the universe. Further, the human situation in relation to these powers characteristically involves impurity or abnormality or injustice which calls for some kind of purification. There are many guises of purification in the texts.

A second general point is also essential for the understanding of Euripides' *Hippolytus* and, for that matter, most of the Greek plays. The Greek conception of divinity is radically different from the Hebraic-Christian idea familiar to Western readers of Greek literature, and is often a source of serious misunderstanding. For example, modern readers of Homer are often mystified by the action in the first book of the *Iliad* when Achilles is about to draw his sword in the quarrel with Agamemnon, but Athena suddenly appears to check him; or in the *Odyssey* by the repeated appearances of Athena to help Telemachus who is struggling to make decisions and to achieve maturity in a difficult personal situation. What is the significance of Athena's appearances? Does Homer expect us to believe that Athena appears physically, or is this simply a metaphorical way of saying that Achilles' better judgment prevailed, or that Telemachus is approaching adult intelligence? The answer seems to be that Homer does ask the reader to accept her appearance as a physical action *and* that a kind of metaphor is involved. Athena is a divine person, she has a personal identity which can be described and recognized; her emotional and intellectual make-up is well defined. But it is equally important to observe that Athena characteristically appears in situations which involve the application of mind to practical situations; on this basis we can understand how her functions as goddess of warfare and as mistress of handicraft could be absorbed into the fully developed conception of her nature. In these Homeric passages she exemplifies the Greek way of saying that active intelligence is more than the thinking mechanism of an individual creature; it is a significant and pervasive aspect of experience. It is bigger than human. It is "divine."

This conception of divinity has a number of important implications for the understanding of the Euripidean *Hippolytus*. For one thing, in Greek literature of the classical period generally, the gods are not pure symbols. One has to reckon with them as personalities and as symbols. For another, one has to be very careful in analyzing the relationship between divine powers and human actions. Much that

has been written about Greek tragedy as "tragedy of fate and deter-
minism" founders on the false assumption that all aspects of divinity
in these strongly religious dramas involve forces which are external
to human affairs and directly determine human actions. Analysis
based on this assumption often produces the conclusion, or the strong
tendency toward it, that the freedom of the human being is severely
restricted by divine control. Bothersome questions arise. Why does
the dramatist devote so much attention to the delineation of human
character if the role and significance of character are so restricted?
If men are close to being puppets manipulated by external forces,
does the human scene have enough status, can it be taken seriously
enough to be "tragic" at all? Or do we have simply pessimism — or
optimism?

It is true that the Greeks were intensely aware of the constant
impact of outside elements upon man's experience. This recognition
is fundamental in their earliest literary document which has survived,
the *Iliad*. But the idea of absolute predeterminism is *not* characteristically Greek. These people keenly felt the instability of human
fortune under the impact of bigger-than-human forces, but they
were also strongly individualistic and insistent upon human preroga-
tives, whether the context be political or intellectual; this is perhaps
one reason why the role of "fate" is a matter for such intense concern. In any event, on this whole matter there is a wide range of
positions taken by individual poets, as well as other thinkers, and
these must be analyzed in terms of the individual poem or drama.
There was no orthodoxy on such issues comparable to that found in
the Christian tradition. One of the points which matters greatly is
the way in which the individual artist uses this conception of the
gods. Are his gods more significant as active personalities? Or as
symbols? Even though exact answers may elude us, at least rough dis-
tinctions are possible, as between the gods of Aeschylus' *Oresteia*
and of the *Hippolytus*. The appropriate answer will matter greatly.
When, as in the *Hippolytus*, the gods function primarily as symbols
of the phenomena which are manifested by the human figures in their
characters and actions, the artist is not saying that human action is
determined by the gods in any absolute sense, but is universalizing
the factors present in the human situation. The notion "tragedy of
fate" is dangerous and intricate.

The prologue of the *Hippolytus* confronts us with these issues immediately. Aphrodite (Cypris), claiming the honor due to her as an
Olympian, announces that she will punish Hippolytus' scorn by death
at his father's hands, and that the process of revenge requires Phaedra's death also. The goddess is heartlessly protecting her own in-

terests. At the end of the drama, Artemis' attitude is comparable:[3]

> Cypris shall find the angry shafts she hurled
> against you for your piety and innocence
> shall cost her dear.
> I'll wait until she loves a mortal next time,
> and with this hand — with these unerring arrows
> I'll punish him.

It is very difficult to state Euripides' religious views clearly, probably because he did not resolve some issues himself. His views are the product of an uneasy, sophisticated, critical mind moved by the rational tendencies of his time. But it seems possible to approach somewhere near the center of his position in this drama, by using the notion of symbolic personalities sketched above. The symbolic aspect of Aphrodite and Artemis is of the utmost importance in the drama. In this aspect the goddesses are, in fact, the whole context of the tragedy. However, *as personal deities* they raise grave doubts for the dramatist. Artemis describes the relationship among the gods as a matter of mechanical protocol:

> For it was Cypris managed the thing this way
> to gratify her anger against Hippolytus.
> This is the settled custom of the Gods:
> No one may fly in the face of another's wish:
> we remain aloof and neutral.

The human reaction to this thought is elsewhere expressed sensitively by the chorus:

> The care of God for us is a great thing,
> if a man believe it at heart:
> it plucks the burden of sorrow from him.
> So I have a secret hope
> of someone, a God, who is wise and plans;
> but my hopes grow dim when I see
> the deeds of men and their destinies.

Professor Kitto interprets Artemis' words this way: "She paints Olympus as a place of moral chaos — which can indicate only that what these deities represent, instinctive passions, is independent of reason and morality." [4] The whole point appears to be somewhat sharper, because Euripides seems also to mean: "If you look to these gods as personalities for comfort and rational concern, you are probably deluded; they seem to be indifferent and irresponsible."

---

[3] The following five quotations are from Grene's translation, pp. 219, 216, 208, 215, 179–80.

[4] *Greek Tragedy*, p. 217.

But at any rate the main function of the goddesses is to represent sexual passion and ascetic purity as "divine" phenomena, that is, as motive forces which are pervasive and persistent. Passion is the force which moves the dramatic action, but the motive of purity is essential for the impasse which produces tragedy. In other words, the phenomena represented by the goddesses are in destructive collision. The Greek way of saying this is found in some more words of Artemis:

> For that most hated Goddess,
> hated by all of us whose joy is virginity,
> drove her with love's sharp prickings to desire
> your son.

Hippolytus and Phaedra are then victims of the force of sexual love. But victims in what sense? The drama has often been interpreted to mean that they are victims of their own extremes. Throughout the text such notions as "moderation" and "excess" are reiterated. But are the characters and actions of Hippolytus and Phaedra (and Theseus) extreme in such a way that their excesses could be resolved by some principle of control?

Essentially the two main characters express humanly the full force of the phenomena figured by Aphrodite and Artemis. Phaedra takes her own life and causes, through Theseus' curse, the death of Hippolytus not because she is weak or irrational, but simply because she is overpowered by love. Every reasonable demand that she try to achieve control is satisfied by her own description of her strong and self-conscious struggle to conquer love "with discretion and good sense." She makes the point herself:

> I think that our lives are worse than the mind's quality
> would warrant. There are many who know virtue.
> We know the good, we apprehend it clearly.
> But we can't bring it to achievement.

Honesty and loyalty are her natural characteristics. The evil which comes from her: the false accusation of Hippolytus and her vindictiveness toward him — these are the products of shame and the desperate attempt to secure her children's future, as the results of being overpowered.

In some respects Hippolytus is one of the most disagreeable figures found in the Greek plays. The Greeks of the fifth-century audience probably felt even more strongly than we do that he is disastrously contemptuous of a fundamental law of human experience. Very obtrusive indeed are his pride, self-love and violence. However, these faults come essentially from his extreme dedication to the purity of forest and meadow, to the chastity of uncivilized nature figured by the Maiden Goddess of Wild Things, Artemis. It is a barren and unnatural commitment, as Euripides clearly feels, but it makes a legitimate claim for attention and respect. Incidentally, these values associated with Artemis could of course be recognized immediately by Euripides' Greek audience; the modern reader has to re-create the original context in this respect.

And Hippolytus is good. This is acknowledged — not only by himself! — by the Messenger (whose statements are factual), Artemis and Theseus. His quality is also demonstrated in the final stages of the action where he is compassionate toward Theseus and frees him of guilt. His death is caused in part by refusal to break his oath of silence. It is typical of Euripides' wry-faced manner to create this disagreeable fanatic whose moral purity is nevertheless authentic.

It is impossible, then, to find in the drama, as the dramatist has shaped it, any means of control or moderation which could be realized. Phaedra has struggled for rational solution, but is overwhelmed by "Aphrodite." Any kind of adjustment by Hippolytus is unthinkable. The *Hippolytus* is not primarily a "tragedy of character" but of the conditions of human existence. Everything points in this direction: the prominent roles of Aphrodite and Artemis, and of what they stand for; the characters of Phaedra and of Hippolytus. Further, in the form of the drama, the power of "Aphrodite" and its collision with the qualities of "Artemis" are represented as a "storm from the sea" (along with related ideas) in a substantial pattern of figurative language throughout the text. For example, Aphrodite's first word in the Greek text of the prologue calls herself "mighty"; by a simple verbal repetition the Nurse later refers to her as coming to men like a "mighty wave" (line 443). Phaedra is tossed by a storm (315) and struggles to swim out (470). The traditional epithet of Aphrodite as the "sea-born queen" is used with special point (415, 522) — whereas Artemis frequents "dry land beyond the sea" (149). In the first stasimon (525-64) Eros and Aphrodite are linked with stormy elements (530, 559, 563). The sound of the conversation of the Nurse and Hippolytus overheard by Phaedra is the sound "of rushing water" (576).

The second stasimon is a brilliant development of this figurative theme. In the first half (732-51) the thought moves from the here and now to distant places around the sea where, in contrast with the flux of the sea, the human grief of the sisters mourning the death of Phaethon is fixed in beauty, and where the gods dwell in brightness and security. In the second half (752-75) the chorus, moving in thought from Phaedra's distant home in Crete to nearby Athens,

identifies the ship which brought her with Phaedra herself, and antici-
pates the suicide of Phaedra who, metaphorically, is "foundering
under bitter misfortune" (769). Theseus looks upon a sea of disaster
(822–24). The final catastrophe is caused by the sea monster sent by
Poseidon.

Euripides clearly communicates his conception that the tragedy of
*Hippolytus* comes from evil which is organic in the natural order of
the conditions in which humans live. It is essentially this "natural"
evil that produces the extremes found in the characters and actions of
Phaedra, Hippolytus and Theseus.

Turning to the *Phaedra* (or *Hippolytus*) of the Roman Seneca
takes us over a wide gap — in time, kind and quality. His plays, of
the first century A.D., are usually thought of as conscious imitations
of various Greek tragedies (apparently Seneca was particularly attracted to the themes dramatized by Euripides), although we suffer
from having little substantial knowledge of Latin tragic drama before
Seneca. In any event we are here interested not so much in the
point-to-point relationship between the Euripidean and Senecan
dramas as in some explanation of the differences between them as
types of drama.

Senecan drama is not directly related to communal ritual like the
Greek. It is the product of the study and presumably — though this
is moot — was written to be recited to literary groups rather than
staged. Condemnations of Seneca the dramatist are commonplace.
His works are, in comparison to the Greek, second-rate melodrama
loaded with rhetoric, mythological and other lore, and violent action
(sometimes, as in the *Phaedra*, horribly violent). They are exces-
sively intense in matter and form.

However, these plays challenge analysis for several important reasons. The striking disparity between the Greek and Roman products
in the same dramatic tradition calls for explanation. Also, the ubiq-
uitous historical influence of Seneca upon English and European
drama of the sixteenth and seventeenth centuries makes it essential
to understand the nature of the source; and it must be remembered
that Senecan influence was not merely a regrettable fact, but in a
number of ways had a positive salutary effect. For example, the
fully developed structure and language of the Senecan play disciplined the drama written under its influence; or again, the device of
introspective monologue, which was shaped by rhetorical and Stoic
elements in Seneca, became a powerful tool for later dramatists.
Finally, most critics appear to take it as a personal insult that Seneca
undertook to write drama, and there has been relatively little effort to
understand what made the plays what they are — for good *and* bad.

The writer has suggested elsewhere that Stoicism formed Senecan drama much more fundamentally than has been realized.[5] It is obvious, of course, that Stoic themes, along with others, appear in the texts. More latently, conceptions from this source seem to have directed the very premises underlying Senecan drama. We are on sure ground in one respect, namely that Seneca was formally a Stoic and wrote a large amount of philosophical essays and epistles which can be brought into relationship with the plays.

A very brief sketch of Stoicism is necessary. It is a very comprehensive, and somewhat paradoxical, system based on the equation "virtue = reason = nature." Virtue is the greatest good for man and is achieved by the exercise of reason, the highest human capacity. But the force of reason is not merely human. It permeates all of nature, producing harmony, system and direction toward the good. This power in nature is also described in religious terms; it is equated with god, it is divine. (It is also, paradoxically, associated with the material fire.) Thus the potential rationality in man stems from his participation in the divine. The human being and the universe are, then, parallel organisms constructed in the best possible way for the realization of good through reason.

One familiar, but crucial, point should be stressed. Tragic drama is, of course, concerned with various forms of evil as they touch humans. A system like Stoicism which is essentially optimistic is hard put to account for imperfections in a world where reason is believed to be the dominant force. The prose writings of Seneca, like all Stoic literature, present a whole battery of arguments attempting to meet the issue: Evil only seems to be evil, and must be part of nature's rational plan; imperfection tests and develops man's mettle; what seems to be evil can be neutralized by man's understanding of "what is in his control" and what is not; evil can be converted to good by endurance, etc. For our purpose the most interesting question is: How does a dramatist with Stoic ideas — or at least this Stoic dramatist — account for catastrophe in tragic drama?

The Stoic philosopher deals with imperfection primarily in terms of the moral condition of the human being. Men's behavior is a battleground of reason vs. passion. The most frequent theme in Stoic writings is that error and evil result when passion overcomes reason. For example, rage, the most common emotion in the Senecan plays, is considered temporary insanity in the first book of Seneca's essay *On Anger*: It is "the most hideous and frenzied of all the emotions," [6] contrary to nature and principal enemy of reason. On the other hand, practice of the virtues of wisdom, courage, moderation

---

[5] "The Stoic Base of Senecan Drama," *Trans. Am. Philol. Assoc.*, vol. 79 (1948) pp. 1–11.
[6] Basore's translation, p. 107.

and endurance not only eliminates weakness within man, but also negates the effect of catastrophe coming from without. The parallel to what is found in the *Phaedra* is very close. Seneca has written a dramatization of criminal psychology, charged with extreme abnormality and irrationality; indeed, this is the main source of the intensity and horror which are Seneca's failings. A few illustrations will show that the formulation of these elements is Stoic. Phaedra recognizes in herself the curse of unnatural love received from her mother (this is only mentioned in Euripides). She introspectively states the moral conflict: "Quid ratio possit? Vicit ac regnat furor." "What can reason do? Passion has conquered and now rules supreme." [7] Theseus is a mad adulterer. Hippolytus can hardly be anything else than a rather colorless victim, for destruction comes wholly from Phaedra, and there is no significant impasse between the two as in Euripides; he speaks as a Stoic when he praises life in the woods and identifies it with the Golden Age.[8] The Nurse both preaches Stoic virtue to Phaedra and urges Epicurean indulgence upon Hippolytus. Perhaps most significant of all is the thought of the Nurse that "base and sin-mad lust . . . has made love into a god and, to enjoy more liberty, has given passion [*furori*] the title of an unreal divinity." [9] Love and passion are moral conditions in men, not conditions of existence. The contrast with Euripides is radical.

Similar features can be found in all the Senecan plays. Also, there are instances where the opposite side of Stoic morality is seen, i.e. where reason prevails and Stoic virtues overcome catastrophe. For example, in the *Troades*, Astyanax and Polyxena face death with such equanimity that they are victors. It seems apparent that Stoicism led Seneca the dramatist to a completely moralistic view of error and catastrophe: Evil is either externalized as the workings of fate or fortune which can be nullified by reason, or is thought to be caused by the deterioration of character which results when passion destroys reason. This is a far cry from the characteristic Greek view that evil is organic in the natural order of things and cannot be eliminated by mere rationality.

In fact, it is very doubtful that the effect of tragedy can be achieved in drama written on these Stoic premises: Such an explanation of human experience is too simple and shallow; it eliminates the possibility of a significant relationship between, on the one hand, what men do and suffer and, on the other, the sources of this experience

[7] Miller's translation, p. 333.
[8] *Ibid.*, pp. 357–61.
[9] *Ibid.*, pp. 333–35.

both within and outside of man. The mystery essential to tragedy is gone.

Other important factors, of course, contributed to making Senecan drama what it is. But Seneca's Stoicism was a source of basic limitations. Composing tragic drama under these limitations and on these premises — whether consciously or unconsciously — the dramatist was restricted in what he could achieve. He chose to intensify, to portray the psychology of behavior, particularly irrational behavior, powerfully and vividly. The center of dramatic attention was turned inward. This new orientation made Senecan drama a landmark in the development of psychological drama, and was carried by Senecan influence wherever it went.

# ❖ ❖ ❖  The Tragedy of Passion: Racine's *Phèdre*

*Henri Peyre*

IT WAS fashionable, in the latter half of the last century and in the early decades of the present one, to lament the death of tragedy. The novel was blamed by some critics, and was to be blamed or envied: it had captured the essentials of tragic emotion, while diluting it and often cheapening it. Others thought the fault lay with the modern democratic public, unable to appreciate the structure, the restraint, and the poetry of true tragedy. One of the pervading myths of the age, the myth of progress, seemed moreover to make tragedy superannuated and superfluous, a remnant of an era of violence and of man's undeveloped ability to control and improve his fate.

Many signs in the last two decades have pointed to a striking reversal of such an attitude. Modern man is no longer sure that he is the free master of his fate and ruler of the sciences and techniques which he practises. The fatality of wars and revolutions crushes him. His struggles are heroic, but he is harried by doubts as to his ultimate triumph. He even clamors, in existentialist language, against the gods who may have loaded the dice in that dubious battle, or he revenges himself by denying their existence. A keener awareness of recent psychology has made many of us readier to admit that there is another kind of fatality, no less implacable, at work within ourselves, made up of evil biological, psycho-physiological or hereditary forces. Several of the greatest writers of our age, Lorca, Claudel, T. S. Eliot, O'Neill, have revived tragedy as an art form. Few novelists since Balzac, Dostoevski, and Hardy had been as tragic as the contemporary ones in Europe and America. The neglected muse nowadays is that of comedy. The ingredient most sorely missed in many a novel is humor. Tragedy abounds. Without a tragic climate, writers like Malraux, Camus, Greene, Faulkner could hardly breathe.

---

Reprinted from *Tragic Themes in Western Literature*, ed. Cleanth Brooks (New Haven, 1955), by permission of Yale University Press and the author. Copyright, 1955, by Yale University Press.

America, where faith in progress and in success was most hardy, where pessimism was long considered a morbid failure of nerves, an unhappy ending a denial of providence, has also fallen a prey to fear, and even to fear of fear. Its novel today is the gloomiest but also the most virile of any western literature. Some of its best plays have staged stories of crime and retribution akin to Aeschylus and Euripides. Even *The Death of a Salesman* or a musical "entertainment" like *The Consul* has been steeped in the tragic. Few topics are more frequently selected by students than the tragic sense of some past or modern book or play. Few titles of courses or lectures prove more attractive than those which promise a treatment of tragedy.

The most tempting peril for a critic is probably that of excessive ingeniousness. The constant study of great works and his impatient reading of other critics, with whom he would like to differ, may drive him to being oversubtle. He often defeats his purpose by attributing too many meanings to the books that he interprets and by reading mysteries into works which thus appear to have been intended only for initiates. The candid admission that occasional disorder and illogic, moments of negligence and of fault, are not absent from works of genius, that "quandoque bonus dormitat Homerus," seems a less romantic conception of greatness in art, and, when all is said, a more modest one than that of the oversubtle critic who depicts the man of genius in his own image. An honest and modest presentation of the truth, the life, and the beauty inherent in a great French tragedy, stressing the significance of that play "hic et nunc," is the sole ambition of this writer.

The tragedy I have chosen to discuss is, but for the religious epic drama of *Athalie*, the last one in the series of masterpieces produced by the French dramatists of the Classical Age. It was produced on January 1, 1677. A common view of literary historians holds that, the very next year, with *La Princesse de Clèves*, the novel asserted itself as the rival of the French tragedy and its heir; only in recent years has tragedy, more freely reinterpreted, caught up with the novel in their symbolic race.

*Phèdre* is not the unchallenged masterpiece of Racine: *Andromaque* has more freshness and more harmony, *Britannicus* is structurally more impeccable, *Bérénice* has occasionally wrenched more tears from some playgoers. Nor is Racine himself the unchallenged master of tragedy in the eyes of the French. Periodically critics, debaters in *salons*, and schoolboys assert that Corneille's genius rose higher. Corneille indeed had more fire, more imaginative inventiveness, a more triumphant mastery of comedy as well as of tragedy; his range was wider than Racine's and he is, with Balzac, the closest approach that French literature had to Shakespeare. But the parallel Shakespeare-Racine is, once for all, to be banished if French tragedy is to be judged aright. *Phèdre* is not a faultless play. But it rises higher than any other French tragedy, it is closer to us today, deeper in its character delineation, more pathetic in its poetical moments. It molded a theme, borrowed from antiquity but filled with new significance, which the modern novel has since enriched further, or perhaps worn threadbare. It is periodically — every three years or so — and always successfully put on the French stage. French males of every generation, like Proust's enraptured hero watching La Berma in the part, have dreamed for years of the great actress — Rachel, Sarah Bernhardt, and a score of others since — who had impersonated Phèdre in their youth. It would be no exaggeration to say that the magnificent love declarations in the play and its burning picture of jealousy have done much to frame the French conception of love and even the behavior of French men and women when possessed by the sacred malady — as all of them are convinced they must be before they become truly civilized and resigned to a serene and dignified existence in the provinces.

The enthusiastic and often uncritical appreciation of Racine which seems to prevail in several countries at present, Great Britain and even America not least of all, is a strange reversal of the attitude of the traditional Anglo-Saxon to the French classical drama. Lytton Strachey, Maurice Baring, T. S. Eliot in his longing for the concentration and tight structure of the French tragedy, and a score of lesser luminaries have made it fashionable for the culture-conscious Englishman to proclaim his admiration for Racine. One of the latest Racinians, Martin Turnell, quoted a Belgian who, in 1945, praised the British people as the most truly civilized in the world because "their bankers spent their leisure hours trimming their rose-bushes and reading Racine." Let us hope they also resorted to other forms of relaxation, including the beneficent Victorian one of spending part of a Sunday morning in church. It is true that some snobbery in literary vogues can work wonders, persuade many people that they actually enjoy and love Racine, Proust, and Paul Valéry, and bring them to such an enjoyment. The *Times Literary Supplement* summed up the striking change in the English opinion of Racine by saying that nowadays if an Englishman did not take to the French dramatist, he would no longer lay the blame on Racine but on himself.

Americans have been less vocal in their Racinian cult. Yet many of the finest studies of Racinian drama to appear in the last twenty-five years have come from the pens of academic writers teaching in this country, and few if any professors complain today of having difficulty in converting their students to a sincere appreciation of Racine. Corneille, Hugo, and Balzac prove to be far worse stumbling blocks to the young American of this generation.

It took a great number of years for English-speaking audiences to rank *Phèdre* unquestioningly on a par with a few other tragic masterpieces. The first adaptation of the play on the English stage was done in 1706 by Edmund Neale Smith. Dryden found fault with the French play in his preface to *All for Love*. Pope speaks coolly of "Exact Racine." Johnson remained silent on, and apparently uninterested in, Racinian tragedy. Coleridge and Hazlitt, in their Shakespearean idolatry, accepted Racine as a mere foil to the Elizabethan giant, and the author of the *Plain Speaker* deemed Racine only worthy of "the frivolous and pedantic nation who would prefer a peruke of the age of Louis XIV to a simple headdress." Landor, De Quincey were still more contemptuous and even presumed to find Racine's verse unmusical and to decree that his ear was defective. The rigid mold of the alexandrine verse, which with Racine is far from rigid if one's ear is attuned to the subtle shades of his music, repelled many Englishmen. Racine's acceptance of the unities was misinterpreted by them as the slavery of a timid courtier daunted by exterior rules laid out by pedants. Racine's language and, strange as it seems today, his characterization were judged to be conventional and pompous. Some French people, during the fiery battles of the Romantics against the belated Classicists of 1820–40 (themselves incapable of understanding Racine), subscribed to similar views. Again lately, Jean Schlumberger and even J. P. Sartre expressed disapproval of Racine on moral grounds.

Our own age, more sensitive than previous generations to the rhetorical excesses of Romanticism and to the formlessness of many Romantic attempts on the stage, has achieved a keener insight into the value of structure, restraint, and purity of form in a work of art. It has gained much in the appreciation of psychology in literary works. Readers of Proust and Mauriac are inclined to miss a certain psychological density in many earlier writers; but Racine, Rousseau, Stendhal stand out among those lucid and profound analysts of the human soul who had nothing to learn from Freud or from Jung. Historical and biographical research has also borne fruit. We have today a much more precise knowledge of the seventeenth century which, even in France, was a century of turmoil, of adventure, of metaphysical and baroque yearnings, of unconventional and brutal behavior. Racine's own life has yielded few secrets: his letters are totally unrevealing, and he wrote no memoirs, kept no diary, left no confession. His prefaces, into which too much has been read, inform us but little as to his esthetic views and still less about the genesis of his dramas. Speculations on his religious feelings and on his so-called conversion have been idle for the most part, and most prudent scholars would today avoid any mention of Racine's Jansenism in his lay dramas, *Phèdre* included.

Racine, the man, remains a mystery. Even more than Descartes, he could have confessed of himself: "larvatus prodeo" — I go forward wearing a mask. But posterity which resents complacency and even happiness in great artists and wants them to have sinned and suffered while they created, has been satisfied in the case of Racine. His biographers (Mary Duclaux, A. F. B. Clark, Geoffrey Brereton among the English ones) have told with evident relish how Racine moved in a Dostoevskian atmosphere of shady liaisons, plots, witchcraft, and poisoning. The French dramatist has appeared to them, and to many others, more "human" for having loved without restraint Marquise du Parc (Marquise was merely her first name), a celebrated actress who was also loved or courted, among others, by Molière, both Pierre and Thomas Corneille, by another poet named Sarrazin and presumably by her own husband. Racine was perhaps involved in an affair of abortion and of poisoning when his mistress died. He then became infatuated with La Champmeslé, for whom he wrote several of his most beautiful women's parts, including that of Phèdre. But he had to share her favors with several other men, and with her husband, who acted some of the men's parts in Racine's own tragedies. When, soon after the performance of *Phèdre* and the hostility which he then encountered, Racine resolved to withdraw from an author's career, it appears that he was moved less by religious fervor or by remorse than by weariness, by some doubts as to his ability to renew his creative power and to retain the public's applause, and by a very worldly desire for security. He found security in a well-rewarded position at the court and in a loveless marriage with an unsophisticated woman who enjoyed the double advantage of having no parents alive and a substantial dowry. His contemporaries failed to see any mystery in his withdrawal from literary life at thirty-eight. But our own age, haunted by Rimbaud's repudiation of literature and by the "broken columns" of geniuses turning insane or entering a life of penance, or even of alcoholism, at forty, are fond of speculating on Racine's retreat after the creation of his most splendid and boldest feminine character. The silence which followed the performances of *Phèdre* and Racine's sudden retreat have enhanced the enigmatic fascination of the play for future audiences.

The theme of *Phèdre*, the main events and even the features of the leading characters, a number of lines and of phrases were borrowed by Racine from Euripides and in a lesser measure from Seneca, perhaps also from Ovid's *Heroids*. No consideration of the play can overlook this essential but often misinterpreted fact. For a comparison between Racinian and Greek drama has long been implicit behind the English charges against Racine's claims to be a true classicist and has been one of the favorite exercises of German critics. Racine knew Greek as well as any man of letters of his age. He professed an unbounded reverence for Sophocles and Euripides and went to the latter for the theme of two or three of his plays. Hasty or malignant critics thus spread the notion that he was attempting to emulate or to repeat a Greek type of tragedy, but that he failed and remained only an imitator and a neo- or pseudo-classical dramatist.

Few commonplaces of the criticism of past ages could be more erroneous. Racine's familiarity with Hellenic writers was real, his artistic sense was akin to that of the Greeks, his exquisite but hardly powerful creative imagination found a valuable support in the subjects already dramatized by ancient writers. An Englishman, R. C. Knight, has lately published a bulky and learned book on the subject. But he has not altered our conviction that the Racinian type of drama is totally un-Greek, that Racine's characterization and especially his delineation of love would have horrified a fifth-century Hellene. In many respects indeed, Shakespeare who probably never had read the Greek dramatists in the original, stands closer to Greek tragedy than does Racine. Racine's classicism is in no way neo-Hellenic but deeply French in its achievement and in its shortcomings.

Of the three great tragic poets of Greece, Euripides is the one who appeared to Racine as the least likely to waylay an admirer. In recent years the characters of Orestes and Electra as first drawn by Aeschylus, then Oedipus and his daughter Antigone, have proved more tempting to many dramatists. Sophocles, of the Greek dramatists the most alien in spirit to Cocteau, Giraudoux, Anouilh, and other moderns, has been the one whom they selected as their patron saint, often to caricature him without piety. Racine's instinct was doubtless right. It was also the instinct of another great poet, steeped in ancient lore, Goethe, who in his talks with Eckermann upbraided Schlegel for his carping criticism of Euripides and exclaimed: "Have all the nations of the world since his time produced one dramatist who was worthy to hand him his slippers?" Poets have as a rule been more sensitive than philologists to the greatness of Euripides. Shelley, Browning,

H. D., Robinson Jeffers have attempted to render him, and Claudel
has strikingly called him "the Greek Baudelaire" and ranked him
among "the poets of the night." They clearly recognized in Euripides not the rationalist reasoner and scoffer into whom some scholars have transfigured him but the most tragic of poets as Aristotle
called him, and a very human dramatist.

Better than his two predecessors on the tragic stage, Euripides
understood women and painted them in their changing and pathetic
truth. Like other friends-in-disguise of womankind, he derided them
occasionally because he both feared and loved them. Sophocles had
sometimes omitted them from his plays or depicted them as rigid
and unnaturally tense: worse still, as in *Ajax* or *The Trachinian
Women*, they were uninteresting. Euripides distrusts them, especially
when they are clever. "Only the narrowness of their brain keeps
some of them incapable of folly," says angry Hippolytus. But with
him they are true. Their emotions often drive them to spitefulness
and revenge; they may be led astray by lustful passion, like Phaedra,
by violence as they are in the *Bacchae*, by jealousy like Medea. But
they stand up to men and can even be superior to them in generosity
as Alcestis is to her selfish and sanctimonious husband. The dramatist
renders the shudder of their flesh and explore the dark recesses of
their souls.

Euripides had devoted two plays to the theme of Phaedra and
Hippolytus. The first one, which is lost except for some fifty scattered lines, caused something of a scandal among the Athenians. In
it Phaedra unashamedly confessed her passion and contrived the
death of her unresponsive stepson. She then put an end to her own
life. The second play, which we have, is more restrained. Her
passion for Hippolytus fills Phaedra with shame. She is a victim of
the goddess of love and the avowal of her passion to her nurse is
half involuntary. She accuses Hippolytus before she dies in order
to spare her own pride but hardly appears criminal to the audience.
She has already atoned for her crime when it is revealed to us, and
Hippolytus himself is not faultless. The drama is a superhuman
struggle between two goddesses.

Racine brought it down to earth; he did not renounce the wealth
of suggestiveness and the remote epic atmosphere which the theme
owed to mythology. Phèdre is "la proie de Vénus" and appeals in her
shame to her father Minos who will judge her in the nether world,
even to her ancestor the Sun from whose eye her incestuous passion
cannot be concealed. But the French drama could hardly be a war
of the gods. Racine, moreover, would have had difficulty in under-

standing the religious character of the Greek theater, as the philology and anthropology of the last hundred years, that of Tyler, Jane Harrison, and Gilbert Murray, have enabled us to do. He had little knowledge of history of religion and even less insight into primitive rituals and cults. His play had to become a purely human drama. Human, but feminine more than masculine. Already in Euripides heroines were often more complex and more noble characters than the men. But Hippolytus, the handsome charioteer ranging about race courses and hunting deer in the forests, scornful of women, impatient of all that seems to him complicated and "fussy" about love, was hardly comprehensible to Racine and his contemporaries. Racine in his preface remarks that ancient critics had blamed Euripides for "having represented Hippolytus as a philosopher exempt from every imperfection." A strange misconstruction indeed, and one that betrays Racine's remoteness from the Greeks. Racine adds that he lent him some weakness (his love for Aricia) which made him somewhat guilty toward his father and his punishment less monstrous. It is hard to believe that Racine remained unaware of the immense gain to the tragic force of *Phèdre* which accrued from Hippolytus' love for Aricia and Phèdre's consequent jealousy. His preface is timorous and diplomatic and hardly consonant with the violence of the play.

In fact, the guilt in Euripides' play as we have it is shared between the young sportsman and his stepmother. The latter is motherly, restrained in her speech and behavior, and neither her husband nor Hippolytus utter any harsh words against her. Hippolytus on the contrary is self-righteous and arrogant. Repeatedly he asserts that no more virtuous man than himself could be found, and he dies boasting of his piety and of his austere reverence for the gods. But he violated the Hellenic ideal of "nothing in excess" by his insensitiveness and his proud exclusiveness. Theseus, before uttering his fatal curse against his son, had taunted him for his pretentious airs. Racine could hardly be expected to understand the implicit blame which the Greek play laid upon Hippolytus. One of the best American critics of Greek and French tragedy, Prosser H. Frye, rightly if sternly noted that Racine "never fathomed the profound moral significance of the great Attic tragedians." Submission to fate, which even Prometheus accepted in the last play of the trilogy by Aeschylus, was the rule with Greek characters but is profoundly alien to those of Racine, who all rebel against the decrees of the gods and the bidding of moderation and wisdom. Shakespearean women, except for a few passionate and arrogant ones like Juliet or Lady Macbeth, are much closer to Greek heroines in their meek acceptance of Lear's, Hamlet's, or Othello's brutality than are Racinian women.

If *Phèdre* deserves to be called a classical masterpiece, it owes it to qualities of its own and not to Racine's fidelity to his Greek predecessor or to any Greek ideal. Racine was like many artists and poets who are at their best when, instead of raising the whole of a new structure with their own hands and setting up their own standards, they work over materials already polished by their predecessors, accept former esthetic ideals and even a certain musical, pictorial, or poetic diction already laden with evocative power. Virgil, Racine, Poussin, Mozart are no less original if less powerfully imaginative than other geniuses who seem to have been born without any ancestor or masters. The originality of *Phèdre* lies in the artistic structure and in the poetry of the tragedy and its splendid and terrifying portrayal of passion.

The inner law of French tragedy has often been defined as one of concentration and of economy of means. Shakespeare and even the Greeks were closer to the epic. A longer span of time was encompassed in their dramas. Lyrics or choruses interrupted the sweep of the plot and afforded a respite to the intensity of the emotions stirred in the audience. Comic and familiar moments, more discreet in the Greeks than in Shakespeare, relieved the horror and the pity. The whole of life invades a Shakespearean drama, and men and women are presented in their varied and contradictory moods, in scenes which appear at first superfluous but enhance the lifelike truth of their characterization. Even *Othello* and *Richard II*, which achieve some structural simplicity, are very remote from the paucity of incidents and the bareness of the plot in *Phèdre*. We learn nothing of the heroine's life before the play began, of her marriage and of her feelings for Theseus, of her maternal affection; a few allusions, indirectly and poetically made, recall to the audience the wrath of the gods which had lighted unquenchable passions in the mother and the sister of Phèdre. But nothing need be known of the growth of the heroine's own loving fury, unlike the development of Othello's or of Romeo's passion, the swift yet gradual corrosion of Macbeth's soul by ambition, or Lear's folly which will lead to his punishment. The audience is thus prevented from sharing the tragic emotions of the protagonists as they grow in them: it is not made their accomplice. But the sudden appearance of the heroine, anguished and tense to the breaking point, ready for the explosion which will work her undoing if her exasperated passion cannot be relieved, produces a strong impact upon reader and onlooker alike. A trigger has been pulled, and all is started: men and women are thrown against each other in fierce outbursts of passion which will easily flare into jealousy, hatred, and destructive impulses. No lyrical appeasement, no rhetorical intoxication with words,[1] no delight in nature or philosophical meditation on love, on life's "walking shadow" or "the sting of death" will bring any abatement to the unleashed fury. There will be no escape but death inflicted or suffered from the infernal machine contrived by the gods.

Very little happens in *Phèdre* and what happens hardly counts. The theme was well known to the audience from the outset, since it had been dramatized by ancient and earlier dramatists: the plot of a drama is in any case easily summarized by the reviewers or in play-goers' talks. As Georges May has proved in his book on Corneille and Racine, the interest of curiosity, primary with the elder French dramatist, dwindles in the younger one to insignificance. Racine never boasted of being inventive or original in his plots. He had little wish to appeal to curiosity. He was chiefly concerned with how characters reacted under the impact of a few very simple incidents.

Hippolytus, having received no news from his father whom many fear to be dead, announces when the curtain rises his plan to embark upon an extensive search for him. He will see his stepmother once before he leaves. Before the interview takes place, Phèdre appears, dying with the fever of her illicit love, struggling between remorse and desire. She yields to the entreaties of her nurse and confidant, Oenone, and confesses to her her love for Hippolytus. After this avowal she yearns only for death. Then the news is spread that Theseus is no longer alive. Phèdre consents to live and to listen to Oenone's argument that her love is no longer monstrous and that her duty is to fight to have her son recognized as heir to the throne.

The news of Theseus' death will be contradicted in the third act, according to a pattern used and abused by Racine. But meanwhile the characters have revealed themselves in several of their facets under the impact of the false report. Hippolytus has been encouraged to open his heart to Aricia, in a delicate scene of confession: he behaves, feels, and speaks like a young Frenchman of the age of

---

[1] Contrary to a common delusion, there is very little rhetoric in Racine's drama and very few tirades similar to those of dying Othello, of Henry V before the battle scene, of Richard II carried away by self-pity. Herbert Grierson rightly observed in *The First Half of the XVIIth Century* (Edinburgh and London, Blackwood, 1906), p. 318: "In no drama is there really so little idle declamation as in the French. . . . Every word from the beginning to the 'Hélas!' at the close helps the action forward a step. And to the end the issue of the action remains uncertain."

Louis XIV, and not at all like a Greek; but far from deserving thereby the irony with which he has sometimes been judged, he reveals himself with graceful dignity and with a shyness which soon gives way to a restrained but winning eloquence. Hardly has he spoken to Aricia than Phèdre steps on the stage and in the third great confession of love in the drama, scaling heights of poetry never before reached by Racine, declares her love to Hippolytus. She accuses herself and accuses the gods, but she secretly hopes that her stepson will be won by the eloquence of passion which burns in every word she pronounces. He has never loved yet, or so she believes, and his shyness might be vanquished by her beauty and her loving avidity. Hippolytus remains insensitive and is bewildered by the furious display of passion. Scorned, Phèdre, probably made conscious of the difference in years between him and herself, aware of the sacrifice of all sense of shame which she has accomplished, takes a bitter joy in proclaiming her own debasement. She oversteps all bounds. She will buy his love if need be through an offer of political power in Athens and dreams already of laying the kingly crown herself on his beloved forehead. She even fancies that he will teach her son horsemanship and be attracted to the mother through the child.

Theseus' prompt return is announced. Fear and remorse triumph for a moment over her wild imaginings. Lucidly, she recalls her advances to her husband's son: "Je connais mes fureurs, je les rappelle toutes." Once again she wishes to die, but agrees in her bewilderment that Oenone may accuse Hippolytus in order to save her honor. Theseus returns, baffled by the cool welcome which greets him. The scenes in which he appears in the third act and later in the fifth are the least inspired of the play. Deceived by Oenone's false accusation, the king implores Neptune to chastise his son whose sole answer, since he will not openly reveal the shame of his father's wife, is a pathetic denial followed by the avowal of his love for Aricia.

Phèdre's remorse fades away when she hears from Theseus that Hippolytus claimed to love another woman, and a younger one. Jealousy revives her love and exasperates it into hatred. She has a rival and was perhaps derided by the two lovers, while she nursed her unrequited love amid remorse and shame. Their love was not a guilty one. "Tous les jours se levaient clairs et sereins pour eux." But she did not even have a right to her tears. In two magnificent speeches which constitute the climax of the tragedy, she vents her wrath and passes alternately from spite to pride and from remorse to a criminal invocation that Hippolytus and Aricia be relentlessly punished. Exhausted, she wants to take refuge in the darkness of the inferno: even there peace will be refused her. Her own father is a judge of the dead and will shudder at his daughter's unheard-of crimes. But her sense of shame is not followed by true repentance. Not once in the play does Racine write the word "sin." Phèdre's last cry is one of regret for never having enjoyed the fulfillment of the criminal love for which she must nevertheless atone.

Hélas! du crime affreux dont la honte me suit
Jamais mon triste cœur n'a recueilli le fruit.

She drinks poison after Oenone has drowned herself and Hippolytus has been killed by his horses, maddened by the monster sent by the god of the sea. The famous narrative of his death, very ingeniously but paradoxically defended by Leo Spitzer, is in our eyes an over-ornate and cool ending to a tragedy which could not maintain the supreme heights to which it had risen.

With the minimum of action and hardly any incidents, Racine has succeeded in blending continuity and psychological surprise, rational causation and mystery. His unequaled skill, and the only achievement at which he avowedly aimed, is the close linking of the scenes. The inevitable artificiality of the characters succeeding each other on the stage at the right moment and opportunely meeting each other no longer seems artificial with Racine. The all too famous classical unities are observed with such ease by the poet that they pass unnoticed or rather become essential to the tragedy. They make for the concentration which is the aim of the French classical drama and which T. S. Eliot missed in Elizabethan plays.

One unity alone matters: that of the continuous and progressive structure of the work of art. The paucity of incidents does not render the action static. Little is done indeed, but much is felt, and emotions and moods of the protagonists change powerfully inside the given situation. Yet Phèdre retains a concentration of purpose and a single-mindedness through her conflicting impulses that are not found in Shakespeare's Cleopatra. The fickleness and the coquettish egotism of the latter seem to many of us more true to life, or more true to the idea that men like to form of women. A greater uncertainty hovers over the Shakespearean play. With Racine, fatality is more imperious: it has marked certain characters with a predestination to misfortune, and all their struggles against that inner fatality (which is that of heredity or of their physiology stronger than their will power) are foredoomed to frustration.

Such a drama, closely knit around one leading theme and very remote from Corneille and even more from the sprawling drama of the more imaginative Spaniards, runs the risk of appearing too elaborately studied and too rational in its structure. Such was the reaction of earlier and more romantic generations, which relished what Keats defined as one of the functions of poetry: to surprise by a fine excess, or to imitate the baffling and variegated pattern of real life. Our contemporaries have momentarily developed such a taste for order in beauty, for geometrical and structural values in art that the appearance of a problem to be solved which is at times assumed by French classical tragedies fills them with delight.

But Racine's plays are rational only on the surface. Their method merely serves to display the triumph of madness. In essence they are poetical. And never did Racine conceive his whole tragedy in terms of poetical exaltation and suggestion more richly than in *Phèdre*. The very coldness of the theme, of which he was aware and by which he was perhaps frightened, demanded it. For illicit love may freely on the stage cast off conventional restraint, be confided by a mature woman to a young man and retain the secret approval of the audience. But incest will not be forgiven. It required the delicate and mythical vesture with which Racine covered Phèdre's physical passion to appease the scruples of the playgoers. Racine did not choose altogether "to temper and reduce passions to just measure with a kind of delight," as Milton puts it in the preface to his own Biblical drama. But he realized with an unerring artistic sense akin to that of the Greeks that inordinate violence verges on melodrama unless it is softened by the beauty of words and enhanced into a "majestic sadness," as he defined it in his preface to *Bérénice*. That restrained and deepened poetry which stylizes the surge of passions has been aptly called by Leo Spitzer "klassische Dämpfung," for it indeed tones down to muffled and subdued music the characters' laments and their vain appeals.

The French contention that Racine is their purest and greatest poet long met with disbelief in readers of other nations, for whom Villon or Verlaine or even Hugo were the true poets of France. The compatriots of Racine, even those among them who had gone through a phase of enthusiasm for Byron, Poe, Keats, or Whitman, cherished their tragic poet all the more jealously as foreigners seemed unable to respond to his music. A keen sensitiveness to Nerval, to Baudelaire, to Mallarmé and Valéry developed, however, among non-French readers of French poetry, and those four poets have many Racinian overtones. Through them and some other modern adepts of pure poetry, an audience grew in several countries for which the indirect lyricism, as we might call it, of Racine and of his successors had a profound appeal. Racine's poetry is indirect because, being

subservient to the dramatic mold, it cannot be and never is the
expression of the self. It does not spring forth into lyrics or into
outpourings of a soul through songs, hymns, and canticles. It suffuses
the speeches of some characters (especially of those who love but
are not loved); but it never invades the play or interrupts the action
or the psychological revelation. It can best be compared to the poetry
in a painting by Vermeer or by Chardin, in a musical piece by
Rameau, Gluck, or even Debussy. A few lines of Wordsworth or of
Milton, of Pushkin and, obviously, of Virgil would be the best
equivalent to those Racinian lines which sound to French ears the
most melodious in their language.

The very setting of *Phèdre* is poetical. Racine's age expressed its
love for exterior nature with great restraint and with a limited and
conventional descriptive vocabulary. It hardly went into raptures
over flowers or rivers or called the moon and the stars to witness or
to assist its passions. The drama took place in a drawing room which
was a prison for the tortured hearts repeatedly faced with their
tormentors or with those who remained deaf to their pleas. Yet
nature was not absent. In *Phèdre*, the struggle in the characters'
emotions is paralleled by an opposition between darkness and light,
"la nuit infernale" into which the incestuous woman would flee and
the sun whose brightness she is ashamed to face. A similar contrast
is suggested between the forest and the sea. "Dieux! que ne suis-je
assise à l'ombre des forêts!" exclaims Phèdre soon after her appearance on the stage; for in those cool forests she might encounter the
hunter Hippolytus and their idyllic meeting there would seem purified
from the guilt which afflicts her. "Dans le fond des forêts votre
image me suit," Hippolytus will confess to Aricia. Later still, in her
jealousy and with the morbidly vivid imagination of one whose
suffering is thus multiplied, Phèdre will wonder how and where her
stepson and the younger woman concealed themselves from her eyes.
"Dans le fond des forêts allaient-ils se cacher?"

The evocation of the sea, from the very outset (lines 10 and 14),
of shores from which ships are ready to set out, their sails unfurled,
and of the banks of Acheron beyond which lies the haven of death
but also of love for ever unfulfilled, is another refrain of the play.
The line most often quoted in French poetry conjures up Phèdre's
sister dying on the shore where she had been abandoned. Elsewhere,
"Ariane aux rochers contant ses injustices" appears as in a romantic
painting. Hippolytus and Oenone meet with death in the sea or on
its shore.

The use of mythological allusion and imagery similarly provides
Racine with a wealth of poetry of which few poets — not even Virgil,

Milton, or Keats — have availed themselves with such effective economy. Erechtheus, Minos, Pasiphae, the Cretan labyrinth and the Minotaur conjure up the atmosphere of an heroic age, when gods and men lived in closer contact, when monsters were challenged by mortals and women ravished by the gods. A new and greater dimension is afforded the play by such allusions to the myths which seventeenth-century audiences revered from their early training in classical lore. The obsessive and destructive passions of the characters appear as attuned to the heroic legends of an early age of human history through the aura of mythology surrounding them.

There is little eloquence in Racine's poetry, far less indeed than in the French romantics who found fault with Racine's language and style, and less rhetoric than in Baudelaire or Claudel. Corneille's characters reason with cogent logic and marshal their arguments in orderly array. Racine has at times (in *Britannicus* or in *Mithridate*) composed long speeches on political affairs worthy of his predecessor. But he is at his best when his speeches express only the eloquence of desire or the self-deception of characters who convince themselves for a fleeting moment that their love is not just folly and may be rewarded by another love kindled by their own glowing words. Very soon, in such tirades, they insert the revealing words "J'aime" which their lips seem to mold with a caress. No sonorous words, no flashes of adjectives or of striking imagery punctuate those high spots of Racinian tragedy. The vocabulary remains almost abstract and the verbs are general and colorless. But an electric current runs through them which multiplies their significance a hundredfold or which transmutes those general words, skillfully parted by ominous pauses, into sensuous pleas or piercing daggers.

> Ma sœur du fil fatal eût armé votre main.
> Mais non, dans ce dessein je l'aurais devancée;
> L'amour m'en eût d'abord inspiré la pensée.
> C'est moi, prince, c'est moi, dont l'utile secours
> Vous eût du Labyrinthe enseigné les détours.
> Que de soins m'eût coûtés cette tête charmante!
> Un fil n'eût point assez rassuré votre amante.
> Compagne du péril qu'il vous fallait chercher,
> Moi-même devant vous j'aurais voulu marcher;
> Et Phèdre au Labyrinthe avec vous descendue
> Se serait avec vous retrouvée, ou perdue.

There are relatively few images in this poetry. The metaphor hunter is at first disappointed and may hasten to proclaim Racine no poet since he does not conform to canons evolved from the practice of Shakespeare or from the Metaphysical poets, by some modern champions of consistency in imagery and of unity reached through the recurrence of so called key words. The modern critic becomes a jailer walking about with his bundle of keys, unlocking captive words and metaphors which had remained meaningless for centuries. It is not impossible to discover such key words in *Phèdre* if one tries assiduously enough. Along with the contrast between light and darkness, between the forest dear to Hippolytus and the sea, one could point to an interplay of two other opposing themes: that of purity and serenity as in a luminous picture of some Arcadia whose love is licit and undisturbed, contrasting with a set of words connoting impurity, stain, poison, groans of pain and remorse. But the only authentic obsession of the tragedy and of Racine's language is with love. The language of passion was conventional and overelegant in Racine's age. The lover was in shackles (*fers*) or under a yoke (*joug*) or otherwise made a slave (*asservi*). He was wounded, or consumed by *la flamme*. Racine, unlike the Elizabethans, is not tempted by luxuriance of vocabulary or by ransacking the world of nature and a rich flora and fauna for similes or images. He accepts the conventions of his age, but endows words which seemed trite with a new resonance: they suddenly spring to life and truth. Thus the image of the prey which suggests an animal hunted down by the relentless pursuit of a tormentor becomes the celebrated line: "C'est Vénus tout entière à sa proie attachée." The simple and colorless verb *aimer* turns into a furious cry when Phèdre realizes that Aricia and Hippolytus shared the intimacy and understanding which were denied her, and that love, once enjoyed, lives on in sensuous memories until the dying day: "Ils s'aimeront toujours!"

A whole body of poetry, including that of some of the greatest among the ancients, is admirable with hardly any recourse to metaphors; it did not appeal to the strangeness of eastern spices and fragrances, rare flowers, or beasts from India, fairy lands, and precious stones. The very original quality of Racine's poetry lies in its smooth continuity. Images, evocative words, sensuous undertones are all merged into or submitted to the dramatic progression and the characterization. Paul Valéry, who emulated that Racinian mastery in some of his long poems, expressed it lucidly when he remarked in his *Rhumbs:* "With Racine, the constant ornament seems to be drawn from the speech itself; therein lies the secret of his prodigious continuity. While with the moderns, the ornament breaks the speech."

France, "Famed in all great arts, in none supreme," likes to believe that she wields unchallenged supremacy in the art of loving — at least in literature, and that her sons hold a saner, more mature, and more lucid view of the passion which rules the world than do citizens of other lands. Let us not generalize from literature to life. It may well be that so many plays, novels, madrigals, paintings, and songs about love have effected in France a catharsis which enables the French to hem passion in prudent guarantees and to protect a man, after he has sowed his wild oats, from the alluring sex whose purpose is "de faire faire des bêtises à l'homme." But the triumph of woman in French letters (very few novels and plays have a man's name for their title) and the universal fascination of the love theme for writers are due in no small measure to Racine. Every French schoolboy, from the age of fourteen on, has been asked repeatedly to analyze the nuances of passion in the character of Phèdre and to assign their relative parts to the senses, the heart, the imagination, Christian influences, in the passionate conflicts within the heroine. The advances of a mature woman to a virginal adolescent, though seldom to a stepson, have become a stereotyped model for many a French novel, and probably for many a love affair in real life. Phèdre is indeed the masterpiece of the tragedy of passion.

Racine's originality is unchallenged in such a realm. Love had little place in Greek tragedy, despite a famous hymn to Love's invincibility in Antigone. Medea, Helen in the Trojan Women are ardent women in love in Euripides, and one of the two plays on Iphigenia rises to great lyrical heights in a splendid epithalamion. But even in Euripides love remains a minor theme. In the Spanish drama and in the English one, in spite of some conspicuous exceptions, sexual passion is secondary to many other motives. Neither Ibsen nor pathetic and anguished Strindberg, neither Goethe nor Schiller has challenged Racine's supremacy as a portrayer of love.

Racine does not stud his tragedy with poetical interludes on the spirit of love whose "capacity receiveth as the sea" or on tender kisses from lips forsworn, "seals of love but sealed in vain," still less on invocations to the eternal feminine or to the Platonic spiritual beauty worshiped behind the alluring flesh. He indulges in no illusion. Even his young men know from the start that love is no game but a mortal disease, and that to be loved too possessively is a curse second to none. Behind the discreet reserve of his vocabulary and some ornamented diction bequeathed by préciosité, he depicts the passion mastering Phèdre as a victory of the senses, as carnal even more than cerebral. Phèdre herself uses the word: "J'ai de mes sens abandonné l'empire." Her first confession to Oenone describes with physiological accuracy the sudden flush and pallor on her face, caused by the violent rushing of her blood to her head, when she saw Hippolytus after a long absence, her eyes suddenly dizzy, her tongue speechless, her whole body alternately burning and shivering. No flowery exuberance covers with an embroidered garb the bareness of her heart and her body, trembling behind her veils. One is very remote from Romeo's exuberance:

> It is the east and Juliet is the sun!
> Arise, fair sun, and kill the envious moon!

Lovers in Shakespeare may hope for marriage. Even Aricia conventionally suggests it when Hippolytus wishes her to flee with him away from Phèdre's hatred. Juliet more impetuously promises to lay herself and all her fortunes at Romeo's feet if his purpose is honorable marriage. Not so with Racine's greatest heroines. We know as they do themselves that never will their burning thirst be quenched. Carnal appeasement is inconceivable in Racine. Not even a semblance of caress or some fleeting tender intimacy will ever draw together loving woman and the man whom she has been driven to pursue. Love is a subjective force which, having rushed toward the other one in full fury, is thrown back upon itself and can only consume the one who loves. Racine profoundly perceived and rendered the fear of passion and of risk in young men, terrified by those violent women who seem to have cast off all shame and rush to devour their masculine youth before their own "démon de midi" is exorcized. They sense hatred or domineering greed behind that carnal love. A line in *Mithridate* which describes the jealous and spiteful love of an old king for a young woman courted by his own sons is applicable to all the lovers of Racine: "Sa haine va toujours plus loin que son amour."

Giraudoux, who like Proust and Mauriac was permeated with Racinian poetry and haunted by Racinian psychology, has brilliantly showed in an essay on Racine how the concentration of classical drama, achieved through the unities, strengthened the obsession with love which Racine wished to create. A few doors open on one hall, which is the classical stage. The characters come and go, hit upon each other while they wish to flee from each other or to inspire a passion or a desire which the other one refuses to share. Behind those doors they dream, moan, sleep, overheard by those whom they hate or whose embrace they covet. To make that stage-prison still more oppressive, there is not the semblance of a tree, of a brook by which to walk, of a cloud in the shape of a camel or of a weasel to watch in the sky. Not a moment of relief is granted them, for the action rushes headlong to the catastrophe and, as Carson McCullers puts it, "Time, the endless idiot, runs screaming round the world." Worse still, a suggestion of incest poisons the stifling air which they must breathe. In *Andromaque*, Orestes and Hermione are related to each other. The relation is closer in *Britannicus*, where Nero elaborately poisons his half-brother and takes his bride by force. Roxane imperiously demands her own brother-in-law's love and in noble but unambiguous language orders him into her bedroom. Incest is more openly suggested in *Phèdre* and "the fury of a woman scorned" which Congreve declares worse than anything in Hell is even more terrifyingly depicted. Jean-Louis Barrault, the actor-director who is also a gifted commentator, published an annotated edition of *Phèdre* in which the words by which French women like to be called, "cannibal," "tigress," "leopardess," "lioness," "wild beast," recur some twenty times. Not once does Phèdre shed a tear. At their dying hour, not once can Racinian characters indulge in a plea for Time to have a stop so that they may forgive the one who drove them to their ruin and repay their lover with supreme caresses.

> I am dying, Egypt, dying; only
> I here importune death awhile, until
> Of many thousand kisses the poor last
> I lay upon thy lips.

Racine's lovers are not truer to life than those of Shakespeare in the sense that a Phèdre or a Hermione are not, let us hope, more frequently to be met with than a Juliet or an Imogen. But the passion which burns them is represented with a power and a depth which are not to be found in Shakespeare. "In this matter at least Shakespeare is an innocent beside Racine," confessed the critic of the *Times Literary Supplement* who, on December 23, 1939, commented upon the third centenary of the birth of Racine. World War II had then broken out. Great Britain had once again witnessed the wreck of her hopes for a civilized, sportsmanlike, and businesslike way of settling the problems of the world. The *Times* commentator added, in very un-English tones:

> It was easy a generation ago to say contemptuously of such a world that it had nothing to do but to make love. But we have lost the confidence that came of the sensation of traveling very fast in the right direction. Now that it has turned out to be the wrong direction, and there is no means of checking the speed, we are readier than we were to listen to the gentle cynics who point out that lovemaking is about the most harmless thing a civilization can be engaged in. Not merely the most harmless, the lover of Racine would say, but the most exciting and, in a sense, the most satisfying . . .

"In a sense" indeed. For the dominant motive in *Phèdre* is *insatisfaction*, as the French language, which hardly knows the word frustration, calls it. The whole of the modern novel, seen in this light, emanates from Racine: Stendhal of course, and Flaubert and Proust and Mauriac, but also Dostoevski who, in a curious letter to his brother Michael in 1840, flew into a temper because Michael had written coolly of Racine, and threatened him with his contempt if he did not "agree that *Phèdre* is the lightest and purest poetry." Racine's theater, which some writers, deluded by appearances, still call today "the theater of reason," is in fact the theater not only of passion but of rebellion, of the annihilation of reason by emotion, of illogic half concealed beneath an orderly mold and artistic restraint. Moderation is the virtue which Racinian heroes and heroines least possess. They always drive their passion to the extreme where only suicide or murder can result. Like the Existentialists today, they seem to consider that life has to be lived constantly on the verge of disintegration. But from their disintegration there is no escape such as philosophical subtleties and the joy of coining new words and of redefining them as soon as readers think they have understood their meaning seem to afford the Existentialist successors of Racine. No one expressed that aspect of Racine's theater more powerfully than an American critic with whose words this essay should conclude: Waldo Frank, in an essay on "The Modern Drama" published in 1929 in *Five Arts* (Van Nostrand):

> Racine is the true father of the modern theatre; and much that has followed — forms so seemingly apart as Ibsen, Dostoevski, Chekov, Shaw — is strictly rooted in him. The modern theme is dispossession and search for repossession: dispossession of the soul that has lost its house — a spiritual, intellectual, social house; repossession through many frantic efforts which indeed trace what we admire as modern "progress." Self-exploration, for example, the gamut of romanticist creeds that sought to replace the lost reality by one within each human spirit. Or science and discovery, which are corollaries of the same romantic movement, quests for a new absolute in natural law or in ideal logic. All of this is implicit in Racine. His reliance on classic molds of Greece and Rome, a trait shared by the entire movement misnamed the Renaissance, is an obvious attempt to discover an external surety of form to replace the crumbling Christian body. Racine "imitates" the subjects of Euripides; he "obeys" Aristotle. This can, however, not conceal the profound and original dissimilarity of Racine from the exploitation of the Greeks by the mediaevals for their own use, and as well from everything that ever shone in Athens. Within the unities of time, place, theme, of such plays as *Phèdre, Bérénice, Iphigénie, Andromaque*, is individual chaos. These creatures are desperate, lawless; and *they are seeking*. In Aeschylus and Sophocles as well were desperate persons; but they accepted, despite their revolt, the supreme, serene authority of Fate. Even Prometheus admits

Olympus. Not so in the great Jansenist Frenchman. The anguish of his person is not due to conflict with spiritual order, but to the weakening, recession, and betrayal of that order. This is why Dostoievski could make Racine his master; why the archetypes of the romantic heroes — those of Stendhal, Chateaubriand, and Ibsen — live already in the outwardly decorous dramas of Racine: and more poignantly than ever since, because the rigid mold of his plays is so plain a compensation for the break within.

# ❖ ❖ ❖ Myth as Tragic Structure
## in *Desire Under the Elms*

### *Edgar F. Racey, Jr.*

It is customary to point to the underlying Oedipal theme of Eugene O'Neill's *Desire Under the Elms* and to link this play with *Mourning Becomes Electra* as evidence of his consuming interest in the Oedipus theme, both as myth and complex. The use of myth, or classical source, in *Electra* is obvious, for O'Neill takes great pains to insure that no one misses the elaborate series of correspondences that his trilogy effects. Less elaborate, but equally effective, is his reliance on the *Hippolytus* of Euripides (and perhaps on Racine's treatment of the theme) in *Desire Under the Elms*.

That the play is a tragedy few will dispute (although early critics tended to see it as a mere shoddy domestic tragedy). It combines a traditional tragic theme (the Oedipus legend) with a dramatic reconciliation in the interests of a higher virtue (Justice). Abbie and Eben, as they are reconciled to their fate (which they *will*), assume a dignity which approaches tragic stature. As they acknowledge their guilt and enter into the process of expiation, their characters tend to become generalized, and O'Neill manages to suggest something approaching the idea of universal justice.

On the bare framework of a New England domestic tragedy, O'Neill has grafted a religious symbology, almost an iconography. The Biblical names, while "locally" motivated (a man like Ephraim Cabot could be expected to name his sons after characters in the Bible), seem to dictate at least some of the actions of the characters, and even take on the beginnings of a dialectic. Thus, Peter ("the rock") is associated throughout the play with rocks and stones:

> Here — it's stones atop o' the ground — stones atop o' the stones — makin' stone walls — year atop o' the year. . . . (I,i)

From *Modern Drama*, V, No. 1 (May 1962), 42–46. Copyright 1962 by A. C. Edwards. Reprinted by permission of the editor.

And it is Peter who first picks up a rock to cast at his father's house. Simeon, on the other hand, reiterates the idea of an eye for an eye (of the Indians which they will presumably meet on the way to California, he retorts that they will repay them "a hair fur a hair") and, in revenge on his tyrannical father, he threatens to rape his new wife. One recalls Jacob's "blessing" of his sons:

> Simeon and Levi are brothers; instruments of cruelty are in their habitations. O my soul, come not thou into their secret; unto their assembly, mine honour, be not thou united; for in their anger they slew a man, and in their self-will they digged down a wall.
>
> Cursed be their anger, for it was fierce; and their wrath, for it was cruel. . . . (Genesis, XLIX,5)

In *Desire*, it is Simeon who "digs down a wall," tearing the gate off the hinges, abolishing "shet gates, an' open gates, an' all gates, by thunder!"

The predominant features of his two eldest sons are combined in Ephraim: he is hard and stony, and embodies the ancient law of retaliation in kind. He is Ephraim, progenitor of the Tribes of Israel, the archetypal patriarch (and for O'Neill, the father-figure). His name ("the fruitful") may be an underlying source of irony by the end of the play, and it is significant that his "fruitfulness" is the greatest source of his *hubris*. He is also identified specifically with God, both in his harshness and solitude. Like Ezra Mannon, he is the embodiment of that blighting New England Biblical tradition which represses life.

Eben (Ebenezer? "store of hope") is a typical O'Neill son. The hope of the line (Simeon and Peter are patently unfit to carry on the name), he is condemned to be placed in constant strife with his father, denying his obvious resemblance to the man he hates. The rivalry is characteristically O'Neill: the father has usurped what the son regards as rightfully his own (the mother and the land). This pattern of rivalry and usurpation is repeated in the male Cabot's relationship with Min, the "scarlet woman"; first Ephraim claimed her, then Simeon, Peter, and finally Eben, who is engaged on learning that here too, they are "his [the father's] heirs in everythin'." The pattern will continue with Eben and Abbie.

While these quasi-religious elements serve to generate a kind of Biblical atmosphere, and perhaps a kind of primitivism, the play says little in the way of definite religious conclusions, save O'Neill's reiterated statement that the restrictive ethic (usually Puritanism) tends to kill off life. Ephraim retires to his stony, solitary existence, submitting once more to the hard God, whom it is his consolation to resemble. The young and life-bearing have been destroyed.

As a classical tragedy, however, *Desire* is both successful and complete. The time is spring, season of awakening and season of ritual. It is the spring which has sent Ephraim out "t' learn God's message t' me in the spring, like the prophets done." It is a spring so compelling in its beauty and life that even Simeon and Peter are moved to utter, from their animal existence, "Purty!" The play will end in late spring a year later.

The situation is the Hippolytus-Phaedra-Theseus plot: the father has returned, bringing with him a young wife, who is immediately attracted to her stepson. The stepson too has responded to the season — his brothers have subjected him to taunts concerning his affair with Min (a possible loose parallel to the gentle banter of Theramenes in Racine's *Phaedra*). Traditionally, Hippolytus was chaste, but the affair with Min affords O'Neill the opportunity to define the usurpation theme.

Like Phaedra, Abbie conceals her growing passion for Eben with the mask of scorn. Like Phaedra, she asks that the son be banished — and for the same reason, plus the fact that Eben is a potential rival for the farm. Like Phaedra, Abbie makes advances, but with more success than her dramatic ancestor. Like Hippolytus, Eben muses constantly on his mother, who was "foreign."

It is in the murder of Ephraim's supposed child that we see O'Neill modifying his prototype to suit his dramatic purposes. The curse on the son, originally uttered by Theseus, is transferred to Eben, who is the rightful father. Ephraim also utters a curse — the curse of God — on his sons, but the crucially dramatic curse is Eben's. Eben's curse is uttered against his son in the throes of error, and rashly; Abbie proves as implacable an instrument of fate as Poseidon. Like Theseus, however, it is Ephraim who is left alone, surveying the wreck of his kingdom.

In the Euripidean version, a sin had been committed against the gods (or rather, Aphrodite imagined herself slighted by Hippolytus' devotion to Artemis). While it is possible to view the "sin" in *Desire* as merely the Freudian sin of repression (leading to symbolic incest), this view, I think, underestimates the design of the play. A sin has been committed, and the sin is Ephraim's. We are reminded of this sin by Eben's continued antagonism, his insistence that the farm is his, and (most strongly) by the "something" which hangs over the play from the opening (and gloriously melodramatic!) stage direction to the final curtain. The "something" is the mother, or rather the wrong done her by Ephraim. Her fiercely maternal presence broods over the play — even the most imperceptive of the brothers feels it. She is sensed most strongly at the moment of Eben's sin, the sin which is the beginning of the retributive process against her oppressor, Ephraim — and she approves of the sin. It is at this moment, of course, that Abbie enacts simultaneously the roles of mother and beloved, and this is the second stage (the first being when he "bought" the farm from his brothers with Ephraim's hoarded gold) of Eben's revenge on his father.

Of frail disposition, gentle, and unused to Ephraim's ways, Eben's mother was forced to work intolerably hard; the work finally killed her. Moreover, there is strong reason to believe that Ephraim has unlawfully taken the farm from the mother, and from the son, on whom it should lawfully devolve. If this is so — that is, if the wrong done the mother hangs over the play like a curse — then Eben and Abbie may be seen as agents of the process of justice, directed against Ephraim. Like Theseus, Ephraim must atone for his rash injustice; it becomes fitting that Ephraim is condemned, ironically, to the land he has stolen.

Without this framework of the curse, the reader is faced with a problem of "dialectical" motivation: Eben and Abbie become simply the victims of their lust, and fail to assume the stature of agents of tragic retribution. They are, of course, "locally" (psychologically, dramatically) motivated: Eben by the Oedipus complex and the desire for revenge, Abbie by her desire to provide Ephraim with an heir, thus assuring her chances of retaining the farm, and both of them by a strong sexual urge. It is precisely in the light of these local motivations that Eben and Abbie are rendered capable of becoming the instruments of a larger process, directed against Ephraim. In this play, the spontaneity with which the characters enter their dialectical roles is ample testimony to O'Neill's dramatic integrity. In some of the plays (particularly *The Great God Brown, All God's Chillun,* and, at times, *Mourning Becomes Electra*), we have the regrettable sense that the characters are being forced more by their dialectical roles than by their psychological drives; in *Desire,* however, this sense is virtually absent.

Tragedy makes its statement in its resolution, and it is here that O'Neill brings together the various threads of the play. Eben and Abbie are reunited in their love, even as they expiate their joint crime of murder. In acknowledging his responsibility in the crime, Eben submits to the ideals of love and justice. In so doing, the two insure Ephraim's complete downfall: his pride in his manhood is destroyed, and he is condemned (after a final effort to escape) to the very thing he has coveted. In the quasi-religious terms of the play, the harsh, puritanical ethic has triumphed — to its own inevitable defeat: Abbie and Eben are destroyed; Ephraim has taken an eye for an eye, but in so doing, he is forced to acknowledge the solitary sterility which has been in fact his lot. Eben is turned from his dream of revenge, for the sake of a higher ideal, but as he turns, he insures the completeness of his mother's revenge. O'Neill's tragic curses do not end with the death of the sinner; they must be expiated in a long and solitary process. Ephraim Cabot, in the rocky solitude of his farm, and Lavinia Mannon, entering for the last time the "whited sepulchre," confront their fates in the only possible way.

Una Ellis-Fermor has pointed out that the symmetry of the tragic form may account for the phenomenon of *catharsis*, that the artistic order of the play may be generalized to a kind of cosmic moral order. With the resolution of this play, justice has been done, even if O'Neill has not achieved the artistic symmetry which apparently he feels is necessary. Eben's and Abbie's last lines (HE: Sun's a-rizin'. Purty, hain't it? SHE: Ay-eh) echo precisely the play's opening lines, and the cycle of retribution, hinted at through use of myth, is artistically completed.

The sheriff, acting as a kind of ironic chorus, underscores the importance of the ownership of the land, which has been the basis of the tragic action. His "wish't I owned it!" is uttered in profound ignorance of the consequences of coveting the farm: desire for the farm prompted Abbie's marriage to Ephraim, and her affair with Eben was initially motivated by her desire to secure her position with Ephraim. Ironically, it is when Eben learns that his father intends to will the farm to his (Eben's) son that he utters the curse. It is when Eben is freed of his desire for the farm, when he returns to Abbie (and the rope), that he assures his salvation. Ephraim, on the other hand, is condemned.

It is perhaps in the tragic aspects of the play that we find sanction for the Old Testament overlay, as hinted in the names of the characters. Throughout the play, it is the Hebraic God who is invoked as a God of wrath and retribution. If O'Neill is attempting to enact a classical tragedy in a modern setting, he needs an ethos which will support a tragic view of life, and the god of inevitable vengeance lends sanction to such an ethos.

In *Desire Under the Elms* and *Mourning Becomes Electra*, perhaps the most extensive explorations of O'Neill's view of the father-son battle/symbolic incest theme, the author has resorted to the use of myth, adopting the structure of classical tragedies. The use of myth, as Eliot has pointed out, affords the artist both the necessary artistic control to explore his subject and the means of generalization. In both plays we see O'Neill creating characters who, by their very natures, are endowed with the necessary motivation to enact the myth; both plays too, though different in many ways, contribute to a unified dramatic vision and testify to the fact that this is the way O'Neill found life.

# Writing Suggestions

Many of the unlimited number of topics concerning these Phaedra–Hippolytus materials suitable for long or short compositions will certainly have occurred to you by this point. Answers to almost any one of the questions posed in the "Study Aids" and "Discussion Topics" could be worked up into good essays. But the following suggestions, first for subjects supported by this book alone, and second, for subjects requiring further investigation or reading may be of help and interest.

## Topics Supported by This Book

I. If you wish to concentrate on one of the plays in this collection, you might develop a topic similar to those in one of the following five categories:

A. Theme, idea, interpretation

The Theme of Greed in *Desire Under the Elms*

Human Volition in *The Cretan Woman*

The *Hippolytus:* A Tragedy of Excesses

B. Character (the qualities of attitude, deed, thought, and statement which define one's personality)

The Motivation of Euripides' Phaedra

A Character Study of O'Neill's Cabot

The Function of Aricia in Racine's *Phaedra*

C. Structure (some formal pattern or principle by which form is established)

The Dramatic Action of Racine's *Phaedra* (an analysis of the events of the play in terms of initial attack, complication, crisis, and catastrophe)

The Structural Function of Cabot's Dancing

Disappointed Desires as Structural Principle in *Desire Under the Elms*

D. Dramatic technique

Foreshadowing in *The Cretan Woman*

Verbal Echoes in the *Hippolytus*

The "Dea ex Machina" in the *Hippolytus*

Expository Technique in O'Neill's *Desire Under the Elms*

Symbolic Gesture in *The Cretan Woman*

The Soliloquy in Seneca's *Phaedra*

Symbolic Setting in *Desire Under the Elms*

E. Language
  Verbal Ornament in Seneca's *Phaedra*
  Images of Natural Violence in *The Cretan Woman*
  The Function of Dialect in *Desire Under the Elms*
  An Analysis of the Choral Odes in the *Hippolytus*
  Mythological Allusion in Racine's *Phaedra*

II. Meaningful comparisons and contrasts may be drawn between two or more of the plays in terms of these five categories. For example: (A) Human Volition in the *Hippolytus* and *The Cretan Woman*; (B) Euripides' Theseus and O'Neill's Cabot; (C) The Crisis or Turning Point in Euripides' *Hippolytus* and Racine's *Phaedra*; (D) The Chorus in Seneca and Jeffers; (E) The Art of the Messenger's Speech in Euripides and Seneca.

III. A critique of one of the critical essays in this book could be developed into an interesting essay in which you can also gain experience in documentation and handling materials from secondary sources. Your problem here would be to summarize the critic's interpretation and to appraise the validity and usefulness of his insights. One does not lightly dismiss the work of an Henri Peyre or a Richmond Lattimore; but do not let the respect due them prevent your taking issue with their views.

TOPICS REQUIRING INVESTIGATION OR FURTHER READING

I. Studies in the Phaedra-Hippolytus Myth
  A. A study of the cult of Hippolytus. (In addition to the views of Frazer and Graves, consult L. R. Farnell, *Cults of the Greek States*, 5 vols., Oxford, 1896–1909, and *Greek Hero-Cults and Ideas of Immortality*, Oxford, 1921.)
  B. A study of the "pattern story" involved in Phaedra and Hippolytus as outlined by Lattimore.
  C. A study of an adaptation of the Phaedra-Hippolytus story other than those contained in this volume. The identification of other versions of the story can be found in the following:
    Karl Heinemann, *Die Tragischen Gestalten der Griechen in der Weltliteratur*. Das Erbe der Alten (Leipzig, 1920), II, 69–79.
    Louis Méridier, *Hippolyte d'Euripide* (Paris, n.d.).
    Winifred Newton, *Le Thème de Phèdre et d'Hippolyte dans la Littérature Française*. Bibliothèque de la Faculté de Philosophie et Lettres de l'Université de Liége, LXXXII (Paris, 1939).

Wilhelm Schmid and Otto Stählin, *Geschichte der Griechischen Literatur.* Erster Teil, Dritter Band, Erste Hälfte (Munich, 1940), pp. 389–90.

Louis Séchan, "La Légende d'Hippolyte dans l'Antiquité," *Revue des Etudes Grecs,* XXIV (1911), 105–51.

The following is a partial list of works dealing with the Phaedra-Hippolytus material:

Ovid, *Heroides* IV and *Metamorphoses* XV
Lope de Vega, *El Castigo sin Venganza* (Justice Without Revenge) (1631)
Richard Brathwait, "The Epistle of Hyppolitus unto Phedra," in *A Strappado for the Diuell* (1615)
Edmund Spenser, *The Faerie Queene,* Bk. I, Canto 5
Nicolas Pradon, *Phèdre* (1677)
Edmund Smith, *Phaedra and Hippolytus* (1707) (See *Spectator* Essay No. 18)
G. S. Marbach, *Hippolytus* (1858)
G. Conrad, *Hippolytus* (1871)
Emile Zola, *La Curée* (1872) and *Renée* (1881)
Algernon Swinburne, "Phaedra," in *Poems and Ballads, First Series* (1866)
Gabriele d'Annunzio, *Fedra* (1909)
S. Lipider, *Hippolytus* (1913)
Sir Lewis Morris, *The Epic of Hades* (1876–77)
Walter Pater, "The Veiled Hippolytus," in *Greek Studies* (1901)
André Gide, "Theseus," in *Two Legends: Oedipus and Theseus,* tr. John Russell (1950)
Robinson Jeffers, *Cawdor* (1928)
"Phaedra," a motion picture (1962) ("a violent drama of profane love") with Melina Mercouri and Anthony Perkins, screenplay by Jules Dassin and Margarita Liberaki. (A "novelized" version of the screenplay was published in 1962 by Pocket Books, Inc.)

II. Euripides
  A. The Theatre of Euripides
  B. Euripides' First *Hippolytus*
  C. Aristophanes' Parodies of Euripides
  D. Modern Translations of Euripides' *Hippolytus*
  E. Performance of the *Hippolytus* in Recent Times

III. Seneca
    A. Roman Stoicism and Seneca's *Phaedra*
    B. Were Seneca's Tragedies Performed?
    C. Seneca's *Phaedra* and the Tradition of Closet Drama
    D. Topicalities in Seneca's *Phaedra*

IV. Racine
    A. The Stage History of *Phaedra*
    B. *Phaedra* in England or America (criticism, translation, or stage performance)
    C. Sarah Bernhardt as Phaedra
    D. Racine's Prefaces
    E. Neo-Classical "Rules" for Tragedy and *Phaedra*
    F. The Theatre of Racine
    G. Jansenism and *Phaedra*
    H. Racine's Use of Plutarch in *Phaedra*
    I. Racine's Biblical Plays

V. Jeffers
    A. Greek Myth in the Work of Robinson Jeffers
    B. The *Oresteia* and *The Tower Beyond Tragedy*
    C. The *Medea* of Euripides and Jeffers
    D. The Hellenism of Robinson Jeffers
    E. A comparison of a theme, character, or technique in *Medea* and *The Cretan Woman*
    F. The Reception of *The Cretan Woman*

VI. O'Neill
    A. The Early Reception of *Desire Under the Elms*
    B. The Influence of August Strindberg on *Desire Under the Elms*
    C. *Desire Under the Elms* as Autobiography
    D. Comparison of T. C. Murray's *Autumn Fire* (1924) and *Desire Under the Elms*
    E. *Desire Under the Elms* as a Naturalistic Play
    F. The Adaptation of *Desire Under the Elms* as a Motion Picture. (See Kenneth MacGowan, "O'Neill and a Mature Hollywood Outlook," *Theatre Arts*, XLII [April 1958], 79–81.)
    G. The Father- (or Mother-) Figure in O'Neill's Plays
    H. Criticism of *Desire Under the Elms* Since World War II